THE FOREIGN POLICY OF HAMAS

SOAS Palestine Studies

This book series aims at promoting innovative research in the study of Palestine, Palestinians and the Israel-Palestine conflict as a crucial component of Middle Eastern and world politics. The first-ever Western academic series entirely dedicated to this topic, *SOAS Palestine Studies* draws from a variety of disciplinary fields, including history, politics, media, visual arts, social anthropology, and development studies. The series is published under the academic direction of the Centre for Palestine Studies (CPS) at the London Middle East Institute (LMEI) of SOAS, University of London.

Series Editors:

Dina Matar, PhD, Chair, Centre for Palestine Studies, and Reader in Political Communication, Centre for Global Media and Communications, SOAS
Adam Hanieh, PhD, Reader in Development Studies and Advisory Committee Member for Centre for Palestine Studies, SOAS

Board Advisor:

Hassan Hakimian, Director of the London Middle East Institute at SOAS

Current and Forthcoming Titles:

Palestine Ltd.: Neoliberalism and Nationalism in the Occupied Territory, Toufic Haddad
Palestinian Literature in Exile: Gender, Aesthetics and Resistance in the Short Story, Joseph R. Farag
Palestinian Citizens of Israel: Power, Resistance and the Struggle for Space, Sharri Plonski
Representing Palestine Media and Journalism in Australia Since World War I, Peter Manning
Folktales of Palestine: Cultural Identity, Memory and the Politics of Storytelling, Farah Aboubakr
Dialogue in Palestine: The People-to-People Diplomacy Programme and the Israeli-Palestinian Conflict, Nadia Naser-Najjab
Palestinian Youth Activism in the Internet Age: Social Media and Networks after the Arab Spring, Albana Dwonch
The Palestinian National Movement in Lebanon: A Political History of the 'Ayn al-Hilwe Camp, Erling Lorentzen Sogge

THE FOREIGN POLICY OF HAMAS

Ideology, Decision Making and Political Supremacy

Leila Seurat

Translated from the French by Martin Makinson

I.B. TAURIS
LONDON • NEW YORK • OXFORD • NEW DELHI • SYDNEY

I.B. TAURIS
Bloomsbury Publishing Plc
50 Bedford Square, London, WC1B 3DP, UK
1385 Broadway, New York, NY 10018, USA
29 Earlsfort Terrace, Dublin 2, Ireland

BLOOMSBURY, I.B. TAURIS and the I.B. Tauris logo are trademarks of
Bloomsbury Publishing Plc

This edition published by arrangement with CNRS editions, France

First published in France under the title "Hamas et le monde"
© CNRS editions, France 2019

English translation © Martin Makinson

All rights to any material included in the Translation provided by the Publishers shall belong to the Publishers

For legal purposes the Acknowledgements on p. xi constitute an extension of this copyright page.

Cover image © Spencer Platt/Getty Images

All rights reserved. No part of this publication may be reproduced or transmitted in any form or by any means, electronic or mechanical, including photocopying, recording, or any information storage or retrieval system, without prior permission in writing from the publishers.

Bloomsbury Publishing Plc does not have any control over, or responsibility for, any third-party websites referred to or in this book. All internet addresses given in this book were correct at the time of going to press. The author and publisher regret any inconvenience caused if addresses have changed or sites have ceased to exist, but can accept no responsibility for any such changes.

A catalogue record for this book is available from the British Library.

A catalog record for this book is available from the Library of Congress.

ISBN: HB: 978-1-8386-0745-6
PB: 978-1-8386-0744-9
ePDF: 978-1-8386-0746-3
eBook: 978-1-8386-0747-0

Series: SOAS Palestine Studies

Typeset by Deanta Global Publishing Services, Chennai, India

To find out more about our authors and books visit www.bloomsbury.com and sign up for our newsletters.

CONTENTS

Foreword — vii
Acknowledgements — xi

INTRODUCTION — 1

Part I
GENERAL ORIENTATIONS OF HAMAS FOREIGN POLICY

Chapter 1
HAMAS AND ISRAEL: CONCILIATION AND CONFRONTATION — 45

Chapter 2
HAMAS AND THE REST OF THE WORLD — 66

Chapter 3
SYRIA, IRAN AND EGYPT — 87

Part II
THE VARIOUS INTERESTS AT THE BASIS OF THE FOREIGN POLICY OF HAMAS

Chapter 4
OUTSIDE: SEEKING RECOGNITION AND LOOKING FOR RESOURCES — 115

Chapter 5
INSIDE: REINFORCING ITSELF AND COMPETING AGAINST ITS RIVALS — 136

Part III
PLACE AND FUNCTION OF IDEOLOGY IN THE FOREIGN POLICY OF HAMAS

Chapter 6
IDEOLOGY AND DEFENCE OF EXTERNAL INTERESTS — 175

Chapter 7
INTERNAL INTERESTS AND IDEOLOGY — 188

Part IV
THE IMPACT OF DECISION MAKING ON HAMAS FOREIGN POLICY

Chapter 8
COLLECTIVE DECISIONS, UNILATERAL DECISIONS 197

Chapter 9
CAUSES OF DISSENT 211

CONCLUSION 232

Postscript 239
Biographies 245
Chronology 259
Bibliography 275
Index 286

FOREWORD

The novelty of Leila Seurat's timely work lies in studying the evolving politics and ideology of Hamas, as well as its 'Islamist foreign policy' from the perspective of International Relations (IR) theorization and conceptualization. By taking the discussion and the study of Hamas into the realm of foreign relations and exploring how the movement has been navigating its external politics, particularly with states, this book stands out as the one and only work that is exclusively focused on Hamas' 'diplomacy' and international relations. Such a perspective has been visibly under-researched in the growing literature not only on Hamas with its specific characteristics but indeed across the board of Islamist movements in general. Sensational accounts aside, serious studies of various Islamist formations, including Hamas, have mostly concentrated on the dynamics and politics of the Islamists within their national context, or within a transcendent 'Islamism-international' that is inherently vague but largely demeaning of the 'state'. This loose transnational 'Islamintern' has significantly differed from the 1919–43 Leninist-Stalinist 'Comintern', for it has lacked organizational structure, global sponsoring superpower and any coherent ideological programme. More to the point of this book, the idea that Islamism and its 'Islamintern' dimension has never exhibited a strong 'statist' component makes it an intriguing case for International Relations study. Either at the national or international level, the 'nation-state' as the foundation of today's world politics has been conceptually contested by many Islamists and has hardly been reconciled with the borderless vision and overarching Islamization process that they have embraced. To challenge the 'nation-state,' the Islamization process and its competing Islamist players have offered, internally and internationally, ambiguous and ill-defined alternatives such as an 'Islamic state,' pan-Islamic unity or the re-establishment of a Caliphate. Against this background, it is truly adventurous to embark on studying any given Islamist movement from a theoretical perspective that is imperatively tied to the concept of a 'nation-state,' as informed by an IR conceptualization, while the subject is neither a practising state in itself nor a strong adherent to the theoretical and philosophical pillars of statehood.

Seurat has set herself out for just such an adventure. The Gaza Strip under Hamas offers a fascinating and perhaps unique case of a territory that is still under official colonization and control but enjoys effective self-rule, as well as some forms of (unsovereign and stateless) foreign policy. Seurat has tackled the many ensuing challenges caused by the elusiveness of the 'state' as a concept in the ideology, politics and world view of Islamists in general and of Hamas in particular. In the latter's case, the challenge has been compounded by the fact that even the idea of any post-colonial state that is contested by many Islamists has been far from being realized in the case of Palestine. Ironically, Hamas has found itself striving for an independent Palestinian state which – in the long term – once achieved and liberated, could be contested and questioned from a strict transnational Islamization perspective. In the immediate term, however, Hamas itself has been a multifaceted player: a liberation/resistance movement of religious ideology and pedigree; a social organization with strong and deeply rooted networks; and a de facto powerholder in the Gaza Strip with whom states and international agencies have been compelled to deal directly or otherwise. Out of these definitions and functions, Seurat has managed to carefully synthesize and locate Hamas as a quasi-state actor whose politics and behaviour can be analysed and measured by concepts and principles that IR theories reserve for the conduct of states.

Hamas' concern in building relations with states started early on, just a few years after the foundation of the movement in 1987. Over the subsequent decade, Hamas managed to secure relations with several countries with varying degrees of 'diplomacy', opening offices and dispatching official representatives in some of those cases. As Hamas' leadership was divided between those living inside and outside Palestine, foreign policy was delegated to the ex-pat contingent. The true turning point in Hamas' political life and in its international relations came about with its victory in the 2006 elections for the Palestinian Legislative Council. For less than a year, Hamas became the Palestinian 'government' in the West Bank and the Gaza Strip, and its prominent leader Dr Mahmoud Al-Zahhar became the Palestinian foreign minister. However, this government was short-lived as tensions between Hamas and Fatah escalated in the Gaza Strip and led to Hamas' forceful takeover of the Strip, which was followed by Palestinian president Mahmoud Abbas's declaration to dissolve the government and the banning of Hamas in the West Bank. Since then, there have been two Palestinian authorities, one in the West Bank led by Fatah and another in the Gaza Strip led by Hamas. Both, however, as Seurat describes, have suffered 'a double denial of recognition', and neither has been recognized as a 'state', although the Palestinian Authority in the West Bank (along with the PLO) has remained the formal and acknowledged representative internationally of the Palestinians.

Since 2007 Hamas became besieged in the Gaza Strip by a 'double blockade' – one geographical by Israel, that controlled land, air and sea access to the Strip, and another diplomatic 'blockade' by the so-called international community led by the United States, as neatly detailed in this book. In the following years, Hamas and the Gaza Strip with its two million Palestinians have had to endure successive Israeli wars that turned the Strip into a miserable and 'unliveable' area, according to some UN reports. Within such conditions, Hamas has maintained its rule up until early 2021, the time of writing, through a complex matrix of politics that knitted internal control with external support and relations.

Seurat's exploration of the overlap between Hamas' domestic and foreign politics reminds us of Martin Hollis and Steve Smith's emphasis on the perspective of combining the 'explaining' and the 'understanding' regarding international relations, where state behaviour is better 'understood' and 'explained' through internally formative and externally systemic factors.[1] That Hamas is neither a state nor the Gaza Strip a sovereign entity raises serious questions about applying IR theorization to either the ruler or the ruled. By insightfully problematizing these questions and conceptualizing Hamas' case and study, Seurat argues that Hamas has ultimately implemented 'a genuine and almost "state-like" foreign policy' and has conducted 'a "classic" foreign policy in accordance with a number of canons listed in the scientific literature'. This argument, supported by a detailed and stimulating array of discussions and evidence throughout the book's chapters, provides a significant contribution to the study of the politics of Islamist movements.

Focusing on the Gaza Strip (and Hamas) from the perspective of international relations theory, as Seurat does, brings back into the discussion the basic rights of Palestinians – such as a Palestinian sovereign state, independence and liberation – which have been completely submerged by constantly having highlighted only the mere misery of their daily realities. As Seurat's book demonstrates, entities that are deprived of state sovereignty and the ability to function at the international level – but capable of effective performance at a local level – can and do survive for years. This is not only by virtue of the internal capacities of both Hamas and the Palestinian people but also because the beneficiary players (Israel, in Hamas' case) would seek to preserve the status quo surrounding these entities as part of the no-solution 'solution', while barely allowing both to survive. A few months after the 2007 Fatah-Hamas/West Bank-Gaza Strip split, I published an op-ed in the leading Palestinian daily *Al-Ayyam* warning that the two parties on both sides of the divide had better reconcile and prevent time from slipping away and further widening the gulf, or the Gaza Strip would end up in a realpolitik situation similar to northern Cyprus. Since the mid-1980s, the status quo in northern Cyprus has been gradually characterized by the internal control exercised by the local authority but a lack of any external recognition (except from Turkey). Over the years, however, the northern Cyprus quasi-state has realistically functioned as an impotent buffer zone between an intractable conflict and finding any lasting solution. Entities of this nature can survive for decades, and the party at the losing end thus keeps compounding its losses as new and newer realities became more concrete and harder to repeal.

In the Palestinian case, Hamas and the Gaza Strip have survived massive challenges and deadly wars – partly because of Hamas' internal capabilities, discipline and grassroots support, but mostly because of Israel's tactics in exploiting Hamas' control in ways that have benefited Israel's own broader strategy. In particular, Israel policies have deliberately prolonged the Gaza status quo and manipulated Hamas' desperation for survival and external recognition. By perpetuating the reality of Hamas' control in the Gaza Strip (and that of the Palestinian Authority in the West Bank), Israel has consolidated its occupation

---

1. Martin Hollis and Steve Smith, *Explaining and Understanding International Relations*, Oxford: Clarendon Press, 1991.

and colonization over both, while effectively ridding itself of any responsibilities for the daily needs of millions of Palestinians.

In pursuit of its own survival and recognition, Hamas' foreign policy has followed a standard realist line of subduing ideology in favour of interest-driven politics. This has been and is still surprising for those who sketchily think of the movement as one blindly driven by a rigid or idealistic religious doctrine. Seurat presents a wealth of evidence in this respect, meticulously tracing Hamas' praxis and intellectual deployment in the domain of international relations. The place and influence of Hamas' religious ideology within its broader project and practice has always been a subject of considerable attention. The early documents and statements of the movement reflected a heavily religious constituting substance, yet this pervasive ideological component has never materialized concretely in the sphere of Hamas' relations either with Palestinian parties (leftist and nationalist) or with other states. In the region, Hamas has nurtured strong relations with a number of 'secular' states; moreover and as Seurat closely explores, Hamas' omnipresent Sunni religious affiliation has been relegated to the back seat as it has enhanced its strategic relations with Iran, the leading Shia power in the region. Internationally, Hamas' has evolved links and contacts with states regardless of 'their religion', enjoying strong relations with Russia, a state that has had a very mixed record and an often brutal history – politically and otherwise – regarding local or international Muslims.

Seurat's book offers the best in-depth investigation of Hamas' international relations and its foreign policy conduct. The scale of research and reliance on original material and interviews is impressive. In particular, the author managed to meet and discuss with dozens of Hamas leaders in the Gaza Strip, the West Bank and outside Palestine – in Syria, Lebanon, Egypt, Qatar, Turkey and even in Switzerland and Cyprus where Hamas members participated in workshops or conferences. This extensive network of interviews near and far afield, coupled with the examination of old and new founding documents of the movement, has allowed Seurat to construct the most precise and balanced picture of Hamas' thinking and practice in foreign policy.

Khaled Hroub

ACKNOWLEDGEMENTS

This research wouldn't have been achieved without the support of my friends in Palestine to whom I am extremely grateful.

I would like to thank Hassan al-Balawi for his patience and attention since the very early stages of my work. I am also grateful to Mohammed Daraghmeh and will always remember the serious – and sometimes lighter – conversations we had in Ankara, Ramallah and Cairo. Last but not least, all my gratitude goes to Hisham Zaqout for sharing his views and making me discover the many faces of Gaza, keeping in memory the convivial atmosphere at the Al-Jazeera offices; these encounters to be revived soon, hopefully.

INTRODUCTION

During a television interview in August 2020, Ismail Haniyeh, the president of the Hamas' Political Bureau, spoke of the sanitary catastrophe provoked by Covid-19 in Gaza. Extending the virus metaphor, he recalled that the Palestinians were fighting several strains of an epidemic apart from the coronavirus itself: the 'corona of division' and the 'corona of the deal of the century'.[1] Also described as the Trump plan for the Middle East, the 'deal of the century' appears as the ultimate curse affecting the Palestinians: it includes moving the US Embassy from Tel Aviv to Jerusalem; Israel's announcement of the annexation of the Jordan Valley and the large settlement blocks, planned for 1 July 2020 and then postponed; the proclamation of normalization accords between Israel and the United Arab Emirates. To each of these announcements, Hamas has distinguished itself by launching rockets towards Israel.[2]

This rocket fire has nevertheless been restricted to its most symbolic dimension. Inversely, Hamas willingly uses its military machine to put forward other – and more short-term – goals related to its political and administrative management of the Gaza Strip. During the whole month of August 2020, the movement did not hesitate to enter into armed confrontation with Israel, by launching incendiary balloons and rockets, to try to lift the blockade. This umpteenth cycle of violence marking the daily life of Gazans since the triggering of the March of Return in spring 2018 thus can be seen as a form of negotiation through violence, a so-to-speak 'dialogue of fire' (*hiwar al-nar*), which allows Hamas to try to secure a few gains in exchange for a pacification of borders: the opening of the Kerem Abou Salem crossing, the extension of the maritime area granted to Gazan fishermen, the provision of working permits in Israel for Gazans, Qatar's payment of electricity bills and $30 million of financial aid handed over by Qatar. The lull beginning in late August, following the visit to the Gaza Strip of the Qatari mediator Mohammed al-Emadi, led to the belief that these concessions, which are the subject of perpetual re-negotiation, were at the time granted to Hamas.

---

1. https://www.youtube.com/watch?v=Cx3wz2YzlsM.
2. As from 25 June, five days before the annexation planned on 1 July, Abu Obeida, the al-Qassam Brigades' spokesman, asserted that the annexation of part of the West Bank would be a declaration of war. On 1st and 2nd July, some twenty rockets were fired at Israel from the Gaza Strip.

Held under the aegis of Egypt and Qatar, these indirect talks between Israel and Hamas have contributed to marginalizing Ramallah's Palestinian Authority in a significant way. The president of the Palestinian Authority, Mahmoud Abbas, has unceasingly denounced these dynamics, accusing both Arab mediators and Hamas of playing into the hands of Israel by acknowledging a permanent separation between the West Bank and the Gaza Strip. However, these separate initiatives did not prevent discussions between Fatah and Hamas. As of July 2020, Fatah's general secretary in Ramallah Jibril Rajoub and Salah Arouri, the deputy chairman of Hamas' Political Bureau (speaking from Beirut), initiated a rapprochement by videoconference. Both made the commitment of uniting Palestinian ranks into a common front to counter Israel's annexation plans in the West Bank. Netanyahu's territorial ambitions and the announcement of Israel's normalization of relations with several Gulf states once more put on the agenda the urgency of Palestinian reconciliation, each of the two parties presenting itself as sincerely engaged in attempts to end division. On 24 September, Fatah and Hamas representatives meeting in Turkey announced the organization of parliamentary and then presidential elections in the near future. As early as 2014, during the signing of the Shati Agreement, then once again in 2017 on the occasion of a new reconciliation deal in Cairo, Hamas had expressed its goodwill in handing over the keys of the Gaza Strip to the president of the Palestinian Authority.

The strategy of Hamas is thus a little enigmatic: involved in indirect negotiations with Israel to ensure the long-term duration of its power over the Gaza Strip, the movement has simultaneously emphasized its readiness to abandon its control of this territory. This book, a study in international relations, is an attempt to go beyond this apparent paradox by showing how Hamas, in its quest for recognition, willingly mobilizes Palestinian internal issues to establish its legitimacy on the international stage. At the same time, its relations with non-Palestinian players allow it to compete against its political rivals on the Palestinian national stage. Foreign and internal policy is therefore not to be understood as two completely unconnected fields of study; quite the opposite, they are strongly intertwined, in accordance with the linkage theory put forward some time ago by James Rosenau.

Despite the boycott Hamas was subjected to since its victory in the 2006 parliamentary elections, it has managed to appear as an unavoidable interlocutor, in charge of an entity akin to a state. Of course, it does not benefit at all from the international recognition Ramallah enjoys, but it can nevertheless boast other requirements of a state, such as a territory identifiable by its borders[3] or internationally recognized cease-fire lines, as well as effective authority over

---

3. Use of the notion of border is a little problematic because Israel and Egypt, the two states that have common borders with Gaza, do not share the same juridical interpretation of this territory. Israel considers that since its withdrawal from the Gaza Strip in 2005, this territory is autonomous and provided with borders, which allows it to criminalize gunfire from Gaza. On the other hand, Egypt considers the Gaza Strip as an occupied territory, whose responsibility rests on the occupying power.

a population.⁴ This consequently begs the question: How should one grasp the nature of this player, which despite not being a state bears no similarities with other non-state entities as defined by the great paradigms of international relations?

Writing Palestine's diplomatic history requires focusing on matters other than the accords and agreements sponsored by the international community, or even the disturbed relations between the Palestinian Authority, the PLO and Israel.⁵ One must also look at the diplomacies of 'intruders', namely the Hamas, which, since its victory in the 2006 legislative elections and its unilateral seizure of power in the Gaza Strip in June 2007, does not embody partisan and asymmetric diplomacy but has succeeded in formulating and implementing a genuine and almost 'state-like' foreign policy.

Strangely, the analysis of Palestinian political parties was a marginal field in scientific works for a long time. In the early 1990s, the attention of academics was more focused on the construction of the Palestinian National Authority, the future of the Occupied Territories marked by colonization and the development of local councils, policy trends towards 'NGO-isation', the question of refugees, memories of the Nakba or Israeli policies relating to prisons. Although Fatah and the Palestinian Left are no longer the subjects of academic attention,⁶ scholars are increasingly interested in Hamas. As from the early 1990s, a first generation of researchers and political scientists began concentrating on the analysis of Hamas' opposition to the Oslo Peace Process, understanding it as a social movement.⁷ From armed struggle to negotiation, the practices of Hamas are, more often than not, the result of internal rivalry between the various Palestinian factions.⁸ This first generation of works was followed by a second one published in the wake of the 2006 Hamas election victory.⁹ The experience of Hamas in controlling the

---

4. The 1933 Montevideo Convention qualifies states as political entities endowed with the four following criteria: a permanent population, a defined territory, a sovereign political authority and the capacity to enter into relations with other states.

5. Augustus R. Norton and Martin H. Greenberg, *The International Relations of the Palestine Liberation Organization* (Carbondale: Southern Illinois University Press, 1989).

6. With the exception of the book by Nicolas Dot-Pouillard, Eugénie Rébillard and Wissam Alhaj, *De la théologie à la liberation? Histoire du Jihad islamique palestinien* (Paris: La Découverte, 2014).

7. Ziad Abu Amr, *Islamic Fundamentalism in the West Bank and Gaza* (Bloomington: Indiana University Press, 1994); Hisham H. Ahmad, *Hamas: From Religious Salvation to Political Transformation: The Rise of Hamas in Palestinian Society* (Jerusalem: PASSIA, 1994); Glenn E. Robinson, 'Hamas and the Islamist Mobilization', in *Building a Palestinian State: The Incomplete Revolution* (Bloomington: Indiana University Press, 1997).

8. Shaul Mishal and Avraham Sela, *The Palestinian Hamas: Vision, Violence, and Coexistence* (New York: Columbia University Press, 2000).

9. Michael I. Jensen, *The Political Ideology of Hamas: A Grassroots Perspective* (London and New York: I.B. Tauris, 2009); Jeroen Gunning, *Hamas in Politics* (New York: Columbia University Press, 2009); Sara Roy, *Hamas and Civil Society in Gaza* (Princeton: Princeton

Gaza Strip has more recently opened other fields of research that see Gaza as a laboratory for the analysis of Islamism in power.[10]

Most of these works reflect interest in the field of sociology of mobilizations and favour an analysis from a local viewpoint. Apart from Khaled Hroub's book,[11] which in his comprehensive study of the Palestinian Islamist movement dedicates a chapter to its foreign relations, there is no systematic approach to the movement's foreign policy. Now, Hamas is not only a party made up of militants; it is also a movement including leaders and involving political decision making, part of a great regional game and the result of specific conditions. Although the movement has certainly developed structured relations with many non-state players, the author's research is above all interested in the relations it has with foreign state players, which are sufficiently varied and complex to be a genuine topic of analysis. These relations also demonstrate that the foreign policy of Hamas is truly oriented towards other states, and therefore towards the type of player favoured by the realist approach, which continues to exert substantial influence on the study of international relations.

The present book, finally, considers itself an invitation to take ideology seriously in the social sciences. It is true that there is a plethora of works, more from experts than from political scientists, that excessively emphasize the ideological factor in order to discredit Hamas. According to this scholarship, the movement, due to the very essence of its transnational religious ideology, is opposed to any form of compromise, or even to the adherence to national borders. This reading rests on no empirical observation whatsoever, and only reappears because of the nuisance capacity of theories based on suspicion: suspicion relating to external allegiances (Hamas is accordingly only the henchman of the Muslim Brotherhood or even Iran[12]) and suspicion of double-talk (Hamas says it is changing, but in fact it is not). This saturation of accusatory writings against the movement has even colonized universities and academia and may legitimately induce among scholars a more or less conscious motivation to leave aside ideology in favour of strictly sociological analyses.[13] Yet beyond biases that are scientifically unfounded and that mistakenly

---

University Press, 2011); Beverly Milton-Edwards and Stephen Farrell, *Hamas: The Islamic Resistance Movement* (Cambridge, UK: Polity Press, 2010); Aude Signoles, *Le Hamas au pouvoir et après?* (Milan actu, 2006).

10. Bjorn Brenner, *Gaza Under Hamas: From Islamic Democracy to Islamist Governance* (I.B. Tauris, 2016).

11. Khaled Hroub, *Hamas, Political Thought and Practice* (Washington: Institute for Palestine Studies, 2000).

12. See Ely Karmon, 'Gaza/Hamastan, plateforme de déstabilisation du monde arabe par l'Iran', *Outre-Terre: revue française de géopolitique* 22, no. 2 (2009): 41–53.

13. See Leila Seurat, Laurent Bonnefoy, 'Les islamistes dans les relations internationales. Des acteurs transnationaux comme les autres?', in *Un monde fragmenté. Autour de la sociologie des Relations internationales de Bertrand Badie*, ed. D. Allès, R. Malejacq and S. Paquin (Paris: CNRS Éditions, 2018).

inform us on the political practices of Hamas, it seemed necessary to rehabilitate ideology and to go beyond binary interpretations considering it either as crucial or as ineffective. Countering these fossilized views, this book tries to grasp ideology and identify the way it is mobilized by Hamas in various contexts, in order to legitimate practices often very far from a supposed original and immutable ideological bedrock.

Genesis of the movement

Hamas is the political and military arm of the Palestinian branch of the Muslim Brotherhood. The links bonding the Muslim Brothers and Palestine go back to 1935, when Abd al-Rahman al-Sa'ati, Hassan al-Banna's brother, visited Palestine and spoke to the Grand Mufti of Jerusalem al-Husseini. In the wake of the Second World War, the Muslim Brothers established their first office in the Jerusalem neighbourhood of Sheikh Jarrah. As of 1947, they had at least twenty-five branches in Palestine.[14] When the first Arab–Israeli war began, they sent volunteers to combat Zionist organizations, thus rallying nationalist factions to war with what was about to turn into the State of Israel.[15]

The 1948 defeat led to a new political configuration where the Jordanians annexed the West Bank and East Jerusalem, while the Egyptians occupied the Gaza Strip. The situation of the Brotherhood in these two territories then developed along distinct lines: in the West Bank under Jordanian rule, the Brothers focused exclusively on their charity mission and abandoned armed struggle.[16] With the exception of a few military operations in the late 1960s in the Jordan Valley under the banner of Fatah, they left the political stage and were no longer part of the liberation effort.[17] In the Gaza Strip, the flow of some 200,000 refugees attempting to return to the lands they were expelled from led to another configuration, where the Muslim Brothers built military training camps to carry out armed operations. They endured fierce and bloody repression by Israel – with incursions, executions and arrests, notably carried out by Unit 101 – without the Egyptians reacting.[18] On the contrary, as of 1954 Nasser was himself bent on repressing the Muslim

---

14. Ziad Abu Amr, 'Hamas: A Historical and Political Background', *Journal of Palestine Studies* 22 no. 4 (1993): 5–19.

15. On the issue of the implication of the Muslim Brotherhood in the national liberation struggle, see Ziad Abou Ghanimah, *Al-haraka al-islâmiyya wa qadiyyat Filastîn* (Amman: Furqan House, 1985).

16. See Milton-Edwards, *Islamic Politics in Palestine* (London: I.B Tauris, 1996). For more details on the situation of the Muslim Brothers in Jordan, see Ammon Cohen, *Political Parties in the West Bank Under the Jordanian Regime, 1949–1967* (London: Cornell University Press, 1982).

17. Hroub, *Hamas, Political Thought and Practice*.

18. Jean-Pierre Filiu, *Gaza: A History* (London: Oxford University Press, 2014).

Brothers, which made him dismantle their paramilitary structures in Gaza. The Brotherhood's dissent would occasionally express itself: in 1955, they massively demonstrated with Communist and Baathist militants against the proposal of settling Palestinian refugees in the Sinai Peninsula and did so once more during Israel's brief occupation of the Gaza Strip between 1956 and 1957; they also formed a national resistance front with the Baathists. They nevertheless went back time and again to their charity and social activities.[19]

From disengagement from armed struggle to the creation of Hamas

In 1967, Gaza and the West Bank were under Israeli occupation. The Palestinian Muslim Brothers took charge of social and educational matters and developed a wide network of dispensaries, schools, clinics and sports clubs. The creation in 1973 by Sheikh Ahmed Yassin of the *Mujam'a al-islâmi* (Islamic Society) also heralded the proliferation of mosques, which rose from 200 in Gaza in 1967 to 600 in 1987.[20] Involvement in proselytizing activities was meant to prepare the next generations to liberate Palestine: only a truly Islamic society was, in their minds, able to efficiently combat Zionism.[21] These initiatives were at the time tolerated by Israel, which saw them as an effective counterweight to the PLO's influence.[22]

This withdrawal from armed struggle would nevertheless generate several splits within Sheikh Yassin's Islamic society. The Brothers' expansion was first of all hampered when many of them dissented and created military cells like the Battalions of Justice, pioneer resistance groups before the founding of Fatah in 1959.[23] Youth at the basis of Fatah wanted to distinguish themselves from the Muslim Brothers for several reasons: on the one hand, they wished to keep Egypt's assistance, while the Brothers were focusing on challenging Nasser's regime. On the other, they projected an alliance with Palestinian Baathists, nationalists and Communists,[24] while the Brotherhood was honing its connections with Saudi

---

19. Jean-Pierre Filiu, 'The Twelve Wars on Gaza', *Journal of Palestine Studies* 44, no. 1 (2014): 52–60. For an analysis of police administration in Gaza under Egyptian occupation, see Ilana Feldman, *Police Encounters: Security and Surveillance in Gaza under Egyptian Rule* (Stanford: Stanford University Press, 2015).

20. Ziad Abu Amr, 'Hamas: A Historical and Political Background', *Journal of Palestine Studies* 22, no. 4 (1993): 5–19.

21. Signoles, *Le Hamas au pouvoir et après?*.

22. Charles Enderlin, *Le grand aveuglement, Israël et l'irrésistible ascension de l'Islam radical* (Paris: Albin Michel, 2009).

23. This was in particular the case of Salah Khalaf (Abou Iyad), one of the most influential figures of PLO officialdom of the 1970s and 1980s. On the matter of links between the Muslim Brothers and Fatah, see Abbu Azza, *Ma'a Al-haraka al-islâmiyya fî-l-aqtâr al-'arabiyya* (Kuwait: Al Qalam, 1992).

24. The Muslim Brothers and other Palestinian political movements stem from the same group of students who were spending time in the early 1950s at Al-Azhar University

Arabia and Jordan. The first Fatah cells were therefore formed while dissenting from the Muslim Brotherhood.

At the end of the 1970s, the Brothers went through other internal rifts. Refusing the pre-eminence of social action over politics, Fathi al-Shiqaqi, who was influenced by Iran's Islamic Revolution,[25] created Islamic Jihad. The creation of this organization then reactivated the debate within the Brotherhood on the movement's priorities:[26] Did the liberation of Palestine have to go through the re-Islamization of Palestinian society, or should it precede it?

The arrest of Sheikh Yassin in 1984 for unlawful possession of weapons is proof that the Palestinian Muslim Brothers were already about to found a new structure meant to take part in armed struggle.[27] It was actually when the First Intifada erupted, however, that they chose to abandon their quietist attitude and change their strategy, by actively taking part in actions of resistance against the occupiers. This event, which occurred on 8 December 1987,[28] marked the creation, on the evening of the following day, of Hamas (an acronym for Movement of Islamic Resistance, which also means 'fervour' in Arabic). The foundation meeting gathered Sheikh Yassin, Abd al-Aziz al-Rantisi, Salah Shehadeh, Abd al-Fattah Dukhan, Ibrahim al-Yazouri, Mohammed Sham'a and Issa al-Nashar. Its first communiqué was written during this gathering but only published a few days later (on 11 December in Gaza and on the 14th in the West Bank). Although some of the Brothers were calling for a continuation of Islamization 'from the bottom', the majority of militants congregating around Sheikh Yassin considered that the time had come to take part in armed operations against the occupier, since not engaging in action meant running the risk of permanently marginalizing the Brotherhood on the Palestinian political stage. While the Israelis had until then been more or less tolerant of Islamist associations, they decided in 1989 to hit hard at the movement by detaining a number of its leaders, Sheikh Yassin in particular.

---

in Cairo. The League of Palestinian Students grouped most Palestinian political currents. See Hassan Balawi, *Dans les coulisses du mouvement national palestinien* (Paris: Denoël, 2008).

25. Fathi al-Shiqaqi, *Al-Humaynî: al-hal al-islâmî wa-l-badîl* (Dâr al-muhtâr al-islâmî, 1979).

26. Thomas Mayer, 'Pro-Iranian Fundamentalism in Gaza', in *Religious Radicalism and Politics in the Middle-East*, ed. Emmanuel Sivan and Menachem Friedman (Albany: State University of New York Press, 1990).

27. Hroub, *Hamas: Political Thought and Practice*.

28. On 8 December, an Israeli truck ran into several Palestinian workers. This event provoked, the same day, massive demonstrations in Jabaliyya camp, from where the three victims came.

Dissent against Oslo and the gradual ascent of the Islamic Resistance

The foundation of Hamas occurred as the first signs of negotiations between the PLO and Israel were emerging. Promulgated on 15 November 1988 in Algiers, the PLO's Independence Declaration was the first outcome of the adoption of a realistic stance towards Israel, which made Yasser Arafat a partner in discussions to come, as compensation for his implicit recognition of the State of Israel and his acceptance of a territorial division of Palestine.[29] From its very first communiqué on, Hamas denounced these Palestinian initiatives meant to solve the conflict: only Islam is an alternative to this 'shaky peace'. To counter the negotiation process, Hamas chose violence.[30] Following the creation in 1992 of its armed branch (the Izz al-Din al-Qassam Brigades),[31] the movement increased the number of operations against Israeli targets, as shown by the assassination of the border guard Nassim Toledano in December. The first attack of any consequence closely followed the Oslo Accords and was a response to the murder in February 1994, in the mosque of Hebron, of twenty-nine Palestinians by Baruch Goldstein, an extremist Jewish settler. Israeli provocations were timely opportunities for Hamas to justify these attacks, which were described as reprisals. This was notably the case in January 1996, when Israel killed Yahya Ayyash, also called 'the engineer', because of the quality of his expertise in the manufacture of explosive powders and substances. The assassination of Ayyash was followed, in March, by a wave of suicide attacks in Jerusalem and Tel Aviv.[32]

Confronted with the pursuit of colonization and delays in the Israeli Army's redeployment schedule in the West Bank, the Oslo process increasingly appeared as a failure in the eyes of the Palestinians. The fact that Hamas was implementing a strategy of armed struggle allowed its popularity to soar. These attacks, however, also damaged the movement's relations with some countries of the region that had recognized the PLO as the sole representative of the Palestinian people and begun talks with Israel.[33] This was the case of Jordan, which in the aftermath of the first Gulf War welcomed several Hamas representatives seeking to settle outside the Occupied Palestinian Territories to protect the movement from the wave of expulsions and detentions.

29. Signoles, *Le Hamas au pouvoir et après?*.

30. For an analysis of Hamas and Islamic Jihad opposition to the process of dialogue and negotiation, see Beverley Milton-Edward, 'Political Islam in Palestine in an Environment of Peace?', *Third World Quarterly* 17, no. 2 (1996): 199–226.

31. The name Izz al-Din al-Qassam was chosen by Hamas in reference to the 'father of Palestinian resistance', the Syrian Izz al-Din al-Qassam, who had gone to Palestine to carry out actions against the British Mandate and who was killed in November 1935, just before the eruption of the 1936 Great Revolt.

32. Rashmi Singh, *Hamas and Suicide terrorism, Multi-Causal and Multi-Level Approaches* (London: Taylor and Francis and Routledge, 2013); Robert A. Pape, *Dying to Win: The Strategic Logic of Suicide Terrorism* (New York: Random House, 2005).

33. In its first communiqué dated to 14 December 1987, Hamas also denounced the signing by Egypt of the Camp David Accords.

During the entire 1990s, the external leadership of Hamas was thus settled in the Jordanian capital. In the eyes of the Palestinian movement, the Hashemite Kingdom was a strategic location, both because of geographical proximity and historical links uniting both Jordanians and Palestinians.[34] As for Jordan, it considered its relations with Hamas as a means of potential pressure, in case negotiations between Israel and the PLO – still in progress for the solving of the final status of the territories – would develop against its own interests. Although Hamas had congratulated the Jordanian Brothers for their victory in the 1989 parliamentary elections,[35] the Palestinian leaders residing in Amman criticized the peace treaty between Jordan and Israel, signed in October 1994, albeit with a measure of caution. Yet despite its efforts to avoid angering and going against Jordanian authorities, Hamas was not able to walk the tightrope of good relations with the Hashemite Kingdom much longer. Several reasons can explain the Jordanian authorities' decision to expel the members of Hamas: one can mention armed operations of Hamas in Israel and the strong pressure on Jordan to close the movement's offices in Amman. Three critical events marked this period: the withdrawal of the passports belonging to Mohammad Nazzal and Hamas spokesman Ibrahim Ghosheh in April 1994, Moussa Abu Marzouk and Imad al-Alami's expulsion in 1995 and finally the arrest of Ibrahim Ghosheh on 7 September 1997. Yet one should note that during the same year, King Hussein had shown strong support towards Khaled Mesh'al, when the latter was the target of attempted murder perpetrated by Mossad agents in Amman.[36] The Israeli commando's pathetic fiasco paradoxically served the interests of Hamas, since Khaled Mesh'al was provided with an antidote delivered by the Israelis, while Sheikh Yassin was being released from jail as compensation. Two years later, in 1999, Hamas was expelled from Jordan and went to settle in Syria.

Concomitant with this expulsion, the failure of the Camp David negotiation process in the summer of 2000 sparked the beginning of the Second Intifada, which, in contrast to the first, was far from being a spontaneous uprising. Hamas would largely gain from this soaring in violence, which carried out spectacular attacks against Israeli civilians. This would later translate into positive results in the 2005 municipal elections.

Hamas and the Muslim Brotherhood: Friendly but non-organizational relations

As stipulated in its Charter, Hamas derives from the Muslim Bortherhood. Article 2 presented the movement as 'the armed wing of the Muslim brotherhood in Palestine'. Nonetheless, Hamas leaders maintain a complex relation with the

---

34. For a discussion of Hamas' political and economic ties with Jordan, see Muhammad Jaradat, 'Islamic Resistance Movement (Hamas) in the Territories Occupied in 1967', *News From Within* 8, no. 8 (1992).

35. Communiqué no 50 published on 27 November 1989.

36. Paul McGeough, *Kill Khalid, The Failed Assassination of Khalid Mishal and the Rise of Hamas* (New York: New Press, 2009).

Egyptian Association. They consider that, depending on the context, it can harm the fulfilment of their interests. Hamas' membership of the Brotherhood can damage relations with many Arab states fighting Islamist forces on their own territory. This is the case of Jordan, which feared that the activities of Hamas on its soil would strengthen the agenda of the Jordanian Muslim Brothers.

Relations between Hamas and the Egyptian Brothers are on the level of mutual feelings of understanding but not at an organizational level.[37] According to the Brotherhood's former Supreme Guide, there is no relationship of command or obedience between the Brothers and Hamas. When the organizations diverge on an issue, however, the Egyptian Brotherhood can intervene.[38] Since the movement's creation in December 1987, Hamas sought to acquire a certain measure of autonomy as regards the Brothers.[39] The memoirs of Salah Shehadeh, one of the founding members of Hamas and the presumed chief of the armed branch before his assassination by Israel in July 2002, illustrate the dilemma of this relationship with the 'parent company': 'In our charter, we have insisted on the fact that Hamas should be a coalition with links not restricted to the Muslim Brothers, but capable of absorbing all Palestinian resistance organizations, their followers and friends.'[40] This distancing did not prevent the consolidation of links between Hamas and the Jordanian Muslim Brothers, until the expulsion in 1999 of the outside leadership from Amman.[41]

During the years after 2000, Hamas would once more minimize its links with the Muslim Brothers, a consequence of the establishment of the external leadership in Syria and Hafez al-Assad's conflictual relations with the Syrian branch of the Brotherhood. At the time of the movement's 2006 election victory, some leaders of the Islamic Resistance around Khaled Mesh'al tried to sever ties between Hamas and the Brothers.[42] In the summer of 2007, when the movement took control of

---

37. For a historical background on the Muslim Brothers and Palestine, see Abd al-Fattah Muhammad Al-Awaisi, *The Muslim Brothers and the Palestine Question, 1928–1947* (London and New York: I.B. Tauris, 1998).

38. Interview of Mahdi Akef in *al-Dustur* on 20 December 2006.

39. Jean-François Legrain stresses that the issue of breaking the links with the Muslim Brotherhood's Association has been raised as early as 1993. Jean-François Legrain, 'Le 'Document' de Hamas (2017) ou l'ouverture comme garante des invariants', *Les carnets de l'IREMAM*, 2017.

40. See the article written by Abd al-Mun'im Mahmoud, a journalist affiliated to the Egyptian Muslim Brothers, in *al-Dustur*, 28 January 2009.

41. Many divergences, however, separate the two organizations, and the Jordanian Brotherhood has for a long time displayed the slogan 'Jordan first'.

42. Following Sheikh Ahmed Yassin's assassination, the website of Hamas introduced him as the 'Supreme Guide' of the Palestinian formation. This title is generally only given to the head of the Egyptian parent branch. The Brotherhood formations of other countries avoid using it as a way of accepting the prominence of the Egyptian branch. Using this title was therefore a kind of declaration of independence.

Gaza, some of its officials apparently refused to meet the Brotherhood's Supreme Guide Mahdi Akef, who was trying to mediate between conflicting Palestinian parties.[43]

On the other hand, the rise to power of the Muslim Brothers in Egypt, in 2012, made Hamas strengthen its ties with the Brotherhood. As from October 2011, Hamas added to its name 'Movement of Islamic Resistance' the mention 'section of the Muslim Brothers'.[44] This process was moreover illustrated by the Brotherhood's interference in Hamas' internal election process.[45] Faced with Mohammed Morsi's discredit on the Egyptian political stage, however, some Hamas leaders then began to question the benefits of such a policy of rapprochement, fearing that the tarnishing of the Egyptian president's image would prolong their regional and international isolation. Mohammed Morsi's fall[46] in the summer of 2013 and the repression of Egyptian Brothers once again raised the question of the future of relations between the Brothers and Hamas.[47] Seeking to brighten its image with the new regime of General al-Sisi, Hamas chose to remain quiet about its affiliation with the Egyptian Brothers when its new Document of General Principles and Policies was published in 2017.

Palestine, foreign policy and political Islam

Diplomacies in search of a state

The classic or 'realist' definition of foreign policy – a tool used by a state to forge and interact with its international environment – is at the basis of international relations theory. Applied to Palestine, this definition raises important questions. Despite not benefiting from state structures, Palestinian political players do nonetheless have a foreign policy, understood as a tool helping in the construction of a sovereign state. This observation seems to support the pertinence of other schools of thought in international relations, which have demonstrated that foreign policy is not the sole privilege of states, and that other players, described as non-state, can also have

---

43. According to *Nahdat Misr*, 2 July 2007.
44. Although the earliest reference to this affiliation appears in a declaration dated 11 February 1988 (i.e. two months after the foundation of the movement), no direct affiliation is mentioned next to the name Hamas. See *Roz* on 11 December 2011.
45. *Maariv* quoted by *al-Masri al-Youm*, 1 April 2013, claims that the Muslim Brothers tried to make Khaled Mesh'al the winner.
46. Mohamed Morsi's fall can be partly explained by his 'interference' in matters relating to Gaza and Sinai, of which the Egyptian military establishment was very resentful.
47. Palestinian Islamists were always dependent on the level of tolerance granted to the Egyptian Muslim Brotherhood on the Egyptian political stage. Nasser's repression as from 1954 had consequences on Gaza's Muslim Brotherhood. Until 1968, this dependency was all the more apparent, since Egypt was administrating the Palestinian coastal strip.

a role in this 'exclusive domain'. This is the case of Bertrand Badie, who refers to an international system that is 'increasingly less run by states',[48] and Christopher Hill who, defining foreign policy as 'the sum of official relations conducted by an independent player',[49] refers not only to states but also to non-state or supra-state players. The PLO's foreign policy was thus largely studied with this perspective in mind,[50] both before and after the November 1988 Declaration of Independence after which many states recognized the state of Palestine.[51]

The Palestinian Authority, a new entity born of the Oslo Accords, saw itself from the very first day of its formation deprived of any powers of diplomacy: it was denied a Foreign Affairs Ministry, because Israel preferred a simple Ministry of Planning and International Cooperation.[52] One had to wait until 2003 to see Israelis finally concede a Foreign Ministry for this new political body. Yet far from favouring the conditions for building an independent state, this parody of sovereignty sparked increased competition between the Palestinian Authority and the PLO, which until then held a monopoly on diplomatic matters. The victory of Hamas in the 2006 parliamentary elections exacerbated this institutional rivalry, since the Palestinian Authority's Foreign Ministry was now staffed with leaders from the Islamic Resistance Movement.

Any attempt by scholars in international relations to order these political players into well-defined categories would seem artificial. Although the classic definition from international relations is not pertinent, applying the concept of a non-state player as defined by the sociology of international relations is also not self-evident. The major part of this literature deals with cases of players in state contexts.[53] Most often, these studies analyse the consequences of external actions led by organizations such as non-governmental, regional and from administrative

---

48. Bertrand Badie and Marie-Claude Smouts, *Le retournement du monde, sociologie de la scène internationale* (Paris: Presses de Sciences Po et Dalloz, 1999).

49. Christopher Hill, *The Changing Politics of Foreign Policy* (New York: Palgrave Macmillan, 2003).

50. Afif Safieh, *On Palestinian Diplomacy*, Palestinian General Delegation to the UK and the Office of the Representation of the PLO to the Holy See, London, 2004; A. Norton, M. Greeberg, *The International Relations of the Palestine Liberation Organization* (Carbondale: Southern Illinois University Press, 1989).

51. This state, whose Declaration of Independence was announced by the Palestinian National Council on 15 November 1988, was then recognized by seventy-five countries. This conferred upon Palestinian representations in these states the status of embassies, and to its representatives the title and status of Ambassador of Palestine.

52. See Annex II of the Declaration of Principles.

53. Brian Hocking, *Localizing Foreign Policy, Non Central Governments and Multilayered Diplomacy* (St Martin's Press, 1993); 'Non-State Actors and the Transformation of Diplomacy', in *Non-State Actors in International Relations*, ed. Bas Arts, Math Noortmann and Bob Reinalda (Ashgate, 2001). Philip Taylor, *Non-State Actors in International Politics. From Transregional To Substate Organizations* (New York: Routledge, 1984).

units, in the framework of decentralized states.⁵⁴ Now, Hamas, just like the PLO or Fatah, are almost state-like non-state players; indeed, these organizations are in many respects more similar to state players than non-state ones (like NGOs).

To be sure, Hamas is not part of the PLO, a body recognized as the sole representative of the Palestinian people. Nevertheless, the movement's overwhelming victory in the January 2006 parliamentary elections allowed it to form by itself the Tenth Palestinian government since the foundation of the Palestinian Authority in 1994. It was able, therefore, to speak in the name of the political entity deriving from the Oslo process which, in its later stages, was to become a state and benefit from international recognition. This conclusion was true even after the seizure of Gaza in June 2007, when Mahmoud Abbas set up a second parallel government in Ramallah and began enjoying international recognition. This institutional split into two parts and loss of recognition did not prevent Hamas from continuing to exercise its foreign policy activities, both from exile and in Gaza: as opposed to Ramallah's political leaders, who saw their authority short-circuited on a daily basis by the always more ominous presence of the occupation forces, Gaza's Hamas leaders could boast that they controlled institutions normally associated with states, such as armed forces and an administrative apparatus. Hamas is thus akin to a semi-state player and, though void of any sovereignty, a 'quasi-state' as understood by Robert Jackson:⁵⁵ that is, more as a territorial jurisdiction surviving thanks to international institutional and material support. Without forming or representing a state, Hamas conducts a 'classic' foreign policy in accordance with a number of canons listed in the scientific literature.

Clarifying a doctrine

Hamas has not really provided an underlying theory for its relations with the outside world.⁵⁶ A few official sources have nevertheless exposed the broad lines of the movement's foreign policy: the Charter, made public on 18 August 1988, the Introductory Memorandum,⁵⁷ an internal document entitled 'The Interim

---

54. Stéphane Paquin, *Paradiplomatie et relations internationales: théories de stratégies internationales des régions face à la mondialisation* (Bruxelles: PIE-P. Lang, 2004); Michael Keating and Francisco Aldecoa, ed., *Paradiplomacy in Action: The Foreign Relations of Subnational Governments* (Portland: Frank Cass, 1999). Panayotis Soldatos, 'An Explanatory Framework for the Study of Federated States as Foreign-Policy Actors', in *Federalism and International Relations: The Role of Subnational Units*, ed. Hans J. Michelmann and Panayotis Soldatos (Oxford: Clarendon Press, 1990).

55. Robert H. Jackson, *Quasi-States, Sovereignty, International Relations in the Third World* (Cambridge: Cambridge University Press, 1993).

56. For an overview of Hamas' political documents, see Menachem Klein, 'Hamas in Power', *Middle-East Journal* 61, no. 3 (2007): 442-59.

57. See Khaled Khroub, *Hamas: Political Thought and Practice* (Washington: Institute for Palestine Studies, 2000), 292.

Policy of Hamas and its Political Relations', written by the members of the outside leadership in the early 1990s,[58] and finally the Document of General Principles and Policies published on 1 May 2017. These documents provide scholars with two conflicting versions of the principles governing the movement's foreign policy.

The Charter emphasizes the necessity of defending Palestine against any foreign usurpation.[59] The Islamic dimension is exposed as the strategic pivot of the movement and the Palestinian cause, which is thought of as a religious cause.[60] Against the enemy, Hamas calls for solidarity from the three circles mentioned in Article 14: Palestinian, Arab and Islamic, each of them contributing to the struggle against Zionism. Although the Charter does not place any restrictions on negotiations with Israel, it does not mention the possibility of establishing specific relations with non-Arab or non-Islamic entities. It also denounces all initiatives aiming for a political compromise and describes them as a 'waste of time', and condemns the West and international organizations for their ties with Israel.[61] In matters of international relations, the Charter is close to classic Islamic doctrine, as elaborated by legal experts between 750 and 900 CE, since it puts forward a dualist vision of the universe, which is divided between Muslim states (*Dâr al-Salâm*) and those that are not (*Dâr al-Ḥarb*).[62]

Since the early 1990s, Hamas began to formulate its foreign policy discourse in a way very different from the binary vision of the Charter. The internal document 'The Interim Policy of Hamas and its Political Relations' discussed by Khaled Hroub reflects a new conceptualization of foreign relations, centred around main international norms. The conflict with Israel is presented as a legitimate clash against an occupation force, and armed struggle towards liberation is portrayed as a practice made legitimate by Resolution 2621 (XXV) of the UN General Assembly. At the heart of this new doctrine is a distinction between 'short-term policy' and the 'long-term solution'.[63] The former, often described as an 'interim' solution, was put forward for the first time in 1988 by Mahmoud al-Zahar, who was addressing

---

58. Quoted by Khaled Hroub who states that he saw this document in April 1995, in Amman. Hroub, *Hamas, Political Thought and Practice*, 50, 191.

59. On modern Islamist discourses on the Palestinian-Israeli conflict, see Beverly Milton-Edwards, 'Political Islam and the Palestinian-Israeli Conflict', *Israel Affairs* 12, no. 1 (2006): 65–85; Iyad Barghouti, 'Islamist Movements in Historical Palestine', in *Islamic Fundamentalism*, ed. Abdel Salam Sidahmed and Anoushiravan Ehteshami (Boulder and Oxford: Westview Press, 1996).

60. Charter, Article 15.

61. Charter, Articles 1–8, 13, 15.

62. This doctrine had seen important changes as from the nineteenth century. The author notes that Islamic theory has accepted the notion of territorial limits and the adoption of the principle of sovereignty. Majid Khadduri, 'The Islamic Theory of International Relations', in *Islam and International Relations*, ed. H. Proctor (London: Pall Mall Press, 1965).

63. Beverley Milton-Edwards and Alastair Crooke, 'Elusive Ingredient: Hamas and the Peace Process', *Journal of Palestinian Studies* 33, no. 4 (2004): 39–52.

Shimon Peres, and then by Sheikh Yassin.⁶⁴ The latter solution, also described as 'historical', emphasizes the sacred aspect of Palestine as a *waqf*, an endowment established under religious law.⁶⁵ This dialectics between tactics (short term) and strategy (long term) is present in an informal manner in many documents and articles written by figures affiliated to Hamas. The aim is to create on a specific territory (*buqʻa*) an authority (*Sulṭa*) that would have relations with the whole world. Making this authority become real would be the start of the fulfilment of Hamas' strategic goals: the return of refugees and the re-establishment of Islamic sovereignty over all of Palestine.

The concept of truce (*hudna*),⁶⁶ borrowed from classic Islamic doctrine, permits implementing the short-term solution without discarding the historical one, which is more akin to a 'self-recognized utopia'.⁶⁷ The movement's leaders consider that a traditional peace treaty like those in the Western tradition would be surrender, while a truce would provide an alternative allowing one to wait for an inversion in the regional ratio of force to the Palestinians' advantage.⁶⁸ According to this doctrine, Hamas is not in favour of pursuing fruitless negotiations (*ʻabathīya*) leading to a rump state without any sovereignty. The refusal of any form of dialogue with Israel is in that sense an unbreakable rule. Although some leaders had spoken to the Israelis during the first years that followed the movement's creation, as early as the 1990s, when the heads of Hamas settled outside of Palestine, the official position consisted in rejecting any contacts with the 'Zionists', except for issues relating to detainees.⁶⁹ As from 1994, Hamas dismissed several Israeli initiatives, considering that with the exception of humanitarian matters like prisoner exchange, the only acceptable language against occupation was resistance.⁷⁰ Yet most interlocutors with whom we were able to speak denied any direct contact

64. *Al-Nahar*, 30 April 1989.
65. According to the Charter (Article 11), Palestine is a *waqf*, a mortmain property.
66. There are several types of *hudna*, distinguished from each other by their duration. These most often last six months, but nothing in theory impedes Hamas from reaching truces that can last up to fifty years.
67. Abdallah Laraoui, *L'idéologie arabe contemporaine* (La Découverte, 1982).
68. Sheikh Yassin mentioned the possibility of prolonging the truce, *Filastin al-Muslima*, March 1995 and November 1997.
69. On 13 December 1993, the IDF general in charge of Gaza mentioned having spoken to Hamas high officials. Hamas denied these statements. Mahmoud al-Zahar, however, claimed not having any objections to talk to Israelis, in the *al-Nahar* daily, on 10 January 1994. See Jean-François Legrain, 'Hamas: Legitimate Heir of Palestinian Nationalism', in *Political Islam: Revolution, Radicalism or Reform?* ed. John L. Esposito (Boulder: Lynne Rienner Publishers, 1997).
70. This rejection of any contact with Israel followed Israeli instructions prohibiting any dialogue with Hamas members. This was one of the results of the transformation of the Intifada into an armed conflict. Communiqué of Hamas on 20 February 1994, quoted by Hroub, *Hamas: Political Thought and Practice*.

with the Israelis, even in humanitarian matters. Simultaneously, some leaders consider that, in case Hamas gathers sufficient forces for real negotiations and upon the condition that Israelis accept concessions to Palestinian people, they are not opposed to the principle of negotiation for a long-lasting truce (*hudna tawîla*). The position of Hamas therefore remains quite ambiguous in this respect. Following the Israeli offensive carried out against the Gaza Strip in summer 2014, Moussa Abu Marzouk declared that Hamas was then favourable to the opening of a negotiation channel, provoking an outcry within the movement.[71]

Concerning the relations of Hamas with other states, the doctrine contained in the Introductory Memorandum, elaborated in the early 1990s, highlights the respect of international resolutions.[72] As opposed to the Charter[73] – which denounces the existence of a two-pronged ('American-Zionist') plot and places at the centre of its rhetoric the question of the failure of Arab policies regarding Palestine – this document makes a distinction between Israel and the states that back it.[74]

A certain caution marked relations between Hamas and other Arab states as early as 1989–90.[75] It was the expulsion in 1992 of the movement's leaders to Marj al-Zouhour[76] in South Lebanon that contributed to this doctrine's formulation. Despite a horrific humanitarian situation, Hamas militants deported to Lebanon took advantage of their plight to gain visibility on the regional and international stages. Thanks to this expulsion, Hamas was able to improve diplomatic relations with many Arab states and thus open its first representation offices in the region.[77] This event is considered by both analysts and players as the 'birth certificate' of Hamas' foreign policy.[78]

The Introductory Memorandum is written around several general principles:

- Hamas seeks to establish good relations with all the forces of these Arab states without taking into account racial or religious differences.

71. *Al-Arabiyya*, 12 September 2014.

72. Hamas accepts Resolution 799, which calls for the return of refugees, but not RES 242 or RES 338. Hroub, *Hamas: Political Thought and Practice*.

73. See the Charter, Article 14.

74. See the Introductory Memorandum quoted by Khaled Hroub, and later in two interviews of Sheikh Yassin, the first in *al-Quds* on 10 January 1998, the other in *al-Hayat* on 3 June 1998.

75. Khaled Hroub has noted in this respect the silence of the movement when Islamists successively won elections, in November 1989 in Jordan and in 1990 in Algeria.

76. After the kidnapping and murder by the Izz al-Din al-Qassam Brigades of Sargent Nissim Toledano, on 13 December 1992, Israel expelled 400 Palestinian Islamists to South Lebanon in Marj al-Zouhour.

77. Ahmad al-Nawati, *Hamâs min al-dâkhil* (Gaza: Dâr al-Shurûq li-l-nashr wa-l-tawzî', 2002).

78. Hroub, *Hamas, Political Thought and Practice*.

- It does not interfere in the internal affairs of these states.
- It is never at war with these states.
- It considers that Palestine is the only location for the struggle against Israel.
- It must clearly show that all relations established with other countries have the clear aim of helping the movement in the struggle against occupation.
- It refuses to join any regional 'axis' or 'front', which would hinder its capacity to establish relations with the entire group of regional and international players.

Finally, on 1 May 2017, Hamas published its Document of General Principles and Policies. As opposed to its 1988 Charter that introduced Hamas as the 'Palestinian branch of the Muslim Brotherhood', this new text did not mention the organizational ties uniting Hamas to the Brothers. Far from relying exclusively on an Islamic environment, Hamas now described itself as a 'Palestinian nationalist Islamist' movement, erasing all links with the Brotherhood. Another noteworthy change: the anti-Semitic overtones of the Charter were entirely scrapped, replaced by a distinction made between the struggle against Zionism and enmity against the Jews. By emphasizing UN resolutions and international law, armed struggle in this document did not appear anymore as the only tool to fight occupation, but only as a means among others, including 'popular and peaceful resistance'. Similarities are striking between this new document and Arafat's 1974 speech to the United Nations General Assembly.[79]

While Khaled Mesh'al, since his departure from Syria and his settlement in Doha in 2013, played a personal part in writing this text, it was the product of a wide consensus among the movement's leaders. Since 2006, they had been debating the opportunity of providing Hamas with a new political document that would reflect the movement's current strategy in a more comprehensive way than the Charter.[80]

Indeed, since 2006, Hamas has unceasingly highlighted its acceptance of the 1967 borders, as well as accords signed by the PLO and Israel. This position has been an integral part of reconciliation agreements between Hamas and Fatah since 2005: the Cairo Agreement in 2005, the Prisoners' Document in 2006, the Mecca Agreement in 2007 and finally the Cairo and Doha Agreements in 2011 and 2012. Yet these compromises linked to the strict framework of

---

79. In a deep analysis of this document, Jean-François Legrain highlights the continuities of Hamas' previous declarations and stresses how it echoes the PLO's positions in the 1970s. Jean-François Legrain, 'Le 'Document' de Hamas (2017) ou l'ouverture comme garante des invariants', *Les carnets de l'IREMAM*, 2017.

80. Although some rejected giving up the Charter for fear of being assimilated to the PLO, which in the person of Yasser Arafat had declared the Charter to be 'obsolete', others on the contrary were prescribing the publication of a new document to tone down hysterical reactions surrounding the Charter, which was a convenient scarecrow for Israel to accuse Hamas of terrorism, allowing the Jewish State to tighten its blockade of Gaza.

reconciliation agreements between Palestinians had never been displayed as an integral part of Hamas strategy. From 2017 on, Hamas would endorse them as its own political stands and not as simple concessions to Fatah. While refusing to speak of a new Charter, Khaled Mesh'al nevertheless stated that this document was now Hamas' political reference: 'The difference is that today, we present this program in a document that is our own.' For all that, the Charter could not be considered obsolete:

> Hamas refuses to submit to the wishes of other states. Its political thought is never the result of pressure from the outside. Our principle is the following: no change of document. Hamas does not forget its past. The Charter illustrates the period of the 1980s and the Document of General Principles presents our policy in 2017. Each document belongs to a specific period.[81]

Although the release of this new document coincided with the departure of Khaled Mesh'al and the renewal of the Political Bureau members – Yahya al-Sinwar had already been elected at the head of the leadership in Gaza – Khaled Mesh'al denied any links with the elections process and stressed that this document reflected a large consensus with Hamas' institutions, which remained stable despite the turnover of its members:

> this document was approved by the *majlis al-shura* and is not related with changes in our leadership. Despite changes relating to our members, our institutions remain stable and there is no such thing as a total change after an election process. We cannot compare Hamas to what sometimes happens after elections in Western countries like America, France, Germany or Great Britain. In those countries when the Left wins, there is a change in policy, both at the national and international levels.

In Khaled Mesh'al's mind, this document enables Hamas to clarify how the movement manages to conciliate attachment to its principles and the ability to adapt to a specific context:

> Adapting doesn't mean disregarding its principles. It is rather a deviation (*inchiqaq*) of sorts, or an adaptation vis-à-vis a specific context. Hamas tries to project this positive image despite two negative representations: firstly immobilism (*joumoud*), while Hamas' attachment to its principles does not imply immobility at all. Secondly, dissolution (*mouyou'*), or the idea that Hamas must leave behind its principles for personal or partisan interests. When faced with immobilism (*joumoud*) and dissolution (*mouyou'*), Hamas has actually chosen a median position (*wasatiyya*), and this it is this position we wanted to reflect in our new document.

---

81. Conversations with the author in Doha, on 17 April 2017.

Foreign policy includes two components, one towards Israel and the other towards other countries. This distinction is also true from the viewpoint of the players themselves, since the movement's diplomatic doctrine revolves around this separation between Israel and other states: Hamas' leaders claim that 'it does not have relations with the occupying power and develops to the utmost its relations with the rest of the world'.[82] During our conversations, the movement's leaders all insisted on the three rules around which the foreign policy of Hamas revolved: the absence of relations with the 'Zionist entity' (including its citizens), the opening of diplomatic relations with the largest amount of states and non-interference in the interior affairs of other countries.[83] Hamas thus embraces the same theory as Fatah on neutrality and non-interference in affairs of Arab states.[84] The movement's leaders, moreover, claim that Fatah has failed in this department, as shown by its conflictual relations with many Arab political players. Their Islamist movement, by contrast, emphasizes that it respects this unbreakable unchangeable rule strictly.

Uses of ideology in foreign policy

The concept of ideology is polysemous and controverted.[85] In its very general sense, it refers to a set of shared values and ideas; in its narrow meaning (as understood here in this book), it is a doctrine meant to become a guide for action.[86] In its link with political action,[87] ideology is a 'more or less coherent set of ideas permitting one to make a value judgement on a social order'.[88] Mental images, religions,

82. Conversations with Osama Hamdan, Damascus, 29 January 2011; Ahmed Yousef, Gaza, 16 March 2013; Mushir al-Masri, in Gaza, 16 March 2013; Ghazi Hamad, Gaza, 17 March 2013; Moussa Abu Marzouk, in Damascus, 1 June 2011; Ayman al-Taha, in Gaza, 19 March 2013; Basem Naim, in Gaza, 18 March 2013; Mahmoud al-Zahar, Gaza, 20 March 2013; Imad al-Alami, in Gaza, 18 March 2013.

83. These three rules are the basis of the movement's official policy, a point that was reiterated many times during our conversations. At the time of his deportation to South Lebanon, Imad al-Alami emphasized the respect for the principle of non-interference in an interview given to the *Filastin al-Muslima* magazine, in May 1995, quoted by Hatina Meir, 'Hamas and the Oslo Accords: Religious Dogma in a Changing Political Reality', *Mediterranean Politics* 4, no. 3 (1999): 37–55.

84. See Hroub, *Hamas, Political Thought and Practice*, 41.

85. Joseph Gabel, 'Idéologie' article, *Encyclopédie Universalis*, 1984.

86. Philippe Braillard, Pierre de Senarclens, 'Idéologie et relations internationales, le cas des relations soviéto-américaines', *Relations Internationales* 25 (Spring 1981).

87. Martin Seliger defends an 'inclusive' conception of ideologies which are applied in political action. Depending on situational response, any ideology may be 'extremist, moderate or conservative'. Martin Seliger, *Ideology and Politics* (New York: Free Press, 1976).

88. Jean Baechler, *Qu'est ce que l'idéologie* (Paris: Gallimard, 1976).

customs and myths[89] are thus not ideological in themselves but can become just that when they are used as a basis for political action.

Hamas claims to take into account political reality by referring to its moral principles and values. It rejects expressions like 'there are no morals in politics' or 'interests are above principles'.[90] Between 2006 and 2013, many speeches given by Hamas leaders, dealing with relations with non-Palestinian players, bore witness to use of varied ideological references. Ideology can be nationalist and/or Islamist and also implies another rhetorical formula based on the 'centrality' of Hamas.[91]

This mobilization of ideology to coincide with the defence of interests was already prevalent when the movement was formed, during the First Intifada of December 1987. The movement was sharpened by foreign policy action, defined as a tool of rebellion against an occupying power.[92] For an organization which had stayed away from armed struggle for many years, this choice was the result of internal interest: to protect the group's structures and avoid it being marginalized on the national political stage. In this endeavour, Hamas largely defended its action as conforming to a certain 'Islamic norm',[93] by notably making use of dates of religious significance or by principally mobilizing during sermons or days of fasting.[94] Resorting to religion was aimed here at distinguishing oneself from the agenda of the National Unified Council, a leadership body created inside the Occupied Territories to implement the Intifada.

Hamas has always oscillated between its attachment to the 'historical solution', which foresees the liberation of the whole of Palestine, and its capacity to recognize the validity of the 'interim solution', which prescribes the creation of a state with the 1967 borders. As noticed by Khaled Hroub, during the post-Oslo period, the movement's leaders resorted to the first option, since it was based on the idea that Palestine was a *waqf*.[95] During the same period, the leaders also tried to be within the scope of the second perspective, the 'interim solution'.

---

89. Myths are representations that support an ideology, see Karl Mannheim, *Idéologie et utopie* (Paris: Rivière, 1957). For a similar acceptation of ideology, see Maxime Rodinson, *Islam et capitalisme* (Paris: Le Seuil, 1966).

90. Hroub, *Hamas: Political Thought and Practice*, 55.

91. Yves Schemeil emphasizes the importance of the amplification of ideological discourse in his *Introduction à la science politique: objets, methods, résultats* (Paris: Presses de Sciences Po, Dalloz, 2010).

92. Beverley Milton-Edwards, 'The Concept of Jihad and the Palestinian Islamic Movement: A Comparison of Ideas and Techniques', *British Journal of Middle Eastern Studies* 19, no. 1 (1992): 48–53.

93. It is impossible, however, to precisely define the term 'Islamic norm'. See Baudouin Dupret, ed., *La charia aujourd'hui: usages de la référence au droit islamique* (Paris: La Découverte, 2012).

94. Jean-François Legrain, *Les voix du soulèvement palestinien, 1987–1988* (Le Caire: CEDEJ, 1991).

95. Hroub, *Hamas, Political Thought and Practice*.

When it was put forward, however, the latter always went together with 'Islamic conditions', which state it must remain in conformity with sharia, since leaders largely resort to concepts from the Qur'an like *sabr* (patience) to give credit to a solution likely to appear as deviant. The Oslo Accords are, according to Hamas leaders, a betrayal of Islam.[96] It was to remain in agreement with this ideological stance that Hamas refused to participate in the January 1996 elections.[97]

These examples illustrate the fact that, regarding Israel, resorting to ideology can serve the movement's interests, by contributing to delegitimize Fatah on the national stage.[98] Like any player coexisting with other formations on the same political stage, Hamas must assert its identity and distinguish itself from its rivals, to positively influence public opinion. This strategy of counter-legitimacy is in addition typical of all Islamist movements when faced with competitors.

Although the movement has employed Islamic discourse to criticize Oslo, its opposition to the accords between the occupying power and Arab states is never formulated in ideological language. In fact, during the signing of Israel's peace treaty with Jordan in October 1994, Hamas merely lamented a 'new crack in the wall of Arab solidarity'.[99] This is mainly explained by the movement's attempt to find backers in a regional environment that favours normalization of relations with the Jewish State.[100] The road of diplomacy Hamas followed during Iraq's invasion of Kuwait also illustrated this sidelining of ideology. The movement managed to balance its stance and thus avoided alienating Palestinian public opinion, which was largely pro-Iraqi. Its communiqués[101] reflected a subtle overlap of multiple positions which, despite their apparent inconsistencies, resulted in a pragmatic posture ensuring the continuation of funding from Gulf monarchies and thereby

---

96. Meir, 'Hamas and the Oslo Accords'.

97. Hamas nonetheless participates in municipal elections, a participation that does not result from populist interest but from a theoretical justification based on the difference with the inner workings of the Palestinian Authority.

98. Ziad Abu Amr, 'Hamas: A Historical and Political Background', *Journal of Palestine Studies* 22, no. 4 (1993): 5–19. See also Hicham Ahmad, *From Religious Salvation to Political Transformation: The Rise of Hamas in Palestinian Society* (Jerusalem: PASSIA, Palestinian Academic Society for the Study of International Affairs, 1994).

99. See the communiqué issued on 27 October 1994, quoted by Hroub, *Hamas, Political Thought and Practice*, 158.

100. Hamas was widely criticized by many Arab states for the kidnapping and murder of the Israeli Sargent Nissim Toledano in December 1992, as well as for the series of suicide attacks against Israeli buses in 1994, and then between February and March 1996.

101. For an analysis of communiqués of Hamas during the Gulf War, see Jean-François Legrain, 'A Defining Moment, Palestinian Islamic Fundamentalism', in *Islamic Fundamentalism and the Gulf Crisis*, ed. James Piscatori (Chicago: American Academy of Arts and Sciences, 1991), 70.

comforted its regional status in relation to the PLO.¹⁰² In addition, keeping friendly relations with oil monarchies was an efficient means to remain inside the community of Arab states at a time when the movement was accused by the PLO of doing Iran's bidding in Palestine.¹⁰³

The adoption of this new language void of ideological reference would enable the movement's leaders to go on many visits to states in the region.¹⁰⁴ Until 1992, Hamas had no official representation in Arab states; nor did it have a spokesman outside the Occupied Territories. In 1991, the visit of a Hamas delegation to Iran, Jordan and Saudi Arabia led by Ibrahim Ghosheh was an opportunity for leaders to become really visible.¹⁰⁵ These leaders seemed from then on, and for the first time, to be diplomats. After his release from jail in 1997, Sheikh Yassin went on a tour lasting from February to June 1998, travelling to Kuwait, Qatar, Sudan, the United Arab Emirates, Yemen, Saudi Arabia and Syria. This was a fundamental episode in the movement's foreign policy, since its charismatic spiritual chief was officially welcomed by many states, despite strong pressure at the behest of some players (the PLO in particular). On 28 April 1998, Sheikh Yassin went to Iran, where he met the Supreme Guide of the Revolution Ali Khamenei, Iran president Mohammed Khatami and Kamal Kharazi (then Foreign Affairs minister), who all reassured him of the Islamic Republic's political and financial backing.¹⁰⁶

Finally, the adoption of a pragmatic foreign policy would also allow the movement to begin speaking to Western states, particularly the United States

102. Regarding Hamas' perspective on the Gulf War of 1990–1, see Andrea Nüsse, *Muslim Palestine: The Ideology of Hamas* (Amsterdam: Harwood Academic Publishers, 1998).

103. With the start of the Iran-Iraq war and Arafat's backing of Saddam Hussein, Khomeini's preferential relations with the PLO rapidly deteriorated until the opening of the Madrid Conference on 22 October 1991, which marked the beginning of Iranian support for Hamas and the opening of an office of the movement in Tehran (in February 1992).

104. According to Khaled Hroub, the birth of Hamas' foreign policy can be mainly explained by changes in tone and the adoption of a new language between 1987 and 1990, *Hamas, Political Thought and Practice*. As early as 1991 Hamas has sought a dialogue with Western nations especially with the US wishing to portray itself as a militant national movement, see Ahmad Rashad, *Hamas: Palestinian Politics with an Islamic Hue*, Occasional Paper serie n.2 (Springfield, VA: United Association for Studies and Research, 1993).

105. His autobiography is available in Arabic Ibrâhîm Ghûshë, *Al-Mi'dina al-ḥamrâ'* ['The Red City'], autobiography, *Markaz al-Zaytûna li-l-dirâsât wa-l-istishârât* (Beirut, 2008).

106. Since the winter of 1992 and the expulsion of Hamas and Islamic Jihad representatives to South Lebanon, the large majority of what Hamas obtained in terms of finances and military backing has come from Tehran. This episode had a crucial influence on the rapprochement between the movement, Iran and Hezbollah.

which, at that time, had no official relations with the PLO.[107] During the Marj al-Zouhour episode, Hamas contacted, via their embassies in Amman, the five permanent UN Security Council members, which were asked to express their opinion on Resolution 799 demanding the immediate return from Lebanon of Palestinian deportees.[108] The movement's representatives then addressed them letters clarifying their political stances and highlighting the legitimacy and conformity with international norms of resistance to occupation, thus trying to prevent the United States from putting their formation on the list of terrorist organizations.[109] For Hamas, Marj al-Zouhour played a part in the new stance towards the community of states and international organizations: it was an opportunity to stress that Hamas was a movement whose struggle was strictly limited to the Palestinian Occupied Territories.

The uses of ideology essentially depend on the movement's degree of integration on the national and regional stages. As opposed to actions against Israel, which are part of an 'Islamic *doxa*' and a wish to reassert itself against the PLO, the actions of Hamas towards other states are bereft of this dimension. The reluctance of many states to open relations with an Islamist movement explains to a great extent Hamas' wish to appear as a player capable of understanding diplomatic stakes and respecting the principle of non-interference in their internal affairs.[110]

An Islamist foreign policy?

The foreign policy of Hamas is of course not as standard as that of players whose ideology is strictly nationalist. Its specificity is nevertheless quite relative. The transnational characteristics of Hamas ideology have modelled its foreign policy in the same way as any transnational ideology shapes that of other players, including states.[111] There are many states whose nationalism encompasses all Arab

---

107. Between January and February, the United States had opened a channel of communication with Hamas via their embassy in Amman. See Hroub, *Hamas, Political Thought and Practice*.

108. Regarding Hamas' perspective on the mass deportation of Islamists to South Lebanon in 1992, see Nüsse, *Muslim Palestine*.

109. In an interview published in *al-Hayat* on 23 January 1994, Hamas leader Mohammad Nazzal stated that the position of the United States was for quite some time hesitant, because the Americans considered that once the Palestinian Authority was established, it would be important to preserve contacts with Hamas. According to him, this issue was still a matter of debate in May 1993.

110. Hamas leaders have recurrently referred to respect for the principle of non-interference, but the bad experience of the Political Bureau in Amman can be explained by the violation of this commitment, since a mobilization of sorts existed in Jordan and was the result of decisions made by the Jordanian Bureau of the Muslim Brotherhood.

111. Many authors consider that a state's foreign policy is partly the expression of social values and norms on the international stage, see O. R. Holsti, 'Foreign Policy Decision

societies, like Syrian and Iraqi Baathism.[112] In addition, its religious aspects do not make it fundamentally different from other players (state or non-state) defending transnational ideologies. Transnational ideological stances of France and Russia themselves have included a religious dimension at various times in their history: France was for a long time considered the protector of Oriental Christians (the Maronites in particular), and Russia was the safe-keeper of followers of Middle Eastern Greek Orthodoxy.

The end of the Cold War encouraged the 'cultural U-turn' of social sciences, a time when 'realist' models lost momentum in international relations theory.[113] Recognizing the part played by ideology, which is now increasingly highlighted, does not mean a consensus has been reached on its importance or on the mechanisms according to which it acts. A central debate in the literature opposes authors defining ideology as a substance and considering that foreign policy is the expression of values of a society,[114] to those who see it only as a factor of legitimation.[115]

Analysis dedicated to the concept of 'Islamic foreign policy'[116] bears witness to this polarization. According to Olivier Roy, this concept was an invention of Iranian dignitaries who were in power in the wake of the 1979 revolution.[117] He has shown that there actually was extraordinary continuity in Iranian diplomacy both before and after the Islamic Revolution. By contrast, Djalili considers that the novel experience of Iran's foreign policy, which has disavowed nationalist peculiarities and sought to export the revolution, is an illustration of a specific model of foreign policy that can be described as 'Islamic'.[118] This diplomacy has resorted to specific types of actions like the abduction of American hostages in November 1979 (the founding act of 'Islamic diplomacy' according to the author) and disseminates

Makers Viewed Psychologically', in *In Search of Global Patterns*, ed. James Rosenau (New York: Free, 1976).

112. Eberhard Kienle, *Ba'th v. Ba'th, The Conflict Between Syria and Iraq, 1968–1989* (London: Tauris, 1990).

113. Dietrich Jung, 'Le retour de la culture: L'analyse des politiques étrangères 'périphériques'?', in *Politiques étrangères, nouveaux regards*, ed. Frédéric Charillon (Paris: Presses de Sciences-Po, 2002); Friedrich Kratochwill and Yosef Lapid, *The Return of Culture and Identity in IR Theory* (Boulder, CO: Lynne Rienner, 1996).

114. Thompson and Macridis, 'The Comparative Study of Foreign Policy', in *Foreign Policy in World Politics*, ed. Macridis (Englewood Cliffs, NJ, 1972); Krasner, *Defending National Interest: Raw Materials Investments and US Foreign Policy* (Princeton, 1978).

115. Walter Carlsnaes, *Ideology and Foreign Policy* (Oxford: Basil Blackwell, 1986).

116. Zachary Karabell, 'Fundamental Misconceptions: Islamic Foreign Policy', *Washington DC: Carnegie Endowment for International Peace* 105, no. 105 (1996): 77–90.

117. Olivier Roy, 'Sous le turban, la couronne. La politique étrangère', in *Thermidor en Iran*, ed. Olivier Roy, Fariba Adelkhah, Jean-François, Bayart (Bruxelles: Éd. Complexe, 1993).

118. Mohammed-Reza Djalili, *Diplomatie islamique, stratégie internationale du Khomeynisme* (Paris: PUF, 1989).

particular ideas on the sovereignty of states and the international order.[119] According to some, it is an autonomous factor likely to determine the behaviour of players in foreign policy,[120] but to others it is nothing more than a disguise enabling one to hide the deeply realist nature of political action.[121] Among this second category of authors, the discussion is still open on the extent of this variable's importance.

In the case of Hamas, some see in ideology the origin and very foundation of its political behaviour.[122] Others imagine it as only a way to respond to needs for pragmatic arrangements and consider that the Islamist movement merely imitates Fatah's policies, hiding them under a 'verbal smokescreen'.[123]

Contrary to Mahmoud Muslih's approach,[124] which dismisses the ideological factor from his analysis of Hamas' foreign policy and considers that the movement's decisions are dictated less by ideology than by politics, the present book is an attempt to demonstrate that seeing these two factors as opposing dynamics is mistaken.[125] Quite the contrary, there is no dichotomy between a movement's interests and its ideology, which most often appears as an essential tool for the

---

119. Brigid Starkey also considers that the Iranian example is the easiest one that isolates Islam as an independent variable, although other ones like the need to strengthen economic links with the West must also be taken into account. Brigid Starkey, 'Foreign Policy in the Muslim World: A Dialogue Between State and Society', *Political Communication* 9, no. 1 (1992): 31–45. On Iran foreign policy and Islam see also Rohallah K. Ramazani, 'Khumayni's Islam in Iran's Foreign Policy', in *Islam in Foreign Policy*, ed. Adeed I. Dawisha (Cambridge: Cambridge University Press, 1983).

120. Vernor Aspaturian, 'International Politics and Foreign Policy in the Soviet System', in *Approaches to Comparative and International Politics*, ed. Barry Farrell (Evanston: Northwestern University Press, 1966); Stanley Hoffman, *Gullivers' Troubles: or The Setting of American Foreign Policy* (New York: McGraw-Hill Book Company, 1968); Henry Kissinger, *Nuclear Weapons and Foreign Policy* (New York: Abridged, 1957).

121. Hans J. Morgenthau, *Politics among Nations. The Struggle for Power and Peace* (New York: Alfred A. Knopf, 1954); Werner Levi, 'Ideology, Interests and Foreign Policy', *International Studies Quarterly* 14, no. 1 (1970): 1–31.

122. Meir Litvak, 'The Islamisation of Palestinian Identity: The Case of Hamas', *Middle Eastern Studies* 34, no. 1 (1998): 148–63; Matthew Levitt, *Hamas: Politics, Charity and Terrorism in The Service of Jihad* (Yale University Press, 2006); Michael Herzog, 'Can Hamas be Tamed?', *Foreign Affairs* 85, no. 2 (2006): 83.

123. Bîsâm ʿAduwān, 'Harakat-Hamâs bayn al-huwiyya al-wataniyya, wa-l-khitâb al-ʿaqîdî', *Seyasat* (Winter 2007), Ramallah, 27–41. See also Ali Jarbawi's interview, 'Le Hamas, un parti politique pragmatique', *Confluences Méditerranée* 4, no. 55 (2005): 105–12.

124. Mohammed Muslih, 'The Foreign Policy of Hamas', *Council of Foreign Relations*, February 2007.

125. Franz Schurmann, *The Logic of World Power* (New York: Pantheon Books, Random House, 1974); Stephen Kirby, 'National Interest versus Ideology in American Diplomacy', in *Knowledge and Belief in Politics: The Problem of Ideology*, ed. Robert Benewick, R. N. Berki and Bhikhu C. Parekh (London: Allen and Unwin, 1973).

fulfilment of these very interests.¹²⁶ Noticing that ideology is often exploited or redefined does not mean, however, restricting its function to a simple window-dressing of interests.¹²⁷ This is an approach shared by Tristan Dunning in one of his articles, in which he analyses the influence of Islam in informing, guiding and legitimizing Hamas' political thought and practice.¹²⁸

Beyond this simple dimidiation, we have identified three types of relationship between interests and ideology: convergence between interests and ideology, conflict between both and finally redefinition of ideology as a function of interests; the latter type of relationship is clearly an example of 'practical rationalization', in the sense meant by Weber.¹²⁹ The fourth possible case (the adaptation of interests to ideology) is not observed at all in Hamas foreign policy. Although the search for interests at the internal level (guaranteeing the Gaza Strip's proper administrative and financial management, and competing successfully against rival nationalist and Islamist factions) is an illustration of these three cases, the search for interests at the external level (looking for recognition and material backers) is obviously an instance of the third case, namely the redefinition of ideology to serve interests. Going beyond a simplistic analysis focusing on the religious coloration of Hamas' political identity, whose sole obsession would be the destruction of the 'Jewish State', the present book tries to disqualify other simplistic approaches.

*Dispersed decision-making leaderships*¹³⁰

The analysis of foreign policy by looking at the decision-making process was an approach with roots going back to the 1950s and the works of Snyder,¹³¹ which

---

126. Mishal Shaul, 'The Pragmatic Dimension of the Palestinian Hamas: A Network Perspective', *Armed Forces & Society* 29, no. 4 (2003): 569–89.

127. Leopold Labedz, 'Idéologie et politique étrangère soviétiques', in *La menace soviétique*, ed. Christoph Bertram (Paris: Berger-Levrault, 1982); Georges Lavau, 'Le rapport entre l'idéologie et la politique extérieure', *Pouvoirs* 21 (1982): 125–38.

128. Tristan Dunning, 'Islam and Resistance: Hamas, Ideology and Islamic Values in Palestine', *Critical Studies on Terrorism* 8, no. 2 (2015): 284–305.

129. Max Weber, *Economie et société* (Paris: Plon, 1971). See also Stephen Kalber, *Les valeurs, les idées et les intérêts. Introduction à la sociologie de Max Weber* (Paris: La Découverte, 2010).

130. Hamas uses the term *qiyâda*, which literally means 'direction', when designating these various geographical locations. It does not seem, however, that the literal translation is adequate at reflecting the geographical dispersion of Hamas. To speak of a 'direction' would introduce a misinterpretation in the understanding of relations between these various locations, which are not autonomous from one another. It is preferable to speak of a leadership.

131. R. Snyder, H. W. Bruck and B. Sapin, *Foreign Policy Decision-Making: An Approach to Study International Politics* (New York: Free Press of Glencoe, 1962).

insist on the need to question the way which leaders perceive a situation, in order to understand their political choices. Theoretical frameworks became increasingly diversified,[132] giving an ever-greater importance to the works of Graham Allison,[133] who demonstrated that a decision is always the result of a compromise negotiated between a set of players who attempt, as a function of their interests, to influence the final outcome.

The present book seeks to illustrate the importance of the negotiation processes between the various Hamas representatives. This seems all the more important, since members of the movement's executive body (the Political Bureau, *maktab al-siyâsî*)[134] are spread out in four locations: the Gaza Strip, the West Bank, Israeli prisons in which some of its members are jailed[135] and finally the outside. The latter, until 2012, was managed by the movement's offices located in Damascus and, later, in Qatar. As a result of the occupation and different waves of expulsion and incarceration, this geographical dispersion has significantly affected the decision-making procedures of Hamas. Though in theory Political Bureau members take their decisions through a consultation process involving all of the leaderships (*mouchawâra*), the distribution of authority of each can vary in accordance with the context and nature of the decisions.

The importance of the external leadership in foreign policy decisions

Decision-making processes cannot, therefore, be analysed through the adoption of a single model; one should instead identify (as stipulated by Margaret G. Hermann)[136] the way in which several configurations coexist within a single

---

132. Bahgat Korany, ed., *How Foreign Policy Decisions are made in the Third World: A Comparative Analysis* (Boulder: Westview, 1986).

133. Graham Allison, *Essence of Decision: Explaining the Cuban Missile Crisis* (New York: Harper Collins, 1972).

134. The Political Bureau is made up of some fifteen members spread out among four leaderships. This body is in charge of implementing decisions in accordance with a line decided beforehand by the *majlis al-shûrâ*, which is akin to a legislative assembly. Hamas members at the local level elect their representatives, who are called upon to sit in *al-shûrâ* consultative council (between seventy and ninety members). The West Bank is divided into seven districts, Gaza into five, each of the districts itself being divided into units. It is the members of the *shûrâ* who elect the members of the Political Bureau. For a detailed analysis of the inner workings of the decision-making process of Hamas, see Jeroen Gunning, *Hamas in Politics: Democracy, Religion, Violence* (London: Hurst and Company, 2007).

135. In Israeli prisons, Hamas is made up of twenty-three members. Until October 2011, its chairman was Yahya al-Sinwar, one of the prisoners freed in exchange for IDF private Gilad Shalit. Of the 5,000 Palestinian prisoners jailed in Israel, approximately 2,000 are affiliated to Hamas.

136. Margaret G. Hermann, 'How Decision Units Shape Foreign Policy, a Theoretical Framework', in 'Leaders, Groups and Coalitions: Understanding the People and Processes in Foreign Policymaking', *International Studies Review* 3, no. 2 (2001), 47–81.

decision-making unit. The case of Hamas testifies to these different configurations: foreign policy decisions, which Hamas leaders willingly assimilate to decisions taken daily (*qarârât yawmiyya*[137]), are also part of the responsibilities of members of the Political Bureau settled outside the Occupied Territories. Hamas justifies this imbalance as being for reasons of convenience and because of the need to take decisions in situations of emergency.

The origins of outside leadership pre-eminence go back to the arrest of Sheikh Yassin in 1989. At the time, Moussa Abu Marzouk, and later Khaled Mesh'al, tried to reorganize the movement by handing over most of the powers to Diaspora Palestinians, who were less vulnerable in terms of security. The same year, the wave of incarcerations affecting the movement forced it to settle part of its leadership outside the Occupied Territories. This process of externalization of power intensified after the 1991 Gulf War, when more than 300,000 Jordanian nationals of Palestinian origin left Kuwait. Among them were several Hamas leaders, such as Khaled Mesh'al, Izzat al-Rishq and Sami Khater. Yet it was above all the 1992 expulsion to Marj az-Zouhour (South Lebanon) that comforted the movement in the idea that it was preferable that a substantial part of it, at the logistical and decision-making level, remains outside the Occupied Territories (in Jordan at the time). Sheikh Yassin's arrest accelerated the rise to power of the Diaspora, at the expense of the rest of the movement. Although his release in 1997 slightly modified the ratio of force in favour of the internal leadership, the outside was still hegemonic in many areas, notably on political and military issues,[138] with foreign donations providing a measure of control over the Izz al-Din al-Qassam Brigades.[139]

The Gaza leadership's power surge

Although the outside leadership has historically additional prerogatives to take decisions in matters of foreign policy, they were tolerated with the proviso that they would not be final. Now, since the death of Sheikh Yassin in 2004, a fraction of Gaza leadership, insisting on increased representation, considered itself hurt by all-powerful external heads of Hamas and demanded a greater part in the movement's decision-making process.[140] Victory in the 2006 parliamentary elections had given

---

137. This seniority of the outside in the elaboration and definition of foreign policy is claimed both by the external leadership and by analysts. According to Osama Hamdan, whom the author met in Damascus on 25 January 2011, issues of daily management of diplomacy were then dealt with by the Damascus leadership.

138. Muhib al-Nawati, *Asharq al-Awsat*, 13 February 2009.

139. According to Shaul Mishal and Avraham Sela, this seniority is related to the aptitude of the outside leadership in gathering material resources. See *The Palestinian Hamas: Vision, Violence and Coexistence* (New York: Columbia University Press, 2000).

140. Jonathan D. Halevi, 'Power Dynamics Inside Hamas: The Increasing Weight of the Gaza Leadership', *Jerusalem Center for Public Affairs* 11, no. 4 (16 June 2011).

Gaza diplomatic weight, as attested by the part played by Mahmoud al-Zahar, who was Foreign Affairs minister of the Tenth Government and went on two tours abroad. He thus granted himself representational prerogatives outside of Palestine, which until then were most often the responsibility of leaders in exile.[141] To this diplomatic capital, one should add the capacity of accumulating material resources from the profits of trade in tunnels linking Gaza to Egypt, which increased in number since the blockade's tightening in 2007. Although historically the various Hamas directions each managed their own resources – the outside one enjoying both diplomatic representation and funds – the Gaza leadership now cumulated several types of these, including those traditionally under the control of leaders outside.

This new balance in favour of Gaza was also the product of a weakening of the outside leadership, in the wake of its departure from Syria: it lost a political and strategic backer. As opposed to Damascus, Doha was not a stable geographical base since, as early as 2015, many of the movement's members were expelled from Qatar with their families and were once more spread out between Lebanon, Turkey and Malaysia. Changes in the regional environment, which turned somewhat hostile to exiled leaders, were paradoxically beneficial for the Gaza leadership, now accumulating on the territory it ruled a capital that was simultaneously symbolic, military, economic and bureaucratic. This change in the balance was above all real in the case of the al-Qassam Brigades, which, thanks to Iranian financial support, became gradually more autonomous vis-à-vis the external leadership. At the height of the crisis between Iranian dignitaries and Khaled Mesh'al, the Brigades benefited from the technological and material backing of the Islamic Republic. The Diaspora leadership's pre-eminence is no longer a reality, the result of a double process of weakening of the outside and rise of Gaza.

Held in 2017, the movement's last internal elections illustrated these fundamental shifts: while the Political Bureau's chairmanship had always been given to a Diaspora Palestinian (Moussa Abu Marzouk and then Khaled Mesh'al), Haniyeh's ascent to the leadership of Hamas heralded a new era. The new head of the Political Bureau was both hailing from Gaza and residing there, even though he was forced to operate largely from the outside.[142]

---

141. With the exception of Sheikh Yassin who when released from jail in 1997 went on a regional diplomatic tour. One should also note that Foreign Affairs minister al-Zahar could not travel to a country without Mesh'al's approval. See al-Zahar's interview, *Palestinian Information Center*, 8 May 2006.

142. Except for Moussa Abu Marzouk, a former chairman of the Political Bureau and member of the outside leadership but coming from Gaza, members residing abroad are almost all from the West Bank or towns and villages conquered by Israel in 1948.

Geographical divides and political conflicts

The foreign policy of Hamas – both its relations with Israel and its regional alliances – has been affected by historical divisions between the internal and external leaderships.

Regarding relations with Israel, the leaders in Gaza had sought in the mid-1990s to find common ground with the very recently established Palestinian Authority[143]. In January 1995, the Gazan leader Ismail Abou Shanab published a communiqué in which he confirmed that a deal had been reached with the Palestinian Authority to implement a truce with Israel. During the summer of 1995, several heads of Fatah met Hamas members from inside Palestine first in Cairo, then in Khartoum. As for the outside leadership in Amman, it was promoting a different agenda, which was less accommodating towards the PLO and the new Palestinian administration.[144] Its hostility to an end to the violence partly explains the fruitlessness of these meetings and the wave of attacks in 1995.[145] Fearing political marginalization, Hamas officials abroad had thus done their best to limit the possibilities of dialogue between their movement inside Palestine and the Authority.[146] This divide – which is reminiscent of different stances within the PLO between exiled leaders believing in the concept of 'historical' Palestine, and those in the territories preferring the option of a 'mini-state' next to Israel – was noticeable during the 2000s: Sheikh Yassin apparently accepted Yasser Arafat's proposal of a cease-fire, while Khaled Mesh'al was adamantly against it and gave instructions to the Izz al-Din al-Qassam Brigades to plan an armed operation in Rafah.[147]

Concerning regional relations, from the early 1990s the Iranian alliance was also the subject of conflict opposing the inside and outside: while the rapprochement with the Islamic Republic was desirable for members of the Bureau residing outside Palestine, the territories' leaders had expressed their reservations, favouring instead

---

143. Wendy Kristianasen, 'Challenge and Counterchallenge: Hamas' Response to Oslo', *Journal of Palestine Studies* 28, no. 3 (1999): 19–36.

144. Jean-François Legrain has explained the outside leadership's stance by the fact that it only had relations with states and organizations and did not have to take into account a popular base; see 'Hamas: Legitimate Heir or Palestinian Nationalism?', in *Political Islam: Revolution, Radicalism or Reform?* ed. John L. Esposito (Boulder, CO: Rienner, 1997).

145. Jamal Salim from Nablus and Mahmoud al-Zahar from Gaza were apparently threatened by the military apparatus of Hamas, see *al-Watan al-Arabi*, 4 November 1994. See also Gunning Jeroen, *Hamas in Politics: Democracy, Religion, Violence* (London: Hurst and Company, 2007).

146. These attacks exposed the inside leadership's weakness and its lack of control over its military machine, see *Haaretz*, 8 janvier1996.

147. Muhib al-Nawati, *Asharq al-Awsat*, 13 February 2009.

the development of more positive relations with Arab countries.[148] Mahmoud al-Zahar had then declared: 'No we are not Shi'is.'[149]

These divergences cannot be understood by merely looking at normative categories opposing a 'radical' outside leadership to a 'moderate' one within.[150] Far from being immutable, the external leadership's opposition to any arrangement of sorts with the Palestinian Authority was a contingent stance that would completely change after 2011, when Diaspora leaders would express their attachment to reconciliation with Fatah, while part of the Gaza leaders would forcefully resist it. In the same vein, the members of the Gaza leadership would be the ones who in 2011 would call for the preservation of the Iranian alliance, when those of the outside were attempting to distance themselves from it. These elements confirm there is no strict overlap between geographical and ideological divide.

The beginning of the Arab Spring in 2011 made these conflicts more visible. Part of the Gaza leadership publicly expressed its disapproval of the policy implemented by the outside. This disagreement crystalized during the signing of the reconciliation agreement with Fatah in Doha, in February 2012. This Gazan discontent did not merely come down to opposition on the contents of policies carried out from Doha by Khaled Mesh'al. Far from being restricted to the two leadership's diverging interests, it was also a reflection of a power struggle between the inside and outside, each asking for more influence in the decision-making process.[151] Dissent from inside erupted because the outside group of players in possession of resources was trying to stop other entities within the government from endangering their position.

Although meaningful, this inside/outside geographical rift must not be overestimated. Coalitions of individual players were sometimes more important than these fault lines, particularly during the movement's internal elections in 2013: some members of the Gaza leadership have thus rallied to the policies promoted by Khaled Mesh'al (for instance, Ismail Haniyeh, the first against the Doha Agreement and then in favour of it), while other members of the outside were unhappy about them (e.g. Moussa Abu Marzouk). Moreover, this divide between

148. *Al-Shira*, 15 April 1993.
149. Mahmoud Zahar, 'No we are not Shi'is. The only country that is governed today in the way we uphold is Sudan', quoted by par Meir, 'Hamas and the Oslo Accords'.
150. This work is different from approaches that consider that ideology has a profound impact on decisions. M. Brecher, B. Steinberg, J. Stein, 'A Framework for Research on Foreign Policy Behaviour', *The Journal of Conflict Resolution* 13, no. 1 (1969): 75–101; Michael Brecher, 'Images, Process and Feedback in Foreign Policy: Israel's Decisions on German Reparations', *The American Political Science Review* 67, no. 1 (1973): 73–102.
151. The conflict surrounding the Doha Agreement appeared to be an illustration of the reality of the divide between Hamas inside and outside Palestine; each side represented a differing viewpoint on what the decision-making location and process should be. See Mohammad Hijazi, 'Hamas Movement between Partnership and Individualism', *Institute for Palestine Studies* 22, no. 87 (2011): 59.

the two leaderships, albeit real, did not seem to affect the culture of compromise characterizing Hamas, allowing the movement to mark its differences with Fatah, an organization often criticized for the authoritarian inner workings of a kernel of its chiefs led by Mahmoud Abbas.

The four watersheds of Hamas foreign policy

During the years spanning from 2006 to 2020, Hamas was affected by several 'shocks', whose effects would overlap: victory in the January 2006 elections, seizure of Gaza in June 2007, the Arab Spring in 2011 and finally Israel military aggression against Gaza which Israel refers to as 'Protective Edge' in the summer of 2014.

Going further back in time, it is possible to grasp the significance of these changes. In 2004, the two charismatic Palestinian leaders Yasser Arafat and Ahmed Yassin were killed, the former probably poisoned, and the latter when an Israeli helicopter gunship fired a missile at him on 22 March. These disappearances left a void the heads of Hamas would try to fill.[152] In summer 2005, Israeli occupation forces withdrew from Gaza; this retreat is of crucial importance to understand the future actions of Hamas and its supposedly legitimate seizure of the Strip in 2007. Preaching that Israel getting out of Gaza was the product of its successful armed struggle and declaring the territory a 'liberated zone',[153] Hamas could hijack the event and describe itself as the guarantor of the preservation of Palestinian interests. Finally, in March 2005, Hamas, together with thirteen other Palestinian factions, signed the Cairo Agreement, whose aim was to facilitate the organization of municipal and parliamentary elections in the entire Occupied Territories, also implying the reaching of a truce with Israel. This document stipulated, moreover, that Hamas was to transfer the file of negotiations with Israel to the PLO. The movement therefore accepted that the president of the Palestinian Authority would manage direct talks with the Jewish State. Hamas had boycotted parliamentary elections in 1996;[154] now, on the contrary, the movement was justifying its participation in the Palestinian

---

152. For an analysis of Hamas political weight after Sheikh Yassin assassination, see Khaled Hroub, 'Hamas after Shaykh Yasin and Rantisi', *Journal of Palestinian Studies* 33, no. 4 (2004): 21–38.

153. BasIm Al-Zubaidi, *Hamas wa-l-hukûm, dukhûl al-nizâm am al-tamarrûd 'alayhi* (Palestinian Center for Policy and Survey, 2010).

154. Hamas criticized the polls for several reasons: first because the Palestinian Authority was a structure without any real power, then because participating in the Authority's elections would come down to legitimating the Oslo Accords and finally because these polls excluded Palestinians from the Diaspora. Hamas made a distinction between these polls and other popular consultations it had actively participated in, such as elections for professional orders, student unions and municipalities, all of these pre-existing Oslo. See Signoles, *Le Hamas au pouvoir et après?*.

Authority's institutions by referring to the failure of the Oslo process and the end of the five-year interim period anticipated by these Accords, which would have supposedly been marked by the building of a Palestinian state.[155] The same year, Hamas won a huge victory in municipal polls. Many analysts interpret these changes as steps in the 'de-radicalisation' of Hamas, steps then ignored both by the Quartet and by the European Union.[156]

The first 'shock' we shall analyse here is that of 2006, when during the January parliamentary elections, Hamas won 74 seats out of a total of 132 (therefore an absolute majority, and 56 per cent of the votes). This result was a testimony of adherence of part of the population to the programme of Hamas. It can also be explained to a large extent by the failure of the negotiation process.[157] The victory of Hamas must be read, therefore, as both a way of sanctioning Fatah and as total adherence to the Islamist movement's line.[158] Since Hamas, following its victory, did not accept the Quartet's three conditions,[159] the latter decided on a series of sanctions that made donor states directly transfer international funds to the Palestinian Authority Presidency, by circumventing the government that was traditionally benefiting from this aid. Although Hamas was very much hindered in its capacity to act, due to the effects of the economic and diplomatic boycott,[160] its management of a Palestinian Authority Foreign Affairs Ministry did yield results, even if only in the balance of power inside the movement: after 2006, governmental management was the prerogative of the Gaza leadership, which could henceforth exert more influence on the movement's decision-making process.

The takeover of the Gaza Strip in June 2007 was the second major watershed in this chronology. Hamas has considered these events as a legitimate response to the coup attempts prepared from Cairo.[161] This explains why some of the movement's

---

155. The decision to participate in the parliamentary elections was taken in 2005. It had led to rifts among Hamas members, some opposed to the movement joining the Palestinian Authority's institutions. This dissent was partially an ideological one, since many Hamas members considered being in power as joining a system that necessarily led to corruption.

156. Are Hovdenak, 'Hamas in Transition, the Failure of Sanctions', *Democratization* 16, no. 1 (February 2009): 59–80.

157. Khaled Hroub, *Hamas, a Beginner's Guide* (London: Pluto Press, 2006).

158. Abdallah Belqiz, 'Azmat-al-machrû' al-watanî al-falastînî, min Fatah ila Hamas', *Markaz dirâsât al-wahda al'arabiyya*, 2006.

159. The Quartet for the Middle East is made up of the United States, Russia, the European Union and the UN.

160. Israeli restrictions on movements of population and goods are in place since the 1990s and were gradually tightened, notably after the First Intifada. As from January 2006, economic sanctions were largely accepted by the international community. Sara Roy, *Failing Peace: Gaza and the Palestinian-Israeli Conflict* (London: Pluto, 2007).

161. In August 2007, to justify its U-turn, Hamas published the *White Book* (*al-kitab al-abyad*), under the title: 'No other option than force', *al-Ittihad*, 16 August 2007; see also Khaled Mesh'al's interview by Ken Livingstone, *New Statesman*, 22 September 2009.

leaders saw this seizure as a 'second liberation', after Israel's withdrawal from the Gaza Strip in 2005. In naming this event, they favour the term *ḥâsim* (a radical but inescapable decision) to that of *inqisâm* (division). On the other hand, adversaries of Hamas largely refer to the term *inqilâb* (coup) when speaking of this episode.[162] One should note on this matter that, since 2006, the Quartet and the European Union had supported a reform implemented by Mahmoud Abbas, which consisted in taking away from government the control of security forces, and this exacerbated the conflict between the two parties.[163] The seizure of Gaza by Hamas also appeared as the consequence of an American plan of action to strengthen Fatah's authority, following the inter-Palestinian reconciliation agreement signed in Mecca in February.[164] In any case, these events deeply shattered the credibility of Hamas. Some inside the movement itself went as far as criticizing the way the situation had been managed.[165]

The new regional context stemming from the Arab Spring was as ominous a transformation as that of 2006. The start of the Syrian uprising incited Hamas to choose to move its outside leadership from Damascus to Doha, despite running the risk of losing the Islamic Republic of Iran's support. Simultaneously, the coming to power of the Egyptian Muslim Brothers was perceived as a historic opportunity to gain recognition, by opting for a regional realignment with Sunni powers. Yet as from summer 2013, Mohammed Morsi's overthrow and his replacement by General al-Sisi (who once in power destroyed all the tunnels between Egypt and the Gaza Strip) made things difficult for Hamas, which caused it to turn once more to its erstwhile Iranian ally.

To this regional rearrangement, which was very detrimental for Hamas, one must add the Israeli offensive against the Gaza Strip in summer 2014. The attack on Gaza was a major U-turn in the political strategy of Hamas: while it had shown itself in favour of a political withdrawal by handing the keys of the Gaza Strip to Ramallah's Palestinian Authority, the latter decided after the Israeli military operation to set up a coordination committee in charge of managing common

---

162. See Naim al-Achab, *Imârat-Hamâs* (*The Hamas Emirate*), Dâr al-tanwîr li-l-nashr wa-l-targama wa-l-tawzî' (Ramallah, 2007); Bakr Abou Bakr, *Hamâs, suyûf wa manâbir*, Dâr al-Shurûq li-l-nashr wa-l-tawzî' (Ramallah, 2008); Ahmad Abd al-Rahman, 'Hamâs khârij al-sirb: wusûlan ilâ-l-hudna l-majjâniyya', *Seyasat* (Summer 2008): 65–70.

163. Are Hovdenak, 'Hamas in Transition, the Failure of Sanctions', *Democratization* 16, no. 1 (February 2009): 59–80.

164. The security component of a plan known as the 'Benchmark Document', written in particular by General Keith Dayton had a clear goal: to prop up Fatah through a massive supply of weapons. According to the plan's schedule, Fatah forces were meant to deploy in June 2007 along the border between Egypt and Gaza and take control of the Strip. See Jean-François Legrain, 'Palestine: un État, quel État?', *Ifri*, January 2010.

165. See in particular Ghazi Hamad's resignation from his position as Prime Minister Ismail Haniyeh's adviser. Nowadays Ghazi Hamad is deputy minister of Foreign Affairs and asserts that he does not wish to again be a minister in a government resulting from division.

affairs in the Palestinian enclave. 'Protective Edge' thus exacerbated the rift between Hamas and Fatah, which assimilated this coordination committee to a government in due form. As from the spring of 2017, Mahmoud Abbas heavily sanctioned Gaza, a measure that would deepen the inter-Palestinian divide.

These four moments (2006, 2007, 2011 and 2014) were turning points in Hamas foreign policy and caused substantial changes, in terms of interests, ideology and decision-making processes.

This research wishes first of all to explore the main interactions between Hamas and non-Palestinian players: first Israel, and then other states. A section is more specifically focused on the trends and changes in relations between Hamas and Syria, Iran and Egypt. Part II explains these interactions by concentrating on various types of interests, both external (loosening the blockade to ensure the Gaza government's survival and ending isolation) and internal (favouring management by its power structure in Gaza, notably by the improvement of its administrative, extractive and military capacities, and competing against Ramallah and the PLO). The means to implement policies in accordance with these interests can of course be redefined as a function of context. The goal of Part III is to present the place and role of ideology in Hamas' foreign policy. Although that is a matter of interest, much more than of ideology, the relation between both factors cannot be seen as a dichotomy. Most often, Hamas succeeds in redefining its ideology to make it correspond to its interests. Always adapted to contexts and interlocutors, ideology thus goes together with the implementation of external interests. It allows the movement to attempt ending isolation and ensuring the loyalty of its economic and political backers. The leaders' interests and ideological stances have repercussions on the movement's foreign policy, via decision-making processes dealt with in last and fourth part of the book. Some decisions were taken by the entire group of members of the Political Bureau and were the product of compromises. Other decisions, taken unilaterally by the outside leadership, were hotly contested. Interests and ideology determining the foreign policy of Hamas are therefore those championed by the members dominating the decision-making process.

Field enquiries

Most academic works favour a sociological analysis of partisan commitment or mobilizations – the main gateway to the analysis of political parties in the Arab world – at the expense of other perspectives. The author has focused, however, on the political direction of Hamas, asking a set of questions to its leading officials and cross-matching their discourse and theoretical and partisan production with the political context, beginning with the victory of Hamas in Palestinian parliamentary elections.

The author's fieldwork began in 2011 in the West Bank, where she spoke to MPs elected in 2006 on the 'Change and Reform' list. These encounters permitted evidencing the paralysis of Palestinian Authority political bodies in the West Bank. Most of these figures (for instance, Ayman Daraghmeh and Mahmoud Mouslih) welcomed the author in their personal offices, and not inside parliament, which has remained shut since 2007. The author could thus take into account their frustrations, related both to parliament being deprived of any means of action and to their geographical distance and the impossibility for them to communicate with their colleagues in Gaza otherwise than by videoconference. These two MPs made the author understand the precautions taken by the movement while separating the function of parliamentarian from that of Hamas representative. Both men mentioned their incapacity to deal with all issues relevant to the movement, since they were cognizant of political files specific to Hamas. The same point led Aziz Dweik, president of the Palestinian Legislative Council, to refuse receiving the author, under the pretext that he did not stand for Hamas but the Palestinian people. During this stay, the author had conversations with other figures close to Hamas, such as Samir Abou Eisheh (an engineer by trade elected in 2006 on the 'Change and Reform' list) and Sheikh Hamid al-Bitawi (a major religious figure of the movement residing in Nablus and deceased in 2012). Under house arrest, Abou Eisheh described to the author his numerous sojourns in Israeli prisons. Despite the fact that Abou Eisheh was under administrative detention, the author became convinced after this interview that Hamas had greater freedom of action in Nablus than in Ramallah, Fatah's headquarters. Finally, this stay was an opportunity for the author to meet many Fatah leaders in Ramallah and take into account the issue of how the movement's foreign policy was perceived in the West Bank.

The foreign policy of Hamas is an official prerogative of its outside leadership: this is why the author travelled to Damascus to speak to two of the movement's major figures: Osama Hamdan and Moussa Abu Marzouk, a historical leader of Hamas and later the Political Bureau's deputy chairman. The relevance of these two stays in Syria was grounded in their timing: the first interview was indeed made in January 2010, before the start of the Syrian uprising. The strategic alliance of Hamas with the Syrian regime was at the heart of our discussions. The second conversation, taking place in June 2011 with Moussa Abu Marzouk, happened while he was very cautious talking about this strategic relationship, but it was still possible to find clues to an inflection of Hamas diplomacy towards other states. What could be perceived, two months into the March 2011 Deraa events, was the ambiguity of a policy regarding Syria expressed in the language of a 'resistance' front against Israel, but where the first signs of a rift with Assad's regime were becoming palpable and would become even more so in June of the same year.

Although the outside leadership enjoys additional prerogatives in matters of diplomacy, it was indispensable to speak to the entire group of players belonging to the Movement of Islamic Resistance, including those in Gaza. At first, the impossibility of travelling to the Strip made dialogue in other countries abroad the only way to pursue this research. The author therefore decided to meet Hamas leaders – both from the movement and MPs – during their travels outside Palestine. What was initially an obstacle turned out to be a prime mover behind the micro-exploration of Hamas diplomacy, with information collected from the players themselves.

In Cyprus, where the author stayed in April 2012 while participating in a seminar organized by the *Revue d'études palestiniennes*, an opportunity to meet Ghazi Hamad (former deputy Foreign Affairs minister of the Gaza government) suddenly arose. His academic experience, his atypical career, his often very entrenched and heterodox stands make this leader one of the movement's paramount figures. Ghazi Hamad had been invited to join several round tables organized by this academic journal's staff. Seeing him interacting for three days with 'Arab intellectuals' who were ideologically closer to Fatah was a chance to directly witness spontaneous reactions from all participants.

In Geneva, the author spoke to two parliamentarians from Gaza invited by the Geneva Inter-Parliamentary Federation: Mouchir al-Masri and Sayed Abu Musameh. Travelling to the Swiss city provided the opportunity to watch the MPs in their interactions with European diplomats, understanding the strategy of players who, in their search for recognition, made use of their status as members of the Palestinian Legislative Council to talk about eminently political issues. This meeting was also an occasion to notice that a leader like Mouchir al-Masri, supposed to be a Gazan hardliner, could, when dealing with foreign interlocutors, introduce himself as a figure with a broad openness of mind. During the interview, he let differences in viewpoints within the movement resurface, by mentioning the existence of 'true divergences in discourse'. The contrast between Mouchir al-Masri and Sayed Abu Musameh made the author clearly understand there was a great diversity of currents within the movement, which could in part be explained by generational differences.

In Turkey, a workshop organized in July 2012 by the Center for Mediterranean Integration (CMI) allowed the author to meet Gaza leaders who had travelled to Ankara to engage in talks with heads of Fatah. It was also during intra-Palestinian meetings held in Egypt that conversations with Gazan leaders were started; it was then possible to contemplate the extent of Palestinian division, but also of internal dissensions within Hamas: during meetings held in February 2012 in Cairo's City Star hotel, four Gaza leaders against the Doha Agreement (signed a few days beforehand by Khaled Mesh'al) were speaking to heads of the outside leadership in an attempt to reach an internal compromise. An opportunity appeared to travel to the Gaza Strip when Ahmed Yousef was planning his return and suggested that the author go with him. Despite this, the author's struggle to get a permit from Egyptian intelligence services proved fruitless, because they requested prior procurement of a formal agreement from France, which had been denied.

It was from Israel that, in March 2013, the author was able to travel to the Gaza Strip, a consequence of the inflection of France's foreign policy, which now called for a lifting of the blockade, but above all a result of the crucial support of Mr Desagneaux, the French General Consul at the time. This stay was absolutely essential for putting into the right perspective the discourse of players residing outside Palestine and comparing them to those of the inside. Our talks with both parliamentarians whom the author had already met during their trips abroad, and erstwhile Foreign Affairs ministers and some of the movement's officials dealing with these matters, provided a chance to map the different levels of representativeness of all. The author was able to observe that the position of Foreign Affairs minister had not been left vacant after the 2007 scission, since this portfolio was given to Ismail Haniyeh in 2013. It was not, however, as a Hamas leader that he was generally welcomed during his trips abroad, because most states recognized the Ramallah government, not the Gaza one. It was soon found out that his son (Abd al-Salam Haniyeh) also had a role in foreign policy: as minister of sports, he was playing an important role while abroad, all the more so since the sports minister was the only one not to be involved in the conflict between Ramallah and Gaza in June 2007. Accompanied by Jibril Rajoub, the Palestinian Olympic Committee and the Palestinian football federation's chairman, Ismail Haniyeh's son travelled to many countries and thus reinforced the personal relations of his father with Arab leaders.

In contrast to the West Bank, Gaza seems to be a 'liberated' region: the control of Hamas on this entity is total. Despite the blockade, which does not permit speaking of any form of sovereignty, Hamas has de facto taken over attributes similar to those of typical states: there are talks on the creation of a future Defence Ministry and the attribution of residence cards to foreigners. Foreign policy is, from this perspective, sovereignty's first attribute. Hamas rule over this territory therefore increases geographical and political chasms between the West Bank and Gaza. Hamas leaders are obviously instructed to display the opposite – Gaza is an integral part of Palestine and there is no plan whatsoever to build what would look like a state – but the presence, after the Eretz checkpoint, of the Hamas border post (*Arba'-Arba'*), a few metres beyond the traditional roadblock controlled by the Ramallah Authority (*Khamsa-Khamsa*), is a case in point of the desire to highlight its presence and control over this territory.[166]

Finally, the author had talks in March/April 2017 with officials in Lebanon and Qatar. In Beirut, she had conversations with Osama Hamdan, whom she had met seven years prior in Damascus. Hamdan confessed that after noticing the changes in the regional context, Hamas had no issues with re-installation in Syria. The talks, which shortly followed Yahya al-Sinwar's victory at the head of the Gazan leadership, partly focused on the movement's organizational evolution and fears expressed in Gaza over the holding of both military and political responsibilities. Hamdan tried to minimize these apprehensions, by comparing Hamas to Israel, whose political leaders had all been officers in the military, from Rabin to Peres and Barak to Netanyahu. On 17 April, the author was finally able to meet Khaled Mesh'al in Doha. At that moment, he had not been the chairman of the Political Bureau for quite some time; the final results of Hamas internal elections were indeed about to determine the name of his successor. This timing also gave a particular coloration to the interview, during which he was able to draw a balance sheet of all his years at the head of the movement. Moreover, our visit preceded the release of the General Principles and Policies Document in which Mesh'al had invested much time and energy.

---

166. Such checkpoints, which can be found at all other crossings separating the Gaza Strip from Israel, are also meant to levy additional duties on products that transit through Israel. See Are Hovdenak, 'The Public Services Under Hamas in Gaza, Islamic Revolution or Crisis Management?', *Prio Report*, 3 (Oslo: PRIO, March 2010).

The Covid-19 pandemic, which drastically reduced the possibilities of travel abroad, was a paradox: it resulted in a multiplication of videoconferences planned by various NGOs, attended by West Bank, Gaza and Diaspora Palestinians. From Paris, the author could easily follow these discussions, such as the one set up by the Masar Palestinian centre, which was held on Zoom in August 2020 and asked Hamas leader Hussam Badran to respond to several aspects of the Trump plan, specifically on Palestinian division, the normalization between Israel and several Arab states, and the future of the resistance programme.

Written sources

The specificity of the author's topic made access to sources highly problematic. The Palestinian Foreign Affairs Ministry was bombed during the November 2012 Israeli military operation, making it impossible to obtain all the documents and sources necessary. Israeli military offensives are partly aimed at making all supportive material or tools of Gazan governmental legitimacy vanish: destruction of archives has been part and parcel of a plan to project the image of an extremist and totalitarian 'Hamastan'. One should also emphasize the unwillingness of some interlocutors to cooperate; using these destructions as an excuse, they provided very few documents, fearing that these would be used against them. Other written sources permitted filling these informational gaps.

Apart from the above-mentioned documents, which relate to the movement's foreign policy doctrine (the Charter, the Introductory Memorandum, the Document of General Principles and Policies), the author also based her research on other sources concerning internal policy, but that also reveal stances towards Israel. The election platform raised the problem posed by Hamas' attachment to armed struggle. This was in particular the case in the speech given by Ismail Haniyeh in parliament, on 27 March 2006, during which he indicated that his government would work 'in conformity with the clauses of Fundamental Law amended in 2003'. This reference to Fundamental Law was significant in that it appeared in the framework of the Oslo Accords. On a legal level, Hamas was therefore abiding by the parameters set up by the 'peace talks'. Signed in June 2006, the National Conciliation Document of the Prisoners[167] was a recognition of the validity of 1967 borders and allowed, just like all the other reconciliation agreements that would follow, grasping the changes in positions of Hamas regarding Israel.

Our visits to MPs also enabled the author to obtain other sources relating to the diplomacy implemented by Hamas parliamentarians. Published by Gaza's Palestinian Legislative Council, the book *Five Years On* thus presents the work of the Gaza parliament since the June 2007 events, including in the field of diplomacy.

---

167. This document was written by Palestinians jailed in Israel, who hoped that their common mobilization and the legitimacy as prisoners would give more weight to their proposals. It was signed by Hamas, Islamic Jihad, PFLP and DFLP three months after the formation of the first Hamas-dominated Palestinian government.

One can find descriptions of many travels abroad, the motives and context of these trips and the interlocutors MPs met. Beyond these descriptions, the document is precious for its self-representation and validates the building of a typology of players active in diplomacy.

In addition, browsing the website of the Gaza government's Foreign Affairs Ministry was useful, because it was a tool for deciphering policies, as well as looking at an effective showcase for foreign readership.[168] The Ministry's aim was to change the Gaza government's image, to make it more acceptable to states and world public opinion, but also to deepen relations between Hamas and Arab states, in order to officially reach a unified Arab stand. This site is no longer in existence. To explain its removal, a plausible hypothesis would be that Hamas no longer wishes to give the impression that it is in charge of a government in Gaza, and that its diplomatic activity is bent on competing against the PLO, or even setting up a separate state in the Strip. In 2013, when the author last consulted the website, she noticed that the section entitled 'the Minister's word' had been left empty. The same year, Hamas created a new website, the Council on International Relations,[169] which introduced itself as the first Palestinian institution in the field of international relations. Managed by Basem Naim, the CIR displayed several intents: to promote the rights of the Palestinian people and guarantee stability in the region; develop relations with regional and international institutions to defend Palestinians' rights; carry out activities and studies to support the Palestinian narrative in its struggle against occupation; provide Palestinian decision-makers with advice in the field of diplomacy; help contribute to dialogue between Palestinians.

Finally, this research is also based on the many speeches relevant to foreign policy, mostly given by the movement's leaders during their travels. One notably thinks of Khaled Mesh'al's speeches in Cairo following Israeli military operations on the Gaza Strip, and his lectures in Tunisia and Turkey, but also his words in Gaza on 8 December 2012. One should, in addition, mention browsing through various websites or newspapers and journals whose opinions are close to the movements, which all allow scholars to delve into deeper analysis. The Palestinian Information centre[170] (*Markaz al-filastînî li-l-i'lâm*), for instance, translates articles into seven languages and is an efficient tool for publishing communiqués and interviews of leaders. The websites of the *al-Zaytouna*[171] centre in Beirut (*Markaz al-Zaytûna li-l-dirâsât wa-l-istishârât*)[172] and *Filastin al-Muslima*[173] (the monthly magazine

---

168. http://www.mofap.gov.ps/new/ last consultation on 15 January 2013.
169. http://coir.ps/en/%d8%a7%d9%84%d9%81%d9%8a%d8%af%d9%8a%d9%88/.
170. http://www.palinfo.com/site/PIC/.
171. http://www.alzaytouna.net/index.php.
172. http://www.alzaytouna.net/index.php.
173. Since early 2013, it has not been possible to consult the site of this journal from France. Articles quoted beyond this date were sent to me via the internet by friends residing in Beirut or Palestine.

published in London) also allow scholars to read interviews and analyses of figures close to the movement.

The remaining corpus selected rests on analyses and studies of the *Alresalah* weekly, the oldest and best-known magazine sympathetic to Hamas, whose chief editor was Ghazi Hamad, prior to him becoming one of the main figures of the Hamas government, and the *Filastin* daily,[174] founded in Gaza in early May 2007, whose chief editor, Mustafa al-Sawwaf, and Fathi Hamad (al-Aqsa TV) are close to the Izz al-Din al-Qassam Brigades. To a careful examination of these journals and magazines, the author would add a reading of the Arab press, with *al-Quds al-Arabi*, *Al-Sharq al-Awsat*, *al-Masri al-Youm*, *al-Hayat* and *al-Ahram* as prime sources of information.

---

174. '*Filastin*' is the title of the most important Palestinian nationalist and liberal daily (1911–67), founded by Issa al-Issa, an orthodox Christian close to the Nationalists, who opposed the actions of the Jerusalem Mufti Hajj Amine al-Husseini and was against the *Mujahidin*'s scorched earth policies during the 1936 revolt.

Part I

GENERAL ORIENTATIONS OF HAMAS FOREIGN POLICY

Chapter 1

HAMAS AND ISRAEL

CONCILIATION AND CONFRONTATION

Hamas has conducted an apparently contradictory policy that at times advocates conciliation, at others armed struggle. As an attempt to end the series of confrontations opposing it to Israel, it opened, as from June 2007, negotiations under the patronage of Egypt, which led to the signing of a *hudna* (truce) in June 2008.

Six months later, in the wake of its numerous incursions in the Gaza Strip, Israel broke the truce and triggered a grand scale military offensive in December 2008–January 2009. The only result of this assault, which Israel refers to as 'Cast lead', was a unilateral Israeli cease-fire.

The year 2011 saw a new sequence of intense interactions between Israel and Hamas. In October, the Islamist movement freed the IDF Israeli private Gilad Shalit, who had been abducted in June 2006. In March and August 2011, the Izz al-Din al-Qassam Brigades fired a series of rockets towards Israel. Two Israeli offensives were then carried out on the Gaza Strip: one in November 2012, 'Pillar of Defence', and one in summer 2014, 'Protective Edge'.

The period that followed the summer 2014 offensive heralded a substantial change in relations between Israel and Hamas. Large-scale recurrent military assaults against the Gaza Strip turned into increasingly routine violent confrontations between the two sides, interwoven with the dynamics of the Great March of Return launched on 30 March 2018.

The election victory's impact: 'One hand builds, the other resists'

Subjecting the exercise of power to the imperative of resistance

The January 2006 elections, won by Hamas (to its own surprise), placed it in an unexpected situation. The refusal of Fatah to form a national unity government led Hamas to constitute the Palestinian government on its own. The movement then considered that, far from abandoning the armed struggle, its entry into the Palestinian Authority's institutions would, quite the opposite, allow it to protect the 'resistance and permanently bury the agreements signed between the PLO and Israel' in 1993 and 1994.¹

The dilemma between resistance and the exercising of power had been clearly exposed before this time.² The election programme, which was the foundation for Hamas' parliamentary election campaign, had led to the writing of two texts dealing with the issue of resistance, each almost contradicting the other. The manifesto published in the newspaper *Minbar al-Islâh*,³ on 8 January 2006, stated that the Palestinian people, still in a state of national struggle, had the right to regain their rights by all means, including armed resistance. In contrast, its draft programme for a coalition government originating from the central committee for the preparation of elections had erased the notion of armed struggle, highlighting other means for the preservation of the Palestinian people's rights.⁴

This dilemma was exposed in exemplary fashion on two occasions: during the 2006 election victory and the kidnapping of Israeli soldier Gilad Shalit. On 27 March 2006, during his inaugural speech in parliament, Ismail Haniyeh mentioned the necessity of founding a Palestinian state within the 1967 borders; he detailed that his government would 'work according to the articles of the Basic Law amended in March 2003'.⁵ This reference to Fundamental Law is significant, in that it appeared in the framework of the Oslo agreements. On the legal level, Hamas was therefore to conform to parameters put in place by the 'peace talks'.

Gilad Shalit's abduction on 25 June 2006, captured jointly by Hamas' armed branch, the Popular Resistance Committees and the Salafi group *Jaysh al-Islâm*, meant the definitive collapse of the truce concluded in March 2005.⁶ During an exclusive interview with al-Jazeera through Tamer al-Mashal documentary programme 'What Is Hidden Is Greater', Marwan Issa, deputy chief of the al-Qassam Brigades, provides details on the manner this operation was prepared, as well as on how it unfolded.⁷ The crisis that followed translated into a campaign of destruction of Palestinian institutions and the arrest of MPs and ministers. In

---

1. The president of the Palestinian Legislative Council Aziz Dweik declared that the Palestinian parliament would review the set of Israeli–Palestinian agreements.

2. Khaled Hroub, 'Conflating National Liberation and Socio-Political Change', *The International Spectator* 43, no. 4 (2008): 59–72.

3. Basim al-Zubaidi, *Hamas wa-l-hukûm, dukhûl al-nizâm am al-tamarrûd 'alayhi* (Palestinian Center for Policy and Survey, 2010).

4. Ibid. See also Khaled Hroub, 'A "New" Hamas through Its New Documents', *Journal of Palestine Studies* 35, no. 4 (2006): 6–27.

5. For an analysis of Hamas' cabinet platform presented on 27 March 2006 see Khaled Hroub, 'A "New" Hamas through Its New Documents', *Journal of Palestine Studies* 35, no. 4 (2006): 6–27.

6. *Al-Sabil*, 25 April 2006.

7. https://primetimezone.com/world/gulf-news/what-is-hidden-is-greater-hosts-marwan-issa-and-broadcasts-an-audio-recording-of-one-of-the-captured-israeli-soldiers-in-gaza-video-a-homeland-tweeting-outside-the-flock/.

July 2006, an Israeli foray in the Gaza Strip provoked the death of the family of Abou Sulmiyya, one of the leaders of Hamas: this was followed in August by an air raid on the al-Shuaja'iyya neighbourhood.

In the wake of this victory, the movement's leaders called for the adoption of a new strategy in which the exercise of power would be subjected to the imperative of resistance. 'How to do things in order to act in an environment where the exercising of power goes against the imperative of resistance? It is a new experiment, that of allying power to resistance, and this is why we must do all we can to carry out this double objective. This situation is provisional, it is not strategic,' Abu Marzouk declared.[8]

The National Conciliation Document of the Prisoners

Three days after Gilad Shalit's abduction, Hamas signed, together with other Palestinian factions, the Prisoners' Document, also called the National Conciliation Document (*Wathîqat al-Wifâq al-watani*). This text implicitly recognized the validity of the June 1967 borders and agreed on limiting resistance to the land occupied in 1967.[9] Since 2005 Hamas had ceased its suicide attacks inside the 1948 territories: this was the period when the movement was preparing its participation in the Palestinian political system. Hamas spokesman Yahya Musa declared: 'Hamas has moved onto a new stage that requires the cessation of martyrdom operations (*istishhâd*), which took place in an exceptional period, that of the Intifada. They have now been brought to an end, for reasons related to circumstances and to our beliefs.'[10]

Just like in the case of the Cairo Agreement of March 2005, the Prisoners' Document transferred to the PLO the file of negotiations with the occupying power. Hamas thereby accepted that the president of the Palestinian Authority carry out direct negotiations with Israel.

However, most of Hamas' leaders tried to minimize the importance of these pragmatic declarations; they were seen as a tactical manoeuvre by the movement, and they did not diminish by any means the validity and legitimacy of its historical strategy. It is possible to notice here a wavering between two fluctuating approaches (*mawâqif moutazabziba*). This policy would be contrary to that of Fatah, for whom the building of a Palestinian state on the 1967 borders constitutes the ultimate goal:

---

8. The truce was concluded in March 2005, during the signature of the Cairo Agreement. According to Gunning, it is very likely that Shalit's abduction was an instruction from the external leadership and was therefore a premeditated act, though this is impossible to verify. See Gunning, *Hamas in Politics*.

9. al-Zubaidi, *Hamas wa-l-hukûm, dukhûl al-nizâm am al-tamarrûd 'alayhi*.

10. *Al-Hayat al-Jadida*, 10 April 2006.

For us, the struggle has not ended, and this is why the building of a Palestinian state on the 1967 borders remains a tactical goal. For Fatah, the conflict is over; this is why for them it is a strategic aim. We do not believe in a two-state solution. Fatah believes in the two-state solution; this is why they have recognized Israel.[11]

Certain clauses of the Prisoners' Document restrict the range of the decision to transfer the negotiation file to the PLO. In the case where an agreement between Mahmoud Abbas and the State of Israel is found, it would obligatorily need to be submitted to the vote of the Legislative Council, where Hamas has a majority. These agreements should, in a later phase, be validated via a popular referendum.[12] Although the movement did show that it was ready to collaborate with Fatah, it thus maintained a more than circumspect stance as regards a policy of peace with Israel at any cost.

The issue of the file's transfer would moreover be the subject of loud disagreements between the two parties during the formation of a national unity government in March 2007. While Fatah insisted on the (Hamas dominated) government's obligation to accept that the PLO be the only decision-maker, Hamas considered that any agreement with Israel necessarily had to be validated by the Legislative Council beforehand.

The Mecca Agreement of February 2007

In 2006, all attempts to form a national unity government failed. During this period, bloody episodes between Hamas and Fatah followed one another, until the signing of the Mecca Agreement in February 2007, which permitted breaking the deadlock and paving the way for this national unity government.

Through this reconciliation, Hamas was endorsing the validity of already-existing agreements between Israel and the PLO.[13] The roots of this acceptance in the framework of the Oslo agreement go back to the period that followed parliamentary elections, when many Hamas leaders had advocated 'respect' of agreements that would not be detrimental to the rights of the Palestinian people. An increasing number of voices in the movement were being heard, asking for recognition of the validity of these agreements, although there was no

---

11. Conversation with Abou Musameh in Geneva on 19 January 2012.

12. During an interview in November 2007, Yahya Musa stated that delegating to Mahmoud Abbas the power to negotiate with Israel was conditional on the Palestinian president addressing his people, listening to the Palestinian street and being inspired by it. See al-Zubaidi, *Hamas wa-l-hukûm, dukhûl al-nizâm am al-tamarrûd 'alayhi*.

13. The Mecca Agreement was signed after lengthy discussions lasting three weeks, which were marked by many conflicts, particularly by disputes on the issue of the candidate to the position of interior minister. Discussions that allowed the formation of the government showed that the confidence crisis was a lasting factor on both sides. See Khaled Safi, *Ittifâq Makka: wâqi' wa tahdiya* (Seyasat: Ramallah, Rabi', 2007).

unanimity on this stand, since others were, indeed, considering that victory in elections provided the possibility of denouncing these accords. The president of the Legislative Council Aziz Dweik had, for instance, declared that the National Assembly would review the Israeli–Palestinian agreements, and that Hamas would only accept those that were in the interest of its people.[14]

Four days after Hamas' victory, Khaled Mesh'al had declared: 'Hamas will take into consideration all established agreements and all realistically and pragmatically voted laws to preserve the rights of its people, but we will take only what is convenient for us; and we shall reject what goes against our interests. We will not pay the price of peace.'[15]

The vice-president of the Political Bureau Moussa Abu Marzouk soon followed in these footsteps and announced that he would take Oslo into account with 'appropriate realism', because from a juridical viewpoint, one must take due note of agreements ratified by an established political regime.[16] He added that although Hamas had entered the contest of parliamentary elections, it had done so 'on the basis of these agreements', despite their diminished weight.[17]

Though attachment to the juridical framework of Oslo preceded the Mecca Agreement, it was really reconciliation in the Saudi holy city in March 2007 that was proof of a break with the previous government. On this occasion, Ismail Haniyeh's speech made clear the change in his stance concerning international and Arab resolutions. The agreement's fourth article suggested the need to put in place a Palestinian plan to unite political discourse on the basis of the juridical legality of international resolutions:

> I call you, as head of the government, to respect the high interests of the Palestinian people, to protect its rights and gains, to make its national goals – as defined by the Palestinian National Council, the Palestinian Constitution as well as the Document of National Entente and the decisions of Arab summits – come to fruition. In one word, I ask you to respect the international juridical decisions of a legal and legitimate nature, and that were signed by the PLO.

Nevertheless, most of Hamas' leaders have tried to minimize this recognition. As concerns the commitment to abide by previous agreements between the PLO and Israel, they have mentioned that there is a difference between respecting agreements and recognizing them. According to them, 'respect' leaves a wider margin for manoeuvre and allows the movement to not 'commit' to their implementation.[18] Moussa Abu Marzouk, at the time the Political Bureau's vice-president, thus expressed this idea in the following terms:

---

14. *Al-Ayyam*, 18 February 2006. See also *Alresalah*, 16 March 2006.
15. *Islam Online*, 5 February 2006.
16. *Alresalah*, 21 September 2006.
17. *Islam Online*, 31 January 2006.
18. Khaled Safi, *Ittifâq Makka: wâqi' wa tahdiya, Seyasat* (Ramallah: Rabi', 2007).

The difference is great between respect (*ihtirâm*) and recognition (*i'tirâf*); I respect does not mean that I implement. This is what happened in the case of the Mecca Agreement; we respect old agreements, but this does not mean we recognize them. For instance, we respect the new Palestinian reality and we participate in it; but this does not mean we are in agreement with Oslo. There is a difference between dealing with reality and accepting this reality. This is exactly the same thing as regards the recognition of Israel. I can recognize the presence of this state as a fait accompli (*amr wâqi'*) or, as the French say, a *de facto* recognition, but this does not mean that I recognize Israel as a state.[19]

The explanation given by Fatah for the respect of these agreements by Hamas is entirely different: for Fatah, this means that Hamas' commitment to respect existing agreements should lead it to a transformation guaranteeing the implementation of the agreements signed by the PLO, which favour the two-state solution, the cornerstone of the 1988 Declaration of Independence of the Palestinian National Council.[20]

The seizure of Gaza and the change in relations with Israel

Three months after signing the Mecca Agreement and the constitution of a national unity government, Hamas seized Gaza by force. Divergences on how to call this event – described by Hamas as 'radical but inevitable decision' (*hâsim*), as opposed to Fatah, which sees it as a real 'coup d'Etat' (*inqilâb*), the commonly used term being that of 'division' (*inqisâm*) – bear witness to the importance of the controversy caused by the taking of Gaza.[21]

In the wake of this episode, the president of the Palestinian Authority Mahmoud Abbas published a set of decrees: Ismail Haniyeh's government was sacked, a state

---

19. Conversation with Moussa Abu Marzouk, Damascus, 1 June 2011.

20. Interview of Jamal Nazzal, Fatah's official representative in the West Bank, Ma'an, 9 February 2007. Interview of Azzam al-Ahmad, *al-Watan*, 10 February 2007, reprinted by *al-Hayat*, 11 February 2007.

21. The author wishes to recall that these events are the consequence of a coup attempt on Fatah's behalf, which was prepared from Egypt, a state player sidelined from negotiations between Palestinians occurring in Mecca. We shall also note the importance of taking into account the international political context: Olmert was trying to circumvent the US president's frustrated desire to reach a negotiated solution with the Palestinians. According to Naim al-Achab, Hamas' forceful seizure of power was in accordance with Israel's interests. See *Maariv* on 1 October 2007, quoted in *Imârat-Hamâs*. This confirms Jean-François Legrain's hypothesis, which postulates that the Israelis precipitated Hamas' military victory in order to weaken Mahmoud Abbas, see Jean-François Legrain, 'Pour une autre lecture de la guerre de Gaza', *EchoGéo* (Sur le Vif, 2009).

of emergency was declared[22] and Salam Fayyad was named prime minister of a Public Salvation government in Ramallah. Gaza's economic encirclement was reinforced, while the West Bank received international promises of economic and financial assistance. Changes in the interior situation led Hamas to seek a truce with Israel, which was finally signed in June 2008. Six months later, following multiple Israeli incursions and due to the prolongation of the blockade, hostilities resumed, and a large-scale Israeli military aggression against the Gaza Strip was launched in December 2008 and January 2009.

The June 2008 truce

Indirect negotiations between Hamas and Israel, which resulted in the June 2008 truce, had begun in August 2007, two months after the Islamist movement's seizure of Gaza. Concluded thanks to Egypt's brokerage, this truce included, apart from the bilateral cessation of all military operations, a commitment by Israel to reopen crossing points and to gradually lift the blockade. It was meant to allow an extension of six months and be renewable.

The truce (*hudna*) is part of the historic tradition of the movement, which was seeking, partly by means of armed struggle, and partly by cooperation, to end the occupation; this dual practice was not new then. It had been initiated by Sheikh Ahmad Yassin in the early 1990s:[23]

> Our understanding of the resistance is extremely broad and unswerving. It can be violent, but can also adopt other forms: information, economics, and diplomacy are so many roads to resistance. At each stage we try to determine what is the most convenient form of resistance. According to context, we insist on one of those aspects, we chose the most appropriate form, political, diplomatic or even peaceful action, as was decided in the last periods.[24]

The leaders of Hamas claim that the main consideration that encourages them to return to the negotiating table and endorse truces is respect for the interest of the

---

22. For an analysis of the decree, the state of emergency and the emergence of a second cabinet, see Jean-François Legrain, 'L'impasse politique et institutionnelle palestinienne', *Critique internationale* 36 (July–September 2007), available online.

23. According to Khaled Khroub, the concept of truce only appeared in the early 1990s, while the duality between the historical approach and the interim one was in existence from the moment of the movement's foundation. The truce dates from Sheikh Yassin's letter written from his cell, in which he indicates that a ten-year truce could become a reality upon the condition that Israel withdraw from the West Bank, Gaza and East Jerusalem, *al-Wasat*, 11 November 1993, then in *al-Hayat* on 3 June 1995. See Khroub, *Hamas: Political Thought and Practice*, 1.

24. Conversation with Sayyed Abou Musameh in Geneva on 19 January 2012.

Palestinian people, who, when faced with too much exhaustion, must benefit from moments of respite:

> Hamas follows only one principle: the aim of the resistance, to liberate Palestine. One can at times increase the momentum of fighting, or diminish it and seek a lull in the fighting. In the frame of the current struggle, the Palestinian people need to regain its breath and this is why we allow it. That does not mean that we abandon resistance, but the orientation is always towards the interest of the Palestinian people. If these resistance efforts are useful for the cause, then that is a good thing, but if the fighting transgresses the Palestinian interest, then we have the right to disagree.[25]

Apart from the need for a respite, it is the unfavourable international and regional context in the struggle against Israel that can explain the lull in fighting at the time. The truce was seen as a way to neutralize the conflict with Israel until the instauration of an outside environment that was more favourable for armed struggle: 'The truce does not mean the recognition of Israel, and is not a peace accord or a permanent policy. When the power ratios change and the Arabs become stronger, we will perhaps get back our land, and we will then buckle down on this.'[26] 'We distinguish armed struggle as the resistance's legitimate right (*haqq*) from the resistance as practice (*mumârasa*). We have the right to resist at the moment that seems the most suitable to us, but this does not mean that we have to have our rifles raised in a permanent fashion.'[27]

As regards accommodation with the 'Zionist entity', Khaled Mesh'al emphasized that his movement has never refused the principle of negotiation as such. According to him, negotiation is a solution that is not unthinkable, since various national liberation movements have done this throughout history. He therefore lists the *hudna* among the series of truces concluded by movements whose rights to self-determination were fully recognized by the international community:

> We do not refuse to negotiate with the enemy, whether from a legal or a rational viewpoint; indeed, there are stages in which negotiation becomes necessary. From both a rational perspective and a juridical one, negotiations, as a means and a tool, can be acceptable and legitimate at a given moment, and rejected and out of the question at another. What you obtain at the negotiating table is a product of your situation on the ground. When you are beaten on the ground, you will certainly also be defeated during negotiations. Just as war requires a balance of power, negotiations and peace require a balance of power, because one cannot make peace when one of the sides is powerful and the other weak. United States did not make peace with Japan and Germany after the Second

---

25. Conversation with Moussa Abu Marzouk, Damascus, 1 June 2011
26. Interview of Mahmoud al-Zahar, al-Jazeera, 12 August 2007.
27. Conversation with Taher al-Nounou, Cairo, 23 February 2012.

World War but, rather, forced their surrender. In short, peace is made by the powerful and not by the weak.[28]

The November 2008–December 2009 assault: 'Cast lead'

Although many analyses accuse Hamas of being responsible for the truce's breach,[29] it seems that Israel, with Egypt's tacit approval, was the side that opened hostilities. A look at chronology confirms this. On 4 November 2008, an Israeli incursion in the Gaza Strip resulted in the deaths of six Hamas militants and was the catalyst of what would lead to the operation in late December. Bill Clinton's former assistant for the Israeli–Palestinian conflict Robert Malley has shared this conclusion on mutual Israeli and Egyptian responsibility. This is also what the French diplomat Yves Aubin de la Messuzière has said: 'The two sides accuse each other of the responsibility for the breach. Yet an examination of the facts forces one to notice that after five months of globally respected cease-fire, it was an Israeli operation against the tunnels dug between the Gaza Strip and Egypt on November 4th that marked the start of the truce's breach.'[30] Sara Roy also shares this analysis: 'Israel's siege of Gaza began on 5 November, the day after an Israeli attack inside the strip. Although both sides had violated the agreement before, this incursion was on different scale.'[31]

Similar analyses detail that Ehud Olmert, Israel's prime minister, needed to once more boost the reputation of the IDF after the substantial losses of the 2006 Lebanon war. Other explanations highlight the holding of parliamentary elections planned for 10 February 2009. The run-up to these elections would have led Israeli political players to up the ante as regards Hamas.[32] Israel may not have sought to destroy Hamas entirely, but its aim would have been to restrict its military capabilities, obliterate as many tunnels as possible and kill a large number of militants.[33] This wishful thinking should not erase the choice made by Hamas, which on 14 December officially announced via Khaled Mesh'al its refusal to renew

---

28. Interview of Khaled Mesh'al by Silvia Catori, *al-Sabeel*, July 2010, English translation by *AMEC (Afro-Middle East Center)*.

29. Abdel Rahim al-Tayeb, President Mahmoud Abbas's secretary general, declared that Hamas was responsible for the breach of the truce, *al-Safir*, 1 January 2009. Qaddura Fares shares this opinion, considering that Hamas acted in emotional and impulsive fashion, conversation, 24 February 2011, Ramallah.

30. Conversation with Yves Aubin de la Messuzière, Paris, 15 January 2010.

31. Sara Roy, 'If Gaza falls . . .', *London Review of Books* 31, no, 1 (January 2009).

32. According to Barak Ravid, Ehud Barak gave Tsahal the responsibility of preparing the operation six months beforehand, despite the fact that Israel was concomitantly negotiating a cease-fire, Barak Ravid, *Haaretz*, 31 December 2008, 'Disinformation, Secrecy and Lies: How the Gaza Offensive Came About'.

33. Muhammad, 'Abd al-Salam', *Nahdat misr*, 25 January 2009.

the truce: 'We, inside Hamas and most of the factions, think that after December 19th, the truce will expire and not be renewed.'[34]

Thus on 20 December 2008 the armed branch of Hamas claimed responsibility for the launching of al-Qassam mortar shells and Grad missiles. Its spokesman Fawzi Barhoum announced that the movement would fight 'Israeli aggression': 'We shall not yield to the logic of threats uttered by Zionist war criminals. Today, we are more ready than ever to thwart any aggression against our people.'[35]

'Cast lead' began on 27 December with a massive air raid. The air force and navy first carried out targeted attacks against Hamas' military infrastructure but also struck the political, social and religious institutions it controlled: ministries, security forces, police barracks, universities, mosques and television studios. As of 3 January 2009, this was followed by a ground offensive. The military offensive lasted three weeks and killed 330 Palestinians and 13 Israelis (including 10 soldiers).

As opposed to June 2008, it was not a real truce that ended hostilities but a unilateral Israeli cease-fire declared on 18 January 2009. Once more, Egypt introduced itself as the indispensable go-between to put an end to the fighting. As early as 6 January 2009, the Egyptians contacted Hamas officials to reach a cease-fire (*waqf itlâq an-nâr*). Hamas then refused to send a delegation to Cairo to meet the chief of the Egyptian intelligence services, Omar Suleiman. Its leaders considered the initiative illegitimate because it was a forerunner for the presence of an international force inside Gaza. In a conversation with al-Jazeera,[36] Khaled Mesh'al declared that any negotiation must result in the lifting of the blockade and the opening of crossing points with Israel and Egypt. Now, the Egyptian initiative did not mention the lifting of this blockade as an essential prerequisite to stop the fighting.[37] As for Ayman al-Taha, who was a Hamas official responsible for relations with Cairo, he had announced that his movement was ready to study all proposals to reach an appeasement (*tahdîya*), on the condition of a halt to the aggression and the lifting of the blockade.[38] The day after the Israeli declaration of a cease-fire, Moussa Abu Marzouk said from Damascus that the various groups belonging to Gaza's Palestinian resistance were in favour of stopping the fighting, while reiterating: 'We insist on our demands, which consist in the retreat of enemy forces, the opening of crossing points, and the entry of humanitarian aid.'[39]

34. Interview of Khaled Mesh'al on *al-Quds* TV channel, 14 December 2008.

35. Quoted by Anne-Laure Egre, *Le recours à la violence par le Hamas à l'aune de l'offensive israélienne sur Gaza pendant l'hiver 2008–2009*, Masters II dissertation in international relations, Université de Paris I Panthéon-Sorbonne, 2008–9.

36. al-Jazeera, 29 December 2008.

37. *Al-Hayat*, 8 January 2009.

38. *Al-Akhbar*, 1 January 2009.

39. *Al-Sharq* on 19 January 2009. According to sources close to Hamas, the movement refused to sign the Egyptian document because it included neither the opening of the crossing points nor discussions on the blockade. Abd al-Hamid al-Kayyali, *Dirâsa*

The turning point of the Arab Spring

The liberation of Gilad Shalit

On 18 October 2011, Gilad Shalit was freed, in the wake of an agreement between Israel and Hamas, with Egypt acting as an intermediary. The Hamas leaders had for quite some time highlighted Israel's responsibility to explain the failure to free the prisoner. Throughout 2009, one could read on the website of the Palestinian centre for Information communiqués of the Izz al-Din al-Qassam Brigades, accusing the 'Zionist Entity' of abstaining from mentioning any compensation in return.[40] Hamas' chief had declared to the Qatari *Al-Watan* newspaper that the talks relating to Shalit's liberation were still going on, squarely placing lack of progress on Netanyahu.[41]

Since 2006, Egypt had introduced itself in this affair as an important broker, capable of leading both parts towards a compromise. Stalled for a long time, the conclusion of an agreement surprised most of the players and their associates. There was undoubtedly a link between the fall of Hosni Mubarak and the conclusion of this agreement. In the wake of the Egyptian president's destitution, it was easier to find a compromise, which had already been facilitated by the German emissary Gerhard Conrad,[42] who was once more visiting Cairo in October.[43] And yet, before trusting the Egyptians, Hamas and Israel had already begun negotiations between the vice-minister for Foreign Affairs of Gaza's government Ghazi Hamad and Gershon Baskin an Israeli academic.[44] Despite denials of the Hamas leadership,[45] it was truly one of their own who was in charge of being an intermediary between Ahmed al-Jaabari, the leader of Hamas' military wing holding captive Gilad Shalit, and the Israelis. According to an Egyptian official:

> The leaders of Hamas and the Israelis came to us to announce that they had made important breakthroughs on this issue and that they wished to resume discussion in Egypt. The Israelis accepted releasing an important number of

fi-l'aduwân al-Isrâ'ilî 'alâ qitâ' Ghazza, Markaz al-Zaytûna li-l-dirâsat wa-l-istishârât (Beirut, 2009).

40. *Palestinian Information Center*, 18 March 2009.
41. *Al-Qassam* Website, 13 August 2009.
42. *Al-Hayat*, 1 October 2011.
43. *Associated Press*, 16 October 2011.
44. Although Baskin is not truly an official representative of the State of Israel but an academic, his designation by Israeli authorities to carry out negotiations with Hamas was a confirmation of direct relations between the two sides, *Haaretz*, 14 October 2011.
45. According to Khaled Mesh'al, Ahmed al-Jaabari may have been part of initial negotiations with the Germans and Egyptians as intermediaries, *al-Quds*, 12 October 2011.

prisoners, including some they had always refused to free, while Hamas accepted crossing out some names on the list.⁴⁶

Although the new Egyptian mediation partly explains the conclusion of this agreement, it is actually the direct discussions between Hamas and a non-official Israeli that brought about this prisoner exchange. Israel and Hamas, each for its own reasons, saw the need to make this exchange project real. This transaction was, moreover, practically the same one as the one previously refused by one party or the other. Israel acceded to some of Hamas' demands by freeing some prisoners it did not wish to let go of, while Hamas accepted to remove some detainees who were on the initial list – for instance, Fatah leader Marwan al-Barghouti and Ahmed Saadat, the chief of the PFLP.

The reconciliation agreements of Cairo and Doha

Four years after the February 2007 Mecca agreement, which had led to the formation of an ephemeral national unity government, on 4 May 2011 the two main Palestinian factions signed a new agreement of national reconciliation in Cairo.⁴⁷ In continuity with what had been conceded to Fatah in 2005 and 2006, this deal included a transfer to the PLO of responsibility for negotiations with the occupying power. It was therefore partly based on the fact that Khaled Mesh'al agreed on an additional one-year extension for Mahmoud Abbas, in order to resume negotiations with Israel. As in 2006, however, this process was followed by clauses specifying limitations. The movement's leader highlighted that it was indeed restricted by Palestinian institutions and popular expression: 'We leave Abbas the possibility of seeking agreements with Israel on the condition that, in the case that this would lead to results, they be submitted to the Legislative Council.'⁴⁸

In November 2011, during a meeting in Cairo between Mahmoud Abbas and Khaled Mesh'al, the latter declared that Hamas would from then on adopt the strategy of 'peaceful resistance' or 'popular resistance'. The leader of Hamas reiterated his commitment to respect 1967 borders, instate a new truce with the occupier and above all endorse a form of resistance described as 'peaceful'. Khaled Mesh'al explained the 'new spirit' (al-rûh al-jadîd) of Palestinian political life: an atmosphere of 'openness towards the other' (infitâh 'ala al-akhar), of taking into account a multiparty system (istî âd al-muhtalif) and finally of political participation (al-mushâraka al-siyâsîya).⁴⁹ In an interview broadcast by the al-Aqs television channel, the president of the Political Bureau also declared that the movement would 'resort no more to other forms of resistance'. He added: 'Do

---

46. Conversation with an Egyptian diplomat, Cairo, in February 2012.
47. 'Palestinian Reconciliation, Plus ça change . . .', *International Crisis Group*, 20 July 2011.
48. Conversation with Moussa Abu Marzouk, Damascus, 1 June 2011.
49. Mahmoud Younes, *al-Hayat*, 26 December 2011.

not believe that popular resistance is nothing, it is very strong, it will have the power of a tsunami.' Yet the rhetoric of transition, from armed struggle only to a different form of resistance described as 'peaceful', was accompanied by the denial of its unprecedented character, since the leaders had guaranteed that 'popular resistance' was by no means an alternative solution and would not occur at the expense of armed resistance.[50]

On 6 February 2012, in Doha, Khaled Mesh'al signed a new reconciliation agreement with Fatah, which implied that Mahmoud Abbas, the current president of the Palestinian Authority, would also accept being the prime minister of a government meant to prepare the organization of the next parliamentary elections. This agreement was also hopeful that the PLO's reactivation would follow, in order to include Hamas and Islamic Jihad.

The November 2012 'Pillar of Defence' offensive on Gaza

Although there was no large-scale military operation against Gaza between 2009 and 2012, this does not mean there was a complete absence of confrontation.

In mid-March 2011, new fighting erupted between Israel and Hamas. On 19 March, in response to an unprovoked Israeli strike, the Izz al-Din al-Qassam Brigades retaliated by firing some fifty shells towards Israeli territory. In reprisal, the Israeli Air Force bombed Gaza. Despite the communiqué of the al-Qassam Brigades calling for respect of a truce if indeed Israel ceased its aggression, another shell was fired on 29 March, sparking Israeli retaliation. On Thursday, 7 April, an anti-tank shell was fired in the direction of a school bus, leading to renewed Israeli reprisals, resulting in nineteen deaths. These events went on until 10 April, when Israel and Hamas declared they were ready to sign a new truce. A second escalation began on 18 August 2011, following a three-pronged attack in the south of Israel ascribed to the Popular Resistance Committee, just as its Secretary General Kamal al-Nayrab was killed near Rafah. Hamas then launched several rockets towards cities of Israel's south; the al-Qassam Brigades, as well as the *Saraya al-Quds* of the Islamic Jihad, announced in an official communiqué on their website the bombing of the settlement of Ofakim by four Grad missiles. On 22 August, a provisional cease-fire was agreed upon, while new rockets were launched by the military branches of two Palestinian factions (PFLP and a dissident branch of the PRC), which had not signed the truce concluded via Hamas. The murder on 24 August of one of the chiefs of the armed branch of Islamic Jihad led those brigades to fire several rockets on the south of Israel.

These episodes of armed confrontation, between March and August 2011, were nevertheless quite restrained. It was the assassination of Ahmed al-Jaabari, second-in-command of the al-Qassam Brigades, on 14 November 2012 that truly marked an escalation. In reprisals, the members of the armed branch of Hamas fired a series of rockets on Israel on 14 and 15 November. This reactivation of the

50. Interview of Izzat al-Rishq, *Palestinian Information Center*, 27 November 2011.

conflict expressed itself in a new large-scale Israeli attack on the Gaza Strip, 'Pillar of Defence'. For the first time, on 21 November, a rocket was sent towards Tel Aviv. Ahmed al-Jaabari, however, was the man who embodied the possibility of signing a long-term truce with Israel. The chief editor of the daily *Haaretz* Aluf Benn had previously described him as Israel's 'subcontractor'.[51] On the eve of his murder, Israelis and Palestinians were mentioning the prospects of signing a new *hudna* under the aegis of Egypt. Contacts with the head of the al-Qassam Brigades were being made via Ghazi Hamad and his Israeli counterpart Girshon Baskin. Defence Minister Ehud Barak knew about these negotiations.[52] Some analyses thus defend the idea of incitement to radicalization, since Jaabari, in charge of Hamas' military wing, was the man who in the early days of 2009 had negotiated the cease-fire and been in charge of its survival. His assassination posted on YouTube may have been a provocation, 'an Israeli tactic for exacerbating the conflict'.[53] Moreover, one can remark that, as in 2008, this war occurred in a context of elections in Israel, which may be an explanation for triggering a conflict with Hamas.

A new truce on 21 November 2012 put an end to Israeli military action, which resulted in 130 Palestinians casualties. Through this agreement, Hamas was reiterating its commitment to abstain from launching any rockets towards Israel, stop all shooting from other groups and halt the arms traffic from the Gaza Strip. As for Israel, it promised to accept brokerage by Egypt. Yet, in contrast with the June 2008 truce, Egypt now had as president a member of the Muslim Brotherhood, Mohammed Morsi. He had expressed his solidarity with Gaza and Hamas, while reaffirming his attachment to the Camp David Agreement signed between Israel and Egypt in 1978.

The Shati reconciliation agreement

On 23 April 2014, a new reconciliation was signed at the residence of the former prime minister Ismail Haniyeh, in the Shati refugee camp. The agreement, with the camp's name, restated commitment to the previous reconciliation agreements signed successively in 2007, 2011 and 2012. In addition to the formation of a unity government and the holding of elections within six months, it provided for the control of the border crossing of Rafah by Mahmoud Abbas's Presidential Guard, the absorption of the Gaza police within the security forces of the Ramallah Authority, as well as payment by the Palestinian Authority of Hamas civil servants, who had not received their salaries for several months. For the first time since June 2007, a PLO deleation led by 'Azzam al-Ahmad travelled to Gaza on the evening of 22 April. On 2 June, Mahmoud Abbas announced the formation of a consensus government led by Rami al-Hamdallah, comprising independent personalities and technocrats: seventeen ministers, including five from Gaza, none of them

---

51. *Haaretz*, 14 November 2012.
52. *Haaretz*, 15 November 2012.
53. Jean-François Legrain, 'Gaza, l'offensive de trop?' *Le Figaro*, 21 November 2012.

affiliated to Hamas. Through this agreement, Hamas thus accepted to pull out from executive affairs and power in Gaza. The overthrow of the Egyptian president Mohammed Morsi and the destruction of tunnels linking the Sinai Peninsula to the Gaza Strip had indeed placed the movement in a situation of ominous financial hardship, since it could no longer bring in funds necessary for the functioning of its government. As for President Abbas, this rapprochement with Hamas enabled him to respond to the Israeli refusal to free a certain number of Palestinian prisoners, as had been agreed nine months before at the opening of the cycle of negotiations under the aegis of the US state secretary John Kerry.

The Israeli reaction was at first expressed by the announcement of economic sanctions against the Ramallah Authority, the construction of new settlements, as well as its withdrawal from negotiations with Mahmoud Abbas, who was accused of choosing Hamas at the expense of peace with Israel. This Israeli withdrawal from bilateral discussions with the Palestinian Authority may (according to several sources) have made the United States officially recognize the new Palestinian 'entente' cabinet. Of course, the latter did not include any official Hamas representative; it is also true, however, that it was the result of an understanding of sorts with the Islamist movement. To this unheard-of recognition by the United States, one can add that of the European Union. Israel then took measures to short-circuit this process of union of Palestinian ranks, by forbidding Gaza ministers from travelling to Ramallah to be sworn into office and threatening President Mahmoud Abbas with sanctions, if indeed he decided to pay salaries to civil servants in Gaza affiliated with Hamas. In this context, hostilities resumed between the two Palestinian factions: in early June, several Hamas militants were arrested in Gaza. The Israeli military offensive carried out as from 8 July 2014 then eliminated any chance of bringing to fruition this agreement, which was already resting on a flimsy basis.

Summer 2014 military assault against the Gaza Strip

'Protective Edge', which lasted some fifty days, is the longest military offensive the Gaza Strip has known. Although officially begun on 8 July, one should nevertheless recall that, as early as 14 June, the search and sweep operation called 'Guardians of our Brothers' was being carried out against Hamas in the main towns and cities of the West Bank; members of the Islamist party were being subjected to an unprecedented wave of arrest. Among these, fifty-six old detainees who had been freed in 2011 in exchange for the prisoner Shalit were recaptured, as well as several MPs of the Palestinian Legislative Council, including the parliament's president Aziz Duweik. These attacks were described by Israel as a response to the kidnapping of three Israeli teenagers on 12 June.[54] An air raid was also decided against the Gaza

---

54. On 12 June, Gilad Saher, Naphtali Fraenkel and Eyal Yifrach were kidnapped in the West Bank, near the Gush Ezion between Bethlehem and Hebron. Their bodies were found on 30 June, in a field 5 kilometres from Hebron. An unknown group introducing itself as the

Strip. On the night of 1 July, a Palestinian teenager was abducted in East Jerusalem and burnt alive by three Orthodox Jews. In reprisals, some 200 rockets were fired into Israel from the Gaza Strip. On 7 July, Israel had a tunnel on the Gaza Strip's border blown up, killing six members of the al-Qassam Brigades. On the following day, these same Brigades fired 150 rockets in the direction of Israel, which in turn officially launched its military assault with a phase of aerial bombing.

Like with 'Cast lead' and 'Pillar of Defence', one should emphasize the difficulties of establishing a fixed chronology on the launch of hostilities. Retaining the official chronology from 8 July onwards means accepting Israeli historiography, making the war an act of legitimate defence caused on that day by the firing of rockets by Hamas; yet these rockets were in themselves an answer to Israel's assassination the day before of the aforementioned six members of the al-Qassam Brigades. Likewise, accepting the date of 12 June (the moment of the kidnapping and murder of three Israeli teenagers) is akin to legitimizing the official Israeli narrative, whose aim is to designate Hamas as the only side responsible for the start of hostilities. One should note that on that day, Hamas did not make any statement on the operation, for which it would claim responsibility only at the end of August, via its representative in Turkey Salah al-Arouri, despite lack of confirmation by the movement's Political Bureau.[55] This is the reason why some analyses insist on the need to reinsert 'Protective Edge' within a longer time frame, its origins thus going back to 23 April, the date of the signing of the inter-Palestinian reconciliation agreement, or on 24 April, the day Mahmoud Abbas anticipated the failure of Israeli-American negotiations under US supervision, and of his attempts at the United Nations to obtain full membership in the Palestinian Authority of the International Criminal Court (ICC).

Other narratives making Hamas the only party responsible for the conflict refer to the reaction, by the Movement of Islamic Resistance, to the first Egyptian cease-fire proposal. On 17 July, Hamas dismissed this Egyptian proposal announced two days earlier, by considering it as 'surrender' and accusing Cairo of not bothering to contact the movement's leadership. This rejection enabled Israel to resume its military actions. It was followed by a second phase of the offensive, which began on 18 July with a land incursion. Israel's stated aim changed noticeably: apart from impeding the Islamist movement's rearming, the goal was now to destroy tunnels

---

Islamic State's West Bank branch claimed the abduction, but this was not taken seriously by Israeli authorities. On 22 August, a Hamas official based in Turkey, Salah al-Arouri, in turn claimed the kidnapping in Hamas' name; the Political Bureau of the movement, however, did not confirm this. In Hebron, IDF forces then murdered Marwan Kawasme and Ammar Abou Aysh, who had been identified by Israel as the killers of the three teenagers.

55. In an interview given to Vanity Fair, Khaled Mesh'al declared that the Hamas leadership had never ordered this operation; having said that, he justified it by emphasizing it targeted settlers and congratulated West Bank Hamas militants for having carried it out. https://www.vanityfair.com/news/politics/2014/10/khalid-mishal-hamas-interview.

separating Israel from the Gaza Strip. Hamas and other armed factions fired more than 1,500 rockets in the direction of Israel.

Between 8 July and 26 August, the dates of the official end of 'Protective Edge', several provisional cease-fires were concluded under Egyptian mediation, to allow humanitarian aid to reach Gaza. On 1 August, a 72-hour cease-fire was agreed on, only to collapse when Israel announced the capture of one of its soldiers in Rafah. On 5 August, a second cease-fire was declared and also failed two days later when rockets were fired from the Gaza Strip by the Ali Mustafa Brigades (the PFLP's armed branch). Most of these cease-fires therefore only lasted a few hours, with the exception of the one beginning on 11 August, which did so for approximately nine days. On 18 August, on the fifth and last day of discussions, three rockets fired neither by Hamas nor by Islamic Jihad fell on Israel. Netanyahu required his delegation to leave Cairo, saying that he 'does not negotiate under fire'. Following the departure of the Israeli delegation, on the 19th, Hamas and Islamic Jihad put forward a cease-fire counter-proposal to the Egyptian authorities that included the complete and immediate lifting of the blockade, the opening of a port and airport, the liberation of detainees who had been released in 2011 in exchange for IDF soldier Gilad Shalit. The proposal was supported by the PLO and Mahmoud Abbas but was ignored by Israel, which decided to pursue its military solution. On 21 August, the day after a fruitless assassination attempt on Mohammed Deif, Israeli forces eliminated two high commanders of Hamas' military branch, Raed al-Attar and Mohammed Abou Shamala.

It was only on 26 August that Egypt and the State of Palestine announced that an agreement had been found, involving the immediate cessation of hostilities, the opening of crossings for humanitarian aid only and the extension of the fishing zone for Gaza's fishermen. Khalil al-Hayya described the document as a piece of paper giving Israelis all rights and implied that thanks to it they would keep control of all of the crossings and monitor Gaza's reconstruction: the issue was to stop any introduction of material or hardware that could potentially reinforce the military capabilities of Hamas. Yet though Israel's objective was to decimate the Hamas leadership, or at least to obtain the demilitarization of Gaza, it was able to gain neither the former nor the latter. In comparison with previous offensives, the human cost for Israel was quite ominous: seventy-three Israelis were killed, sixty-seven of them IDF soldiers. Hamas still has the remains of two of them, Hadar Goldin and Oron Shaul. On the Palestinian side, the operation resulted in the deaths of 2,200 people, mostly civilians, and left the Gaza Strip in a state of unprecedented humanitarian disaster.

The post-2014 turning point

The Document of General Principles and Policies and the conclusion of a new reconciliation agreement

Khaled Mesh'al describes the Document of General Principles and Policies published on 1 May 2017 as a new political benchmark for Hamas. Although the recognition of 1967 borders goes back to the Cairo Agreement and the Prisoners'

Document, respectively, signed in 2005 and 2006 and is an integral part of all intra-Palestinian agreements signed since then (2007, 2011, 2012, 2014), this document introduces for the first time the recognition as an integral part of the Islamic resistance's programme, and not simply as a programme shared by the set of Palestinian political players. As mentioned in the Introduction, the text describes armed struggle in euphemistic terms; it does not appear as the only tool to fight occupation, but only as one among others, which include 'popular and peaceful resistance'. Hamas is always attempting to show that the struggle against occupation is legal, namely that fighting for liberation is a legitimate self-defence activity, and part and parcel of the natural right to self-determination (paragraph 39).[56] Khaled Mesh'al, however, refuses to consider this document as a new Charter: he maintains that this document amends but does not abrogate the original 1988 Charter. Some analysts have explained Hamas' reluctance to amend the Charter by the will to not lose its base, with some of its members joining other Islamist factions.[57]

Despite the Shati agreement and the formation of a unity government in June 2014, 'Protective Edge' ended all perspectives of a union of Palestinian ranks. Although on 9 October 2014, the unity government met for the first time since its formation, this was nothing more than an attempt to show an appearance of consensus and make donating countries meeting in Cairo agree in providing international aid for Gaza's reconstruction.

It was only three years later, in October 2017, that Fatah and Hamas signed a new reconciliation memorandum in Cairo. Like what had been conceded during the Shati agreement, Hamas reiterated its desire to pull out of governmental affairs and hand the keys of Gaza to Mahmoud Abbas. Since September, it had announced the dissolution of its administrative committee, a body in place since 2014 to manage the strip's current affairs (a body considered by Fatah to be a government in all but name, and that it saw as a factor increasing divisions and leading to the separation of Gaza from the West Bank).

A solution was from then on put forward for each of the points of litigation paralysing previous agreements: Hamas would accept that its officials be paid only 50 per cent of their salaries before anticipated retirement and agree on the fusion of Gaza's police with that of Ramallah under the new government's authority,[58] and

---

56. For a deep analysis of Hamas' new document, see Qossay Hamed, 'The Constant and Variable in the Ideology of Hamas (2006–2018)', Thèse de science politique, Université de Bordeaux, sous la direction de Laetitia Bucaille, soutenue le 30 mars 2021.

57. Bilal Shobaki, 'Hamas: Three Though Hurdles in 2015', *Alshabaka* (2016), quoted by Hamed, 'The Constant and Variable in the Ideology of Hamas (2006–2018)'.

58. The issue of control of security apparatuses had since Hamas' victory in the 2006 elections opposed it violently to Fatah. Mahmoud Abbas had denied Sayyid Siam, the interior minister of the Ismail Haniyeh government, any authority on public coercion forces, naming Rachid Abou Shabbak as director general of Interior Security Forces. In response to this, Hamas created its own security agency (the Executive Force), which was dissolved and integrated to Gaza's civilian police in 2007.

finally approve of Palestinian Authority taking control of the main crossing points – with only the Rafah border as a matter of contention, since Hamas had suggested that some of its employees remain there. Very quickly, though, disagreements became obvious, not only over the Kerem Shalom crossing, a central place for commercial merchandise generating important revenue via taxes, but also the Rafah one, which Ramallah's AP employees left after January 2019. Fatah claims to have been expelled by Hamas, while the latter accuses the former of having deliberately sought confrontation, in order to favour the closure of the crossing and accelerate the bankruptcy of the Gaza Strip, already bled dry by Mahmoud Abbas's sanctions. One must indeed place this agreement in a context in which since April 2017 Mahmoud Abbas has imposed heavy sanctions against the Gaza Strip, from the reduction of civil servant wages to the diminution of the sum paid to Israel for electricity provided to Gaza.

The March of Return and the beginning of cycles of negotiation and confrontation

The launch of the March of Return on 30 March 2018 was a new page in the relations between Israel and Hamas. Meant to last only five weeks – until the transfer of the US Embassy from Tel Aviv to Jerusalem on 14 May – it commemorated not only the seventy years of the creation of the State of Israel but also the expulsion of the Palestinians (the Nakba). In this framework, the weekly mobilizations of Gaza's inhabitants, who meet along the land and sea borders with Israel, are still alive and well. The announcement of the transfer of the American embassy to Jerusalem took place while a bloodbath was occurring in Gaza. Sixty Palestinians were killed by Israeli forces along the security fence. At the end of May, rockets were fired jointly by Hamas and Islamic Jihad, deeds condemned by the UN Security Council and answered by dozens of Israeli strikes against military targets of the two Palestinian factions. Under the aegis of the Egyptians, an initial cease-fire was then implemented, paving the way for an uninterrupted cycle of negotiation and confrontation.

Implicating the entire spectrum of Palestinian factions, all united under a high coordination committee, the Great March of Return has also been used by Hamas as a lever to obtain the lifting of the blockade. Although some factions created by Gaza's youth can of course escape Hamas' grasp, the latter largely controls the dynamics of the protests, perceived as a means to extract concessions from Israel. It would be quite difficult here to make a precise inventory of the confrontations opposing Israel and Hamas, since they are so numerous and also involve other Palestinian players that do not always coordinate with this Islamist movement (Gaza's youth or other armed factions). It is possible, however, to distinguish two great moments in the confrontation: summer 2018 and spring 2019. Between these two moments, one must mention the botched-up Israeli incursion into the Gaza Strip.

On 13 July 2018, Israel attempted to prevent attacks by kites on fire from the Gaza Strip, which were stoking arson on the Israeli side of the fence. On 20 July, after the killing of one of its soldiers during demonstrations near the border (the first IDF serviceman killed since the 2014 war), Israel began intense bombings on the military command of Hamas in Khan Younis, in the south of the enclave. Four Palestinians were killed, including three members of the al-Qassam Brigades. A truce was agreed following mediations by the UN and Egypt. On 7 August, however, two other militants of the brigades died during an Israeli strike, this time in the Gaza Strip's north, a strike which according to IDF command may have been the result of a blunder. In response, more than 180 rockets were fired at Israel, with the Israeli Air Force retaliating by hitting more than 150 military sites supposedly belonging to Hamas. A young pregnant woman was killed with her eighteen-month-old daughter. This escalation, the most important one since the 2014 war, took place while indirect negotiations between Israel and Hamas were being mediated by Egypt and the UN. These talks, which aimed at establishing a long-lasting truce between the two parties, were successful in that they agreed on a cease-fire on 15 August that broadly restated the points accepted by the August 2014 one: cessation of hostilities, widening of the fishing zone, reopening of the Kerem Shalom crossing (sealed since early July).

The level of confrontation at the border has greatly diminished since the summer of 2018 and negotiations continue between Israel and Hamas: since November, the two parts have made an agreement projecting the delivery by Qatar of petrol and cash, the setting up of an electrical plant, Gaza's reconstruction and a decision to launch talks to find an agreement in the long run. Yet on 11 November, an Israeli commando was located near Khan Younis, when a local commander of the al-Qassam Brigades was killed during crossfire. Quite low key at the beginning (a few rockets only, fired towards enclaves close to the border and not causing any damage), Hamas' response intensified the flowing day. The IDF then retaliated with tens of air raids on the Gaza Strip.

In March 2019, tensions flared up once more. As from the 8th and 9th of March, the IDF retaliated against the launching of incendiary balloons from the Gaza Strip. On 14 March, two rockets were fired in the direction of Tel Aviv, hitting a settlement to the north of Israel's largest city, something unheard of since 2014. Hamas then tried to calm the situation by indicating via the Egyptians that this was a mistake linked to a maintenance operation. On 25 March, however, a new rocket landed in Mishmeret to the north of Tel Aviv, causing damage (the destruction of a house and seven wounded civilians). No Palestinian faction claimed this new attack. The same day, Israel responded with a huge campaign of bombings on the Gaza Strip, causing damage to both military and civilian locations. On 30 March, during the anniversary commemorations of the March of Return, Hamas was looking for a respite, deploying men in orange uniforms to stop demonstrators from engaging in confrontation with Israeli forces. While the protests had already killed 260 people, the demonstrations on 30 March resulted in the deaths of 4 Palestinians. On 1 April, a compromise was reached thanks to Egyptian brokerage and was supported by the UN and Qatar. The great principles of the November 2018 agreement were reiterated: opening of the Kerem Shalom crossing, closed since 25 March; delivery by Qatar of $40 million to officially finance the health sector and mitigate unemployment by putting in place a programme of cash payments for work in UN organizations; supplying of the Gaza electric plant; the creation of two industrial zones in the enclave's east and north; the lifting of the restrictions affecting fishermen.[59] In exchange for all of this, Palestinians consented to forbid the launching of incendiary balloons and creating a 300-metres-wide buffer zone in front of the security fence separating Israel from the Gaza Strip.

On 3 May 2019, a new cycle of violence erupted following crossfire between Israel and Islamic Jihad. IDF forces carpet-bombed the Gaza Strip, killing twenty-five Palestinians, including two pregnant women. Seven hundred rockets were fired from Gaza, targeting urban centres in Israel's south, such as Ashkelon, Ashdod and Beer Sheba, causing four Israeli deaths. In this context, Israel resumed its targeted assassinations, killing Hamad al-Khodori, who was driving his car in downtown Gaza. He had been accused of being responsible for Iranian money transfers to the enclave. A new cease-fire was ratified on 6 May, restating the main clauses of previous agreements.

The resumption of talks on prisoner exchange

Indirect discussions between Hamas and Israel also include another component, negotiations around an exchange of prisoners. Since the 2014 war Hamas has kept the remains of two soldiers, Hadar Goldin and Oron Shaul, as well as of two civilians, Avera Avraham Mengistu and Hisham al-Sayed. Since then, many mediators have attempted to reach a compromise. The German press has recently exposed the part played by German Federal Intelligence (better known under the name BND) in talks between Israel and Hamas in the summer of 2018.[60] Other players have also tried to reach an agreement between the two sides, such as Qatar, Egypt and even the UN.

In April 2020, the Covid-19 pandemic provoked an increase in the regularity of talks and stimulated the goodwill of Israel and Hamas in reaching an agreement as soon as possible. The virus has allowed discussions to be redirected towards more humanitarian concerns, with Yahya al-Sinwar now claiming the priority release of old and sick prisoners, in addition to detainees freed in 2011 at the same time as Shalit and re-imprisoned in 2014.[61] Ismail Haniyeh spoke in a similar fashion during his interview on 14 April: without confirming the precise figure of 250 prisoners, he mentioned the need to free women, children and sick people, as well as prisoners re-incarcerated in 2014.[62]

---

59. http://eng.alzaytouna.net/2019/05/13/political-analysis-gaza-understandings-snatching-rightsor-mined-gains/#.X0gpKyHgq2x.
60. Revelations broadcast by al-Jazeera on 6 May 2020.
61. Sarah Daoud, 'Gaza. L' "apaisement" contre la sécurité sanitaire', *Orient Xxi*, August 2020.
62. https://www.youtube.com/watch?v=Cx3wz2YzlsM.

Chapter 2

HAMAS AND THE REST OF THE WORLD

Visits abroad and the welcoming by Hamas of representatives of other states have always taken place, alternately, in Gaza and Damascus, the latter the seat of the movement's outside leadership until 2012. We shall present here the main aspects of these interactions, by following the same chronological breaks as for the previous section: from 2006 to the seizure of Gaza in 2007, from June 2007 to the Arab uprisings, from 2011 to 'Protective Edge' and finally after the assault against Gaza in summer 2014.

The imposition of the blockade in 2006 drastically limited the opportunities of Hamas interacting with Western countries. With the exception of infrequent visits to Europe, which have remained secret, contacts with these countries were and are still very limited. Mahmoud al-Zahar, the Foreign Affairs minister, and Prime Minister Ismail Haniyeh have both made many trips to Arab countries, but also beyond. Khaled Mesh'al has also travelled to several states and has welcomed foreign dignitaries in Damascus.

After June 2007, the blockade of the Gaza Strip became stricter. That is why Hamas' external head office took charge of main diplomatic activities, as seen in the tour of the external leadership's delegation, between 2009 and 2010.

The Arab Spring temporarily reinstated the complementarity between these two centres. From Qatar, where he now lives, Khaled Mesh'al travelled to Jordan, Turkey and Tunisia. Thanks to the relative reopening of the Rafah crossing, Ismail Haniyeh regained a visibility of sorts by going on two diplomatic tours in the region. Many official representatives of other countries also travelled to Gaza: these include the emir of Qatar, the Egyptian former prime minister, the Tunisian Foreign Affairs minister and even Sheikh Youssef al-Qaradawi.

'Protective Edge' opened a new era of difficulties for the Gaza leadership, which, since the rise to power of General al-Sisi in Egypt, saw its possibilities of travel drastically restricted. From Qatar, Khaled Mesh'al resumed his bilateral meetings before announcing his withdrawal from the Hamas leadership, which did not prevent him from remaining active. The movement's internal elections, which were held in February 2017, in fact, inaugurated substantial change in the distribution of tasks between the internal and external leadership since, for the first time in Hamas' history, a member of the Gaza leadership (Ismail Haniyeh) was nominated as the head of the Political Bureau. Because he was under house arrest by the decision of Egyptian authorities, diplomatic activities were taken care of by external leadership members, in particular the movement's vice-president Salah al-Arouri. In December 2019, after two-and-a-half years of immobility, Ismail Haniyeh was finally authorized by Egypt to go on his own diplomatic tour, joining on several occasions his colleagues of the outside leadership. At the time of writing, he has not returned to Gaza.

Carrying out diplomacy despite the boycott

Limited interactions with the West

In the wake of its victory, Hamas has displayed pragmatic stances in order to appear as a credible partner in the eyes of Western countries. As early as January 2006, Ismail Haniyeh sent a letter to the Quartet[1] calling for the acceptance of cooperation with Hamas and the creation of an 'open dialogue'. Dated to 31 January 2006, this letter followed a meeting during which Quartet members had debated the attitude to adopt towards the Islamist formation the day after its victory. The conclusion from this discussion was that Hamas would be considered a legitimate partner once it fulfilled three conditions: an end to violence, the recognition of Israel and the acceptance of previous agreements between the latter and the PLO, all unacceptable demands in the eyes of Hamas.[2] The aim of Ismail Haniyeh's inaugural speech, in March 2006, was to gain the trust of international players and Arab regimes, as testified by points six and seven focusing on the necessity of mobilizing the Palestinian people's interests. In these points, the prime minister asked the international community to respect the choices made by the Palestinians who had elected Hamas and reconsider initial negative reactions.

In March 2006, MP Sayyid Abou Musameh travelled to London with Ahmed Yousef, Prime Minister Haniyeh's adviser, to reaffirm the 'legalist' nature of Hamas.

> We have explained to British MPs our concept of the truce. They then welcomed us once more with Khaled Mesha'al and Moussa Abu Marzouk. We insisted on the fact that it was necessary to broaden negotiating circles and finalize them with action on the ground, in order to exit the tunnel.[3]

---

1. Carolin Goerzig shows how the three conditions imposed by the Quartet were originally intended as a basis of framework but in really have acted as an impediment. Carolin Goerzig, 'Transforming the Quartet Principles: Hamas and the Peace Process', *Institute for Security Studies*, Vol. 85 (Western European Union, 2010).
2. *Al-Riyadh*, 31 January 2006.
3. Conversation with Sayyid Abou Musameh, Ankara, 19 January 2012.

Ahmed Yousef holds American citizenship and perfectly masters the English language. He is a central figure in the establishment of contacts with the international community.

> I have sent letters to world leaders, as well as the Quartet. We have done much in the hope that the world opens its doors to us. We have travelled and explained to people where we are, what our stances are, and what is our political vision.[4]

During the first months of the 'Tenth Government', Ahmed Yousef sent tens of letters to many chiefs of state and international organizations, in which he detailed the movement's political vision and reaffirmed its inescapable role in any solution to the conflict. These initial contacts were fruitless, for Western Foreign Affairs Ministries did not wish to normalize their relations with Hamas, despite its election victory. This refusal has indeed greatly frustrated Ahmed Yousef: 'I met many people and all said to me "we are sorry that Hamas was placed on the list of terrorist organizations, while its demands are acceptable and the Palestinian people's resistance is legitimate".[5]

On 9 May 2006, Ismail Haniyeh sent a new letter to the Quartet, requesting its members to go back on the decision of imposing three conditions to Hamas as preliminary to any discussion.[6] This pragmatic posture as regards Western powers was also shared by Khaled Mesh'al in the Italian daily *Corriere della sera*, where he spoke of the importance taken by Hamas on the Palestinian political stage and its key role in the search for a solution to the conflict. As for Moussa Abu Marzouk, he declared that there are many relations between the movement and the United States concerning a number of issues, and that Hamas was ready to broaden these discussions and make them official.[7]

Hamas consider that the European stand is subtler than the American one.[8] Mahmoud al-Zahar welcomed the stance of Romano Prodi, who compared the freezing of international aid to collective punishment of an entire people. Al-Zahar hoped that this position would encourage other European Union states to reconsider the boycott.[9] According to Moussa Abu Marzouk, Europe understands better certain questions, for instance, the juridical impossibility for a movement to recognize a state.[10] The leaders of Hamas, hence, see the importance of showing

---

4. Conversation with Ahmed Yousef, Ankara, 19 May 2011.
5. Ibid.
6. *Bahrein News Agency*, 9 May 2006.
7. *Al-Joumhouriyya al-Masriyya*, 3 January 2006.
8. Nathan Brown shares the same view even though he considers that this more nuanced policy towards Hamas has not necessarily produced better results. See Nathan Brown, 'Principled or Stubborn? Western Policy towards Hamas', *The International Spectator* 43, no. 4 (2010): 73–87.
9. *Ma'an News*, 12 April 2006.
10. Interview of Moussa Abu Marzouk, *al-Hayat*, 26 December 2006.

there are important divergences in opinion among European countries. According to Mahmoud al-Zahar, France, Germany, Norway and Switzerland have a posture that distinguishes them from the British one, which is seen as more negative.[11] Yet the Quartet's refusal to inflect its position and recognize Hamas has significantly limited any possibility of interaction with these countries.[12] The European Union has joined the hard line espoused by the Quartet, in refusing to recognize election results,[13] even though it had encouraged the process of democratization and sought to broaden the dialogue with some elected members of Hamas in the wake of the 2005 municipal elections.

Mahmoud al-Zahar and Ismail Haniyeh's tours

For the first time since the government's formation, visits abroad were made by Gaza leaders, in tandem with the traditional tours made by the external leadership based in Damascus. Together with Mesh'al's visit to Moscow,[14] which took place in March 2006, Mahmoud al-Zahar (then Foreign Affairs minister) went on two diplomatic tours in April and May of the same year. On 14 April, he travelled to Saudi Arabia, Syria, Kuwait, Bahrein, Qatar, the United Arab Emirates, Yemen, Libya, Algeria, Sudan and Egypt.[15]

> In Saudi Arabia, I was welcomed by the Foreign Affairs Minister Prince Faysal. In Syria I met president Bashar al-Assad and his Foreign Affairs Minister, and we were able to adopt a common stance as regards Palestinians stuck on the Syrian-Iraqi border after the American invasion of Iraq. The visit to Bahrein where I was welcomed by the Foreign Affairs Minister was also very important; then in Qatar, I met the Emir and delegations of Western Europe who do not wish that these visits be made official. I met the Ministers of Foreign Affairs of the Emirates, Yemen (as well as its President), Libya, Algeria, and also Sudan, where I also met the President.[16]

On 27 May, he began his second tour in Asia and travelled to Indonesia, Malaysia, the Sultanate of Brunei, Pakistan, China, Sri Lanka and Iran. During a conversation with this book's author, he enjoyed insisting on the high level of protocol of his

---

11. See the interview of Mahmoud al-Zahar in *al-Arabiya*, republished by the IPC on 8 April 2006.
12. *Al-Riyadh*, 31 January 2006.
13. Are Hovdenak, 'Hamas in Transition, the Failure of Sanctions', *Democratization* 16, no. 1 (February 1999): 59–80.
14. For an analysis of relations between Russia and Hamas between 2006 and 2010, see Wissam Abou Issa, *Hamâs wa Rûsiyâ, Markaz al-filstîni li-l-dirâsât wa-l-ishtishârât* (Beirut, 2011).
15. See the interview of Mahmoud al-Zahar, *Markaz al-filastîni lil-l-i'lâm*, 8 May 2006.
16. Conversation with Mahmoud al-Zahar, Gaza, 20 March 2013.

partners:[17] 'During the second tour, I met the Indonesian and Malaysian Presidents, as well as the Sultan of Brunei. In Pakistan, I met the Vice-President, as well as the Prime Minister and the Minister of Foreign Affairs.'

Mahmoud al-Zahar's approach consisted in sending a series of letters to all Foreign Affairs ministers of countries he wished to visit;[18] he would then plan his agenda according to their answers. The countries contacted for diplomatic visits reacted in very different ways, as al-Zahar himself confessed: he indeed mentions having been very warmly welcomed in most countries, yet some expressed reluctance, like Egypt, and others simply refused to receive him, like Venezuela.[19] Among countries considered by Hamas as important players, but with which it maintains poor relations, there are Egypt and Jordan.[20]

Concerning Egypt, its Interior Ministry state Habib al-Adli had at the time denounced the implication of two members of Hamas' armed branch in the Dahab attack on 4 April 2006. These declarations had led Cairo to refuse to welcome Mahmoud al-Zahar on his first trip. Avoiding any form of conflict, the Hamas leadership had then sent its Interior Minister Sayyid Siam to the Egyptian capital to speak to Omar Suleyman, then chief of intelligence services.[21] Despite this crisis, Mahmoud al-Zahar was finally received by Ahmed Abou al-Gheit, then Egyptian Foreign Affairs minister, while returning to Gaza. Al-Zahar had insisted on the importance of this meeting and the existence of positive relations between the two sides.[22]

Another crisis explains tensions with Jordan: the discovery of arms caches belonging to Hamas, according to Jordanian authorities. These accusations had caused the postponement of Mahmoud al-Zahar's visit to Amman, planned for 20 April.[23] Ghazi Hamad, at the time spokesman for the Gaza government, had expressed his astonishment at the fact that Jordan was the only Arab state to cancel the visit.[24]

Mahmoud al-Zahar also mentioned his participation in several multilateral bodies: the Forum for Cooperation between China and the Arab States, the one for ministers of Foreign Affairs of Arab States, and the Islamic Forum in Saudi

17. *Alwatanvoice*, 27 May 2006.
18. Several letters were sent to Egypt, Saudi Arabia, Syria, Kuwait, Bahrein, Oman, Qatar, the United Arab Emirates, Yemen and Libya. See the interview of Mahmoud al-Zahar, *Markaz al-filastînî lil-l-i'lâm*, 8 May 2006.
19. Ibid.
20. *Ma'an news*, 7 May 2006.
21. Mohammed Jam'a, 'Al-Azma al-falastînîya wa 'ilâqât-Hamâs al-iqlîmîya', *Al-Siyasat al-dawlîya*, October 2007, 42.
22. *Al-Mustaqbal*, 5 May 2006.
23. This announcement, made by the Jordanian government spokesman Nasser Jawdeh, occurred the day after a suicide attack in Tel Aviv, causing nine deaths, an operation firmly condemned by Amman.
24. *Al-Riyadh*, 20 April 2006.

Arabia.[25] Mahmoud al-Zahar's participation in these summits nevertheless was sometimes peppered with incidents, as witnessed by his barring from the Summit of Non-Aligned States, at that time in Kuala Lumpur: he attributes this to manoeuvres of Mahmoud Abbas, who wished to impose the PLO's Foreign Affairs minister Farouq al-Qaddoumi as chairman of the Palestinian delegation.[26]

As for Prime Minister Ismail Haniyeh, he travelled at the end of 2006 to Egypt, Syria, Kuwait, Iran, Lebanon, Qatar and Saudi Arabia (while on the pilgrimage to Mecca).[27] This was the first time that a Hamas prime minister made a diplomatic visit. His departure in the winter of 2006 was more awkward, since, during his crossing of Rafah, the Egyptian authorities made him wait several hours in the cold for the green light to enter their territory. On the day of his departure, just before leaving Gaza on 28 November 2006, he gave a speech: 'This is the first time since the government's formation that I set foot outside my homeland. The aim of these visits is to deepen relations between the "Tenth Government" and Arab and Muslim governments, and do everything necessary to make the Palestinian people able to confront the unjust blockade forced upon it.'[28]

The actions of Hamas MPs

Concomitantly with the diplomacy of the 'executive' branch of Hamas, the movement's MPs elected in 2006 as part of the 'Change and Reform' group also made visits abroad, as well as welcoming foreign MPs into the Gaza Strip.[29]

On 28 March 2006, MPs Mahmoud al-Zahar, Sayyid Siam and Azzam al-Ahmad travelled to Jordan to meet the Arab Parliamentary Federation. On 30 December 2006, Ahmad Bahar accompanied Prime Minister Ismail Haniyeh during a journey to Saudi Arabia to visit King Abdullah, just before making his Hajj pilgrimage. Some MPs also participated in several summits: the Summit of 'Victory of Jerusalem and of the Palestinian people', held on 4 April 2006 in Iran, the Islamic Summit in Turkey on 10 April 2006, the Summit for Democracy in Doha on 29 October 2009 and finally the International Asian Summit for Peace in Iran on 11 November 2006.[30]

As of February 2006, members of the Palestinian Legislative Council were able to welcome a series of delegations, particularly a British one from the House of

---

25. Conversation with Mahmoud al-Zahar, 20 March 2013.
26. *Globalnewscombined.com*, 31 May 2006.
27. *Ma'an News*, 28 November 2006.
28. Ibid.
29. Following Aziz Dweik's arrest on 29 June 2006, Ahmad Bahar took charge in the interim. The Palestinian Legislative Council also includes representatives from other factions. We shall mention here only the interactions that were from members of the 'Change and Reform' political platform.
30. *Arba' sanawât min al-'ita raghma l-hisâr, 2006–2010*, Majlis al-tashrî 'î al-falastînî, 2010.

Commons led by Iain Wright (on 28 February 2006), and another of the European Union (on 2 March). Prior to his arrest, which took place on 29 June 2006 during operation 'Summer Rains', the President of parliament Aziz Dweik also met: the Indian ambassador to Palestine Ohm Prakash, a Belgian parliamentary delegation, the Swedish MP Gieri Mille, the Chinese ambassador Yang Wei and his Egyptian counterpart Ashraf Aqel. On 10 June, it was the turn of Ahmad Bakr to welcome the Tunisian ambassador. According to sources inside the Legislative Council,[31] the aim of these visits was 'to extend relations regionally and internationally, strengthen relations with politicians and MPs of various states of the world and build real bridges to explain the Palestinian perspective to centres of global political decision'. The visits of European delegations to Gaza were loudly criticized by Israel, which considered they should not have been made in the EU's name, since that institution considers Hamas a terrorist organization.[32]

The reinforcement of the blockade and the rise in power of the external leadership

A curtailed but quite active diplomacy

As from 2007, the toughening of the blockade limited the travel capabilities of the interior leadership. Until 2011, no visit was made by Gaza government ministers, now competing with another newly established government in Ramallah. The creation of this other executive, moreover, weakened Gaza's Ministry of Foreign Affairs, since some of its officials accepted to stop working in exchange for the payment of their salaries by Ramallah.[33] Many letters addressed to Western heads of state bear witness to this lock-up endured by the members of the Hamas Gaza centre. In December 2007, Hamas addressed a letter to the White House via the media. Ahmed Yousef, who was the prime minister's adviser, denounced the continuation of Gaza's isolation and insisted on the fact that Hamas was ready for dialogue with the West.[34] One should also note Ismail Haniyeh's letter addressed to French president Nicolas Sarkozy on 11 January 2008, a letter that provided the Quai d'Orsay (the French Ministry of Foreign Affairs) with the opportunity to give details on its official position: if Hamas did not submit to the aforementioned three conditions, then the opening of a dialogue with the movement would be impossible.[35]

---

31. Ibid.
32. Al-Riyadh, 31 January 2006.
33. Over a total of 172 civil servants belonging to this ministry, 15 apparently no longer came to work. Hamas appointed six new civil servants to replace those who preferred to stay at home. Are Hovnedak, *The Public Services under Hamas in Gaza*.
34. *Marebpress*, 9 December 2007.
35. *Al-Ayyam*, 11 January 2008.

Israeli offensive on the Gaza Strip in December 2008 and January 2009 and the assault on the Turkish *Viva Palestina* flotilla in May 2010, all played a part in the relative opening up of Gaza. A surge in solidarity from new players came about in the wake of Israeli aggression during 'Cast Lead', which led to the launch of a new tour of Gaza MPs.[36]

The June 2007 events, which had led to the Palestinian government's paralysis, made Hamas resume the sessions of the Palestinian Legislative Council with only MP's from Gaza.[37] Faced with the emergency of reconstruction after 'Cast Lead', this new assembly received many invitations on behalf of the parliaments of Arab states. The delegation headed by Ahmad Bahar visited Syria, Iran, Sudan, Oman, Indonesia, Bahrein, Saudi Arabia, Lebanon and Ethiopia. According to official sources originating from the Gaza parliament, the delegation's role was to honour media institutions and personalities who had supported Gaza during the Israeli aggression, such as the al-Jazeera TV channel. This delegation spoke with very high-level partners, such as the former Sudanese president Omar al-Bashir, the emir of Qatar and the Iranian president. It was in Tehran, moreover, that this delegation attended the Fourth Jerusalem Summit, named 'Victory of Gaza', on 4 and 5 March 2009. Activities at popular level were also important for this delegation, which organized meetings with Palestinian communities in these countries, particularly in Qatar and Saudi Arabia, but also festivals in refugee camps.[38]

Gazan diplomacy also remained active at the time, as seen in the reception of foreign representatives to the Strip:[39] Ahmad Bahar welcomed delegations,

---

36. The first tour of parliamentaries took place at the end of March 2007, at the moment when the national unity government was in power, and when the Palestine Legislative Council (PLC) had received invitations from several Arab parliaments. Heading the delegation to Egypt, the emirates, Oman and Sudan, were Ahmad Badr and MPs such as Rajah Baraka, Hissam al-Tawil, Abdel Rahman al-Jamil and Salah al-Bardawil. Its results are summarized by PLC sources in the following terms: success in the approval of official cooperation between the Egyptian parliament and the Palestinian Legislative Council; creation of an assembly for parliamentary friendship between the Sudanese national assembly and the Palestinian parliament; official agreement by the Sultanate of Oman to finance the construction of a hall for the parliament in Gaza; agreement in principle to open a Palestinian consulate in al-Arish (Sinai) to alleviate the suffering of Palestinian citizens (*Arbaʿ sanawât al-ʿita raghma l-hisâr, 2006–2010* (Majlis al-tashrîʿî al-falastîni, 2010)).

37. The first session of this assembly took place in September 2007. Each of its members had the right to stand for one or two members of parliament imprisoned in Israel. See Are Hodevak, Public Services under Hamas in Gaza.

38. In the Nahr al-Bared camp near Tripoli in Lebanon, and in that of Yarmouk in Damascus for the 'victory' of Gaza. Hamas appears to have distributed $100 to each family in these camps during its visits.

39. Most of the receptions were organized in Gaza, with the exception of the welcoming of a delegation of European MPs by Aziz Dweik in al-Khalil/Hebron, on 15 December 2009. *Arbaʿ sanawât al-ʿita raghma l-hisâr, 2006–2010* (Majlis al-tashrîʿî al-falastîni, 2010).

including one from the Egyptian Workers' Party (on 26 January 2008) and another of European parliamentarians travelling on 26 January 2008 to discuss reconciliation. After inviting former US president Jimmy Carter to speak of the arrest of Palestinian MPs and demand an international campaign for their release, Ahmad Bahar met a delegation of the AKP (Turkey's ruling Justice and Development Party) on 16 June, another from South Africa on 28 June, and one of Human Rights Watch on 27 July. As for Aziz Dweik, on 16 January 2010, he welcomed the most important European delegation since the start of the blockade, headed by British MP Gerald Kaufman, with fifty-seven members from twelve countries.

In May 2010, the killing of nine Turkish nationals by the Israeli forces during the *Viva Palestina* flotilla episode set similar dynamics in motion. Arab League general secretary Amr Moussa's trip to Gaza in June 2010 was an illustration of this. It was the first visit in four years to the Gaza Strip made by an official political representative (but not a chief of state).[40] Israeli acts of aggression have allowed Hamas to mobilize international public opinion and participate in the organizations of humanitarian convoys in the framework of European campaigns for lifting the blockade.[41] On 10 August 2010, Ismail Haniyeh focused on welcoming the delegation of the 'Miles of Smiles 2' European caravan to the Palestinian Legislative Council in Gaza, doing likewise for Malay delegations at the seat of the government presidency. According to Ahmed Yousef, the raid against the Turkish flotilla was a real turning point and projected Hamas to the centre of the international community's attention.

The centrality of the Hamas Damascus head office

After 2007, relations with Tehran were significantly strengthened, as shown by the multiplication of bilateral meetings between the Hamas leadership based in Damascus and Iranian authorities: on 21 July, a month after Gaza's seizure, Khaled Mesh'al and Izzat al-Rishq met Iranian president Mahmoud Ahmadinejad in the Syrian capital. Six months later, in January 2008, it was the turn of the Islamic Republic's authorities to welcome Hamas leaders to Tehran. In January 2009, little after the announcement of the unilateral Israeli cease-fire, the president of the

---

40. Hedi Ahmad, Fislastin al-Muslima, July 2010, 26–7. The author mentions scepticism surrounding this visit, which could not put an end to the blockade. He quotes two university professors, Talal 'Oukil from Gaza University and Abd al-Sitar Qassam from al-Najah University in Nablus, who described Amr Moussa's stance as 'weak'.

41. Anwar al-Gharbi, who was spokesman of the European campaign for the lifting of the 'Zionist embargo', mentions the possibility for European parliamentary delegations to travel to Gaza. Among the participants coordinating the Swiss convoy, the lawyer Idir Dimertis and the former British MP George Galloway, who claimed he would manage a new convoy despite Egyptian prohibition, see the *Palestinian Information Center*, 22 September 2010.

Iranian Legislative Council Ali Larijani and Seed Jalili (president of the Iranian National Security Council) both spoke to Khaled Mesh'al in Damascus.[42] Finally, Iran was the first state to which a Hamas delegation travelled to after operation 'Cast Lead'. During this last visit, Khaled Mesh'al had a conversation with the Guide of the Islamic revolution Ali Khamenei, as well as with President Ahmadinejad.[43]

During the same period, members of the external head office residing in Damascus reinforced their links with Qatar. The emirate indeed appeared as an influential mediator for setting up contacts with the Americans. In November 2008, Khaled Mesh'al had done his best behind the scenes to make a letter reach US president Barack Obama during the latter's visit to Qatar.[44] This document, which congratulated the new American president for his victory in the elections, requested setting up a meeting between Hamas and American officials in a country to be chosen by the US State Department. Bilateral meetings with Qatari authorities gained new momentum during the Arab League Summit in Doha on 16 January 2009. Though the quorum of Arab heads of state required for this summit to take place was not reached, the Qataris decided to let it happen.[45] It was the absence of the delegations from Saudi Arabia, Egypt and Kuwait,[46] and that of the Palestinian Authority's president, moreover, that enabled the Qataris to welcome Hamas and Khaled Mesh'al and let them represent Palestine.[47] In sources close to Hamas, this Arab League Summit was considered the signal for the end of isolation.[48]

Damascus was also a useful platform to welcome foreign figures like Amr Moussa (in April 2010[49]) and South African vice-president Kgalema Motlanthe (On 22 October 2010).[50] Finally, between the springs of 2009 and 2010, the heads

42. *IRNA*, 9 January 2009; see Adnan Abu Amer, *Iranian Influence in the Gaza Strip, Evidence and Implications* (Jerusalem: Friedrich Ebert Stiftung, 2011).
43. http://www.youtube.com/watch?v=a33itaDX18k.
44. *Al-Akhbar*, 29 November 2008.
45. The quorum of fifteen states was not reached, since twelve states only were present out of the twenty-two of the Arab League. Egypt, Saudi Arabia, Kuwait and Mahmoud Abbas boycotted the meeting. Countries present included Syria, Sudan, Algeria, Iraq, Libya, Lebanon, Qatar and Iran. See *Info-Palestine*, 19 January 2009.
46. Hamas nevertheless saluted the stance of the Kuwaiti government, which, in response to the massacre of the flotilla, chose to withdraw from the Arab initiative. Its stand was described as an 'Encouraging Approach that Expresses the Will of the Kuwaiti People', *Filastin al-Muslima*, July 2010, 35.
47. *Jarida al-Arab* (Qatar), 17 January 2009.
48. Abd al-Hamid al-Kayyali, *Dirâsa fî-l-aduwan al-isrâ'îlî 'alâ qitâ' Ghazza*, Markaz al-Zaytûna li-l dirâsât wa-l-istishârât (Beirut, 2009).
49. During his meeting with Amr Moussa, Khaled Mesh'al gave details on his views regarding the failure of reconciliation, mainly denouncing the US stance. Khaled Mesh'al asked for his support to encourage the implication of Arab states in this matter, in tandem with Egypt, *Markaz ak-filastînî li-l-i'lâm*, 23 October 2010.
50. *Palestinian Information Center*, 23 September 2010, Damascus.

of the external office travelled on a tour led by Khaled Mesh'al and visited Sudan, Libya, Yemen,[51] Iran and Russia. While in the wake of 'Cast Lead', Moscow was contented with merely expressing its reservations regarding support for Hamas,[52] the Kremlin now gradually returned to the policy of openness launched in 2006. Three months after this February 2010 visit to Moscow,[53] Khaled Mechal met President Dimitri Medvedev for the first time in Syria.[54] On this occasion the Russian head of the executive told the Hamas Political Bureau president of many means to solve various affairs and issues, notably advising on the release of IDF private Gilad Shalit. This meeting provoked the anger of Israelis, who then considered that Russia was about to make a distinction between 'good' and 'bad' terrorists.[55]

The Arab Spring: The end of the lockdown or an increase in isolation?

Gaza and the outside leadership: Towards a new complementarity

The context of the Arab Spring created a new atmosphere favourable for the travels of Gaza leaders who, thanks to the temporary reopening of the Rafah crossing, could now go on visits abroad. Profound regional changes, moreover, allowed more countries to welcome a movement inspired by the 'Brotherhood', who maintained influential relations with other Islamist groups or regional governments with an Islamist majority. In order to take advantage of this new regional environment, Ismail Haniyeh decided to appoint, during a ministerial shuffle in March 2011, Mohammed Awad as foreign minister, who then travelled to Egypt, Iran and Turkey. During a conversation with the author, Awad compared this period to that of 2006, when Mahmoud al-Zahar was in charge of Foreign Affairs: 'I was on an official visit to Iran and Turkey, where I was received by the Foreign Ministers of these countries. I visited Egypt and I was welcomed by the President. In short, the period when I was Minister of Foreign Affairs looks a lot like 2006.'[56]

By comparing his period of office at the head of the ministry with that of 2006 (when the only Palestinian Foreign Affairs minister was from Hamas), Mohammed Awad gave his portfolio a legitimacy and importance that political division since 2007 had considerably weakened. In fact, the duration of his mandate did not exceed eight months, during which he only made three visits

---

51. *Filastin al-Muslima*, January 2010. Discussions between Khaled Mesh'al and Ali Abdullah Saleh also dealt with means to break the political fracture between Sanaa and Tehran regarding the Houthi rebellion in northern Yemen.
52. *Al-Khalij*, 17 December 2008.
53. http://www.hanein.info/vb/showthread.php?t=156449.
54. *Alresalah*, 9 February 2010.
55. *Al-Sharq*, 25 May 2009.
56. Conversation with Mohammed Awad in Gaza, 19 March 2013.

outside of Gaza, while Mahmoud al-Zahar, in one year, had made more than ten. It was the awareness of the increasingly superfluous aspect of this portfolio that led the Gaza government to abolish it several months later and to attribute its duties to Prime Minister Haniyeh. This decision put an end to what appeared to be a parenthesis in a continuous dynamic of weakening of the Gaza government's diplomacy since June 2007.

The period opening in 2011 with the Arab Spring was also marked by Ismail Haniyeh's new regional tour. Five years after his first diplomatic experiment, the prime minister travelled to Egypt, Sudan, Turkey and Tunisia[57] to congratulate the Egyptian and Tunisian people on the success of their revolutions.[58] When he arrived at Tunis' airport, he was greeted by a crowd of young men screaming anti-Jewish slogans.[59] On 24 February 2012, he gave a sermon at Al-Azhar University in Cairo.[60] The contrast between his long wait at the Rafah crossing in the midst of winter 2006 and the way he was welcomed by the prestigious Islamic institution was quite striking. During a later tour, he went to Qatar, Bahrein, Kuwait, the emirates and Iran. When he visited Tehran on 11 February 2012, he reiterated the movement's maximalist strategy by refusing any form of agreement (*taswiya*) with Israel.

The same week, Moussa Abu Marzouk met Hassan Nasrallah in Beirut.[61] The departure of the external Hamas leadership from Syria occurred a year after the beginning of the Arab Spring. The year when Khaled Mesh'al was still in Damascus was marked by his trip to Jordan, a gesture of mending bridges bit by bit with a state that had broken its relations with Hamas in 1999. Jordanian prime minister Awn Khawasneh had prepared this visit by announcing as early as October that Hamas' expulsion from Jordan had been a mistake. Contacts between Mohammad Nazzal, settled in Amman since the summer of 2011, and Jordanian intelligence services had both helped in organizing the visit, also been facilitated by the personal intervention of Qatar's emir to King Abdullah II.[62] The fact remains that the Hashemite Kingdom appeared to be very cautious about this visit due to pressure exerted by US authorities, who were opposed to it.[63] Khaled Mesh'al travelled once more to Jordan in spring 2012, on the occasion of the funeral of

57. Larbi Sadiki, 'Hamas and the Arab Spring', al-Jazeera, 29 December 2011.
58. Ismail Haniyeh congratulating the Tunisians for the victory of their revolution, *Palestinian Information Center*, 26 November 2011.
59. Alain Gresh, 'La Tunisie, le Hamas, la Palestine et les juifs', *Le Monde Diplomatique*, 10 January 2012.
60. 'I salute all the Arab peoples and I salute the courage of the Syrian people, who looks for freedom, democracy and reform', *Ismail Haniyeh, al-Azhar*, Cairo, 24 February 2012.
61. Top Hamas officials visit Teheran, *The Daily Star*, 15 March 2012; 'Sayyed Nasrallah Received Hamas Delegation: Syria, Gaza on the Table', *al-Manar*, 14 March 2012.
62. *Al-Hayat*, 22 January 2012.
63. Attempts to make a rapprochement apparently met with American and Israeli pressure. Jordanian authorities sent a letter to Hamas, in which they requested the

one of Hamas' founders, Sheikh Omar al-Ashqar. A year later, on 28 January 2013, Mesh'al asked Jordan's king to transmit a message to President Barack Obama that stated that Hamas accepted the 1967 borders.[64]

After the external leadership's departure from Damascus in February 2012, Khaled Mesh'al resumed his diplomatic activities. He also made a visit to Tunisia, during which he met President Moncef Marzouqi. Mesh'al had been invited to participate in al-Nahda's congress on 12 July;[65] he advised Tunisian leaders to not insert the criminalization of normalization with Israel into the new Tunisian constitution.[66] On 30 September, the Political Bureau's president also went to Turkey to attend the AKP's caucus. A first meeting had already taken place on 16 March, in Ankara, with Turkish prime minister Recep Erdogan. In September, the severing of ties was definitively consummated with the Syrian regime, since during his speech Khaled Mesh'al had shown his support for the 'Syrian revolution', stating that 'reform and democracy' were at the heart of the movement's internal politics, while 'resistance and confrontation with Israel' was at the top of its foreign policy agenda.[67]

Khaled Mesh'al's other travels essentially took place in Egypt. On 16 March 2013, he visited the Muslim Brotherhood offices in Mokattam (a Cairo suburb) to meet the Supreme Guide of the Brotherhood, Mohammed Badie. Mesh'al gave insurances there that Hamas would not meddle in the internal affairs of Arab countries[68] and said that the movement was in contact with the Egyptian presidency and intelligence services to state this policy of non-interference.[69]

Visits by MPs

In a similar fashion, MPs also made several visits to Arab countries. Heading a delegation, Ahmad Bahar travelled to Tunisia, Morocco and Qatar. In Morocco, he met the prime minister and general secretary of the Justice and Development Party, Abd al-Ilah Benkirane, in order to discuss the Israeli policy of Judaization of Jerusalem, the issue of reconciliation and the arrest of MPs. Ahmad Bahar handed over an urgent letter on this matter to the president of the Arab Parliamentary Union, demanding the inclusion, in the following session's agenda, of the issue of incarceration of MPs and the Palestinian Legislative Council's president Aziz Dweik. In Qatar, Ahmad Bahar emphasized that the victories of Islamists translated their hopes and ambitions for political, economic and social reform and

---

postponement of Khaled Mesh'al's visit to a date subsequent to that of Abdullah II to Washington, where he met Barack Obama.
    64. *Al-Ayyam*, 31 January 2013.
    65. *Al-Quds al-Arabi*, 12 July 2012.
    66. *Al-Quds al-Arabi*, 29 October 2012.
    67. https://www.youtube.com/watch?v=ROBrYNcEyzE.
    68. *Al-Masri al-Youm*, 16 March 2013.
    69. *Ahram Online*, 28 March 2013.

the struggle against American hegemony in the region. In Doha, Bahar confirmed that the Palestinian–Qatari relationship was grounded in religion and recalled that its history was marked by the generosity of Qatar's prince, who had provided aid and assistance to the Palestinian people facing the blockade and confronted with the practices of 'Zionist terrorism'.[70]

Europe was also visited by Gaza MPs. On 18 May 2013, Jamal al-Khoudari went to Brussels to attend a conference for the right of return on the occasion of the Nakba's sixty-fifth anniversary.[71] Many European members of parliament were present, together with the former British minister for International Development Clare Short,[72] as well as Rashid al-Ghannouchi, who recalled that one of the Tunisian people's slogans, after 'The people want the fall of the regime', was 'The people want the liberation of Palestine'.[73]

In January 2012, the International Parliamentary Union invited the head of the parliamentary block for Foreign Affairs, Mouchir al-Masri,[74] as well as Sayyid Abou Musameh and Khamis al-Najjar. During this visit, they spoke to a number of political officials, in particular with the Swiss ambassador to Syria. Swiss officials had suggested that Hamas abrogate the death penalty;[75] the discussion also notably focused on the fate of common criminals. On 13 February 2013, other MPs from Gaza travelled to Sofia, but were then expelled by Bulgarian authorities, who considered that 'their activities in the country were not in accordance with the reason for which a visa was issued to them'.

Hamas at the gates of recognition

The November 2012 offensive against Gaza sparked a wave of solidarity, which translated into many official visits to the Strip. Until then, the territory had welcomed only a few foreign political representatives, the most notable being Qatar's emir Sheikh Hamad ben Khalifa al-Thani, who travelled there (for the first time since 1999) on 23 October 2012. This broad wave of diplomatic activity was seen by some analysts as a chance for the recognition of Hamas on a regional, and

70. *Palestinian Information Center*, 3 December 2011.

71. This term literally means 'catastrophe' and is a reference to the expulsion of the Palestinian during the first Arab–Israeli war of 1947.

72. *Alresalah*, 18 May 2013.

73. http:///www.alwada.eu/index.php./conference/news/548-2013-05-18-16-26-44.

74. Mushri al-Masri's predecessor was Ahmad Abou Halabiyya, and his successor Salah al-Bardawil.

75. The author was informed of these discussions by one of the members of the delegation, who told her that since 2006 Hamas has executed very few people, always doing the utmost to avoid implementing death penalties. He claimed that, quite the opposite, Hamas tries to find other alternatives like cutting off the hands of the guilty or increasing detention so that the families of victims change their minds.

perhaps even international, level.[76] On the operation's third day, President Morsi sent his Prime Minister Hisham Qandil to Gaza.[77] Following the cease-fire, the Tunisian foreign minister Rafiq Abd al-Salam and his Turkish counterpart Ahmet Davutoglu both went to Gaza.[78] In January 2013, it was the turn of Malaysian prime minister Mohammed Najil Abd al-Razzak. Renewed Israeli aggression also brought the Arab League general secretary to Gaza.

Finally, a last visit of importance on the evening of 8 May 2013 was that of Sheikh Yusuf al-Qaradawi, the president of the International Federation of Muslim Ulemas, who went to Gaza accompanied by a delegation of thirty-nine men of religion from fourteen various countries, among which were Egypt, Qatar, Saudi Arabia, Syria, Tunisia, Morocco, Pakistan, India, Sri Lanka, Australia and the UK. Many Hamas figures were present to greet Qaradawi at the Rafah crossing, Ahmad Bahar in particular. During his visit, Yusuf al-Qaradawi gave a sermon in the great al-Omari mosque in the centre of Gaza and visited the home of Sheikh Yassin.[79] This was the first time since 1958 the preacher had returned to Gaza.

Diplomacy in deadlock?

The summer of 2013 appears to have seen a turning point that closed the window of opportunity had opened for Hamas at the start of the Arab Spring. The administration that came after Mohammed Morsi undertook the destruction of the tunnels and imposed a diplomatic blockade preventing steps towards representation outside Gaza.[80] In tandem with these restrictions, which provoked a renewed debilitation of the Gaza leadership and government's diplomacy, the external leadership was also affected, following its territorial fragmentation in the wake of its departure from Damascus. Whereas in 2007, as Hamas members residing in Damascus were able to take over diplomatic activities and consequently become more visible, their geographic dispersion in 2012 inaugurated a period of great hardship.

The perception affecting some of the most important of the movement's figureheads – Khaled Mesh'al in particular – gives a peculiar scope to Hamas' diplomatic activity. Iran's refusal to welcome Mesh'al in Tehran in October 2013 is

76. Jean-François Legrain, 'Gaza, novembre 2012: une victoire pour quoi faire?', *Carnets de l'IREMAM*, 3 February 2013.

77. Sending Hisham Qandil to Gaza had been very badly perceived by the Egyptian military establishment, who considered that Mohammed Morsi had gone way beyond the part he could play as a normal go-between.

78. Turkish prime minister Recep Tayyip Erdogan cancelled his visit to the Gaza Strip on several occasions: a first time in September 2011, a second in April 2012 and finally in May 2012. The third visit was postponed following a request by the US state secretary, *Markaz al-Filastînî li-l-i'lâm*, 22 April 2013.

79. *Al-Safir*, 10 May 2013.

80. *Markaz al-Filastînî li-l-i'lâm*, 1 December 2013.

an illustration of this. Mesh'al could only travel to Lebanon while other members of the external head office could land in the Iranian capital.

On 1 December 2013, Khaled Mesh'al, Ossama Hamdan, Mohammed Nasr and Sami Khater travelled to Kuala Lumpur. Hamas sources emphasized the unusual aspect of this meeting, which was the first official visit of the Political Bureau's president to Malaysia, illustrating the rapprochement of the movement with this country since Malaysian prime minister's 'historic' visit to the Gaza Strip.[81] Analysts close to the movement have considered that this initiative was symbolic of a new era of international openness following Egypt and Syria's negative trajectories.[82]

One had to wait for the end of 2014 to see the inception of this end in Hamas' isolation. On the occasion of the annual Justice and Development Party (AKP)'s congress, held in Konya on 28 December, the president of the Political Bureau was met by Foreign Minister Ahmet Davutoglu. A second official visit to Turkey by Mesh'al took place on 10 January 2015. On 8 December, a delegation of the external head office, comprised of Mohammed Nasr and Ossama Hamdan, travelled to Iran. Khaled al-Qaddoumi, Hamas' representative in Tehran, coordinated the visit. In an interview with the *Alresalah* newspaper, Qaddoumi highlighted the existing positive relations between Iran and Hamas and the importance of the Islamic Republic's support for the resistance. He also stressed that Iran would not be opposed to Khaled Mesh'al's arrival, and that this would take place shortly at the appropriate moment.[83] Although the Political Bureau's president has still not been authorized to travel to Tehran, on 11 March 2015, he was able to meet the Islamic Assembly's president Ali Larijani in Doha. That was the first time that the Palestinian Islamist movement's head was able to talk officially to Iranian authorities since the beginning of the Syrian uprising in March 2011.[84]

Finally, Khaled Mesh'al made a visit to Saudi Arabia on 17 July 2015. This meeting had been in preparation since the death of King Abdullah in January; it was described by the Hamas Political Bureau's president as a 'step on the right path'.[85] It was seen as a benchmark in a process of regional recomposition, through which the Kingdom of Saudi Arabia was attempting to bridge the gap between Hamas and Egypt and estrange the movement from the Islamic Republic, in the wake of the signing by Tehran of the deal on its nuclear programme. The impact of this visit was nevertheless mitigated by the Saudi foreign minister, who described it as 'religious' and not 'political'.[86]

81. *Markaz al-Filastînî li-l-i'lâm*, 2 December 2013.
82. *Markaz al-Filastînî li-l-i'lâm*.
83. *Alresalah*, 9 December 2014.
84. *al-Jazeera*, 12 March 2015.
85. *Al-Hayat*, 23 July 2015.
86. *BBC Arabic*, 23 July 2015.

Earning a place in an increasingly complex regional game: The post-2014 turn

Consolidating the Doha leadership

Material destructions caused by 'Protective Edge', as well as the humanitarian disaster suffered by the Strip, led several UN and EU envoys to travel to Gaza in late 2014: the UN general secretary Ban Ki-Moon, the Swiss ambassador to the Palestinian Authority Paul Garnier and the German Foreign Affairs minister Frank-Walter Steinmeier. Apart from these visits, whose nature was essentially humanitarian and which did not lead to meetings with Hamas official representatives, two encounters took place in Doha between Khaled Mesh'al and the Quartet's Emissary to the Middle East, Tony Blair. On the occasion of these two meetings, which were held in May 2015 with the EU, Washington and Israel's consent, discussions focused on the lifting of the blockade, the conditions of implementation of a truce between Israel and Hamas, as well as an eventual prisoner exchange.[87] These discussions thus marginalized the Palestinian Authority, excluding it from any debate on the Gaza Strip's reconstruction and plan to reach a negotiated solution with Israel. In Hamas' mind, this was a recognition of its inescapable role, as well as proof that the Quartet's conditions forced on the Gaza Strip in the last eight years had not yielded any results whatsoever. Hamas communiqués very much highlighted the fact that neither the recognition of Israel nor Gaza's demilitarization was considered as precondition for the instauration of exchanges, thereby signalling that the inclusion of their movement on the list of terrorist organizations was an aporia leading to nowhere. A few months earlier, on 17 December 2014, Hamas had expressed its satisfaction at the European Court of Justice's decision (which resulted from the analysis of a procedural flaw) to overturn Hamas' inscription on the EU's blacklist. The movement's hope sank again in July 2017, in the wake of the Court of Justice's ruling to keep it on the European Union's list of terrorist organizations.[88]

Despite the emir's backing, the Qatari haven of Hamas was precarious. As of 2015, subjected to Israeli and US pressure, Qatar had to expel Salah al-Arouri and six other Hamas members, who then were spread out from Turkey to Lebanon and Malaysia.[89] In June 2017, subjected to renewed pressure from Saudi Arabia and the United Arab Emirates, two states accusing Qatar of supporting terrorism, Doha was again forced to throw out several Hamas representatives. Ahmed Yousef, speaking from Gaza, attempted to minimize this incident, by arguing that these officials were already outside Qatar at the time of the proclamation

---

87. *Al-Quds al-Arabi*, 12 June 2015.
88. For thoughts on the classification of Hamas as a terrorist organization by the European Union, see Catherine Charrett, *Hamas, the EU and the Palestinian Elections: A Performance in Politics* (Routledge, 2019).
89. *Al-Monitor*, 20 December 2019.

of this decision and consequently had not been evicted. As for Khalil al-Hayya, he stated that the provisional departure from Doha could be explained by the context of Hamas' internal elections and the need to unite the movement's various leaderships.[90] Without wanting to give any credit to these justifications, it is true that the expulsion from Qatar took place while February internal elections were being held, officially confirming Ismail Haniyeh in the Hamas' presidency.

This did not prevent Khaled Mesh'al from continuing to meet international dignitaries in Doha. Particularly noteworthy, for instance, was Russian foreign minister Sergei Lavrov's visit on 18 February 2020. The encounter occurred with Mikhail Bogdanov (president Putin's emissary for the Middle East and Africa), as well as that of the Russian ambassador to Qatar, being present.[91]

Salah al-Arouri's diplomatic tour

By propelling Ismail Haniyeh to head of the movement's Political Bureau, the 2017 internal elections made more complex the traditional divide between the internal and external leadership. Although until then the presidency of Hamas' executive body had always been given to a representative of the foreign leadership, it was now a representative of the Gaza one who took charge of the movement's direction. Now, it so happened that Ismail Haniyeh, who had already gained experience from his diplomatic tours in 2006 and 2011, first as prime minister of the Palestinian government and then of Gaza's, was prevented by Egyptian authorities from leaving the blockaded Strip. It was only in November 2017, some five months after his election at the head of the movement, that he was finally allowed to leave Gaza for a simple return journey to Cairo.

Since it was forbidden for Haniyeh to go beyond Egypt's capital, it was the Political Bureau's vice-president Salah al-Arouri who took charge of Hamas' diplomatic action. In July 2019, he led a Hamas delegation, which included Moussa Abu Marzouk, Maher Saleh, Khaled Qaddoumi, Hussam Badran, Izzat al-Rishq, Ismail Redwan and Osama Hamdan. When in Moscow, the delegation spoke to the Russian president's special adviser for the Middle East Mikhail Bogdanov. By raising both the conditions for a cease-fire between Israel and Hamas and the issue of inter-Palestinian reconciliation, Russia was presenting itself as an alternative to the 'deal of the century' put forward by US president Donald Trump.[92] On 21 July, during a conversation in Iran with Kamal Kharaji, president of the Assembly for Strategic Affairs, Hamas insisted on the need to counter Israeli attempts to normalize with some Gulf emirates, in particular Bahrein and the UAE. Al-Arouri described the meeting with Ali Khamanei as historic, emphasizing that relations between Hamas and Iran had once more become strategic.[93] Ismail Haniyeh

---

90. *RT Arabic*, 18 June 2017.
91. *Al-Monitor*, 1 March 2020.
92. https://www.youtube.com/watch?v=WNb7f2KX0xA.
93. *Arabi21*, 25 July 2019.

expressed his satisfaction from Gaza regarding this visit, hoping it would yield positive outcomes.[94]

Ismail Haniyeh's departs from Gaza for an unspecified period

In December 2019, Haniyeh was finally permitted to travel beyond the Egyptian capital. From Cairo's airport, he flew to Istanbul, where he met Turkish president Recep Tayyip Erdogan. His tour then took him to Qatar, Oman, Kuwait, Lebanon, Mauritania, Indonesia and Malaysia, where he met several important officials in Kuala Lumpur, Iranian president Hassan Rohani among them. In parallel, one should note that former Political Bureau chairman Khaled Mesh'al himself participated on 18 December in the Kuala Lumpur Islamic Summit, where his delegation and he met Malaysian prime minister Mahathir Bin Mohammed, Qatar's emir Tamim Bin Ahmad al-Thani, Turkish president Erdogan and Iranian president Rohani.[95] This visit, which sidelined Haniyeh, raised a number of questions on Mesh'al's political ambitions, both regarding Hamas and the Palestinian Authority's presidential elections in the future.[96]

As noticed, Ismail Haniyeh's freedom of movement, however, depended on Egyptian goodwill. Although Egypt finally accepted his departure from Cairo on a historic diplomatic tour, it could also exert control on Haniyeh by preventing his return to the Strip. This in fact occurred when, after his trip to Tehran on 6 January to attend the funeral of General Qassem Soleimani,[97] killed by the United States at Baghdad airport, Egyptians impeded his return home.[98] In order to minimize what was indeed punishment, Hamas announced through Khalil al-Hayya that the chairman of the Political Bureau's tour was meant to last an entire year, thus belittling Egyptian restrictions and presenting the president's absence from home as a deliberate choice. The presence of a Hamas delegation at Soleimani's funeral also hindered the attempts at a rapprochement with Saudi Arabia. Despite Saudi pressures to make Hamas recognize Israel,[99] added to Saudi press publications describing the movement as 'terrorist' and the jailing of Hamas members,[100] Ismail Haniyeh expressed his wish to visit the Saudi kingdom to its authorities. This request has remained unanswered until today, since his visit to Tehran became

---

94. *Al-Arabiyya*, 21 June 2019.

95. *Al-Monitor*, 9 January 2020.

96. Mesh'al's delegation during the Kuala Lumpur summit included Moussa Abu Marzouk, Izzat al-Rishq, Hussam Badran and Khalil al-Hayya.

97. General Qassem Sulaymani, the commander of the al-Quds force of Iran's Islamic Revolutionary Guard was killed on Iraqi territory by an American strike, on 3 January 2020.

98. *Independent Arabia*, 12 January 2020.

99. *Arabia 21*, 9 January 2020.

100. Saudi Arabia detained some sixty Palestinians accused of supporting terrorism, in particular Mohamed al-Khudari, the principal Hamas representative in the kingdom.

a major impediment to a visa to Riyadh.¹⁰¹ In order to facilitate his rehabilitation among Saudis, Hamas is now hedging its bets on a reconciliation between Doha and Riyadh.

On 1 March, Haniyeh went to Moscow. His delegation was received by Russian Foreign Affairs minister Sergei Lavrov. This meeting was meant as an answer to the Warsaw summit, which had been held on 13 and 14 February, during which the United States had announced their new vision for peace in the region.¹⁰² Beyond its military and political intervention in the civil war in Syria, Russia was thus trying to deal with Palestinian issues to curtail US influence in the region.¹⁰³ While restating Hamas' good relations with Russia, Moussa Abu Marzouk mentioned, in an interview with *Alaraby TV*, Russia's strategic importance in countering the 'peace process' paradigm of the United States. He said Russia was favouring inter-Palestinian reconciliation and recalled it had welcomed President Mahmoud Abbas beforehand and was about to receive other Palestinian delegations in Moscow. Haniyeh, in a televised interview, expressed his satisfaction at the positive nature of these visits, which made Hamas open discussions around various subjects, among them Palestinian reconciliation, humanitarian aid, resistance and the urgency of fighting against the 'Deal of the Century' American project.¹⁰⁴ Haniyeh highlighted that his home was not in Qatar but in Gaza; as Hamas president, however, his duty was to guarantee the representation of his movement outside the Occupied Palestinian Territories. He hoped he would continue his visits after the disappearance of the coronavirus pandemic. Haniyeh insisted that the sanitary lockdown ordered by several countries would in all likelihood not stop him from pursuing his diplomatic activities.

On 22 August, Ismail Haniyeh and Saleh al-Arouri were welcomed in Istanbul by President Erdogan to speak of the dangers of the 'Deal of the Century'. This trip provoked the ire of the American State Department, which accused Erdogan of complicity with terrorism, as well as the irritation of the Israeli *chargé d'affaires* in Turkey, who said Ankara had handed passports to twelve Hamas members in order to carry out terrorist attacks.¹⁰⁵ This was the second meeting that year between the Turkish president and Hamas since Erdogan had welcomed Haniyeh on 1 February. On 2 September, Ismail Haniyeh was in Lebanon to participate in an anti-normalization symposium at the Palestinian Embassy in Beirut where all Palestinian political factions were gathering.¹⁰⁶ During his speech, Haniyeh warned against the dangers of the US plan for the region and emphasized the

---

101. *Al-Monitor*, 21 January 2020.
102. https://www.youtube.com/watch?v=LGwa6Ujnwpo.
103. https://www.youtube.com/watch?v=LGwa6Ujnwpo.
104. https://www.youtube.com/watch?v=Cx3wz2YzlsM.
105. *Al-Monitor*, 7 September 2020.
106. This meeting which gathered both Islamic Jihad and the FPLP was meant to condemn the peace accord between the United Arab Emirates and Israel. Mahmoud Abbas also participated by videoconference from Ramallah.

urgent necessity of confronting it with a common front of resistance.[107] This visit was also the occasion for him to speak to several Lebanese politicians, including the president of the parliament, Nabih Berry, the director of Lebanese Security Services (*Sûreté Générale*) and the leader of the Druze community Walid Jumblatt. Received with great pomp in the Palestinian refugee camp of Ain al-Hilwa in Saida (South Lebanon), he also met Hezbollah secretary general Hassan Nasrallah. Both leaders highlighted the dangers of any form of normalization with Israel and spoke of the solidity of links between the two organizations.

107. https://www.youtube.com/watch?v=yHXmO5TjqYg.

Chapter 3

SYRIA, IRAN AND EGYPT

Several elements explain Syria's central role in Hamas' foreign policy. Until February 2012, the members of the external leadership were settled in Damascus. This strategic location allowed leaders to meet foreign chiefs of state during their visits to Syria, a country outside Israeli control; yet this fact also makes its foreign policy more complex by creating a dualism. With the launching of the popular uprising in Syria, relations with the regime soured until the closure of the movement's offices in February 2012. The change in the relationship with Damascus has always been a central issue in that it has also determined relations with the Islamic Republic of Iran.

As for Egypt, it has most often played the part of intermediary between Israel and Hamas, in particular for the signature of truces. The only country with a land border abutting Gaza (apart from Israel), its geographical location explains its central role, not only in terms of possibilities for travel but also more generally when it comes to access and exchange. Tunnels between Egypt and Gaza have enabled Hamas to levy import taxes, which are custom duties of sorts. Between 2006 and 2011, relations between Hamas and Hosni Mubarak's regime significantly deteriorated. January 2011, in contrast, saw a rapprochement between Hamas and Cairo, until Mohammed Morsi's ousting on 3 July 2013 and his replacement by Marshal Abd al-Fattah al-Sissi. The new Egyptian administration wanted to prove itself especially harsh with Hamas, as shown by the systematic destruction of tunnels and the total closure of the Rafah border crossing during 'Protective Edge', in summer 2014. Yet despite this enmity on display, Egypt understood that Hamas was an effective partner in the struggle against Sinai's Takfiri. In addition, Cairo's investment in Palestinian reconciliation brought Egyptian intelligence to meet Hamas leaders on Egyptian territory; these meetings also allowed Egypt to become involved in negotiations between Israel and Hamas aimed at a return to calm (*tahdi'a*).

Hamas and Syria: From strategic alliance to disunity

Damascus, capital of Hamas diplomacy

Despite the antagonism between the Muslim Brotherhood and the Syrian regime, culminating with Hafez al-Assad's bloody repression of this organization and the

Hama massacre in February 1982, al-Assad chose to welcome Hamas leaders in Damascus as of 1999, providing the Palestinian movement with considerable material and political support. According to Ali Sadr al-Din al-Bayanouni (the former general secretary of the Syrian section of the Brotherhood), this alliance between Hamas and the Syrian president did not prevent the Palestinian Islamist organization and the Syrian Muslim Brotherhood from maintaining amicable relations.[1] These relations have remained, however, more friendly than organizational, since the mere affiliation to the Syrian Muslim Brotherhood after 1982 entailed the death penalty. Understandably, this relationship is therefore difficult to describe in detail through independent sources while written documents are somewhat lacking.

We previously saw that a part of Hamas' visits abroad were made by representatives of the external leadership residing in Syria. They would regularly leave Damascus for destinations as different as Russia, Iran and many Arab capitals. Damascus, however, has been particularly important in Hamas' diplomacy, in that living there gave leaders of the movement the possibility to approach foreign leaders coming to Syria to meet people of Bashar al-Assad's regime. The members of head offices outside could therefore take advantage of their permanent stay in Damascus to converse with heads of state and other political representatives. Describing once more all the visits by foreign diplomats and meetings with Hamas representatives would be tedious; one cannot overrate, however, the importance of the Damascus platform, when it comes to relations with the Russians and with European diplomats residing in Syria.

In Hamas offices in Mashru' Dummar, a department specifically focusing on international relations was founded under the direction of Osama Hamdan, who had been the movement's representative in Lebanon.[2] On this matter, Hamdan told the author: 'Thanks to foreign policy, we can have access to relations with the outside world, without necessarily going through state diplomatic channels. Our objective is to build positive relations with the greatest amount of players, and to change the attitude of certain states towards us.'[3] According to Khaled Mesh'al, the aim of this new structure was to develop an ambitious and coherent foreign policy by integrating Hamas into solidarity networks that were not exclusive to one another.[4] This department was a 'factor of strength, openness and in gaining international support to the cause and for the movement'.[5]

1. https://www.youtube.com/watch?v=2bLQNg19Qp0.
2. The creation of this position offered to Osama Hamdan was largely publicized. During our conversations, the two MPs of the 'Change and reform' list, who were present in the West Bank, both mentioned the importance of the position of Hamdan, an ex-representative of Hamas in Lebanon.
3. Conversation with Osama Hamdan, Damascus, on 29 January 2011.
4. Interview of Khaled Mesh'al by Silvia Catori, *al-Sabeel*, July 2010, English translation by AMEC (*Afro-Middle East Center*).
5. Ibid.

Osama Hamdan and his adviser Khaled al-Qaddoumi regularly spoke to various diplomatic figures living in Damascus. A Norwegian diplomat[6] confirmed the existence of these regular contacts: 'There was a meeting in the month of December 2010 organized by Osama Hamdan, who gathered the ambassadors of Switzerland, Norway, Cuba, South Africa, China, Venezuela, etc. . . . The aim of the meeting was to update their relations and explain the positions of Hamas and the conflict's developments.'[7]

Damascus was thus a strategic location to make contact with players who, theoretically, are not authorized to develop relations with Hamas or who do not wish that these relations, when indeed they exist, be known and appear in the open. Talal Naji, the representative of PFLP-General Command of Ahmed Jibril,[8] was a figure close to Syrian authorities, but above all close to Hamas. He was at the time an important intermediary for many figures, including European ones, who wished to open a form of dialogue with the Movement of Islamic Resistance.[9]

Tawâjud or 'presence in absence'

The start of the popular uprising in Syria placed Hamas in front of a crucial dilemma. Witnessing the torture and massacres perpetrated by the regime against its own people, the movement could either keep quiet and run the risk of being accused of supporting Bashar al-Assad or openly express the hopes for freedom and justice of demonstrators, and by doing so be seen by the regime as an enemy. Now, it was impossible for Hamas to criticize the repression by a regime that had granted it unfailing protection since its expulsion from Jordan in 1999. Simultaneously, Hamas did not forget the PLO's costly siding with Iraq in the 1990s[10] and could not, as requested by Syrian and Iranian authorities, officially support Damascus. The main economic backer of Hamas, Iran, was hoping that the movement would officially express its support for Assad. Three moments punctuated the relations between Hamas and the Assad regime from March 2011 onwards: hoping at first to play the part of a mediator, it finally closed its offices in Damascus after a brief period of 'wait-and-see'.

6. Although they had no contacts with Hamas representatives at government level, the Swiss and Norwegians did not implement the boycott policy imposed by the European Union.

7. Conversation with the Swiss diplomat Thomas Oertle, Damascus, 20 January 2011.

8. The office of Talal Naji was located in PLO offices in Damascus, because the PFLP-General Command is officially still a part of the PLO, even though it does not participate in its Executive Committee.

9. Conversation with the Swiss diplomat Thomas Oertle, 20 January 2011.

10. During Iraq's invasion of Kuwait in 1990, the PLO chose to side with Iraq. This choice was very costly, since a large proportion of its financial resources were from Gulf states. This choice was also very awkward for Palestinians residing in Kuwait, who were expelled from the country in the wake of Iraq's defeat.

Hamas first tried to position itself as a mediator in the Syrian conflict when Nabil al-Arabi, the Arab League's secretary general, asked Khaled al-Mesh'al to use his influence on Bashar al-Assad in order to find a peaceful solution to the crisis.[11] The very day after the fall of Hosni Mubarak, and foreseeing the emergence of popular dissent in Syria, Khaled Mesh'al met the Syrian president and explained to him that although his foreign policy was excellent, some reforms in his internal policy were warranted.[12] According to Nabil al-Arabi, Khaled Mesh'al probably played an important part in attempting to convince Damascus to accept the mission of Arab League observers in Syria.[13] Returning from his trip to Cairo and his meeting with the Arab League general secretary, Mesh'al carried a letter that stated that an Arab solution was preferable to foreign intervention; high Syrian officials were furthermore encouraged to accept this initiative. He also emphasized that he did not understand Syria's suspension from the Arab League, expressing his irritation at seeing states that the Assad regime had supported (like Sudan) breaking away from their old ally. Salah al-Bardawil argued that Hamas has frequently expressed its hopes of seeing Syria exit the crisis and sought a political solution to implement reforms, respect of fundamental freedoms and human rights.[14]

Some sources also emphasize the role played by the Syrian Muslim Brotherhood in attempts to make Hamas a mediator, in order to incite Bashar al-Assad to carry out reforms. These attempts occurred a few days before the triggering of the uprising in Dera'a, on 18 March 2011. Ali Sadr al-Din al-Bayanouni and Mohammed Riyad al-Shaqfa, who then was general secretary of the Syrian Section of the Muslim Brotherhood, met Khaled Mesh'al in Khartoum on 6 and 7 March 2011, requesting him to transmit a message to Bashar al-Assad: if the latter wanted to save his regime, he had to take swift measures to prevent an uprising from occurring in Syria.[15]

The declarations of Hamas leaders draw a parallel between the mediation's failure and Hamas' departure from Damascus: 'We tried to explain to the regime that a political solution had to be imagined, but when we saw that it was rejecting this, we left.'[16] This chronological connection must, however, be questioned, since, several months after the end of discussions, Hamas was still in Syria. It appears that the movement at first chose to remain in Damascus and adopt a more 'wait-and-see' attitude. In December 2011, many sources referred to a decision by the Political Bureau calling for a gradual evacuation of its representatives to locations

---

11. 'Arab League asks for Hamas Help with Syria', *Reuters*, 6 January 2012.

12. 'Mesha'al Failed to Pass on Arab League's Message to al-Assad', *Asharq al-Awsat*, 20 January 2012.

13. *Al-Safir*, 27 December 2011.

14. *Al-Safir*, 9 January 2012.

15. *Arabi21*, 'Al-Bayanouni Clarifies Mesh'al's Speech Concerning the Mediation Between the Brotherhood and the Assad Regime', 16 November 2020.

16. Conversation with Imad a-Alami in Gaza, 18 March 2013.

outside Syria.[17] Most of them, born in Gaza, went back to their town or village of origin in the Strip, while others settled in Turkey, Jordan, Egypt, Lebanon or Qatar. Only leaders of lower rank in charge of the collection of funds and the families of leaders left the country, while high-ranking officials continued to travel episodically to Damascus to preserve their relations with Syrian leaders. A letter was apparently sent by Khaled Mesh'al to the executives of the outside offices to make them continue going to Syria provisionally in order to avoid a fuss. Many sources confirm that it was in an atmosphere of utmost secrecy that the decision to evacuate Syria was taken in December,[18] together with the choice of leaving some leaders there and preserving relations with Damascus. Other sources revealed that all elements of the military structure had left the country, and the only personnel still there were influential leaders.[19] The choice of leaving Syrian territory was made during the first year, simultaneously with keeping a presence of sorts there.

In order to overcome the dilemma resulting from the necessity of preserving the support of its Syrian and Iranian allies while making a rapprochement with Egypt and Qatar, the movement was able to find a compromise by effecting the departure of high executives from the outside leadership, while maintaining the symbolic presence of its main chiefs. In Arabic, there is a specific term to designate this presence next to other people, without implications of any form of allegiance: *tawâjud*.[20] Though this policy of 'presence in absence' allowed minimizing the political costs of a break with the Syrian regime, it may have also expressed Hamas' will to appear as a player opposed to Bashar al-Assad, a posture which would have been interesting for the movement on two accounts: on the one hand, to respond to the demands of a part Gaza's population, who very firmly supported the Syrian revolution,[21] on the other, preserve a space in post-Assad Syria, in case the latter was to endure the same fate as Mubarak, Ben Ali or even that of Gaddafi.[22] This desire to leave a 'presence in absence' was a way for Hamas to observe changes in the situation on the ground in Syria and minimize the cost of a bold or even rash political choice in favour of one side or the other. *Tawâjud* nevertheless was undeniably risky because the Syrian regime and Iran saw this as indirect backing

17. 'Hamas leadership Evacuates Families from Syria as Violence Escalates', *Haaretz*, 17 January 2012.

18. Ibid.

19. *Al-Sharq*, 12 February 2012.

20. The term was used in a *Haaretz* article, on 6 December 2012, and was adopted by Al-Quds. Derived from the verb *wujida*, 'to be present', this passive form implies recognition of a presence, but does mean an intention to take it into account. This noun is used, for instance, to describe the way religious minorities in Lebanon are living together.

21. For Valentina Napolitano, Hamas's decision to ban demonstrations in support of the Syrian revolution in the Gaza Strip bitterly disappointed the population. See Napolitano, V. (2013). Hamas and the Syrian uprising: A difficult choice. *Middle East Policy*, 20(3), 73-85.

22. Even though Syrian dissident Burhan Ghalioun announced in several declarations that after Bashar al-Assad's fall, the new regime would sever diplomatic relations revolving around the axis of Iran, Hezbollah and Hamas, *Wall Street Journal*, 26 March 2011.

of the opposition, while other regional players that Hamas was trying to woo considered this attitude as indirect backing of the Assad regime.

Siding with the Syrian uprising

Hamas had difficulties in maintaining a neutral stance when faced with pressure exerted on it by different sides to the conflict or by their backers, for instance, Sheikh al-Qaradawi, for whom the movement's inertia in Syria meant solidarity with Damascus,[23] or Bashar al-Assad himself, who demanded answers from Hamas about those critical of him. Asked to clarify its allegiances, Mesh'al was able to preserve an ambiguity of sorts: yet he neither managed to satisfy the Syrian president's requests nor did he explicitly condemn the Egyptian sheikh's words,[24] holding on to a sufficiently vague attitude to spare all sides:

> We consider what is happening in Syria to be an internal issue concerning our Syrian brothers. Hamas, abiding by its principles, nevertheless respects the aspirations and will of Arab and Islamic nations, and hopes this crisis will be overcome in [a] way that is favourable to the aspirations of the Syrian people, and which will preserve the country's stability and internal cohesion.[25]

Neutrality, or at least non-interference, was difficult to maintain when violence affected Palestinian refugees. On 6 June 2011, Syrian armed forces fired on demonstrators who were attempting to enter the occupied Golan Heights on the day of commemoration of the Naksa.[26] In August 2011, regime bombing in the al-Ramel camp in Latakia caused between 5,000 and 10,000 people to flee.[27] On 2 August, the Syrian Army bombed the Yarmouk camp, killing twenty-two people.[28] Some analysts stressed that Hamas, in the Yarmouk camp in particular (where the movement has social and familial connections), incited Palestinians to rebel against the Syrian regime.[29] Close to Hezbollah and the Lebanese Left, these sources remain, however, questionable.

It was only in February 2012 that Hamas permanently evacuated Syria, and even then, spokesmen did not officially acknowledge the departure and continued to deny any break with the regime: 'No, we have not left Syria, our leadership is still in Damascus. Some of the leaders have travelled during more or less long periods,

---

23. 'Qaradawi Condemns Atrocities Against Protesters in Syria', *Gulf Times*, 26 March 2011.
24. 'Khaled Mesha'al did not criticize Sheikh Qaradawi', *Ma'an News Agency*, 3 April 2011.
25. 'Hamas Stands by Syrian Brothers', *Ahram Online*, 3 April 2011.
26. The day of the *Naksa* commemorates on 5 June of each year the exodus of Palestinians resulting from the Israeli victory in the Six-Day War of 1967.
27. 'Syrian Enclave of Palestinians Nearly Deserted after Assault', *The New York Times*, 16 August 2011.
28. 'Syrian Army Resumes Shelling Yarmouk Camp', *Ma'an News Agency*, 4 August 2011.
29. https://al-akhbar.com/Arab/80493.

but the offices in Syria remain open. Hamas has not closed anything, not a single one of its offices.'[30]

Except for Ismail Haniyeh's sermon at the al-Azhar mosque in February 2012[31] and Salah Bardawil's declaration in Gaza during celebrations in the Khan Younis refugee camp,[32] both statements of support for the Syrian opposition, no official words were ever clearly uttered against Bashar al-Assad. It was only off the record that some leaders would give their opinion:

> Although relations with the Syrian regime were good, Hamas had no illusions about it. When the Americans occupied Iraq and threatened Syria, the Syrian president authorized thousands of Islamists to travel to Baghdad to fight the Americans, which led the Americans to retreat from the border with Syria. But when these fighters returned to Syria, Assad put them in jail. We have tried to help their families financially, but the regime has prevented us from doing this. This war will be very brutal and will only finish with the end of a long civil war, unless the West attacks Bashar al-Assad's palace to eliminate him.[33]

On 30 September 2012, while in Turkey, Khaled Mesh'al expressed for the first time his support for the Syrian 'revolution'.[34] According to some sources close to the Syrian regime and Hezbollah, the Izz al-Din al-Qassam brigades were participating actively in the war in Syria, on the side of the rebellion. They apparently shared their expertise with the Free Syrian Army by helping it dig tunnels during the Battle of al-Qusayr in May 2013.[35] As early as November 2012, a video broadcast by Syrian television was accusing Mesh'al of high treason. In it, one could see three Hamas fighters found dead in Syria with Ahmad Yassin's photograph. The funeral of one of the al-Qassam fighters, Mohammed al-Qneita, killed in Idlib, took place in Gaza in Ismail Haniyeh's presence.[36] Although Khaled Mesh'al has utterly rejected these allegations and claimed that the fighter killed in Idlib had left Hamas, these elements of information were reprinted by *Times* and *al-Ahram* as from the summer of 2013,[37] when several Western diplomats confirmed the

---

30. Conversation with Taher al-Nounou, the spokesperson of Hamas, Cairo, 25 February 2012.

31. '*I salute all Arab peoples, and I salute the courage of the Syrian people seeking freedom, democracy and reform*', Ismail Haniyeh, al-Azhar, Cairo, 24 February 2012.

32. Salah al-Bardawil sent a message of support to 'All Peoples That Are Not Yet Liberated, Their Blood Continuing *to* Flow Day After Day', CIP, 29 February 2012.

33. Conversation with a Hamas official who wishes to remain anonymous, Cairo, February 2012.

34. https://www.youtube.com/watch?v+ROBrYNcEyzE.

35. *Al-Akhbar English*, 21 June 2013.

36. https://www.youtube.com/watch?v=MqpzizljYKk.

37. *Al-Ahram*, 4 May 2013.

presence of Hamas combatants in the Palestinian camps of Damascus, Aleppo and Jaramana (an eastern suburb of the Syrian capital).[38]

It would be a mistake, however, to think that the presence of al-Qassam fighters in Syria was the result of coordination between Hamas and the Syrian Brotherhood. It is moreover simplistic to assume that the armed resistance to Assad in Syria, from 2011 onwards, was merely the result of decisions on the ground taken by the Muslim Brotherhood and its sympathizers. By providing military assistance to the Syrian rebels, Hamas nevertheless took a stance that was radically different to other organizations such as Islamic Jihad, which is indeed not affiliated to the Muslim Brotherhood. But its political stance in favour of the rebellion should not be understood as an ideological one. While Islamic Jihad considers that Qatar, Turkey and Egypt cannot ever replace the relations built among Palestinian factions, Syria and Iran in the last two decades, Hamas on the contrary considers the changing regional environment as conducive to support for its movement.[39]

The pro-revolution stance of Hamas, as formulated in September 2012, went through a major shift a year later, when, in October 2012 in Beirut, Khaled Mesh'al declared in front of journalists affiliated to the official Syrian TV channel al-Mayadeen: 'People have the right to rebel to defend their rights, but they must do so peacefully. Organizations fighting in Syria must point their rifles in the direction of Palestine.'[40]

Changes in the ratio of power on the ground were part of the explanation of this regional re-positioning of Hamas. The seizure of the Yarmouk Palestinian camp by Islamic State in April 2015 made the movement question more seriously the rationale of its military engagement on the rebels' side. The Jihadi threat led Khaled Mesh'al to open a dialogue with Ahmad Jibril, the general secretary of the Popular Front for the Liberation of Palestine – General Command (PFLP-GC) – Bashar al-Assad's loyal ally. This reorientation made the Syrian opposition doubt the sincerity of Hamas' commitment to the revolutionaries, and dissidents began to criticize, increasingly, its links with Tehran and Hezbollah. In an interview given on the internet site of *Orient-News* (one of the Syrian opposition's main TV channels), Melhem Daroubi, a member of the Syrian Muslim Brotherhood, estimated that Mesh'al's movement was stuck 'between the hammer of Iranian support and the anvil of al-Assad's oppression.'[41] In addition, the storming of Yarmouk by Islamic

---

38. *Al-Mayadeen*, 3 October 2013.

39. Nicolas Dot-Pouillard, 'Les Palestiniens déchirés par la crise syrienne', Orient Xxi, October 2013.

40. The Aknaf Beit al-Maqdis Brigades were the main conduct for Hamas' military intervention and may have then gathered 200 fighters. They fought the regime, but also PFLP-GC forces, as well as Fatah Intifada, Saiqa, which are factions nevertheless linked to Hamas within the Alliance of Palestinian Forces opposing the Oslo Agreements since 1993. See Nicolas Dot-Pouillard, '*Yarmouk,* Divisions Palestiniennes Face à l'organisation de l'Etat islamique*'*, Orient Xxi, April 2015.

41. See Wissam al-Haj and Nicolas Dot-Pouillard, *Orient Xxi*, March 2015.

State may have been facilitated by the reversal of the al-Nosra front's stand. Al-Nosra, the official branch of al-Qaeda in Syria, appears to have chosen to sever links with Hamas after the Mesh'al/Larijani meeting in Doha on 11 March.[42]

The 'Rejectionist Front' weakened by the Syrian crisis

The Islamic Republic: An unfailing partner

Though the first signs of a meaningful rapprochement with Iran appeared as early as 2006, it was above all in the wake of the events of June 2007 that the movement consolidated its alliance with the Islamic Republic, as seen in the various above-mentioned meetings.

According to some observers, this alliance went through a brief chill during 'Cast Lead'. This suggests that Hamas may have been disappointed with the lack of Iranian support during Israel's aggression of Gaza, in comparison with the backing Tehran had provided Hezbollah in July 2006.[43] These observations echo Israeli analyses, which consider that 'Cast Lead' was a disaster for Iranian interests.[44] This cold spell, nevertheless, did not put an end to diplomatic activity between the Palestinian movement and the Islamic Republic.

Iranian leaders were the first foreign politicians Hamas encountered after 'Cast Lead'. The meeting took place in January 2009 in Damascus. Khaled Mesh'al thanked Iran for its vital role in the victory.[45] Likewise, Iran was the first state Hamas travelled to after the war, when, in February 2009, a delegation from the movement went to Tehran to talk to Ali Khamenei and Mahmoud Ahmadinejad. Mesh'al then emphasized: 'All Islamic parties will form a united front with Iran against Israel, if Israel decides to attack the Islamic republic. Regional resistance is capable of confronting the Israeli danger. It is the honour of Palestine and the Umma.'[46]

In February 2010, Khaled Mesh'al met Ahmadinejad once more in Bashar al-Assad's presidential palace and declared that any renewed aggression on Gaza would be considered as an 'aggression of the three components involved in the resistance'.[47]

---

42. Nicolas Dot-Pouillard, 'Yarmouk: divisions palestiniennes face à l'organisation de l'État islamique', *Orient Xxi*, April 2015.

43. These interpretations consider that Hamas had acquired a real expertise in smuggling networks, which would have reduced its dependence on Iran. Abu Amer, *Al-monitor*.

44. Alex Fishman, 'So that the Iranians won't Reach Gaza', *Yediot Aharonot*, 17 January 2009.

45. 'Hamas Leaders Praise Iran for Help in Gaza Fight', *Associated Press*, 2 February 2009.

46. *Filastin al-Muslima*, January 2010.

47. *Filastin al-Muslima*, April 2010.

Ismail Haniyeh also confirmed his solidarity towards Iran in case of an Israeli attack against Tehran. In September 2010, he declared: 'We are a single united front against the enemies of Islam.'[48] Two months later, in November 2010, Ahmed Yousef sent an invitation to Mahmoud Ahmadinejad to visit Gaza. These elements illustrate the resilience and permanency of a strong alliance between the two Middle Eastern players.[49]

The time of dissent

The breaking of relations with Bashar al-Assad's regime immediately raised the issue of the continued alliance with Iran. Many Iranian leaders warned Hamas: if links with Bashar were severed, Hamas would suffer an end to subsidies, weapon deliveries and military training provided to its armed branch in Iran.[50] These threats, however, did not materialize. Despite the departure of the external leadership from Damascus in February 2012, Iran continued to fund Hamas. Leaving Syria coincided furthermore with Ismail Haniyeh's visit to Tehran, during which the latter reiterated the maximalist stance of his movement and his unswerving support to 'the rejectionist front'.

Decline in Iranian backing occurred later in two stages. In the summer of 2012, approximately five months after Hamas' permanent departure from Damascus, Iran apparently reduced by half the economic assistance provided to the movement, which decreased from 150 million to less than $75 million yearly.

The second stage of wavering Iranian links occurred several months after 'Pillar of Defence'. Once more, Iran decided to reduce by half its financial aid to Hamas. This decision coincided with the Battle of al-Qusayr in May 2013, during which militants of the al-Qassam Brigades fought Syrian regime forces and those of Hezbollah. Faced with this military interference, it was very awkward for Iran and Hezbollah to continue supporting Hamas, since the Hezbollah had actively participated in the aforementioned battle, therefore fighting the al-Qassam Brigades on Syrian territory. This episode was a heavy blow to the axis linking Hamas, Iran and Hezbollah.

On 3 May 2013, Yusuf al-Qaradawi's sermon in the mosque of Doha, in Khaled Mesh'al's presence,[51] made Iran very unhappy. The Egyptian sheikh described the Shia Lebanese Party as the 'party of Satan' and the Islamic Republic as 'the ally of

---

48. Interview with Ismail Haniyeh, *Markaz al-filastînî li-l-i'lâm*, 7 September 2010.

49. 'Hamas invites Ahmadinejad to visit Gaza Strip', *Jerusalem Post*, 8 November 2010.

50. Conversation with Sayyid Abou Musameh, Geneva, 19 January 2012.

51. *Al-Quds al-Arabi*, 3 June 2013.

Zionism'.⁵² Then on 17 June 2013 another event was the source of much irritation for the Iranians: in an official communiqué, Khaled Mesh'al called on Hezbollah to pull out of Syria and stop fighting side by side with Bashar al-Assad's forces. Wafiq Safa (the Lebanese Hezbollah's man in charge of security) then ordered Ali Barakat (the representative of Hamas in Lebanon) to close his seven offices in the southern suburbs of Beirut and leave Lebanon as soon as possible.⁵³ Safa apparently told Hamas' representative that the latter's movement had chosen to side with Qatar and therefore with 'Israel's side'. The cooling of relations with Iran was moreover confirmed by the Gaza government's vice-minister of Foreign Affairs Ghazi Hamad, who declared on 19 June 2013 that links with the Islamic Republic were not as fundamental as in the past, although contacts had not been cut.⁵⁴

Towards a warming up of relations with Shia partners?

In the summer of 2013, Hamas tried to re-establish good relations with the Islamic Republic. In June, the movement's leaders decided to set up two delegations, one travelling to Beirut and the other to Tehran.⁵⁵ In mid-October of that year, however, while Khaled Mesh'al had planned to visit Iran after his stay in Lebanon, Iranian authorities asked him to postpone his trip. Despite a speech in Beirut calling on Syrian rebels to surrender their weapons, Iran refused to receive the Political Bureau's president. Official sources have confirmed this request for cancellation, while adding that it solely concerned Khaled Mesh'al. According to Ahmed Yousef, a secret visit did nonetheless take place, but no precisions were given on the identity of the leaders invited.⁵⁶ Osama Hamdan, the ex-representative of Hamas in Lebanon, may have gone to Beirut's Iranian embassy to deliver a message of friendship on behalf of Khaled Mesh'al.⁵⁷ On 9 December 2013, Mahmoud al-Zahar congratulated Iran for recent progress in negotiations on its nuclear programme and stated that relations between his movement and the Islamic Republic had been re-established.⁵⁸

On 10 March 2014, the resumption of relations was officially announced by the Iranian parliament's president Ali Larijani: 'Iran supports Hamas because it is a resistance movement. [. . .] Our relationship with Hamas is good and has gone back to what it was. We have no problem with Hamas.'⁵⁹

On 8 December 2014, a delegation from Hamas led by Mohammed Nasr travelled to Iran. This two-day meeting's goal was to prepare Khaled Mesh'al's

52. *Al-Shourouk Online*, 4 May 2013.
53. *Al-Quds al-Arabi*, 11 June 2013.
54. *Al-Masri al-Youm*, 19 June 2013.
55. *Al-Quds al-Arabi*, 3 June 2013.
56. *Al-Quds al-Arabi*, 23 October 2013.
57. *Alalam*, 30 November 2013.
58. *BBC Arabic*, 9 December 2013.
59. *Noqta*, 11 March 2014.

visit.⁶⁰ He, however, was still persona non grata in Tehran. The Mesh'al-Larijani meeting on 11 March 2015, which took place in Doha, marked the beginning of normalization of relations with the Hamas Political Bureau president who, in the eyes of many Syrian and Iranian dignitaries, continued to appear as a traitor. Full reconciliation with Tehran seemed to require Bashar al-Assad's prior consent.

The incipient warming up followed reconciliation with Hezbollah, sanctioned by Hassan Nasrallah during his TV interview on *al-Mayadeen* channel on 15 January 2015. Hezbollah's general secretary declared that relations with Hamas had never been severed and had actually improved since 2012. In addition, he confirmed that it was Hamas that wished to distance itself from Hezbollah and not the reverse. He nevertheless emphasized that Hamas and Syria, partners in the 'rejectionist front', did not wish to re-establish their relations for the moment.⁶¹ This speech was given a few days before the Israeli attack in the Syrian Golan Heights, during which several Iranian high-ranking officials and others from Hezbollah (including Jihad Mughniyeh, son of ex-leader Imad Mughniyeh assassinated in Damascus in 2008) were killed. This military strike was followed by several declarations of support from Hamas to Hezbollah.⁶² Ismail Haniyeh and Mohammed Deif sent two letters of condolences to Hassan Nasrallah, highlighting once more the strategic convergence with Hezbollah in its confrontation against Israel.⁶³ The warming of relations with Iran was upset, however, by Khaled Mesh'al's visit to Saudi Arabia in July 2015, which was interpreted as a sign of a growing rift with Tehran.⁶⁴ The Iranian Fars Press Agency, moreover, confirmed that Riyadh had demanded that 700 al-Qassam Brigade combatants participate in the fighting against the Houthis in Yemen, an information officially denied by Hamas' spokesman.⁶⁵ According to a source quoted by the Arabic version of the Huffington Post, Iran cancelled the planned visit of a Hamas delegation to Tehran as a reaction to the meeting between Khaled Mesh'al and King Salman.⁶⁶

The war in Yemen was a factor explaining Iranian irritation with Hamas. Although formulated with much caution to avoid accusations of bias in favour of either one of the two sides, Hamas' communiqué on 30 March 2015 was interpreted by Iranian authorities as tacit support for President Mansour Hadi and Saudi Arabia. While Islamic Jihad and the PFLP had clearly condemned Saudi aggression, the neutrality of Hamas, which emphasized 'the right of Arab states to make their own countries secure', was tantamount to the Iranians' opinion to tacit approval of the military coalition headed by the Saudis. Though Iran did not officially react to Hamas' communiqué, a former member of the Iranian Shoura

60. *Alresalah*, 9 December 2014.
61. *Al-Mayadeen*, 15 January 2015.
62. Adnan Abu Amer, *Al-monitor*, 27 January 2015.
63. *Al-akhbar*, 20 July 2015.
64. *Al-Nahar*, 27 February 2015.
65. Official communiqué of the Movement of Islamic Resistance, 19 July 2015.
66. *Huffpostarabi*, 8 August 2015.

Council apparently stated that Hamas 'has not learnt any lessons from its previous stand on Syria', and that its position demonstrated 'a bias in favour of Saudi Arabia, which means that Hamas is turning its back – for the second time – on the one supporting it with money and weapons'.[67] Torn between the necessity of restoring relations with Iran and not alienating the Gulf states, Hamas likewise remained silent when faced with GCC countries naming Hezbollah a terrorist organization.[68]

The position of Hamas regarding Yemen should be understood as a response to the decrease in Iranian backing, which, if one is to believe the declarations of Palestinian leaders, has apparently not returned to past levels. In January 2016, an excerpt from a telephone conversation of Moussa Abu Marzouk, which stated that 'all they say on support for the resistance is nothing but a lie' was leaked to the press.[69] The leader of Hamas declared that Iran would continue to make its financial aid conditional.[70] On 15 March 2016, Khaled Mesh'al followed suit by declaring that Iran had put an end to its assistance to the Movement of Islamic Resistance because of the latter's stance on the Syrian revolution.[71] These words, however, did not prevent Hamas leaders from visiting Tehran in February and March 2016, on the occasion of the thirty-seventh anniversary of the Islamic Revolution.

Bombings of the city of Aleppo in December 2016 reactivated tensions. On 14 December, after condemnation by, respectively, Mahmoud al-Zahar[72] and Khalil al-Hayya of the massacre of Syrian civilians,[73] Hamas published an official communiqué denouncing the 'genocide' in Aleppo, while stopping short of clearly pointing out the Assad regime's responsibility.[74] Hamas security services in Gaza simultaneously arrested several figures who had expressed their satisfaction at the retaking of Aleppo by Hezbollah and the Syrian regime's army.[75] Although Hamas leaders claimed to refuse to take sides, emphasizing their statements expressed only humanitarian considerations supporting displaced populations affected by the bombings, Iranians saw it as another sign of an alignment on foreign powers, namely Qatar and Turkey.

As profound as they were, these disagreements did not prevent Iran and Hamas from introducing themselves as partners of a common resistance front.

---

67. *Info-Palestine*, 12 April 2015.

68. The mention of Hezbollah as a terrorist organization occurred on 2 March 2016. It was nevertheless denounced by the PFLP and Islamic Jihad, which publicly expressed their support to the Lebanese movement; *Al-Monitor*, 10 March 2016.

69. The excerpt of this phone conversation can be head on the *Al-Arabiya* website, 31 January 2016.

70. *Al-Sharq Al-Awsat*, 31 January 2016.

71. *Arabi21*, 15 March 2016.

72. *Safa*, Palestinian Press Agency, 16 December 2016.

73. https://www.youtube.com/watch?v=CuMriM7BKRQ.

74. https://hamas.ps/ar/post/6529/%D8%AA%D8%B5%D8%.

75. This was the case of Hicham Salem, the representative of Al-Sabireen in Gaza. *Al-Monitor*, 29 December 2016.

The year 2017 favoured this rapprochement, facilitated by the renewal of leading bodies inside Hamas. Khaled Mesh'al's replacement by Ismail Haniyeh, and the ascent to power of leaders like Yahya al-Sinwar and Salah al-Arouri, reputed to be close to Iran, favoured this renewed alliance.[76] This was mentioned by the Hamas representative in Iran, Khaled al-Qaddoumi.[77] According to him, although no official visit had gone to Tehran since February 2016, meetings outside this country never ceased.

The rapprochement between Iran and the Islamic Resistance was also eased by the renewed friendship between Hamas and Hezbollah. Between January and June 2017, Moussa Abu Marzouk spoke several times with Hassan Nasrallah.[78] While Hamas had not condemned the GCC states' inclusion of Hezbollah on the list of terrorist organizations, it displayed its support for the Lebanese Shia Party when on 20 November 2017 the latter was labelled once more 'terrorist' (this time by the Arab League). Links with Hezbollah allowed Hamas to consolidate its relationship with Tehran, and Iran was an unavoidable entrance point to re-establish relations with Bashar al-Assad's regime. In February 2018, when the Syrian Army shot down an Israeli F-16 warplane over Syrian territory, the al-Qassam Brigades officially expressed their support for Damascus. On the occasion of Salah al-Arouri's visit to Tehran in July 2019, Ismail Haniyeh mentioned the 'lesson' of the departure from Damascus and hoped for return to a strong Syria.[79] At the same time, from Moscow, Moussa Abu Marzouk was emphasizing that relations with Iran had never been severed.[80]

Egypt: Between revolution and return to the old order

A conflictual relationship under Hosni Mubarak's rule

Already at a very low ebb in 2006, relations between Hamas and Egypt further deteriorated following the June 2007 events, when Cairo imposed a severe embargo on the Gaza Strip.[81] From this date, Hamas began accusing Egypt of all sins. The

---

76. At the end of May 2017, several Iranian officials congratulated Ismail Haniyeh for his victory in elections, particularly Ali Larijani, the president of the Islamic Consultative Assembly, Mohammad Javad (the minister of Foreign Affairs), General Qassem Soleimani (the commander of the al-Quds force of the Iranian Revolutionary Guards). See *Al-Monitor*, 2 June 2017. As for Salah al-Arouri, he has apparently travelled to Iran more than five times since his election in February 2017. *The Times of Israel*, 22 July 2019.
77. *Al-Monitor*, 9 February 2017.
78. http://www.alquds.com/articles/1497448393934968300/.
79. *Al-Arabiyya*, 21 July 2019.
80. *RT Online*, 16 July 2019.
81. The embargo put in place following Gaza's seizure by Hamas in June 2007 dramatically debilitated the Strip's entire economy. All crossing points, including that of

main statements of the movement's leaders were particularly full of insults against Mubarak's regime, blaming it for the closure of the Rafah crossing.[82]

The first episode illustrating this deterioration occurred on the night of 23 January 2008, when an explosion, attributed to Hamas, made a gap in the barrier separating Gaza from Egypt, near Rafah. Clashes had begun the day before between Egyptian armed forces and Hamas militants demanding the opening of the Rafah border crossing. Seeking to prevent Palestinian activists from taking advantage of the barrier's breach to reinforce their stocks of weaponry, the Egyptians deployed troops around the border, gradually restricting circulation. According to UN estimates, this hole in the fence provoked the sudden entrance of hundreds of thousands of Palestinians into Sinai, searching for various foodstuffs. The border between Gaza and Egypt was totally sealed on 3 February 2008.

Sources confirmed the rapprochement between the Egyptian Muslim Brotherhood and Hamas at the moment of the opening of the breach.[83] The Brothers apparently exerted much pressure on Egyptian authorities, mobilizing the population in favour of Hamas at a moment when the latter were damaging the fence with explosives. In their attempt to weaken Hosni Mubarak's regime, they seem to have used the Brotherhood's international network to support Hamas and obtain the lifting of the blockade, particularly during trips of some leading Muslim Brother figures from Europe.[84] Various sources have thus mentioned Khaled Mesh'al's demand to the Brotherhood's Supreme Guide to 'excite' Egyptian public opinion in order to mitigate pressures suffered by Hamas in Gaza.[85] Before forcing the border, Hamas explicitly asked the Brothers to plan demonstrations so as to 'prepare the atmosphere', as a way of forcing the authorities to take the Egyptian street into account.[86]

The Brothers then organized a series of protests supporting Hamas in various regions of Egypt in order to prepare public opinion.[87] This does not automatically mean they were doing the bidding of Hamas. Quite the opposite, these meetings

---

Rafah, were sealed, except for the importation of humanitarian aid. Are Hovdenak, *Prio Report*, 3. Oslo: PRIO, March 2010.

82. Jihad al-Khazin, *al-Hayat*, 10 January 2009.

83. According to the *al-Khamis* newspaper, in its edition of 12 July 2007, which claims to have obtained its sources from the Brotherhood's Guidance Bureau.

84. This was in order to lobby embassies, NGOs and civil society in the Arab and Muslim world, in particular in Yemen, Algeria, Syria, Iran, Pakistan, Indonesia, Sudan, Malaysia and South Africa.

85. On 31 January 2008, in the newspaper *al-Masri al-Youm*, Khayri Ramadan formulated specific allegations on coordination between the Egyptian Brothers and Hamas.

86. *Al-Mussawwar*, 8 February 2008.

87. According to scholar Tewfik Aclimandos, precautionary measures taken by security officials in Cairo were impressive, but the regime could also display a certain laxness in the provinces, where the deployment of policemen was more low-key, 'La onzième plaie d'Egypte', *Outre-Terre* 22, no. 2 (2009): 159–66.

were organized by the Brotherhood in accordance with its own interests. Although as from January 2008 the Egyptian Brothers made Hamas' main claims their own, notably those related to the opening of border crossings, it was essential to compete with the Egyptian regime. Looking for a part to play in the resolution of the conflict between the two main Palestinian factions, the Brothers also tried to substitute for Hosni Mubarak by appearing as the most capable of organizing a dialogue between Fatah and Hamas. Mohammed Habib, the vice-supreme guide of the Brotherhood, appears to have met Khaled Mesh'al, Mahmoud al-Zahar and Fatah representative Nabil Shaath on several occasions.[88] Sami Abou Zouhri, the Hamas spokesman, emphasized that though the Brotherhood played a central part in the wall's explosion, it was to allow the Brothers to sponsor an attempt at reconciliation between the two main Palestinian factions. He added that Khaled Mesh'al and Mahdi Akef were in permanent contact to determine the Brothers' contribution to the Palestinian cause.[89]

Relations between Cairo and Hamas underwent serious deterioration prior to 'Cast Lead', since both sides blamed the other for the failure of Palestinian reconciliation and the truce with Israel. Egypt accused Hamas of launching hostilities, while the latter excoriated Egypt's silence, furious in particular at Tzipi Livni's presence in Cairo a few hours before the Israeli offensive.[90] Hamas spokesman Fawzi Barhoum insisted on the fact that these raids began just after the meeting between Hosni Mubarak and Tzipi Livni. It was from this moment that the threat of Hamas' destruction took shape. The spokesman also accused Cairo of high treason, stating that Egyptian intelligence services had provided false information, informing him on 26 December of the possibility of a truce as early as the following day. Yet 27 December was the date of the start of the offensive. As for Mohammad Nazzal, he declared that the Egyptian Foreign Affairs minister Ahmad Abou al-Gheit had adopted during the first days of the offensive an attitude of 'double standards', putting the onus of responsibility solely on the victims.[91]

After the military assault against Gaza, new crises punctuated Egypt's relationship with Hamas, particularly during the pilgrimage to Mecca (*Hajj*). Hamas accused Egypt of not letting pilgrims exit Gaza, while Cairo and the Ramallah authority alleged that Hamas was responsible for the closure of the crossing points by prohibiting pilgrims not affiliated with the movement to get out of Gaza.[92] In March 2009, Egyptian authorities confiscated the goods of Hamas leaders who

88. *Al-Mal*, 10 February 2008.
89. *Al-Masri al-Youm*, 29 January 2008.
90. Tewfik Aclimandos, 'La onzième plaie d'Egypte', *Outre-Terre* 22, no. 2 (2009): 159–66.
91. Abd al-Hamid al-Kayyali, *Dirâsa fi-l-'aduwân al-isâ'ilî 'âla qitâ' Ghazza, Markaz al-Zaytûna li-l-dirâsat wa-l-istishârât* (Beirut, 2009).
92. The Egyptian viewpoint is defended by the political commentator Jamal 'Abd al-Jawwad in the *Nahdat Misr* issue of 3 December 2008.

were attempting to import them into the Strip through tunnels.[93] According to Ismail al-Ashkar, Egypt has seized some fifty million dollars from Hamas since the imposition of the blockade.[94] In December 2009, Egypt's construction of a metal barrier on its border with Gaza was aimed at stopping smuggling[95] going through Hamas-controlled tunnels[96] and stoked new tensions between the Islamic Resistance and Cairo.

Limited coordination during Mohammed Morsi's presidency

Although the link between Hamas and the Egyptian Muslim Brotherhood is explicitly mentioned in the Charter,[97] the filiation of the movement was emphasized in October 2011: Hamas joined the Muslim Brotherhood, adding to its acronym 'Movement of Islamic Resistance', the mention 'Section of the Muslim Brothers'.[98] The Arab revolts therefore 'clarified' this relationship. Sayyid Abou Musameh thus details: 'We, Hamas, have always been Muslim Brothers, this is not new. This appears like it's something new, but is in fact quite old. It is nevertheless true that the Arab revolutions have helped clarify this situation.'[99]

On 29 October 2011, a high-level delegation of the Brotherhood went to Gaza. Yet it was following the victory of the Egyptian Muslim Brothers in the parliamentary and presidential elections (in succession, in January and June 2012), that the rapprochement became more obvious. This victory coincided with the departure of the external leadership from Syria, enabling Hamas to more

---

93. According to *al-Dustur* on 19 March 2009, they seized in Mohammed Hajjaj's personal effects 452,000 euros and $260,000, three compasses, two GPSs, a suitcase for solar energy, mobile cell phones in those of Mohammed Mahmoud Jindiyya and finally two pairs of night-vision goggles in Wa'il Abou Diyab's luggage.

94. '*Ashkar says Egypt has confiscated $50 million from Hamas' smuggled money over the years*', '*Gaza: A castle in the Sand*', *al-Ahram*, 2 September 2010.

95. Egypt may have built the wall to secure American economic aid. See House Report 110–497, Section 690, Making Appropriations for the Department of State, Foreign Operations, and Related Programs for the Fiscal Year Ending 30 September 2008, '11th Congress, 1st Session' 17 December 2007.

96. According to Graham Usher, during the year 2009 Hamas collected between 150 and 200 million dollars, thanks to the revenue from tunnel traffic; 'Gaza: A Castle in the Sand', *al-Ahram*, 2 September 2010. In total for 2008 and 2009, traffic transiting through the tunnels was estimated to be between 200 and 400 million dollars, and would represent between 65 and 90 per cent of supplies for the interior market, 'Smuggling Fuels Gaza's Stalled Economy', *BBC*, 31 December 2009.

97. See Khaled Khroub, *Hamas, Political Thought and Practice* (Washington: Institute for Palestinian Studies, 2000), 148.

98. See *Roz*, 11 December 2011, which confirms Nathan Brown and Mahdi Abd al-Hedi's analysis.

99. Conversation with Sayyid Abou Musameh in Geneva, 19 January 2012.

easily get closer to the Brotherhood in Cairo.[100] On 16 March 2013, Khaled Mesh'al travelled to the Brotherhood's headquarters in Mokattam to meet Supreme Guide Mohammed Badie and reaffirm the principle of Hamas' non-interference.[101]

> The Muslim Brothers have a working method, which is that of total decentralization. We do not take common decisions with them: they do not meddle in our affairs and we, likewise, stay outside of theirs; if not this would mean that we would enter into the politics of the states they are in. Nowadays, even in Egypt, they do not intervene in our politics, there is a form of empathy. There are visits but no coordination.[102]

Notwithstanding the last part of this statement, relations between Hamas and the Muslim Brothers have been marked by deep coordination. The issue of holding internal elections inside Hamas in Cairo illustrated this solidarity and the warm connections between both parties. While Mohammed Morsi had at first demanded from Hamas that it postpone elections, in order to reduce tension in Egypt,[103] he finally decided to allow them to go ahead in Cairo on 31 March 2013, despite the Egyptian Army's reluctance.[104] Mohammed Badie, moreover, was present during the opening ceremony of the elections. The Egyptian president therefore chose to validate Mesh'al's demand against the Egyptian Army's will.[105] The armed forces criticized Morsi for his proximity with Hamas and was opposed to Hamas holding elections in Egypt for its Political Bureau.

Apart from organizing elections in Cairo, Moussa Abu Marzouk, vice-president of the Political Bureau of Hamas, was able to settle down in Cairo in February 2012 and open an office. These political gains for Hamas and this renewed diplomatic coordination with the Egyptian executive did not, however, prevent the Egyptian armed forces from acting against Hamas. Indeed, the rapprochement with Morsi could be a cause for a stiffening of the Egyptian Army's position, namely Gaza, forcing the closure of tunnels linking the Strip to Sinai. The first wave of destructions took place in the summer of 2012,[106] a second in early 2013. This was

---

100. Nathan Brown, 'Is Hamas Mellowing?', *Carnegie Endowment*, 17 January 2012.
101. *Al-Masri al-Youm*, 16 March 2013.
102. Conversation with Sayyid Abu Musameh in Geneva, 19 January 2012.
103. *Ahramonline*, 31 March 2013.
104. Internal elections inside Hamas take place every four years. Prior to the departure of the external leadership from Damascus, these elections used to take place in Syria. The members of the consultative *majlis al-shûrâ* assembly meet to choose the Political Bureau's chairman. These internal elections had begun in April 2012.
105. *Ma'an News*, 1 April 2013.
106. The Kerem Shalom attack in August 2012 provoked the temporary closure of tunnels and the Rafah border crossing, which caused a price hike in construction materials of 40–60 per cent.

done by the deliberate flooding of the tunnels.[107] President Morsi has indeed very restricted control over the tactical decision of the Egyptian armed forces.

The campaign against Hamas and the ousting of Mohammed Morsi

As of March 2013, a huge anti-Morsi campaign also hurt Hamas: Morsi's 'favours' to the Islamist movement were hotly disputed by a sector of Egyptian society, in particular by the army. This institution had always been apprehensive and extremely distrustful of Hamas, worried by the movement's supposed plan to administratively detach Gaza from the West Bank. The army also reproached Morsi for his protection of Hamas, which, according to the armed forces, was responsible for the Kerem Shalom attack that killed sixteen Egyptian border guards on 5 August 2012.[108] Associated with Mohammed Morsi, Hamas became, in Egypt, and as of March 2013, the favoured target of an anti-Brotherhood media campaign.

Many in Egypt denounced the involvement of Hamas in the February 2011 'Battle of the Camel', during which many demonstrators were killed on Tahrir Square. The movement was also blamed for being involved in the forceful storming of prisons, notably the one in Wadi al-Natrun where Mohammed Morsi was jailed.[109] With the latter's election to the presidency, the rise of anti-Brotherhood feelings in Egyptian public opinion accelerated the discredit of Hamas.[110] A hostile campaign was led by a number of Egyptian newspapers, and it became particularly wide ranging as from 14 March 2012, when the *al-Ahram* daily published the names of three political and military officials belonging to Hamas, allegedly involved in the attacks against the Kerem Shalom border post: Mohammed Ibrahim Abou Shamala, Raed Attar (one of the men responsible for Gilad Shalit's abduction) and Ayman Nofal.[111] The assault on the border post may have been a revenge for the destruction of many smuggling tunnels by the Egyptian Army a few days earlier. An anonymous military source quoted by *al-Shourouk* confirmed that the sponsors of these attacks had entered Egypt from Gaza through these very tunnels. In the opinion of the Egyptian military chief-of-staff, the involvement of Hamas

---

107. Khalil al-Hayya demanded that Egypt open the Rafah crossing. He emphasized that tunnels were the people's only choice to confront the blockade, *al-Arabiyya*, 16 February 2013.

108. A border post between Egypt and Israel was attacked by thirty-five armed men, an operation which led to the death of sixteen Egyptian border guards and the loss of an Egyptian armoured vehicle, which was captured to attack the Kerem Shalom crossing at the intersection of the borders of Gaza, Egypt and Israel.

109. *Ahramonline*, 12 May 2013.

110. *Al-Masri al-Youm*, 26 April 2013.

111. A member of Hamas' military wing, this prisoner had managed to escape during an attack against the prison on 28 January 2011.

and its armed branch in the attacks was absolutely certain. Mohammed Morsi was accused of silencing the names of officials to protect the Palestinian organization.

This campaign was also based on the alleged presence of training camps in Northern Sinai, where Hamas appeared to have banded with al-Qaida and the *Ansar al-Jihad* Egyptian armed group.[112] Many Egyptian media became increasingly receptive to the theory that there was a project to increase the surface of the Gaza Strip and make it a viable territory at Sinai's expense. They were anxiously following the statements of certain Israeli and American think tanks on the matter.[113] Hamas thus appeared as a 'third force' involved in the confrontation between pro- and anti-Muslim Brothers.[114] A number of newspapers also spread the news that 7,000 Hamas fighters were in charge of guaranteeing President Morsi's security on Egyptian territory. These rumours contributed to paint an extremely negative picture of Hamas, described as a foreign militia attempting to play a part in the protection normally entrusted to the country's police.[115] At the bottom of this campaign was the issue of respect for Egypt's sovereignty – which Hamas was accused of having violated – and the fear that Hamas would drag Egypt under Muslim Brotherhood rule into a catastrophic adventure (*tawrît*), which Hamas was accused of having violated. Thus the discredit affecting the Brotherhood also hurt the Islamic Resistance Movement until Morsi was deposed by the army on 3 July 2013.

Egypt extends the 'war against terrorism' to Gaza

Since Mohammed Morsi's fall, Hamas leaders have energetically denied any meddling in Egypt's internal affairs. As of July, the declarations of the movement's leaders reiterated the principle of non-interference[116] and Egypt's right to do everything to safeguard its national interests.[117] Ahmed Yousef declared that Hamas had sent a letter to the new administration with the hope that Cairo change its attitude with respect to Hamas.[118] And yet, these same Hamas leaders

---

112. *Ahramonline*, 28 March 2013.

113. According to Mohammed Qadri Said, one of the experts in military affairs of the *al-Ahram* Centre for Strategic Studies, Hamas has always kept an eye on Sinai and does not consider this territory as falling within Egyptian sovereignty.

114. Accusations particularly focused on the supposedly nefarious role played by Hamas during the confrontation between pro- and anti-Morsi demonstrators in December 2012, in front of the Presidential Palace (an accusation not substantiated by facts), see *Ahramonline*, 29 March 2013.

115. *Ahramonline*, 22 March 2013.

116. Hamas spokesman Abou Zouhri has denied that Hamas members were jailed in Egypt, *Palestinian Information Centre*, 4 September 2013.

117. Speech in Gaza by Ismail Haniyeh on the occasion of the Aid al-Adha holiday, 19 October 2013.

118. *Al-Quds*, 23 October 2013.

had officially emphasized that the overthrow of President Morsi was nothing more than a military 'coup' (*inqilâb*).

Faced with these contradictory statements, General Abd al-Fattah al-Sissi chose to strike the Palestinian Islamist movement harshly.[119] He began destroying smuggling tunnels, which placed Hamas on the verge of bankruptcy, with losses estimated at more than 230 million dollars. Simultaneously, Cairo drew closer to the political adversaries of Hamas in the Gaza Strip by sponsoring new coup attempts. Fatah indeed saw an opportunity to reinforce itself from Egypt and backed the popular mobilization of the movement of rebellion (*tamarrud*) against Hamas, planned in Gaza for 11 November 2013 (the anniversary of Yasser Arafat's death). According to the rebellion movement's spokesman, who dismissed all implications of Egyptian intelligence or of Ramallah's Palestinian Authority, the mobilization was finally cancelled to allegedly avoid a bloodbath.[120] For Hamas, however, the absence of any demonstrations on this day was proof that it still enjoyed substantial popularity in Gaza. General al-Sisi, moreover, has not excluded the possibility of a limited military intervention in the Strip, should the internal situation in the territory threaten Egypt's security. By asphyxiating more than 1,800,000 inhabitants, the Egyptian military expected that they would all turn against their leaders. This strategy recalls that of the years 2006–7 when, in the wake of Hamas' election victory, Quartet members had imposed a blockade with the hope that economic suffocation would lead to political collapse.

The new Egyptian administration finally accused Hamas of collaborating with al-Qaida. While one of Mohammed Morsi's goals had been to convince the United States to remove Hamas from the list of terrorist organizations, it was now the turn of the Egyptian Muslim Brotherhood to be designated as such by the new Egyptian government. Identified with the Egyptian Association, Hamas has suffered from this assimilation.

The equivalence of Hamas with terrorism was also staunchly put forward by several Fatah leaders, such as Yasser Abed Rabbo, who has excoriated Hamas for backing Jihadi extremists in Sinai. President Mahmoud Abbas apparently even provided Egypt with a number of documents proving Hamas' guilt. Although it is difficult to verify the truth of these allegations, one can nevertheless stress that the 'war' declared against Hamas has allowed the Egyptian Army to reinsert its struggle against the Brotherhood within a regional perspective, providing it with more credibility. By emphasizing the 'collaboration' between the Egyptian Brotherhood and Hamas, the al-Sissi regime has hence tried to brandish the scarecrow of the terrorist threat.

The deterioration of relations between Egypt and Hamas was an explanation for some of the motivations of 'Protective Edge' in summer 2014. General al-Sisi's

---

119. Mahmoud Jaraba, 'Hamas in the Post-Morsi Period', *Carnegie Endowment*, 1 August 2013.

120. Fatah spokesman Ahmad Assaf also denied any involvement of his movement in the rebellion in Gaza, see *al-Masri al-Youm*, 11 November 2013.

animosity towards Hamas undoubtedly jeopardized the mediation, resulting in a war longer and costlier in human lives.

For some, 'Protective Edge' cannot be considered as a simple face-to-face confrontation between Israel and Hamas, because General al-Sisi played such a central role in it, which he saw both as the extension of an internal conflict against the Muslim Brotherhood and as a means to consolidate a regional axis associating Egypt with the United Arab Emirates and Saudi Arabia.[121] Only a few hours before the beginning of the bombing of Gaza, Muhammad Farid al-Tohamy (the head of Egypt's general intelligence services) was in Tel Aviv. From the very start of the military operation, Cairo chose to close its border with Gaza, only episodically permitting a limited evacuation of the seriously wounded and the entry of minimal food supplies. The attention focusing on the cease-fire proposal offered by the Egyptians also allowed identifying differences between General al-Sisi's administration and previous ones. In itself, the proposal's content did not fundamentally differ from cease-fires formulated by the Mubarak or even Morsi administrations. The main difference resided in the absence of a 24-hour extension granted to Hamas before its implementation. Yet the form of this cease-fire significantly differed: unlike previous proposals, the one of 15 July 2014 was coordinated with Israel without ever consulting Hamas. This strategy, which incited Hamas to refuse the deal, permitted designating the movement as the main party guilty of prolonging the conflict, thus giving Israel scope to pursue its military operation. The narrative that consisted in making Hamas the main problem was now shared by the Palestinian Presidency, as well as by some Fatah representatives. Finally, by refusing to directly speak to Hamas leaders, Egypt transformed the movement into a simple player within a Palestinian delegation gathering Fatah members, left-wing organizations and Islamic Jihad, the latter now a favoured interlocutor of Cairo.

Hamas, from enemy to partner in the fight against Takfiris

On 28 February 2015, an Egyptian court of law declared that Hamas was now a terrorist organization.[122] In its attempt to give a regional tone to its war against the Muslim Brotherhood on Egypt's national soil, Cairo accused Hamas of participating in a series of attacks against Egyptian security forces in the Sinai Peninsula. Yet as of June 2015, Egypt reconsidered its decisions, officially reverting this classification on the grounds of a lack of competence of the court that had issued it. Although Hamas leaders expressed their satisfaction, this decision nevertheless did not prevent the continuation of attacks against the Islamic Resistance, now accused of trying to establish a state in Sinai and even of ordering the murder

---

121. Jean-François Legrain, 'Gaza 2014, les paradoxes d'une guerre pas comme les autres', *Orient Xxi*, 8 July 2015.

122. This decision was taken a month after the al-Qassam Brigades were listed as a terrorist organization.

of General Attorney Hisham Barakat.¹²³ These accusations, which were part of a cabal against Hamas in the Egyptian press, coincided, however, with a round of discussions between Khaled Mesh'al and the head of Egyptian intelligence Khaled Fawzi, centring on the possibility of a visit of a Hamas delegation to Cairo. The latter, which took place on 12 March 2016, led to talks that essentially covered security matters, with Hamas reiterating its commitment to ensure Egypt's stability and protect its borders.¹²⁴ By drawing closer to Hamas, Cairo was seeking to fight more effectively against Takfiris in Sinai, organizations that Hamas knows well. Of course, the Egyptian president still saw Hamas as an 'enemy', but for al-Sisi a Hamas under control was more useful to guarantee Egypt's security than an isolated Hamas.

This rapprochement should not be overestimated: despite concessions made by Hamas – the removal of Mohammed Morsi's photographs from Gaza's central square;¹²⁵ the arrest of 'terrorists' supposedly plotting against Egypt – the Rafah crossing has remained shut. Quite the opposite, the Egyptian executive continued to pressure Hamas, as illustrated by the abduction of four Palestinians by the Egyptian security services after their crossing of the Rafah border post illegally, in August 2015.¹²⁶ Cairo indeed wanted Hamas to contribute more in the repression of Takfiris, especially by deploying its own security forces in Egypt, which the Palestinian movement has refused to do. This tension was exacerbated by the declarations of Egyptian Foreign Affairs minister Sameh Shoukry, who said Israeli military operations against the Palestinians could not be considered acts of terrorism.¹²⁷ As relative as it was, the rapprochement between Egypt and Hamas was also for General al-Sisi an attempt to exercise pressure on Palestinian president Mahmoud Abbas, to make him once more accept the return of his rival Mohammed Dahlan to the political stage.

Getting involved in Palestinian reconciliation and soothing tensions between Israel and Hamas

Understanding Cairo's attitude regarding Hamas also requires focusing on Palestinian reconciliation, an issue that enables Egypt to play a major diplomatic role in the region. Conscious of the difficulty of finalizing reconciliation, which none of the Palestinian parties involved were particularly attached to, Egypt

---

123. Appointed Attorney general in 2013, Hisham Barakat had ordered the freezing of assets belonging to several members of the Muslim Brotherhood, including those of Supreme Guide Mohammed Badie. He was killed in a car bomb attack on 29 June 2015. The Egyptian executive accused in turn, the Egyptian Muslim Brothers, Hamas and even an official of the security services, see *Al-Monitor*, 11 March 2016.
  124. See Khalil al-Hayya 's communiqué: https://hamas.ps/ar/post/5110/.
  125. http://www.alquds.com/articles/1458462450860956300/.
  126. al-Jazeera, 24 August 2015.
  127. https://www.youtube.com/watch?v=kLksFALEQWQ.

continued, however, in its approach, presenting the Palestinian reconciliation as a prelude to any attempt to solve the Israeli–Palestinian conflict. Mahmoud Abbas was now sidelined because of his refusal to reintegrate Mohammed Dahlan. Conversely, Egypt was hoping to obtain a number of concessions from Hamas, among which was the return of Dahlan, the former Fatah head of security in the Gaza Strip.

This was how in June 2017, after a five-week visit to Cairo by Yahya al-Sinwar, the Egyptians agreed on opening the Rafah crossing, letting cement and tankers filled with millions of litres of fuel for Gazans go through. The Strip's inhabitants had been deprived of electricity following Mahmoud Abbas's default on payments of fuel bills.[128] This Egyptian goodwill towards Gaza should thus be seen as a sign of gratitude, because Hamas consented to important concessions, in particular better relations with its former enemy. Now, it was this Hamas–Dahlan rapprochement that largely contributed to the conclusion of a new Palestinian reconciliation agreement signed in Cairo on 12 October 2017: weakened by this new coalition Cairo/Hamas/Dahlan front, Mahmoud Abbas saw himself obliged to reach compromise with Hamas, the only way to retake Gaza before it fell into Dahlan's hands.[129] Yet, just like previous agreements, this reconciliation fell on deaf ears: the management of the Gaza Strip was sufficiently complex to make Mahmoud Abbas avoid taking risks on this matter; as for Hamas, it did not wish to grant Ramallah the control of all of the crossing points.

Without any illusions as to the probability of an accord in the near future between Palestinians, and having duly noted the unrealistic prospects for reconciliation, Egypt was, in practice, committed to other bilateral negotiations between Hamas and Israel. This reinforced Fatah's feeling of marginalization which accused Egypt of widening division. It was, thus, Egyptian mediation, backed by the United Nations and Qatar, that allowed, in November 2018, the conclusion of a first agreement between Israel and Hamas aimed at defusing tension; the Palestinian movement committed to stop the launching of incendiary balloons, obtaining in exchange a loosening of the blockade, permitting the delivery of oil and money by Qatar. Once more on 1 April 2019, a new deal was reached under the aegis of Egypt, which restated the principles of the previous one: in exchange for no more incendiary balloons, Hamas, in theory, got the reopening of the Kerem Shalom border crossing; the delivery by Qatar of $40 million to finance the health sector and fight unemployment;[130] the supplying of fuel for Gaza's electric plant; the lifting of restrictions on fishermen and also, at a later stage conditioned by a truce

---

128. Since March 2017, President Abbas has imposed heavy sanctions on the Gaza Strip, reducing the share of the Palestinian budget allocated to this territory, refusing in particular to pay Gazan electricity bills to Israel.

129. Leila Seurat, Mohamed Younes, 'Un accord entre le Fatah et le Hamas à l'ombre du parrain égyptien', *Orient Xxi*, October 2017.

130. It consists in setting up a programme of payments in cash by Qatar, via work done by the poorest Palestinians hired by UN bodies.

of longer duration, the possibility of creating two industrial areas to the east and north of the enclave.

Such agreements indicate that Cairo's approach became relatively conciliatory towards Hamas, as shown during Ismail Haniyeh's stay in Cairo between 3 and 27 February, as well as by the release of the four Gazans jailed in Egypt after their abduction in Rafah in summer 2015.[131] Ismail Haniyeh's presence in Tehran during Qassem Soleimani's funeral resulted in a cold spell in relations with Egypt, but this did not stop Egyptians from pursuing their mediation between Israel and Hamas. The period of the Covid-19 pandemic was marked by the reopening of negotiations aimed at defusing tensions, this time including humanitarian clauses; for Hamas, the goal was to obtain both medical kits and the release of prisoners, essentially old and sick people, in exchange for the bodies of two dead soldiers killed in 2014 during 'Protective Edge'.

131. *Al-Monitor*, 20 March 2019.

Part II

THE VARIOUS INTERESTS AT THE BASIS OF THE FOREIGN POLICY OF HAMAS

To escape its isolation, Hamas wants to be seen as both a political organization and a government. Thomas Lindemann[1] has extensively discussed the case of state players that despite the official recognition they receive, they look for a more symbolic acknowledgement. The case of Palestine in general, and Hamas in particular, illustrates a double denial of recognition: the Palestinian Authority's institutions are not considered as state institutions, and Hamas, as a player, is subjected to a boycott.[2] According to Lindemann, these denials of recognition enable one to explain the escalations in violence.

To these symbolic interests, one must add economic and local political ones. Indeed, in the context of the blockade, the activities of Hamas leaders (both members of the government and MPs) are a search for economic backers. Wished for as early as June 2007, the truce signed in June 2008 allowed Hamas to reinforce its domination of the Gaza Strip. This assessment thus supports a 'realist' approach as developed by Morgenthau, who has stressed the link between the interior capacities of players and their margins of manoeuvre in the field of foreign policy.[3] They also confirm the hypothesis of a linkage, as defined by Rosenau:[4] the liberation of Gilad Shalit and armed actions are evidence that Hamas tries to compete with its political adversaries on the internal Palestinian political stage, which illustrates the important interconnection of the internal and external environments.[5]

1. Thomas Lindemann, 'Théories de la reconnaissance dans les relations internationales: enjeux symboliques et limites du paradigme de l'intérêt', *Cultures et Conflits*, n° 87, 2012, p.7–25.

2. In Kelsen's opinion, acts of recognition between states are only an empirical assessment and do not imply any show of respect. They are thus more acknowledgements rather than true recognitions, 'Recognition in International Law: Theoretical Observations', *The American Journal of International Law*, 35, 1941, n°4, p. 605–17.

3. See the realist school's definition put forward by Carlnaes in the *Handbook of International Relations*, edited by Walter Carlsnaes, Thomas Risse-Kappen and Beth A. Simmons, Sage, 2002.

4. James Rosenau, *Linkage Politics, essays on the convergence of national and international systems*, New York, The Free Press, 1969.

5. R. Puttman, H. Jacobson, P. Evans, *Double-Edged Diplomacy, International Bargaining and Domestic Politics*, Berkeley, University of California Press, 1993.

Chapter 4

OUTSIDE

SEEKING RECOGNITION AND LOOKING FOR RESOURCES

Diplomatic visits of leaders and members of government are meant to obtain recognition, which was increasingly difficult after the events of June 2007 that led to the establishment of a second government in Ramallah, considered as the only legitimate one. Hamas, however, has also gone after an unconventional form of recognition. For instance, the launching of hostilities through the opening of a gap in the border fence with Egypt was aimed at obtaining symbolic recognition.[1] Attempts to end isolation also materialized in the signature of reconciliation agreements with Fatah. The Prisoners' Document and the Mecca Agreement of 2006 and 2007, respectively, can be explained by the search for new outside backers. Following the beginning of the Arab Spring in January 2011, Hamas redefined its network of alliances to benefit from the support of Egypt and Qatar, countries that contributed to committing Hamas to reconciliation. Though this attempt to break its isolation necessarily exposed Hamas to outside pressure, engaging in compromise and deals with states was nevertheless always perceived as a lesser evil, given the situation of lockdown the movement found itself in.

The other aim was, in the context of a blockade, to look for material sources. When returning from their stays abroad, Hamas leaders would often carry suitcases containing millions of dollars. Faced with the impossibility of getting hold of enough financial backers in Arab countries, Hamas courted Iran to ensure the survival of its government. The alliance with the Islamic Republic was thus a result of the tightening of the blockade, since Iran was the only state providing Hamas with substantial economic support to pay its public sector employees. We shall see that like the strategies chosen to end isolation, the means used to obtain material resources have also changed with time: the rapprochement with Qatar is explained by financial promises formulated by Doha during the emir's visit to Gaza and the attempt to establish a substitute alliance in the framework of decreasing links with Tehran. Yet, once more, this did not lead to the expected results, and Hamas again had to warm up its alliance with the Islamic Republic to ensure its

---

1. Thomas Lindemann, *Causes of War: The Struggle for Recognition* (Colchester: ECPR Press, 2010).

survival, particularly after the summer of 2013, when the Egyptian military closed the Rafah crossing and destroyed most of the smuggling tunnels into the Strip.

The triggering of the March of Return in March 2018 heralded new terms in the provision of Qatari aid to Hamas. This aid was now indexed to war and peace dynamics: the nuisance capacity of rockets and incendiary balloons allowed Hamas to ensure that Israel would authorize, in return for calm, the monthly sending of tens of millions of dollars to Gaza.

Going after double recognition

Searching for diplomatic recognition

Visits made by Hamas outside the two main centres of activity (Gaza and Damascus), and the welcoming of foreign representatives in these two cities, were attempts to obtain the lifting of the encirclement and the recognition of its two successive governments ('Tenth Government' until March 2007, and Gaza government as of June 2007). The main stake of the trips abroad was the acceptance of results of the Palestinian elections that consecrated Hamas' victory.[2]

In the wake of the formation of the 'Tenth Government' in March 2006, many countries agreed to receive Foreign Minister Mahmoud al-Zahar, thus legitimating the principle of governmental diplomacy carried out by Hamas. Al-Zahar emphasized that all the states he travelled to officially recognized him as minister.[3] He even claimed that the Egyptian administration, which at the time did not recognize the Hamas government and had refused to meet him during his first stay in Cairo, finally accepted to see him during his return to Gaza, on 4 May 2006:

> In Egypt there was at first a problem, since the Egyptians gave the pretext that the Foreign Affairs Minister was late for this meeting. I instead met members of the Arab League, as well as ministers from Arab countries. During my second trip, however, I was able to meet Ahmad Abou al-Gheit, the Egyptian Foreign Affairs Minister.[4]

Most people with whom we were able to discuss this topic (including Fatah representatives) agree that in 2006 Hamas' diplomacy was recognized as the Palestinian Authority's official foreign policy.[5] It allowed most Fatah leaders to claim that this stage was the only moment when the Hamas government had any

---

   2. Conversation with Taher al-Nounou, the spokesman of the Gaza government, Cairo, 25 February 2012.
   3. See Mahmoud al-Zahar's interview, *Markaz al-filastini li-l-i'lâm*, 8 May 2006.
   4. Conversation with Mahmoud al-Zahar in Gaza, 20 March 2013.
   5. With the exception of Ziad Abu Amer, who considers that even in 2006 attempts at recognition as the Palestinian people's representative government at the diplomatic level

legitimacy.⁶ In 2006, during the visit of a delegation of European MPs to Gaza, its president certified that collaboration was direct, and that this testified to a recognition of Ismail Haniyeh's government.⁷

Following the events of June 2007, this recognition was no longer forthcoming. The tightening of the blockade and the formation of another government in Ramallah significantly isolated Hamas. The *inqisâm* provoked the departure of the majority of diplomatic representations in Gaza,⁸ to Ayman al-Taha's great regret:

> Before 2007, all diplomatic representations were in Gaza and consulates in the West Bank. There were diplomatic representations of a number of countries such as China, Tunisia, Argentina, Norway, Egypt, South Africa. The only country that did not withdraw its representative after the *hâsim* [the 2007 events] was Qatar. Other countries have consular antennas in Gaza, for instance Germany, France and Switzerland, but we do not have official relations with these.⁹

The departure of all diplomatic representations was, moreover, very often mentioned by Hamas' political rivals, in an attempt to demonstrate that the Islamist movement's coup in Gaza had damaged its credibility, hampering any possibility of official diplomatic action: 'The only people who remained after the coup [*inqilâb*] were representatives of these countries' security services. From this date on, each time a Palestinian from Gaza wants to travel anywhere, he must send all his official papers to Ramallah to obtain a visa.'¹⁰

Between 2007 and 2010 there was no diplomatic tour by Gaza government members, whether the Foreign Affairs minister or the prime minister:

> From March 2006 to March 2007, the 'Tenth Government' was legitimate and recognized by many countries, like those in Latin America and some Arab countries. Mahmoud al-Zahar travelled as Foreign Affairs Minister, and participated in many summits. During the rule of the national unity government, it was Ziad Abu Amer who took charge of this ministry; the government also enjoyed a measure of legitimacy. After *inqisâm*, it was more difficult, because Abou Mazen [Mahmoud Abbas] set up another government, and the one in

---

failed because of the nature of relations between these countries and the PLO (conversation on 23 March 2013, in Ramallah).

6. Conversation with Khader Mahjiz, an ex-member of Hamas, Gaza, 17 March 2013.

7. *Al-Riyadh*, 31 January 2006.

8. Are Hovdenak, 'The Public Services Under Hamas in Gaza, Islamic Revolution or Crisis Management?', *Prio Report*, 3 (Oslo: PRIO, March 2010).

9. Conversation with Ayman al-Taha in Gaza, 19 March 2013.

10. Conversation with Rafiq al-Masri, an academic who is not a Hamas sympathizer, 19 March 2013.

Gaza became illegitimate, although the presidential decree establishing Abbas' government has no legitimacy at all.[11]

This change was also manifested by the withdrawal of the Foreign Affairs minister from the Gaza government. Conscious of the fact that this minister had difficulties in representing Palestinians in the context of the blockade's tightening, Hamas decided to leave this position vacant from then on. In a more symbolic manner, it was Ismail Haniyeh who ensured the interim as concerns Foreign Affairs.[12] The cancellation of this position, however, did not mean the end of the Foreign Affairs Ministry. Quite the opposite, the latter remained active, its direction being taken care of by a vice-minister, in the person of Ahmed Yousef, and then Ghazi Hamad.

Aware of the difficulties of states previously recognizing the PLO as the sole representative of the Palestinian people, Hamas' leaders claimed to respect these 'contradictions', and not bicker on issues of protocol. They thus expressed that they would see no inconvenience in being welcomed in a non-official manner, since establishing this sort of relation is always preferable to the total absence of relations:

> We do not want to delve into the question of knowing whether they recognize us or not. We accept all levels of representation that countries want to have with us. Some players want recognition or nothing at all, but we do not agree with this approach; we proceed in this way in order to not break relations we already have.[13]

Despite these declarations of intent, Hamas did not give up on obtaining recognition. For this, it played on the various levels of representation it held in order to multiply relations and make them official. In parallel with the two levels of governmental foreign policy – the one conducted by the Foreign Affairs minister and the other by the prime minister – Hamas has carried out other types of diplomacy. Playing on various 'stages', by introducing themselves as representatives of a government, or alternatively as members of a political group, allows Hamas to go on many visits without forcing their hosts to run the risk of conferring recognition on the government based in Gaza. This double activity characterized Hamas diplomacy during the entire period studied in this book, not only the time immediately after the division between Gaza and the West Bank. For example, in April 2006 and February 2007, Russia welcomed a Hamas delegation as a political movement, not as a group of government representatives. This ambiguity allowed the various hosts to avoid offending Ramallah and permitted Hamas leaders to pretend that it

---

11. Conversation with Basem Naim in Gaza, 18 March 2013.
12. Ismail Haniyeh was at the time in charge of the Finance and Foreign Affairs Ministries, as well as being prime minister. Are Hovdenak, 'The Public Services Under Hamas in Gaza'.
13. Conversation with Imad al-Alami, Gaza, 18 March 2013.

was a form of implicit recognition. The same dilemma was obvious to Jordanian authorities during Khaled Mesh'al's visit in 2012.[14]

Hamas leaders have insisted on the existence of a complementarity (*takammul*) between these two levels. They have often invoked the same example: when the movement talks to popular groups in the Arab world, these groups put pressure on their respective governments to make them recognize Hamas. In turn, therefore, the government gains from the movement's recognition.[15] As for Mahmoud al-Zahar, he mentioned the existence of common goals between the various different levels and insisted on the greater margin of manoeuvre of the movement's members, who can speak to the people they wish during their visits. This explains how the movement's delegations met popular groups (for instance, the *dîwânîyât* in Kuwait) or were able to participate in many festivals in refugee camps, particularly in Yarmouk in Damascus.

The role of the external leadership was always crucial in making good use of contacts with players who are not authorized to develop relations with Hamas, or who do not wish them to be leaked.

Hamas representative offices abroad, moreover, can also participate in the organization of visits, like Khaled Mesh'al's to Jordan in 2012, which was prepared beforehand by Mohammad Nazzal from Amman:

> Every time a delegation from Gaza or outside arrives in a country, we set up contacts and we organize meetings between this delegation and official representatives of this country.[16] When the Foreign Affairs Minister wants to travel, it is the Hamas movement that organizes the visit. It has the role of an embassy.[17]

> The three levels are independent from each other, but there is of course a complimentarity (*takammul*): only one *marja'îya* (reference) but several *ikhtisâsât* (specialties). When the government seeks to develop relations with foreign governments, its global aims are the same as the movement's: to break the blockade and remove Hamas from the list of terrorist organizations.[18]

The removal of the position of Foreign Affairs minister of the Gaza government, after June 2007, is to be partly explained by the wish to not embarrass host countries. The title of 'Vice-Minister of Foreign Affairs' (*Wakîl wâzîr al-khârijîya*) is more in agreement with the rationale announced by the movement's leaders. This status does indeed make trips outside Palestine easier and allows leaders to be welcomed abroad.[19] As of June 2007, it was Ahmed Yousef, a former adviser to the

---

14. *Arabtimes*, 30 January 2012.
15. Conversation with Walid al-Mdalal in Gaza, 15 March 2013.
16. Conversation with Imad al-Alami, Gaza, 18 March 2013.
17. Conversation with Ayman al-Taha, Gaza, 19 March 2013.
18. Conversation with Mouchir al-Masri, Gaza, 16 March 2013.
19. Conversation with Ghazi Hamad, Gaza, 17 March 2013.

prime minister, who was in charge of this. After 2011, following the brief interlude during which Mohammed Awad became Foreign Affairs minister,[20] Ghazi Hamad was nominated to this position. This status enables the government's foreign diplomatic action, supervised by a representative who is not a minister, to continue operating. It is actually because Ghazi Hamad was not a minister that he could move around Europe. The author met him in Cyprus in May 2012, on the occasion of a symposium on the repercussions of the Arab Spring in Palestine. Had he been a minister, it would have been difficult for him to obtain a visa, even though his visit was not official. One knows that when a minister, Mohammed Awad, was refused a visa, even though he had even been invited by the International Parliamentary federation to travel to Switzerland as an MP. Questioned on the reasons for this cancellation, Awad explained it by mentioning his ministerial status.[21]

Finally, the diplomatic role of MPs invited by foreign parliaments, particularly in Europe, allows Hamas to capitalize on these visits to try to gain a form of recognition. Switzerland has thus regularly invited Palestinian Legislative Council representatives. Hamas leaders welcomed as parliamentarians describe these visits as taking into account the movement in an official way. Mahmoud al-Zahar thus highlighted the topic of discussions with his Swiss interlocutors during his January 2012 visit, in the context of a parliamentary trip: 'I went to Switzerland as member of Parliament, but it was really to represent the movement, since we did not even mention the Parliament's role. There were many officials and former ministers.'[22] While in Geneva in early January 2012, the author noticed that discussions dealt with political matters, such as human rights and conditions imposed by the Quartet; in addition, people present during the meetings were not parliamentarians, but ministers or ambassadors. Some countries wished in this manner to welcome Hamas and open a dialogue with its leaders, so as to be able to play the part of mediator in the future, if needed. To this end, the status of MPs is of paramount importance: a country like Switzerland would have not been able to receive government members were they not parliamentarians. Hamas has willingly mobilized its various levels of representation, according to the preferences of relevant players, and tried to make good use of the visits of these MPs, which are all described as a 'victories'.[23] The movement uses the legitimate status of the Palestine Legislative Council's members in an attempt to establish the foundations of an official diplomacy with Western states, with the goal of one day being recognized by Europe or the United States.

20. Mohammed Awad became minister in the wake of a cabinet reshuffle in March 2011. He remained minister until March 2012.
21. Hamas tried to send Mohammed Awad as representative of parliament when he was the Foreign Affairs minister.
22. Conversation with Mahmoud al-Zahar, Gaza, 20 March 2013.
23. Mouchir al-Masri said that parliament never had a problem of recognition, since there is no other parliament in Gaza.

The nomination in 2011 of Mohammed Awad as Foreign Affairs minister is a testimony to the wish to respond to the new regional context and reach a new stage, which would resemble that of 2006. Mohammed Awad thought that the evolution of the regional context permitted ending the complete isolation after June 2007. He compared this period to 2006 when Mahmoud al-Zahar was in charge of Foreign Affairs. He was nevertheless aware of the long path still ahead before recognition:

> There is a recognition (*i'tirâf*), even if there is no real collaboration on the ground (*ta'âmul haqîqat-'al-'ard*). To reach true collaboration on the ground, we must have relations with ambassadors. Now, this is not the case. The juridical framework (*itâr tatbîq al-qânûn*) is left to Abbas.[24]

Ismail Haniyeh's diplomatic tours from 2011 finally gave some satisfaction to the wish of appearing abroad as the head of a 'legitimate' government. He was indeed welcomed in various Arab countries as prime minister and as chief of government with all diplomatic prerogatives. Since June 2007, Haniyeh had already held these two powers but was unable to travel. After the Arab uprisings, Hamas leaders would not speak of recognition but nevertheless said they expected progress from the Foreign Affairs ministers in terms of foreign diplomacy.[25] All highlighted the fact that Ismail Haniyeh was welcomed in all countries of the region as prime minister:

> Ismail Haniyeh was officially welcomed as head of the government. Those who received him have done so officially (*al-tartîbât al-brûtûkûlîya*), for instance in Egypt, Tunisia and Turkey, and this is a reflection of the Arab uprisings, which have opened new relations with Hamas. These changes have incited other countries to follow the same path. Before the Arab uprisings, yes, it was different: between 2007 and 2011, there was no official visit.[26]

Hamas, however, can hardly publicly claim that its movement has been recognized in an official manner, since by doing so it runs the risk of seeing its emissaries expelled from the countries concerned. This is what happened during the trip of MPs to Bulgaria in March 2013.[27] Likewise, on 19 March 2012, the visit of MP Ismail al-Achqar, who had been invited to give a speech at the UN Council for Human Rights on the issue of parliamentarians jailed in prisons of occupation forces, was cancelled.[28] Even though several MPs accompanying Mahmoud

---

24. Conversation with Mohammed Awad, Gaza, 15 March 2013.
25. Conversation with Mouchir al-Masri, Gaza, 16 March 2013.
26. Conversation with Mouchir al-Masri, Gaza, 16 March 2013.
27. *Al-Monitor*, 20 February 2013, Adnan Abu Amer.
28. *Markaz al-filastînî li-l-i'lâm*, 19 March 2012.

al-Zahar had gone to Geneva beforehand, Israeli pressure finally got the better of the Swiss decision.[29] This was also Huda Naim's experience:

> There were diplomatic contacts with the West, Europe, America, but this is still shadow diplomacy. In five years, I was invited only twice, by Switzerland and Norway, and these invitations were cancelled even though I am a woman, a person considered less dangerous.[30]

> Hamas' capacity to stay in power for more than five years has made many Arab countries have relations with Hamas; both with the movement and the government, but there is a difference between the recognition of a government as a reality (*amr wâqi'*) and the recognition of a government as legal authority (*tanfîdpiya qâ'ima*).[31]

Symbolic recognition

Faced with the difficulty of gaining diplomatic recognition through these visits and meetings, Hamas has sought less conventional recognition by other means: the launching of hostilities against Egypt.

The opening of a gap on the border between Gaza and Egypt in January 2008 can in part be explained by Hamas' wish to be seen as an unavoidable stakeholder, forcing Arab states that had criticized Gaza's seizure (such as Egypt, Saudi Arabia and Jordan) to consider the movement as a true player, or even as a political partner.[32]

In this quest for recognition, Hamas largely based itself on the solidarity of the Muslim Brotherhood, which mobilized the 'Egyptian street' in its favour during the opening of the hole in the border wall. This support confirms the importance of the notion of *linkage*, theorized by Rosenau then reintroduced by Yaacov[33] to explain the foreign policy of Syria between 1960 and 1970. In their attempt to weaken Hosni Mubarak's regime, the Muslim Brothers used their international network to try to force the lifting of the blockade. The travels of several Muslim Brother executive leaders to Europe were used to defend Hamas' cause.[34]

By placing the Egyptians in front of a fait accompli, the explosion breaching the border wall obliged them to open a dialogue with Hamas to solve the crisis swiftly. On 29 January, the Islamist movement thus cooperated with Egyptian

29. *Haaretz*, 19 March 2012.
30. Conversation with Huda Naim, Ankara, 19 May 2011.
31. Conversation with Adnan Abu Amer in Gaza, 24 March 2013.
32. Beverly Edwards, 'The Ascendance of Political Islam: Hamas and Consolidation in the Gaza Strip', *Third World Quarterly* 29, no. 8 (2008): 1585–99.
33. Bar-Siman-Tov Yaacov, *Linkage Politics in the Middle East: Syria between Domestic and external Conflict, 1961–1970* (Boulder: Westview, 1983).
34. *Al-Khamis*, 2 July 2007.

security forces to fill in the gaps in the wall.[35] On the following day, Hamas officials went to Cairo to deal with the issue of the crossing of the border.[36] The crossing was completely closed on 3 February, since Hamas had rejected the demand for the redeployment at the Rafah crossing of forces loyal to Mahmoud Abbas's Palestinian Authority and requested that the border be controlled only by themselves and Egyptians. In exchange for this collaboration, which was capable of making Hamas appear as a responsible partner, the movement hoped to obtain the Rafah crossing's partial reopening.

The decision of Egyptian authorities to collaborate with Hamas in the control of the border was therefore seen as a victory by the movement. In such circumstances, confrontation appeared as a means to convert its weakness into a resource, as emphasized by Lindemann. As for the mobilization of a linkage group, it proved to be beneficial, since Cairo reacted in a positive fashion to Hamas' claims, which were conveyed by the Egyptian Muslim Brothers.

Armed struggle towards Israel also appeared as an unconventional means to end isolation,[37] as shown by Hamas' stand during 'Cast Lead'. While the movement did not actually expect an Israeli reaction on such as scale,[38] that robust military response allowed it to activate the strategy of the weak versus the strong, while showing that, despite its superior technology, Israel's forces were not entirely unbeatable. According to Lindemann, the absence of recognition incites the offended political entity to re-establish its self-esteem through violent actions. By emphasizing the profound inequality in the ratio of force between 'oppressors' and 'victims', the aim was also to obtain a certain form of recognition on the international stage.

The Palestinian reconciliation: A means to break isolation

The Prisoners' Document and the Agreements with Fatah from 2007 to 2012

In the wake of its election victory, Hamas committed itself to following the path towards an agreement with the other Palestinian parties on the international stage, particularly with Fatah. By accepting to sign the Prisoners' Document and

---

35. *IRIN*, Cairo/Jerusalem, 30 January 2008.
36. Ibid.
37. Laetitia Bucaille has shown that suicide attacks can be explained as an attempt to obtain symbolic gains, Lateitia Bucaille, 'L'impossible stratégie palestinienne du martyre: Victimisation et attentat suicide', *Critique Internationale* 20, no. 3 (2003): 117–34.
38. According to Alex Mintz, Hamas acted in this way, believing that Israeli leaders, preoccupied by elections, could not launch a large-scale operation in the Gaza Strip. The movement apparently acted as a result of misperceptions. See Alex Mints and Karl DeRouen, *Understanding Foreign Policy Decision Making* (New York: Cambridge University Press, 2010).

the Mecca Agreement, Hamas was trying to become an indispensable partner on Palestinian issues and end the international quarantine on its government. Through deals with Fatah, Hamas wished to earn the sympathy of international powers interested in the 'peace process', in particular the Quartet, which had forced a financial and political lockdown on the Hamas government.[39]

As opposed to the 2006 and 2007 inter-Palestinian reconciliation agreements, whose initiative rested on Hamas, in 2011 pressure for reconciliation came from state agencies with which the movement wanted to create a rapprochement. Hamas' leaders, however, thought that by signing a new deal with Fatah, Western countries, gradually launching talks with the region's Islamist parties, might change their stance and open official channels to deepen dialogue with them.

Statements concerning the 1967 borders, the transfer of the file on negotiations with Israel to the PLO and the adoption of peaceful resistance during Mesh'al's meeting with Abbas in Cairo in November must be interpreted as an attempt by Hamas to break its isolation and appear as a respectable and pragmatic player. Ahmed Yousef thus said of the 2011 Cairo Agreement: 'Hamas wanted to test the international community to see if it has accepted a government of technocrats in order, if this were the case, to earn recognition and receive funds.'[40]

Nathan Brown also considers that Khaled Mesh'al saw regional opportunities for Hamas and tried to adopt a 'sanitized' version of political Islam, which would permit integrating Hamas into a process of Western recognition of the Muslim Brotherhood. Brown elaborated on the Cairo Agreement: 'The leaders of Hamas in charge of the reconciliation committed themselves to a process that would enable incorporating Hamas as a diplomatic player into Palestinian executive structures in exchange for a voice and a part in these structures.'[41]

The adoption of 'peaceful resistance' was justified by the search for new regional backers, but also international ones, all the more so because some states had normalized relations with Islamists since the election victories of parties originating from the Muslim Brothers in Egypt and Tunisia.[42] The choice of such an approach was all the easier because its implications were in agreement with the Egyptian Brotherhood's line: it was critical of armed struggle. It thus allowed

---

39. al-Zubaidi, *Hamas wa-l-hukûm, dukhûl al-nizâm am al-tamarrûd 'alayhi*.

40. Conversation with Ahmed Yousef, Ankara, June 2011. One should note, moreover, that this agreement came approximately a fortnight after the murder in Gaza of the Italian activist Vittorio Arrigoni, a crime that seriously damaged the image of Hamas, which has tried to suppress any form of assimilation to Jihadi movements.

41. Nathan Brown, 'Is Hamas Mellowing?', *Carnegie Endowment for International Peace*, 17 January 2012.

42. One should recall that to minimize the cost of such an announcement, which ran the risk of appearing in the eyes of its base as a strategic U-turn, Hamas leaders were denying its unprecedented character by asserting that 'popular resistance' would never be at the expense of armed struggle; see Izzat al-Rishq, *Markaz al-filastînî li-l-i'lâm*, 27 November 2011.

Hamas to emphasize its ideological kinship with an organization on the verge of normalizing relations with the United States and the European Union. After the advent of the Arab Spring and the victory of Islamist parties in Tunisia and Egypt, Hamas leaders thought that the West could soften its stance and open a dialogue with their movement, particularly so because the latter was focusing on Palestinian reconciliation. This hope was comforted by the existence of already old underground contacts, now likely to be given an official dimension that would go hand in hand with the end of the status quo in the region. Taher al-Nounou confirmed this analysis with the following words:

> With the Arab Spring, we can now seize the occasion to broaden our relations with this kind of state: European countries that had recognized the national unity government in 2007 in the wake of the Mecca Agreement. We nowadays think that several of these countries are ready to establish direct relations with Hamas, and this is not an analysis I make, but originates from genuine sources: this concerns several states, but we cannot reveal their identity. It is up to them to do so if they wish to, but we cannot publicly identify them because of American pressure on them, and pressure of the Zionist lobby. But I can assure you that many European countries have direct relations with us.[43]

These declarations illustrated the search for Egyptian support in a post-revolutionary context where the Muslim Brotherhood opposition had great chances of winning most votes in the next elections. Hamas then hoped that this victory would lead to the Rafah crossing's opening and the creation of a commercial zone between Egypt and Gaza. The Doha Agreement was also derived from the will to end isolation, since Qatar had told Khaled Mesh'al it was committed to help Hamas establish links with the United States and Europe.

Constraints related to regional realignment

At a first glance, it is true that the existence of ideological kinship with Egypt and Qatar made these countries more acceptable than an alliance with a Shia republic.[44] This rapprochement was also a means for Hamas to avoid being affected by the consequences of the Assad regime's isolation from the moment the Arab League had decided to suspend Damascus's membership and impose sanctions on Syria.[45] There were many Arab capitals then threatening Hamas with a veto on opening offices if the movement did not leave Syria.[46] Egypt and Qatar from then

---

43. Conversation with Taher al-Nounou in Cairo, 25 February 2012.
44. According to Matti Steinberg, 'Hamas Went Back to its Earlier Policy of Alliances', *Reuters*, 1 February 2012.
45. 'Hamas Is Looking for an Alternative to Damascus', *Times*, 6 December 2011.
46. *Al-Quds al-Arabi*, 5 March 2012.

on became alternatives to Damascus: Moussa Abu Marzouk set up an office in Cairo, while Khaled Mesh'al chose Doha as his main residence.

In a personal interview with the author, Khaled Mesh'al confessed that the presence of a leadership outside Palestine was not an easy thing to deal with, but denied any sort of interference in Hamas' decision making, quoting the departure of Syria as an example to stress this high level of autonomy:

> We were in Amman at the beginning of the 1980s, then for a brief time in Qatar in 1999, prior to settling in Syria, and then once more in Qatar. During these times, we were able to preserve a total independence in our decision making, strategy and political line. Our decisions are not linked to political geography. When we were subjected to pressure, we actually left these countries, both Jordan and Syria. We are guests (*diouf*) in these countries, but if invitations come with strings attached, we just leave. These countries are not humanitarian agencies; they take advantage of our presence because the defence of Palestine is a winning cause.

Despite this discourse, this new configuration of alliances imbued with ideological affinities served the interests of Hamas only superficially: it implied both an inflection of practices and a loss of decision-making autonomy.

The rapprochement with Qatar forced a marked distancing with Bashar al-Assad's regime and binding support for the Syrian uprising. Yet in taking sides in the conflict in Syria, Hamas distanced itself from its principle of non-interference and became exposed to major risks in the case of Iran winning in Syria. One can notice, for that matter, that the departure from Damascus and Ismail Haniyeh's speech at the Al-Azhar University in Cairo advocating support for the Syrian revolution coincided with the signing of the Doha Agreement in February 2012. The emir of Qatar's visit to Gaza on 23 October 2012, followed by the opening of a representation office were gestures of gratitude towards Hamas after the severing of relations with the Syrian regime. As Hamas welcomed Yusuf al-Qaradawi in Gaza and, once again, openly displayed an anti-Assad stance, Mohammed Morsi was also in June stating his engagement with the Syrian rebellion.[47]

One should also note that the rapprochement with Qatar was not necessarily well accepted by the entire Palestinian population, because the new Gulf godfather was perceived as a US ally.[48] During Yusuf al-Qaradawi's visit, demonstrators in Khan Younis displayed the ulema's crossed-out portrait, together with the ones of Bashar al-Assad and Hassan Nasrallah. As for Fatah, the PFLP and the DFLP, they had refused to participate in the welcoming ceremony.[49]

47. *Al-Safir*, 10 May 2013.
48. *al-Jazeera*, 7 May 2013.
49. *RT Arabic*, 9 May 2013.

Rallying to the Muslim Brotherhood also demanded an ideological and strategic inflection from Hamas. Quoting American sources, the *Roz* newspaper claimed there were proofs that the Brotherhood controlled some crucial decisions taken by Hamas in Gaza. On 17 August 2011, when Khaled Mesh'al went to the head offices of the Guidance Bureau to discuss Palestinian reconciliation, the real order of the day was Gilad Shalit's liberation. Hamas apparently needed the Brothers' blessing.[50] On 29 October 2011, a high-level delegation of the Brothers appears to have travelled to Gaza. As from early 2013, the rapprochement with the Palestinian Islamist movement enabled Morsi to show a moderate and pragmatic face to the Arab world, and above all to the United States. Morsi made his approach part of a Qatari and Egyptian plan backed by Saudi Arabia and Jordan, whose aim was to take advantage of changes occurring in the region to transform Hamas and make it resemble much more other Muslim Brotherhood movements not listed as terrorist organizations.[51] This domestication of Hamas became a reality when the Brotherhood interfered in Hamas' internal election process. Influential Egyptian leaders, such as the former Supreme Guide Mahdi Akef and the current one Mohammad Badie (in jail since 2019), in fact sent a letter to the Hamas Gaza leadership backing Khaled Mesh'al's re-election.[52]

Finally, beyond the issue of loss of political autonomy, this rapprochement with Egypt ran the risk of seriously hurting Hamas. Morsi was very much contested in his own country. As of March 2013, a broad anti-Morsi campaign also targeted the Palestinian movement. Though this rapprochement was an opportunity to end its international isolation, Hamas feared that Morsi's discredit on Egypt's internal political stage could damage its own agenda. This fear was later proven justified. Having minimized the importance of popular dissent, which denounced Morsi's political management of the Gaza Strip and his relations with Hamas, the Egyptian president-elect was ousted by the army on 3 July 2013. Assimilated to the Egyptian Brotherhood, the Palestinian Islamist movement became the favoured target of the new power structure in Cairo, which had declared open war on the Brothers. Trying to avoid the serious consequences of Morsi's destitution and the emergence of an axis hostile to the Muslim Brotherhood, headed by Saudi Arabia, the United Arab Emirates and Egypt, Hamas began to think of the opportunity of writing a new document, in which its affiliation with the Muslim Brotherhood would not be mentioned.[53]

---

50. *Roz*, 11 December 2011.
51. *Al-Masri al-Youm*, 1 April 2013.
52. Maariv, quoted by *al-Masri al-Youm*, 1 April 2013, which states that the Muslim Brothers attempted to impose Khaled Mesh'al's victory.
53. Hroub Khaled, 'A Newer Hamas? The Revised Charter', *Joural of Palestine Studies* 46 (2017): 100–11. See also Leila Seurat, 'Révolution dans la révolution au Hamas', *Orient Xxi*, May 2017.

Looking for material resources

The inadequacy of Arab support

The needs of Hamas are made all the more pressing by Gaza's disastrous economic situation and the impossibility of generating sufficient resources for its weaponry and government. All this entails a foreign policy essentially guided by the search for material backers. As of March 2006, Ismail Haniyeh's inaugural speech invited potential Arab donors to set up mechanisms to ensure the appropriate use of donations.

Mahmoud al-Zahar thus described the goals of his diplomatic tours in April and May of 2006: make Hamas better known outside, since the movement's specifics are often ignored by international players, emphasize the 2006 election results and, above all, obtain financial support.[54] He insisted on the crucial necessity for these countries to remain loyal to the line adopted by the Arab League during the Khartoum Summit in March 2006, during which participants had taken the decision to economically back the 'Tenth Government'.[55]

Interactions with organizations from civil society were also of fundamental importance. Mahmoud al-Zahar concluded that his visit to Egypt had led to reactivation of wide-ranging solidarity networks and to donations of approximately 600,000 Egyptian pounds.[56] He was referring to the creation of a specific programme allowing, thanks to the payment of a dollar by each of the world's Muslims, collection of a billion-and-a-half dollars, enough to fund the entire government budget.[57]

Beyond the quest for funds, the Foreign Affairs minister had to confront the logistical challenge of bringing this aid to Gaza, since most banks were subjected to huge pressure, leading them to refuse carrying out these transactions. Mahmoud al-Zahar took suitcases containing $20 million with him to Gaza. Two weeks before, Ahmad Bahar and Mouchir al-Masri had returned to the Strip with US$4 million.[58] The minister's activities went therefore well beyond the normal and traditional prerogatives of the function. The diplomat became a funds escort, guaranteeing the transport of cash: Mahmoud al-Zahar confessed that 'due to the refusal of banks to transfer the money, we were obliged to transport ourselves twenty million dollars in cash to pay the government's civil servants'.[59]

---

54. According to Mahmoud al-Zahar, many countries like Algeria, Qatar, Saudi Arabia and Iran had promised aid to the movement. Conversation in Gaza on 20 March 2013.

55. This summit was an attempt to provide economic aid to the Hamas-led government. The summit echoed the one taking place in August 1967, which adopted the three 'nos': no to reconciliation with Israel, recognition and normalization, *al-Jazeera*, 29 March 2006.

56. See the interview of Mahmoud al-Zahar, *Markaz al-filastînî li-l-i'lâm*, 8 May 2006.

57. Ibid.

58. *Markaz al-filastînî li-l-i'lâm*, 28 November 2006.

59. Conversations with Mahmoud al-Zahar, Gaza, 20 March 2013.

A number of analyses emphasize Hamas' capacity to develop wide-ranging contacts at a popular level, both with individuals and NGOs: 'Hamas benefits from important backers, not only inside Islamist groups, but also in the anti-American and anti-Israeli camps. Sympathy for Hamas in Gulf states and other Muslim and Arab countries reaches important levels, which allow local partners of Hamas (organizations and individuals) to collect a considerable amount of funds.'[60]

Leaders and Hamas sympathizers frequently boast about the efficiency of this foreign policy in providing for the government's financial needs. For instance, Ayman al-Taha, who was in charge of relations between Egypt and Gaza, mentioned that these initiatives allowed the Gaza government to survive financially for approximately six years.

Although it is impossible to verify whether all these promises of assistance were indeed kept, one can nevertheless be sure that they were not sufficient for the government to survive. Indeed, most Arab countries remain Western allies in the region and therefore indirectly support the blockade, which has led Hamas to draw closer to Iran. While during the entire 1990s Hamas was receiving funds from diversified sources and did not solely depend on Iranian aid, the period that followed Hamas' victory in the January 2006 elections illustrated increased economic dependency on the Islamic Republic.[61]

The unavoidable Iranian manna

Iran was the first country to provide Hamas with political and military support.[62] In March 2006, a delegation led by Khaled Mesh'al was welcomed in the Iranian capital, prior to Mahmoud al-Zahar and Ismail Haniyeh's visits. In December 2006, the prime minister of the 'Tenth Government' reaffirmed in Tehran that Hamas' goal was to fight Israel, and that to this end, the only conceivable strategy was resistance. During this visit, which apparently translated into $250 million being handed over, Haniyeh dismissed any likelihood of submitting to the three conditions of the EU.[63] According to some sources, Egyptian customs let Mahmoud al-Zahar go through the border, despite knowing at the time that the money was from Iran.[64] Our conversations with the movement's leaders confirmed this correlation between the economic blockade and the rapprochement with Iran:

---

60. Hroub, 'A Newer Hamas? The Revised Charter'.

61. Beverly Milton-Edwards, 'The Ascendance of Political Islam: Hamas and Consolidation in the Gaza Strip', *Third World Quarterly* 29, no. 8 (2008).

62. Râ'id Kamâl Aḥmad Ashniyûr, 'Al-taqqarub bayn Îrân wa Ḥamâs: Bayn al-ḍarûra wa-l-khiyâr' ['The Rapprochement between Hamas and Iran: Between Choice and necessity'], Kânûn al-awwall, Birzeit University, 2010.

63. Ismail Haniyeh's visit took place between 7th and 11th December 2006, *Iranian ISNA News Agency*, 10 December 2006.

64. *Masress*, 17 June 2006; *Miftah*, 29 November 2006.

Hamas has gone through very difficult moments following the 2006 election victory: the suspension of funding was a means to prevent it from exercising power. Many states closed their doors to Hamas and adopted a policy of isolation to bring the movement to its knees. This made Hamas knock on other doors, like those of Iran for instance.[65]

The need for Iranian funds became more urgent after the events of June 2007, when Hamas alone took responsibility for managing the government in Gaza. Public sector employees of Fatah who accepted to stay at home were the only ones to receive their salaries from Ramallah.

Iranian financial backing came in the form of annual budgets and occasional additional payments. These amounts may have amounted to $20 million a year, added to 50 million provided during the 2006 election campaign. From the time of the government's formation in March 2006 until the war in Gaza in December 2008, Iran apparently handed over more than $100 million a year to cover the wages of civil servants, providing another $45 million for the families of prisoners.[66]

While the movement had to take responsibility for the government's entire annual budget (reaching $300 million for 20,000 public sector employees, including 16,000 working as security personnel),[67] Iran was a considerable source of support, donating between $100 and $150 million a year. Independent sources attest that, though not regular, this backing is assessed at approximately $120 million yearly, a sum absolutely vital for Hamas: Ahmed Yousef told the author that 'Iran has offered a hundred million dollars a year to pay its public sector employees, and additional sums of money for other aspects, for example forty-five million for families of detainees in Israeli prisons'.[68]

Beyond financial support, Iran has also provided military support to Hamas via a transfer of scientific and technological knowledge. Hamas' military industry is apparently in full progress courtesy of its close cooperation with Tehran, which also supplies weapons and trains fighters.[69] At the organizational level, the movement increasingly resembles Hezbollah, particularly at the level of the *'manzuma'* structure supervising military training and smuggling.[70]

65. Conversation with the academic Adnan Abu Amer in Gaza, 24 March 2013.
66. Adnan Abu Amer, *Iranian Influence in the Gaza Strip*, Evidence and Implications, Friedrich Ebert Stiftung, Jerusalem, 2011.
67. For 2010, the Finance Ministry announced a global budget of $540 million, *Associated Press*, 18 March 2012.
68. Conversation with Ahmed Yousef in Gaza, 16 March 2013.
69. According to Israeli sources republished in *al-Khalij* on 11 July 2007, Hamas had approximately 10,000 fighters at its disposal.
70. *Al-Ittihad*, 12 July 2007.

Searching for alternative backers and retaining old ones

Faced with a redefinition of its regional alliances, Hamas also had to make sure its new Egyptian and Qatari political backers would also become financial ones. The severing of relations with Syria did in fact raise the issue of the resilience of the alliance with Tehran. Many Iranian leaders had announced that, in case of a break in links with Bashar al-Assad, Iran would end its funding, delivery of weapons and military training in Iran for Hamas' armed wing. As from the summer of 2011, Tehran asked Hamas to officially support the Syrian regime[71] by organizing pro-Assad rallies in Palestinian neighbourhoods in Syria.[72] The Palestinian leaders' refusal to submit to this injunction did not put a final stop to funds, as witnessed by the presence of many Hamas leaders during the International Congress in support of the Intifada, organized in Tehran on 1 October 2011. In Moussa Abu Marzouk's opinion, Khamenei's speech was a sign of the unflinching support for his organization.[73] According to what he said in talks with the author, the first decrease in economic backing was visible in the summer of 2012: 'Hamas was punished by Iran and Syria because it refused to adopt an official stance of support for the al-Assad regime: Iran with money and Syria by other means.'[74] 'The Iranians put pressure on us to make us back al-Assad, but we replied "sorry, this is not possible". They then reduced funds for a while, but then resumed their financing, because they could simply not take upon themselves to lose us.'[75]

Momentarily deprived of Iranian manna, Hamas then considered it essential to find alternative backers. The signing of the Doha Agreement in February 2012 derived from the need to diversify sources of aid in the context of Iranian threats to put an end to funding.[76] In addition to the commitment to open communication channels with the United States and Europe, Doha also said to Khaled Mesh'al that it wanted to help in lifting the blockade and reconstructing Gaza. The Qatari emir's visit to Gaza on 23 October 2012 was a reflection of these promises of investment.[77]

During a conversation between the author and Ahmed Yousef, however, the latter mentioned the inadequacy of Qatari support and its broken promises, while the reconciliation agreement implied new investments from the Gulf emirate to help in Gaza's reconstruction:

71. Mustafa al-Sawwaf claimed that economic support was always given under certain conditions, *Palestine* newspaper, 6 September 2011.
72. This happened at the time the Syrian regime was attacking Latakia and in particular the neighbourhood of al-Ramel, forcing more than 10,000 Palestinians to flee and go into exile.
73. *Al-Alam*, 1 October 2011.
74. Conversation with Ahmed Yousef in Gaza, 16 March 2013.
75. 'Hamas out of Syria', *Associated Press*, 27 February 2012.
76. According to Jonathan-Simon Sellem, more than 40,000 public sector employees in Gaza did not receive their pay in July 2011, *JSSNews*, 22 August 2011.
77. *Le Monde*, 24 October 2012.

> When Fathi Hamad and Ghazi Hamad visited Qatar, we told them: 'You can send your men and start rebuilding Gaza.' But they answered: 'Sorry, we cannot transfer the money.' We in turn told them: 'You can have your own banks in Gaza.' But they declined the offer. These false promises partly explain why Hamas did not cut its relations with Iran. We asked Qatar to send us oil to Gaza via Egypt, but they also declined. They will do as in Darfur, they only care about their image in the media.[78]

According to Moussa Abu Marzouk, the Gulf states suggested that the movement sever its relations with the Islamic Republic but, when they were asked to replace financial assistance until then provided by Iran, they refused. He claimed that Hamas had proposed that a rich Gulf emirate become its main 'godfather', in exchange for economic support to an extent of $150 million per year, but this proposal fell on deaf ears.

> During a meeting, the Saudis asked us to cut ties with Iran. We asked the Saudi Foreign Affairs Minister Saud al-Faysal to give us a comparable sum each year to sever our relations with the Islamic Republic, but he made no promises. We had good relations with King Abdullah when he was prince. He supported us. He liked Sheikh Yassin. He would visit him every day when he was in hospital in Saudi Arabia. He liked his way of thinking, his charisma. When he became king, he stopped all of this, probably due to American pressure.[79]

Faced with broken promises and with changes in the regional context, Hamas saw itself obliged to mend ties with Iran. Some sources have mentioned the first trip to Tehran of Hamas leaders in the summer of 2012, the first period of significant decrease in Iranian support. Between 8 and 13 September 2012, Mahmoud al-Zahar and Marwan Issa may have signed in both Beirut and Tehran detailed military protocols stating the commitment of Hamas to join a common front in case of an Israeli attack against Iran.[80] The Iranians apparently introduced demands specific to Hamas, explaining that if these requests were not accepted, Hamas would leave Tehran with empty hands. As compensation for these agreements, Iran apparently agreed to resume its economic support, as well as the supply of missiles and technology. The same sources have also reported that the Iranians trusted Hamas so little that they obliged its delegation to go through Beirut to meet Hassan Nasrallah before returning to the Gaza Strip.

The second decrease occurred much later, in May 2013 during the Battle of al-Qusayr, when members of Hamas fought Syrian regime forces and Hezbollah. This renewal of tension between Iran and Hamas was confirmed on 19 June by

---

78. Conversation with Ahmed Yousef, Gaza, March 2013.

79. Conversation with a Hamas figure who preferred to remain anonymous, Cairo, February 2012.

80. *Debka*, 27 September 2012.

the Foreign Affairs vice-minister of the Gaza government, Ghazi Hamad.[81] From then on, Hamas has sought to 'make up' for Khaled Mesh'al's initiatives, which, to say the least, were not very appreciated by Tehran (for instance, his presence next to Sheikh al-Qaradawi, when the latter described Hezbollah as 'the party of Satan', or when he published an official communiqué on 17 June 2013, calling for a Hezbollah pull-out from Syria).[82]

The need to re-establish good relations with the Islamic Republic has become increasingly acute, all the more so since the ousting of Egyptian president Mohammed Morsi and the implementation by the new al-Sissi administration in Cairo of a very strict policy towards Hamas. Confronted with the closure of the Rafah crossing and the sealing of most tunnels linking Gaza to Sinai, Hamas found itself for the first time since 2006 on the verge of collapse.[83]

Breaking the deadlock

Handing Gaza's keys over to Mahmoud Abbas: The Shati and Cairo Agreements

The various inter-Palestinian reconciliation agreements signed since 2006 were a means for Hamas to try to obtain recognition through political union with Fatah: the Mecca Agreement, which had enabled the formation of a national unity government, collapsed during the June 2007 events; the Cairo and Doha Agreements (2011 and 2012), which did not gain consensus within the movement, depended on an uncertain regional context. As of 2014, reconciliation agreements were not in the opinion of Hamas, all part of the same strategy of normalization. Conscious of difficulties in gaining recognition through union with Fatah, Hamas now chose to withdraw from the political game and decided, in order to break the deadlock, to hand over the keys of Gaza to Mahmoud Abbas.

This was what occurred during the Shati Agreement of April 2014. Economically weakened by the destruction of smuggling tunnels between Egypt and Gaza, Hamas left Fatah with the responsibility of forming the Palestinian Authority government on its own. The government formed in the wake of the signing of the agreement did therefore not include any minister affiliated to Hamas, a crucial factor which, moreover, allowed the European Union and the United States to recognize it. Yet these dynamics stumbled over Israel's robust opposition. The Jewish State vetoed the permission for Qatari aid meant to pay 40,000 Gazan public servants to transit via Ramallah's Palestinian Authority. This refusal would be later expressed in a more brutal way by the launching of 'Protective Edge', during the summer of 2014.

---

81. *Al-Masri al-Youm*, 19 June 2013.
82. *Al-Quds al-Arabi*, 3 June 2013.
83. According to the Minister of Economy Ala al-Rafati, the sealing of tunnels since July would have caused the loss of $230 million and cost more than 20,000 jobs in Gaza. The Kerem Abou Salem crossing would only account for 30 per cent of the Gaza Strip's needs.

In October 2017, Hamas reiterated its wish to hand over Gaza's keys to the Palestinian Authority's president, since it was cornered by new sanctions, this time decided as early as April by Mahmoud Abbas himself.[84] The decision to return to Gaza was also eased by a double dynamics: on the one hand, the efficiency of Egyptian mediation and, on the other, the ascent to the Gaza leadership of Yahya al-Sinwar, who was sincerely committed to the implementation of a reconciliation process that he imposed on intractable elements in his party.[85] Thus, on the eve of the Cairo Agreement, Hamas announced the dissolution of its coordination committee, a decision that was interpreted as Gaza's complete surrender to Fatah.[86] Yet once again, these dynamics stumbled on the hesitations of Mahmoud Abbas, who did not see the appropriateness of once more taking responsibility for the administration of two million Gazans living under blockade. Conscious of these obstructions, Hamas then had to think of other strategies to obtain the lifting of the embargo.

Guaranteeing the monthly payment of Qatari aid: The dynamics of war and peace

Although the March of Return was part of the dynamics of popular protest organized via the mediation of various political factions, it very quickly became an instrument of pressure used by Hamas to oblige Israel to negotiate. Considered as tools complementary to rockets, incendiary kites and balloons were now associated with a global strategy of armed struggle, mobilized as a function of the progress in negotiations held simultaneously in Cairo: when the talks were going smoothly, Hamas would keep the peace, but when they stalled, it would use these tools to force Israel to return to the negotiating table. Launched in July 2018, these talks led to a first agreement reached in November under the aegis of the United Nations, Egypt and Qatar. Since then, the goal of Hamas has been to force Israel to implement the terms of this deal.

Hamas has various instruments to coerce Israel into implementing the agreement. It can, for instance, refuse to accept Qatari payments when Israel tries to impose new conditions on the movement: this is what happened when, following

---

84. Mahmoud Abbas justified these sanctions by denouncing Hamas' announcement of the formation of a coordination committee in March. Yet Abbas' sanctions began as early as April, first affecting his own public servants, whose salaries decreased by 30–50 per cent, and then hitting impoverished families who became deprived of assistance (including medical insurance), as well as the Gazan population as a whole, whose electricity was cut since the Palestinian president had decided to refuse paying to Israel bills for electricity meant for Gaza. Ahmad Melhem, 'Abbas sanctions fit into peace project', *Al-Monitor*, 30 June 2017.

85. Mohamed Younis, Leila Seurat, 'Un accord entre le Hamas et le Fatah à l'ombre du parrain égyptien', *Orient Xxi*, le 17 October 2017.

86. Official communiqué of Hamas, 17 September 2017. https://hamas.ps/ar/post/7917/.

the reception of the first two payments of $15 million in November and December,[87] Hamas rejected the third one, accusing Israel of demanding new restrictions,[88] which included the transiting of Qatari money through the Palestinian Authority's official banks, and even the halting of the March of Return.[89]

Tired of waiting for the implementation of the agreement, Hamas could also choose to intensify the dynamics of the March on the Northern and Eastern fronts. For instance, this occurred in March 2019, when the movement incited protesters to carry out operations of 'night disturbances' to scare Israeli civilians and pressure their government during a time of elections. This strategy would go as far as firing rockets in the direction of Tel Aviv on 14 and 25 March. Yahya Musa mentioned the deliberate choice of reactivating the March of Return, at a moment when the April Israeli elections were being held. Netanyahu could not allow himself to launch a military operation of great magnitude against Gaza and had no choice but to negotiate.[90]

This reactivation of 'violent' means went in tandem with a dynamics of appeasement. On 30 March 2019, during the first anniversary of the March of Return, Hamas, in the midst of negotiations in Cairo, deployed its men in orange suits to secure the security fence separating Gaza from Israel and prevent Gazan youth from walking into a confrontation.[91] It thus obtained an increase in Qatari aid, which rose from US$15 to US$40 million, without interrupting the March: the mobilization could remain in the form of a march per week, which would never go beyond the security perimeter extending 300 metres from the security barrier. It was the same logic of appeasement that prevailed during the violent clashes opposing Israel to Islamic Jihad in November 2019: staying away from confrontation, Hamas obtained the opening of the Kerem Shalom crossing, the supply of fuel by trucks and an extension of the maritime territory granted to fishermen.

The provision of various compensations to Hamas – either in the form of Qatari aid meant for public servants and Gaza's impoverished population, or as solutions to fight against unemployment, or even in the guise of a gas pipeline construction project to provide Gaza with electricity, or a water treatment plant – is the product of the search for global solutions to try to make the Gaza Strip viable. Hamas, the only guarantor of stability in the territory, has thus acquired, via negotiations under the aegis of Egypt, Qatar and the United Nations, the status of an unavoidable interlocutor.

---

87. Over the $15 million granted to Hamas, $10 million were used to pay the salaries of public servants, and $5 million were meant for humanitarian aid.
88. https://www.youtube.com/watch?v=rs0CVszO2ZY.
89. *al-Jazeera*, 24 January 2019.
90. Tareq Baconi, 'Stopping an Unwanted War in Gaza', *International Crisis Group*, March 2019.
91. *Al-Monitor*, Rasha Abu Jalal, le 2 avril 2019.

Chapter 5

INSIDE

REINFORCING ITSELF AND COMPETING AGAINST ITS RIVALS

On the local Palestinian stage, Hamas seeks to instore a truce with Israel to ensure its control over the Gaza Strip's administrative and financial management and to compete with its nationalist and Islamist rivals.

As regards nationalist forces, Hamas is above all competing with Fatah, the dominant political force within the PLO and one of the Palestinian Authority's institutions. In its speech, Hamas constantly tries to distance itself from Fatah and the PLO's diplomacy. In practice, this distinction also allows it to vye against Ramallah. In this regard, Gilad Shalit's release and, more generally, armed struggle against Israel are victories against Mahmoud Abbas's government. Visits abroad also appear as attempts at delegitimizing the PLO, a contributor to Hamas' isolation from official Palestinian diplomatic bodies.

The Islamist forces against which Hamas is competing are Islamic Jihad and various Salafi groups threatening the prolongation of the truce between Israel and Hamas. However, Hamas has oscillated between two contradictory priorities: though it has to respect the truce with Israel and the resulting calm on the borders, it cannot show itself as a force repressing actions of the 'resistance'. This is why it is sometimes forced to tolerate and even participate in armed operations carried out by rival factions. Islamic Jihad is an important competitor, particularly because it benefits from solid backing by Iran. Since it did not close its offices in Damascus and has refrained from criticizing Hezbollah for its participation in the fighting on Syrian soil, it is able to benefit from Iran's favour at the expense of Hamas. The summer 2014 war in Gaza nevertheless opened a period of collaboration between these two factions.

Good governance and foreign policy

Re-establishing order and reforming the security system

From the moment Hamas dominated the Strip politically, guaranteeing the security of Gaza's population became a means for the movement to reinforce its credibility.[1]

---

1. Conversation with Hassan Balawi in Ramallah on 16 February 2011.

In 2003 and 2004, the Gaza Strip was a hotbed of all dangers. Various armed groups which had become stronger in the wake of the Second Intifada were fighting each other, creating an atmosphere of extreme violence (*falatan amni*).[2] In this context, it became Hamas' priority to put an end to insecurity by 'cleansing' Gaza of the various clans, which constituted a threat to the consolidation of its power.[3] Tareq Mukhimer has emphasized: 'The Hamas government began a process of consolidation of its power and centralization of its authority by reducing the military and economic capabilities of the clans, militias and criminal gangs in Gaza.'[4] This purge particularly affected the Helles, a family known for its ideological proximity with Fatah, as well as the Dughmush.

Following a deadly attack blamed on Fatah in July 2007, Hamas police launched repressive operations and attacked the bastion of the Helles clan. Responding to the requests of Mahmoud Abbas, Israel agreed to save 180 members of this family by allowing them to take refuge in the Jewish State.[5]

A few months later, when a policeman was shot dead in Gaza by members of the Dughmush family, Hamas security forces attacked the clan and made many arrests. In the autumn of 2007, most weapons of these groups were requisitioned.[6]

With the same aim of re-establishing order, the movement focused on freeing Alan Johnston, the BBC correspondent detained in Gaza by the Salafi *Jaysh al-Islâm* group. Johnston had been captured in April 2007, two months prior to the seizure of Gaza. At the time, however, Hamas had neither demanded his release nor tried to be a mediator. Yet as from 15 June, it did all it could to free the hostage, going as far as to use force against the Salafi movement.[7] On 17 June, *Jaysh al-Islâm* dismissed the demands of Hamas and published a video of the correspondent, still alive, a broadcast requesting in exchange for his liberation that of Abou Qatada

---

2. Jean-François Legrain has noted that the use of the term *falatan* is recent. It replaces that of *fawda* employed during the Second Intifada to describe exacerbated violence. The *falatan* springs from the confrontations occurring as early as 2003 between Mohammed Dahlan's Palestine Preventive Security (PPS) and Moussa Arafat's Military Intelligence Services. It exposed the Palestinian Authority's incapacity to guarantee the population's security. See Jean-François Legrain, 'La dynamique de la "guerre civile" en Palestine', *Critique Internationale* 36 (2007): 147–65.

3. According to Naim al-Achab, insecurity in the Gaza Strip was a pretext that Hamas took advantage of. The movement considered it had to seize Gaza to re-establish order, *Imarât-Hamas, Dâr al-tanwîr wa-l-tarjama wa-l-tawzî'* (Ramallah, 2007).

4. Tariq Mukhimer, *Hamas Rule in Gaza: Human Rights under Constraint* (Basingstoke: Palgrave Macmillan, 2012).

5. Yezid Sayigh, 'Policing the People, Building the State: Authoritarian Transformation in the West Bank and Gaza', *International Crisis Group*, February 2011.

6. *Asharq al-Awsat* of 24 August 2007 mentions the improvement of the situation in Gaza on the level of security.

7. 'Radical Islam in Gaza', *International Crisis Group*, Middle East Report, n. 104, 20 March 2011.

al-Filastini, who was jailed in the UK because of his alleged affiliation to al-Qaida.[8] Via the Executive Force, Hamas then proceeded to this group's leader's arrest and freed Alan Johnston.

This affair severely hurt the Dughmush, since most members of *Jaysh al-Islâm* were part of this family. During the months that followed, the relations between Hamas and the family continued to sour. Gaza government police forces began attacking the Dughmush neighbourhood, which was bombed for the first time on 25 July 2008,[9] then again in August. Nine *Jaysh al-Islâm* activists were killed on this occasion, and Hamas ended the clan's autonomy.[10] This outcome made the movement appear, on the external and above all the internal stage, as the guarantor of order, in addition capable of eradicating ideological thought jeopardizing the Brotherhood's doctrine.[11] This repression was carried out concomitantly with the signing of the June 2008 truce: focused on the struggle against the 'enemies' within, Hamas wanted a lull in the fighting with Israel.

The search for a truce was also an opportunity for Hamas to start reforming its security system.[12] Despite the restricted material resources that is dedicated to this goal, this reform allowed the movement to appear, in the eyes of its base and, more broadly, Gaza's population, as capable of administering the coastal strip and providing adequate public services.[13] In contrast to reforms decided simultaneously by Mahmoud Abbas as an answer to pressure from Western donors, restructuring the security apparatuses was an initiative of the Gaza government only, during a period of intensification of the financial blockade. According to Yezid Sayigh, it was this freedom of action that explained the improvements to the security sector. Sayigh highlighted the importance of the autonomy given to Interior Minister Sayyid Siam in this project's implementation.[14]

8. Demands for Qatada's liberation (his real name being Omar Mahmoud Othman) were not a proof of *Jaysh al-Islâm*'s affiliation to al-Qaida.

9. Fighting caused the death of 13 people, including 11 members of the Helles clan, and at least 100 wounded. International organizations described excessive use of force, hindrances to human rights and summary executions. Mukhimer, *Hamas Rule in Gaza*.

10. 'Radical Islam in Gaza', *International Crisis Group*, Middle East Report, n. 104, 20 March 2011.

11. In an interview given to *Asharq al-Awsat* on 24 August 2007, a leader of Hamas declared that though the organization was very firm with *Jaysh al-Islâm*, this was not to please international opinion, but because this group's ideology was *takfiri*, that is, close to that of al-Qaida.

12. Mukhimer, *Hamas Rule in Gaza*.

13. Yezid Sayigh, 'Policing the People, Building the State: Authoritarian Transformation in the West Bank and Gaza', *International crisis Group*, February 2011.

14. According to Yezid Seyigh, tens of security and police agents were sent to Syria, Iran and Sudan to be trained, even before Hamas' show of force in the Gaza Strip.

In order to limit the defections of public servants who, answering Salam Fayyad's injunction,[15] were not coming to the workplace, Sayyid Siam recruited 5,000 policemen. He then included professionals and old Fatah officials ready to work for Hamas.[16] Officer Tawfiq Jabr took charge of the new section of the police and became responsible for reorganizing security forces in the Gaza Strip.

His main achievement was the official separation of the Izz al-Din al-Qassam Brigades from the police forces. In fact, at the time of the creation of the Executive Force[17] in April 2006, 2,500 members of the Brigades were included in it. The 2007 reform led to the dissolution of this force, which was integrated into the Palestinian Authority's legal structures; its members were once more part of the Palestinian Civilian Police,[18] while the role of the Brigades was now restricted to the defence of borders and the struggle against Israel. According to Yezid Sayigh, the participation of al-Qassam Brigade members in the operations of police forces was one of the causes of the deterioration of Hamas' image among the public and various NGOs on the ground. This was also confirmed by the chief of the Executive Force Abou Ubayda al-Jarra. He granted that the Brigades did play a significant part, particularly during the 'military decision' to seize Gaza, and that an interference (*tadakhkhul*) may have occurred in jurisdictional terms, but they were asked to gradually go back to their positions, public order being the business of the police. He mentioned having attempted, moreover, to pass this message to Israeli authorities by providing Brigade members with unmistakable uniforms and requesting them to stay clear of Israel's border zones.[19] These declarations reveal that this restructuration was for Hamas a major priority, the movement's image having been tarnished in the wake of the 2007 show of strength. In the frame of this reorganization of the internal stage, the truce appeared as fundamental since it allowed the movement to implement its specific goals and to enjoy greater credibility among Palestinians.

---

15. In the wake of Hamas' show of force in the Gaza Strip, Gaza's public servants still had their wages paid by the Ramallah Authority, on the condition they stay at home. This policy resulted in many defections, which allowed Hamas to create its own security service, making any hostility towards it vanish. See Are Hovdenak, 'The Public Services under Hamas in Gaza'.

16. *Al-Watan al-Arabi*, 22 August 2007.

17. The Executive Force (*al-qiwa al-tanfîdîyâ*) had been created by Hamas in April 2006, because security forces refused to cooperate with the new Hamas interior minister. Comprising 5,800 men, it was a Hamas police of sorts. See Beverley Milton-Edwards, Order without Law? An Anatomy of Hamas Security: The Executive Force (*Tanfithya*), *International Peacekeeping*, 15:5, 2008, 663–76; See also Are Hovdenak, 'The Public Services under Hamas in Gaza'.

18. Yezid Seyigh, 'Policing the People, Building the State: Authoritarian Transformation in the West Bank and Gaza', *International Crisis Group*, February 2011.

19. *Al-Nahar*, 5 September 2007.

Hamas has tried to dissolve the Executive Force by absorbing its personnel into four agencies inherited from the Fatah's regime: civilian police (*shurta*), the National Security Force (*quwat al-amn al-watanî*), Civilian Defence (*al-difâ' al-madanî*), and Special Security (*al-amn al-khass*). These forces were integrated into those of the Interior Ministry, following the Prime Minister' orders. Intelligence services, the Presidential Guard and the military police were also dissolved and replaced by a new structure, the Agency for National Security, whose responsibility was internal security and protection of the Hamas regime; this agency was also under the Interior Minister's orders.[20]

To implement this reform, Hamas had to ensure conditions for a relative calm on the Israeli front; such an initiative could not succeed in a context where rockets were being fired at Israel.

Basim al-Zubaidi also considered that through this policy of appeasement, Hamas wanted to reorganize the Palestinian internal stage in its various aspects. His analysis of the stances of the movement's leaders as regards the truce has shown that it was after the coup in Gaza that declarations in favour of a lull in the fighting increased in number.[21] He noted that, paradoxically, it was also the moment when the embargo was tightened and Gaza was regarded by Israel as an 'enemy entity'.

Planning financial management and rearmament

Gaza's economy evidently depends on Hamas' financial backers – Iran in particular – and on the Ramallah Authority, which continues to pay the wages of its former public servants, as well as on international organizations, UNRWA in particular. After 2006, decreasing aid from Hamas' traditional supporters resulted in a lack of cash flow, hence the need to find alternative sources of funding. Many American NGOs were declared guilty of supporting a 'terrorist organization':[22] the arrest of five chairmen of Islamic associations depending on the Brotherhood in New Jersey and Texas restricted financial transfers for charity reaching Damascus.

20. Seyigh, 'Policing the People, Building the State: Authoritarian Transformation in the West Bank and Gaza'.
21. Basim al-Zubaidi has proven in his analysis published in the *Alresalah* newspaper the weekly increase in announcements in favour of the truce, going from a quarter of declarations in 2005 to more than half in favour of appeasement in 2006. The year 2007 saw the disappearance of the opposition of the truce, after Hamas occupied the Gaza Strip. al-Zubaidi, *Hamas wa-l-hukûm, dukhûl al-nizâm am al-tamarrûd 'alayhi*.
22. Ali Mufid 'Abd al-Qadir, Khaled Mesh'al's half-brother, was apparently sentenced to twenty years in jail, and Mohammed al-Muzayyin, Moussa Abu Marzouk's cousin, to ten years. Shukri Abou Bakr and Ghassan al-'Ishi, the founders and managers of 'Holy Land Institutions' (*mu'assat al-ard al-muqaddassa*) were sentenced to sixty-five years in prison on 29 May 2009, according to *Asharq al-Awsat*.

Other institutions had already closed shop following the 9/11 attacks.[23] Since they could not count on their internal charity networks and their *zakat* committees only, Hamas tried to multiply duties and taxes, exploit lands freed by the departure of Israeli settlers, encourage investment and recover high-value land seized by Hamas officials.[24]

After the events in June, Hamas above all attempted to safeguard its control of the economy, in particular by dominating the informal sector. Tunnels were the main channel of commerce.[25] Thanks to the levying of substantial taxes, the emergence of this underground economy allowed the movement to generate sizeable profits: in 2009, 80 per cent of imports into Gaza apparently came in via tunnels employing some 15,000 Palestinians who had lost their jobs in the wake of the embargo.[26] This situation lasted until June 2010, when the loosening of the blockade permitted passage of goods through the land border with Israel.[27]

The al-Qassam Brigades had established strict control over these tunnels previously managed by other factions,[28] thus replacing the old merchant elite.[29] This smuggling, of course, generated confrontation with the families owning the tunnels: the increase in the number of tunnels had lowered prices and resulted in the payment to Gaza's municipality of a fixed fee of $3,000 for the delivery of a yearly permit. Hamas leaders also levied taxes of 15–20 per cent of the value of goods transiting through the tunnels.[30]

Taxes were also levied on the conventional trade of products coming from Israel. The collection of compulsory duties on imports enabled Hamas to earn

23. According to *Asharq al-Awsat* (29 May 2009), one of their main charity organizations was the *jam'iyat al-islâh al-hayrîya*, whose main funder is the *i 'itilaf al-hayr*, presided by Sheikh al-Qaradawi.

24. *Al-Watan al-Arabi*, 22 August 2007.

25. Peter Spiegel, 'Tunnels Allowing in Food, Medicine also Help Fuel Fighting in Gaza', *Los Angeles Times*, 11 January 2009.

26. Nicolas Pelham, 'Diary in Gaza', *London Review of Books* 31, no. 20 (22 October 2009).

27. According to Liam Stack, the informal economy emerging since 2008 is responsible for approximately 80 per cent of imports into Gaza, and employs more than 15,000 people, 5,000 tunnel owners, plus a number of merchants, in total some 50,000 people. In 2009, Hamas would have collected between 150 and 200 million dollars. Liam Stack, 'For Hamas, an End to Gaza's Tunnel Trade May be Only the Beginning', *The Christian Science Monitor*, 15 August 2010.

28. 'Ruling Palestine I', *International Crisis Group*, Middle East report n. 73, 13 March 2008.

29. Though the tunnels were existence prior to June 2007, their number increased in the wake of Gaza's seizure by Hamas in June 2007. Their number in 2008 was thought to be between 400 and 1,100. See Saleh al-Naimi, 'Gaza Underground World', *Asharq al-Awsat*, 13 October 2009. Omar al-Shabban from *Pal Think* estimated their number to be 1,200.

30. Eric Cunningham, *The Christian Science Monitor*, 17 August 2009.

some $4million a month, that is, 17 per cent of monthly government expenses, which are assessed at $30 million. These taxes are quite unacceptable for Gaza's population, since commercial exchange is already taxed beforehand by Israel, money then handed over to Ramallah's Palestinian Authority. Levies occur at checkpoints created a few metres away from those controlled by Ramallah's Palestinian Authority.[31]

These tunnels, whose construction became systematic as from June 2007, are doubly useful for Hamas: they gather sympathy from Gaza's inhabitants but also permit obtaining rare products, particularly medicine and enable the movement to renew its stock of weapons.[32] The tunnels have indeed contributed to increase its military capability[33] and monopolize the arms traffic by only tolerating weapons coming out of its own ones.[34] The *hudna* also allowed the arrival of 300 armoured cars, hundreds of jeeps and Landrovers and even hundreds of vehicles tailored for the needs of high officials. Hamas, moreover, seized the personal property of Fatah officials, some 5,000 bullet-proof vests and modern means of communication.[35] The lull in the fighting with Israel provided Hamas with an opportunity to 'digest' its victory, as emphasized by Beverly Milton-Edwards, who noted the chronological correspondence between Hamas' huge military preparation and this period of calm.[36]

The January 2008 *hudna* was for Hamas a means to fulfil its various internal policy interests, such as the fight against banditry, the reorganization of its security and the accumulation of wealth and weaponry. These positive outcomes, particularly 'good governance', naturally allowed the movement to strengthen its relationship with its regional backers and restore its credibility abroad. On this matter, Ahmed Yousef has indicated that Turkey offered Hamas a secret mediation, which at the time was in addition welcoming many European delegations, officially for 'security' or 'academic' reasons, but in fact for political motives. These visits led to the publication of reports calling for the lifting of the blockade.[37] Confidential meetings with Italian intelligence officials occurred on 27 August 2007 in Ismail

---

31. 'Ruling Palestine I', *International Crisis Group*, Middle East report n. 73, 13 March 2008.

32. David Schenker, 'Gaza Tunnels no Path to Peace', *The Washington Institute for Near East Policy*, 14 January 2009. According to the statements of American official Gary Ackerman published in the *New York Times* on 8 November 2007, Egypt may have allowed Hamas to obtain weapons and let various armed group go to train in Iran; republished by *al-Ittihad* on 7 November 2007.

33. Nicolas Peltham, 'Gaza Tunnel Complex', *Middle East Research and Information Project* 41 (winter 2011).

34. Rex Brynen, 'Gaza's Tragically Peculiar Economy', *Foreign Policy*, 18 March 2010.

35. Maryam Robin, *Uktubar*, 29 July 2007.

36. Beverly Milton-Edward, 'The Ascendance of Political Islam: Hamas and Consolidation in the Gaza Strip'.

37. *Al-Hayat*, 3 September 2007.

Haniyeh's office, with Mahmoud al-Zahar and Ahmed al-Jaabari being present. During these talks, Hamas leaders apparently asked the Italians to soften the stances of other European countries on the issue of the blockade and requested the provision of visas for their leaders. In general, however, these attempts were not very fruitful.[38]

Vying with Ramallah

Hamas is mainly competing with Fatah, an influential political force dominating both the PLO and part of Palestinian Authority institutions. The Islamist movement thus tries to delegitimize institutions controlled by its rival by pointing the finger at Fatah's grip on them. In order to do this, Hamas has not hesitated to mobilize Palestinian Authority institutions to assert itself against the PLO.

A diplomacy of demarcation

The narrative of Hamas opposes the PLO's project of 'surrender', in which truce is equivalent to the end of war, to its own 'resistance program', which sees the *hudna* as nothing more than a provisional agreement aimed at the cessation of Israeli military actions. By making negotiation a form of management of war, Khaled Mesh'al can continue to display his differences with Fatah and the PLO, the latter conceiving negotiation with Israel as an end in itself, and not a means:

> What you obtain at the negotiating table is a product of your own situation, and the result of the balance of forces on the ground. If you are beaten on the ground, you will also certainly be defeated at negotiations. Just as war requires an equilibrium of power, negotiations and peace require an equilibrium of power, because one cannot make peace when one of the sides is powerful and the other one weak; in the latter case, this is surrender. The United States did not make peace with Japan and Germany after the Second World War, but they rather forced these two countries to surrender, and the signing of a pact of respect of what had been decided and submission. In short, peace is made by the powerful and not by the weak.[39]

In its discourse, Hamas use comparisons that integrate its strategy into existing categories and clarifies it by using historical precedents through which organizations that are neither Islamist or ideologically close to it have passed. The

---

38. According to *al-Khalij*, 6 August 2007, Haniyeh tried to make his audience forget about the refusal to recognize Israel's existence by insisting on the democratic nature of Hamas.

39. Khaled Mesh'al's interview by Silvia Catori in the Jordanian *al-Sabeel* newspaper, in July 2010.

Political Bureau's chief referred to the situations in which victor's justice is forced upon the defeated, the archetypal example being the end of the Second World War, imposed on the losing side by the atomic destructions of Hiroshima and Nagasaki.[40]

According to Hamas leaders, the main lines of their diplomacy are based on the permanent preoccupation of rectifying Fatah's 'mistakes'.[41] In contrast to Mahmoud Abbas, who puts up with occupation, Hamas tries to convince international players to change their opinion towards Israel. This is what Mahmoud al-Zahar said when describing his visit to Kuala Lumpur: 'the Indonesian president wanted to take steps to establish relations with Israel and I managed to dissuade him from doing so. Abou Mazen [Mahmoud Abbas] went there after I did and convinced him of the opposite.'[42]

Hamas leaders also claim to have re-established links with Kuwait, Libya and the Sultanate of Oman, states that according to Mahmoud al-Zahar no longer have relations with Fatah. One of the successes of his visit appears to have been renewed contacts with Oman and the first official visit of a Palestinian delegation. He added:

> In Kuwait, our visit was a victory [*ziyâra nâjiha*], because the Kuwaitis did not want to have official relations with the Palestinians since the first Gulf War. While they were asking for official apologies from the PLO, they welcomed me in a very dignified way, and I was met at the airport and directly taken to the Emir's palace, where I received forty million dollars (lost by the Palestinian authority) in favour of our government.[43]

Non-interference in the internal affairs of Arab neighbours has a central place in this diplomacy of demarcation.[44] Mahmoud al-Zahar thus reckoned that 'Hamas does not interfere in the internal affairs of any country, and is not part of any "axis" in the Arab world. Respecting these rules allows us to avoid reproducing the errors of Fatah, for example during the first Gulf War, which had caused the departure of al Palestinians from Kuwait.'

These words echoed those of Osama Hamdan:

> Fatah has had a much longer political experience than ours (with positive and negative aspects). When our movements took shape, we drew lessons from these experiences. Our policy of not interfering in the internal affairs of Arab

---

40. Ibid.
41. Hroub, *Hamas, a Beginner's Guide*, 153.
42. Conversation with Mahmoud al-Zahar in Gaza, 20 March 2013.
43. Ibid.
44. This claim to correct or not repeat Fatah's mistakes must of course be questioned: at the time, Yasser Arafat was acting without a territory, while, from the very moment of its formation, Hamas benefited from a territory and a militant base. This partly explains the fact that the movement had better success at avoiding confrontation with host states.

states originates precisely from the study of Fatah's experience. There was a step backwards in Palestinian politics because of Fatah, which, instead of fighting the Israelis, began fighting Arab peoples and other Palestinians, for instance in Lebanon. We have undoubtedly benefitted from these mistakes, and we have succeeded in not repeating them.[45]

As for Mahmoud Al-Zahar, he asserted that

The greatest crime perpetrated by Palestinian leaders was to enter the game of axes. Abou Ammar [Yasser Arafat], when he played this game, got closer to Iraq in its war against Kuwait. Who lost in the end? The Palestinians. This is why the game of axes is a blind game, and we do not wish to play it. If this were the case, interest would have led us to side with Egypt.[46]

We are not a movement of mercenaries who strengthen their relations with the one who gives, and break them with the one who does not. Our relations must be good and courteous with the entire group of Arab and Muslim countries. We are not in an axis, and we hope for the end of the policies that consist in toeing the line spread by United States and the occupation.[47]

The last characteristic of this diplomacy of demarcation is the supposed respect for the principle of separation between the movement's representatives and members of the government. Basem Naim, in charge of the movement's foreign policy in Gaza, highlighted the fact that, as opposed to Fatah, Hamas abides by this rule: 'There is a collaboration (*tansîq*) with our brothers working in the government, but no interference (*tadakhkhul*). The government represents all of the Palestinian people, while the party represents only itself.'[48] He emphasized the difference with Fatah's experience, which totally conflated government and movement. This is also what Ayman al-Taha (the former official in charge of relations between Egypt and Hamas) has asserted.[49]

Although they accept the idea of complementarity between the various levels of representation, the movement's leaders nonetheless dismiss any attempt to interfere: parliament members are said to be Hamas representatives, like any MPs in the rest of the world belonging to a political party; members of the government, however, are clearly dissociated from the movement's leaders.[50] This description

---

45. Conversation with Osama Hamdan, Damascus, 29 January 2011.
46. Mahmoud al-Masri's interview in *al-Masri al-Youm*, 3 May 2011.
47. Mahmoud al-Masri's interview in *markaz al-filastînî li-l-i'lâm*, 6 December 2010.
48. Conversation with Basem Naim in Gaza, 18 March 2013.
49. Conversation with Ayman al-Taha in Gaza, 19 March 2013.
50. Many ministers are also influential members of Hamas, for example, Ismail Haniyeh, Mahmoud al-Zahar, Ghazi Hamad. According to Mohammad Hijazi, Hamas made the same mistake as Fatah by not dissociating members of its movement from those of its government, *madkhal li-qirâ'a tajribat hamas f-i-l-hukm*, *Awrâq falastinîniya*, 2 (Summer 2008): 99–101.

is far from real. Quite the opposite, there is intense interdependence, since government representatives are most often important members of the movement or even members of its executive body (the Political Bureau). In the opinion of some analysts, it is precisely this interdependence that explains the success of Hamas in consolidating its power over the Gaza Strip in such a short time after the June 2007 events.[51]

In 2006, it was Mahmoud al-Zahar, one of Hamas' founders and a Political Bureau member, who was chosen to become Foreign Affairs minister. Questioned on the matter, Mouchir al-Masri confirmed that when he was minister, he did not officially represent the movement. Ismail Haniyeh's case is more problematic: he has been simultaneously vice-president of the Political Bureau, MP, Foreign Affairs minister and prime minister. Al-Masri justified this situation by the exceptional context of occupation. Basem Naim, in charge of the movement's foreign policy in Gaza, emphasized that in contrast to Fatah, Hamas strictly respects this principle of dissociation.[52]

Gilad Shalit's release

Hamas widely criticized the first attempt by Mahmoud Abbas to request Palestine's membership in the UN Security Council in November 2011. The reason given was that this request had no legitimacy, since it was not made in the name of a government of national unity but of the PLO only. The Hamas Foreign Affairs minister Mohammed Awad considered that any plan aiming for the success of such an initiative had to be based on the unity of Palestinian ranks:

> With our unity, we can address the world with a unified discourse, to make everybody understand what we want and that we deserve a state. We fear that Palestinian Authority President Mahmoud Abbas' determination to travel to the UN in the coming month of September, to obtain the recognition of a Palestinian state on the basis of the 1967 borders, is only a media campaign which will yield no result whatsoever.[53]

---

51. Yezid Sayigh, 'Hamas Rule in Gaza: Three Years On', *Crown Center for Middle East Studies*, Middle East Brief 41, March 2010, and Beverley Milton-Edwards, 'The Ascendance of Political Islam: Hamas and Consolidation in the Gaza Strip', *Third World Quarterly* 29, no. 8 (2008).

52. Conversation with Mouchir al-Masri on 16 March 2013 in Gaza, and Basem Naim, on 18 March. As for Ayman al-Taha, he considered this phenomenon as one of the problems encountered by Hamas. In his mind, dissociation must not be an intangible rule (conversation on 19 March 2013 in Gaza).

53. Conversation with Mohammed Awad, Gaza, 17 March 2012.

At the time, only Ahmed Yousef had declared that his movement was wrong to be against the demand for recognition at the UN,[54] deploring Hamas' opposition when the Islamic Conference Organization, Turkey and many states throughout the world were backing it. In his letter addressed to the Palestinian president, published on the internet on 23 September, he stated that Hamas had good reason to be very critical of Mahmoud Abbas, but that it was more appropriate to make good use of the sympathy of various states for the Palestinian cause.

The personal and unilateral aspect of Mahmoud Abbas's initiative, in a way, benefited Hamas, allowing it to construct its narrative of dissent around a claim that could appear as legitimate to other Palestinian factions, also opposed to the recognition process. The denunciation of this unilateralism, however, was diluted in other disapprovals concerning this recognition's adverse impact: renunciation of 80 per cent of Palestinian land, Fatah's commitment to the principle of negotiation at any cost and renunciation of the Palestinian people's legitimate rights. The fact that Abbas acted on his own was of secondary importance in the light of the many criticisms expressed towards him.

It was in this context that the liberation of IDF private Gilad Shalit happened. President Abbas's new popularity following his speech at the UN General Assembly worried Hamas, which wanted to claim responsibility for the release of more than a thousand Palestinian prisoners. Hassan Balawi confessed: 'Hamas needed this deal and it was for this reason that it made concessions on a number of points, like the issue of Marwan Barghouti's liberation, that of the head of PFLP, as well as the deportation of many prisoners outside Gaza and the West Bank.'[55]

Shalit's liberation occurred at a time when Hamas' popularity was at a low ebb. Many Palestinians were indeed questioning the inefficiency of its supposed resistance and saw it as a movement similar to Fatah that was looking for political gains but was incapable of lifting the blockade depriving the population of construction materials and essential medical supplies.[56] One should note that in this particular case, the interests of Israel and those of Hamas converged.

According to an Egyptian diplomat, this situation made the agreement possible.[57] He emphasized the rivalry of other groups such as Salafis and Islamic Jihad, both with doubts on Hamas' role in resistance against Israel.

---

54. Ahmed Yousef had publicly declared this during a radio talk on '*Sawt Falastin*' (*The Voice of Palestine*), on 18 September 2011.

55. Conversation with Hassan Balawi, Paris, 15 December 2011.

56. 'Curb your Enthusiasm: Israel and Palestine after the UN', *International Crisis Group*, Middle East Report No. 112, 12 September 2011.

57. 'Egypt played the part of an accelerator, because it wished to close this file as a first stage in the lifting of the blockade, and join Gaza with the West Bank. Indeed, Gaza represents a major problem for the security of Sinai and of Egypt in general, as shown by the Eilat attacks of the month of August'; conversation with an Egyptian diplomat, Cairo, February 2012.

Military escalation

While being a means to break Gaza's isolation and obtain recognition,[58] 'Cast Lead' also guaranteed Hamas' interests on the local stage and helped it compete with the Palestinian Authority.

In January 2009, Khaled Mesh'al felt he had gained enough legitimacy through armed resistance on the ground; because of the Israeli aggression's intensity, he felt he was able to question the Palestinian Authority's president, who was pressing Hamas to accept the UN resolution. This was an attempt to discredit Fatah by emphasizing the illegitimacy of Abbas, who had sided with Israel though his mandate was over, preventing international aid from going through administrative bodies controlled by Hamas: 'Mahmoud Abbas must permanently break peace negotiations with Israel if he really wants Palestinians to reconcile with each other.'[59]

Hamas, moreover, may have 'needed' this war to delegitimize the Ramallah Authority, which was on the verge of signing a deal with Ehud Olmert.

Indeed, in November 2007, while the siege of the Gaza Strip had tightened and as the West Bank was receiving promises of economic support, Mahmoud Abbas and Salam Fayyad had travelled to the Annapolis summit to speak to Ehud Olmert. The idea of a permanent settlement to the conflict had been submitted on the occasion of this meeting. Bilateral Israeli and Palestinian groups had been formed to deal permanently with the following issues: refugees, borders, settlements, Jerusalem and water. Though these talks had not led to concrete solutions, since Israel was continuously creating what is called 'new facts on the ground' regarding West Bank settlements, both sides were keen to conclude an agreement in November 2008.

Hamas' sources on this war were describing Mahmoud Abbas as a traitor and Fatah as Israel's ally.[60] Mouchir al-Masri accused Mahmoud Abbas of being informed of an imminent Israeli offensive against Gaza.[61] Hamas also claimed that a crisis unit was set up in Ramallah by the president's secretary general al-Tayeb Abd al-Rahim, whose mission was to collect information on Hamas' arms caches and find the locations of its leaders to hand them over to the enemy.[62] The Islamist movement's spokesman Fawzi Barhoum, moreover, refused Mahmoud Abbas's invitation, considering that it was formulated too late and was a means to make the president's actions on this matter be forgotten.

In March 2011, through reactivation of conflict with Israel, Hamas wanted to snuff out any possibility of national reconciliation by drawing attention to other priorities. The al-Qassam Brigades' firing of rockets thus were aimed at making

58. Ismail Haniyeh, 'My Message to the West', *The Independent*, 15 January 2009.
59. Quoted by Egre, *Le recours à la violence par le Hamas*.
60. *al-Jazeera*, 1 January 2009.
61. *Al-Quds*, 30 December 2008.
62. Al-Safir, 1 January 2009.

people forget about the popular revolts of 14 and 15 March, which had demanded 'the end of occupation' and 'the end of division'.[63] While Prime Minister Haniyeh had given his consent to the organization of demonstrations on the Square of the Unknown Soldier, demonstrators had walked to Katiba Square. This initiative sparked the anger of Hamas leaders, who then called on security forces to repress the demonstrators.[64] Many of these protesters were wearing insignia of other Palestinian groups, violating the instructions on unity that forbade any other symbol than the national flag.

While on 16 March Mahmoud Abbas had favourably answered Haniyeh's invitation to discuss new bases on which inter-Palestinian reconciliation could take place, ten days later several Hamas military leaders let it be known that the security of the Palestinian Authority's president could not be guaranteed were he to go to Gaza. This warning cast doubt on the sincerity of Ismail Haniyeh's proposal[65] and on his room for manoeuvre in the movement's decision-making process. It is relevant here to formulate the idea of a causal relation between military escalation and reconciliation. By reactivating the process of armed struggle, Hamas was apparently dismissing discussing the issue of national unity, and in order to do this, was trying to draw attention to other priorities.

The November 2012 assault on the Gaza Strip was widely analysed as a victory over Ramallah. Hamas then sought to minimize rallying of the people around Mahmoud Abbas's next approach to the UN,[66] whose goal was the recognition of Palestine as a non-member state. This second attempt, planned for 29 November, had many more chances of success[67] compared to the first one. It was for this reason, in particular, that Hamas leaders did not denounce it this time. Khaled Mesh'al saluted the initiative as a 'small' positive 'step' in his speech in Gaza on 8 December.[68] As for Osama Hamdan, he believed it paved the way for the official recognition of Palestinian delegations, not only at the UN but also in other international bodies.[69] This inclusion as a non-member state was, according to

---

63. These mobilizations came after two attempts, the first being 'Gaza Youth Breaks Out' and the other 'The Revolution of Dignity'. The latter was planned for 11 February and was meant to be against Hamas, but it never took place.

64. 'Gaza: Stop Suppressing Peaceful Protests', *Human Rights Watch*, 19 March 2011.

65. When Abbas expressed his wish to go to Gaza, some of the Strip's leaders, such as Ismail Haniyeh and Aziz Dweik, favourably received this initiative, while most other high Hamas officials questioned this trip's goal and motivations and harshly criticized the PA's president; see Usama Hamdan's statements in *Asharq al-Awsat* on 23 March 2011.

66. Jean-François Legrain, 'Gaza, novembre 2012: une 'victoire' de Hamas pour quoi faire?', *Carnets de l'Iremam*, 3 February 2013.

67. 29 November was chosen symbolically, because it is also the day when, sixty-five years earlier (in 1947), the UN General Assembly adopted Resolution 181 that partitioned Palestine into two states.

68. *Markaz al-Zaytûna*, 10 December 2012, Beirut.

69. *Markaz al-Zaytûna*, 8 February 2013, Beirut.

him, very useful in invalidating the juridical claims of the Israelis, particularly those concerning refugees. The goodwill of Hamas regarding this second approach did not prevent it from using the armed struggle to hamper Abbas's increasing popularity.[70] Victory over Ramallah was naturally not just the result of Hamas' strategy. Many analysts[71] have also highlighted the Israeli tactic consisting in widening the gap between Hamas and Fatah, an example of traditional 'divide and rule'.[72] Netanyahu also wished to undermine the Palestinian Authority's president on the eve of his attempt at the UN.[73] Once more, one can notice the occasional match between the interests of Hamas and those of Israel. This strategic convergence can be explained by the will to contain Fatah's progress. Israel, keeping Ramallah at bay, had tolerated the wide-scale diplomatic manoeuvres taking place in the wake of the November offensive against Gaza.[74]

Competing with the PLO

Since 2006, Hamas has mobilized Palestinian Authority institutions it controls in Gaza, including those duplicated in 2007, in order to assert its legitimacy and compete with the PLO. The rapprochement with Iran, as well as with Qatar, has favoured these attempts to delegitimize its main Palestinian rival.

The Palestinian Authority, a tool to delegitimize the PLO

The Oslo Accords had taken good care to impede the Palestinian Authority's right to create a Ministry of Foreign Affairs:[75] diplomatic relations and negotiations with

---

70. Khaled Diab, 'Israelis and Gazans: Don't Buy your Leaders' Rhetoric', *Haarezt*, 17 November 2012.

71. Yossi Alpher, 'Israël va devoir compter avec l'islam politique', *L'Orient-le-Jour*, 25 November 2012.

72. There is also a common expression in Arabic to express this rule: '*Farq tasûd*' ('divide and you win').

73. Raghida Derham, 'The Gaza War Reinforces Palestinian Division and Threatens Abbas's Palestinian Authority', *al-Hayat*, 24 November 2012.

74. Jean-François Legrain, 'Gaza, novembre 2012: une "victoire" de Hamas pour quoi faire?' *Carnets de l'Iremam*, 3 February 2013.

75. Annex II of the Declaration of Principles, initialled at Oslo on 20 August 1993. Now, the capacity to create contacts with other states is, according to the Montevideo Convention, one of the conditions for a state's existence. Israel had authorized the creation of a Ministry of Planning and International Cooperation directed by Nabil Shaath, whose role was to preside over commercial and financial deals with other states and manage aid for development. The aim of the 2002 reform was to rectify limitations to the peace accords by handing over more stately attributions to the PLO.

Israel were left to the PLO, whose offices remained in Tunis.[76] The founding of a Foreign Affairs Ministry of the Palestinian Authority in 2003[77] provoked very serious tensions between Farouq al-Qaddoumi, the PLO Foreign Affairs minister and Nabil Shaath, the National Authority's Foreign Affairs minister between 2003 and February 2005. By multiplying the number of diplomats, this reform had exacerbated tensions between the PLO and the Palestinian Authority, since Farouq al-Qaddoumi, the president of the PLO's Political Department, saw himself as the foreign minister of the State of Palestine from the moment of the Palestinian Declaration of Independence in Algiers, on 15 November 1988. As for Nabil Shaath, he was nominated as the Authority's Foreign Affairs minister. Between 2003 and 2006, al-Qaddoumi many times reasserted his superiority over Nabil Shaath and Nasser al-Qidwa (who were ministers in succession).[78] For instance, when the latter had wished during the first week of 2005 to reorganize the diplomatic agenda by appointing twenty-two Palestinian Authority ambassadors, Farouq al-Qaddoumi rejected this reform to maintain his control over diplomatic personnel.[79] This coexistence of two personalities claiming the same status created a form of schizophrenia, since there were two ministers to represent a country not recognized as a state.

The conflict was partly solved by the adoption of the law regulating the diplomatic corps, which was enacted by Nasser al-Qidwa, a law reinforcing the prerogatives of the Palestinian Authority at the PLO's expense. Mahmoud Abbas, who did not expect to lose the 2006 elections, had indeed given more power in this field to the Palestinian Authority. Yet faced with the Hamas' victory, Abbas reversed his decision: he prescribed a change in strategy and remobilized the PLO on issues of foreign policy to reduce the manoeuvring space of the Hamas-led government.[80] Although a complete U-turn seemed impossible, the Palestinian president added a motion stipulating that, in all matters relevant to ambassadors, Third World summits and Europe, Farouq al-Qaddoumi would be able to overrule the Authority's ministry.

76. One should recall that the Oslo Accords were signed between Israel and the PLO, which was recognized by Israel as the 'representative of the Palestinian people'. Letter of recognition of Itzhak Rabin, September 1993, in Mahmoud Abbas, *Le chemin d'Oslo*, Paris, Edifra, 1994, 295.

77. Mamdouh Nofal has denounced the Palestinian Authority's negligence towards PLO ambassadors and representations, Mamdouh Nofal, 'La crise entre l'Autorité Nationale et l'OLP', *Revue d'études plaestinienne*s 56, no. 4 (Summer 1995): 3.

78. Nasser al-Qidwa was from 1991 to 2005 the Palestine's observer at the UN, prior to becoming the Palestinian Authority's minister of Foreign Affairs, in February 2005.

79. 'Sirâ' bayn Fatah wa Hamâs "ala al-tamthîl al-khârîjî"', *Rojava*, 15 May 2007.

80. This rivalry between the two institutions led Hamas to create a Ministry of Refugees while, theoretically, relations with the Diaspora were a prerogative of the PLO. Conversation with Hassan Balawi in Ramallah, on 20 February 2011.

Mahmoud Abbas, however, could not simply consider the Authority as the PLO's simple executive body. Had he not favoured the rebalancing in favour of the Palestinian Authority's government? Hamas would largely benefit from the reforms carried out by Abbas before the 2006 elections to claim a capacity to represent Palestinians as legitimate as that of the PLO, displaying its presence as an attribute of the Foreign Affairs Ministry it now embodied.[81]

Mahmoud al-Zahar's withdrawal from the Summit of Non-Aligned States in Malaysia bore witness to the intensity of the conflict between the two Palestinian institutions, a conflict by then concealing an opposition between two political factions. Farouq al-Qaddoumi had come to lead the delegation[82] as Palestine's '"legitimate" representative',[83] while Mahmoud al-Zahar was the Palestinian Authority's Foreign Affairs minister. Al-Zahar was moreover already present in Kuala Lumpur on the occasion of his diplomatic tour in the region. Faced with the PLO's insistence, he then announced his withdrawal from the Summit of Non-Aligned States. Such an event would have probably not occurred had the Palestinian Authority's Foreign Ministry been a Fatah representative. Beyond the continuation of institutional rivalry, these splits acquired another dimension with the rise to power of Hamas. In Mahmoud Abbas's mind, Farouq al-Qaddoumi had to continue representing Palestinians in Third World countries, and as a minister of the Palestinian Authority, Mahmoud al-Zahar could be part of the delegation if he wished so but, nevertheless, could not lead it. Together with his role inside the PLO, Farouq al-Qaddoumi was in addition Fatah's general secretary, a role that confirms the idea that confrontation on such a scale would have never happened had the Palestinian Authority's minister been a member of Fatah.

In his statements, al-Qaddoumi denounced Mahmoud al-Zahar's diplomatic inexperience and his lack of expertise. He described the latter in an extremely condescending manner, depicting him as a simple intern heading a local government (*mahallîya*). He added that he was ready to give him 'lessons in diplomacy' before handing him the portfolio.[84] According to al-Qaddoumi, the problem was not political[85] but only related to the contrast between his thirty years of experience and al-Zahar's complete inadequacy.[86] He also asserted that 'the highest level of representation of the Palestinian people is the PLO', and that 'Mahmoud al-Zahar does not want to understand this'.

---

81. This institutional confusion also allowed Hamas to justify its refusal to participate in peace negotiations with the Israelis, arguing that this task was the PLO's.

82. *Al-Mustaqbal*, 29 May 2006.

83. During Mahmoud al-Zahar's visit to Syria, Farouq al-Qaddoumi could not act in the way he did in Malaysia, since Syria does not recognize the PLO and had never welcomed Palestinian diplomats before 2006.

84. Farouq al-Qaddoumi's letter, addressed to Mahmoud al-Zahar and dated to 29 May 2006, is accessible online: http://www.paldf.net/forum/show-thread.php?t=64296.

85. *Al-Ahram*, 30 May 2006.

86. *BBC Arabic*, 29 May 2006.

Despite its obvious inferiority in comparison to the PLO, Hamas contested its monopoly, claiming that while that structure is indeed in charge of representing Diaspora Palestinians, it does not represent those of the West Bank and Gaza. According to the leaders of the movement, this was truly a political conflict, since Fatah has taken advantage of the PLO to confiscate all foreign policy prerogatives from Hamas.

Among other examples, the presence of Hamas at the Congress for the Right of Return in Brussels illustrated this wish to delegitimize the PLO and rival it. The speech of Suleyman Abou Seta, who was this summit's general coordinator, was bent on denouncing the security cooperation between Ramallah's Palestinian Authority and Israel, emphasizing that the PA was only protecting the 'Zionist Entity'. He also castigated the absence of the Palestinian ambassador, stating that the latter had never answered the invitation.[87] He finally condemned the PLO's attempts to scuttle the summit.[88]

Mohammed Awad, who was Foreign Affairs minister between 2011 and 2012, has confirmed the amplification of institutional rivalry between the PLO and the Palestinian Authority after 2006. According to him, Mahmoud Abbas took advantage of the fact that Hamas was not part of the PLO, in order to impose a representative of this institution in international summits and forums:

> The problem of the Hamas government's Foreign Affairs Ministry is linked to two phenomena: the fact that the President of the Authority belongs to Fatah and is personified by Abou Mazen (Mahmoud Abbas), and the problem of the PLO's jurisdiction, of which Hamas is not part, and whose president is also Abou Mazen (Mahmoud Abbas). Although each Palestinian Authority minister had to theoretically share the task of running foreign affairs with the PLO, and all ambassadors abroad had to systematically consult the President and the PLO, the problem became worse with the arrival of Hamas. This issue already existed before 2006, but became far more acute after 2006.[89]

Though Fatah leaders insisted there is no Hamas foreign policy, since contacts developed by the movement do not go beyond partisan relations,[90] the movement's foreign relations were, all the same, a sensitive matter for Mahmoud Abbas, who feared witnessing increasing recognition of Ismail Haniyeh's government from 2011 onwards. The very fact that Ismail Haniyeh was welcomed as prime minister

---

87. *Alresalah*, 18 May 2013.
88. *Al-Awda*, 18 May 2013.
89. Conversation with Mohammed Awad in Gaza, 17 March 2012.
90. In the opinion of Ziad Abu Amer, former Foreign Affairs minister of the national unity government between March and June 2007, Hamas enjoys only partisan relations (*hizbiyyan*) with some parties or states and has only a few representation offices in some countries. Ahmed Yousef is alone in sharing this view: 'We are strong in Palestine but not outside. We do not have the support of the Arab and Muslim world.'

outside Palestine was in itself a problem not only for Ramallah but also and above all for the PLO.

Haniyeh thus denounced Fatah's pressures exerted on Arab chiefs of state to make him unwelcome during his first tour, which began in late December 2011. During the 12 January parliamentary session, Haniyeh stated that these countries' leaders had fortunately ignored the president of the Palestinian Authority's attempts: 'I was informed by the Tunisian presidency that Mahmoud Abbas had addressed a request to avoid meeting me, but the Tunisian president answered that in his state, rule of law prevailed, and that he would receive me as legitimate Prime Minister, in conformity with Palestinian law, pending the designation of a new Prime Minister.'[91]

Ismail Haniyeh's second tour in the United Arab Emirates also provoked the dismay of Mahmoud Abbas, who was surprised at his rival being welcomed as a minister and not as a simple Hamas delegate.[92]

The reception of foreign representatives in Gaza was also a problem for Ramallah and the PLO. In January 2013, the visit of Malaysian prime minister Mohammad Najil Abd al-Razak once more provoked the ire of Mahmoud Abbas. He fumed: 'This visit undermines my status and that of the PLO as sole representatives of the Palestinian people.'[93] The same occurred during the May 2013 visit of the president of the World Federation of Ulemas, Sheikh Yusuf al-Qaradawi. The Gaza minister of Waqf and Religious Affairs Ismail Redwan insisted that this initiative was proof of Arab and Muslim support for Palestine[94] and marked a stage towards another visit to Jerusalem once the holy city would be liberated.[95] Ramallah's Waqf minister Mahmoud al-Hibash, however, declared that Yusuf al-Qaradawi should have gone to al-Aqsa instead of Gaza, in a context of Palestinian division. In the eyes of Fatah, this visit deepened *inqisâm*.[96]

Hamas nonetheless denies going after recognition, for fear of appearing as an alternative to the PLO.[97] Ayman al-Taha referred to Khaled Mesh'al's worry of seeing foreign heads of state officially travel to Gaza and give the impression that the Hamas government behaves as if representing a state. Mahmoud Ahmadinejad's invitation to Gaza, in November 2010, had indeed hurt the movement enough.[98] Ghazi Hamad thus explained: 'Our goal is not to deepen division, but quite the

---

91. Jacques Benillouche, 'L'étrange réconciliation entre le Fatah et le Hamas', *Slate*, 7 February 2012.
92. 'PA Denies to Obstruct Arab Tour', *Wafa*, 14 January 2012.
93. *JSSNews*, 23 January 2013.
94. *al-Jazeera*, 7 May 2013.
95. One should note that the year before Sheikh al-Qaradawi had forbidden all visits to Jerusalem by any Muslim.
96. *Syrianow*, 11 May 2013.
97. Conversation with Imad al-Alami in Gaza, 18 March 2013.
98. 'Hamas Invites Ahmadinejad to Visit Gaza Strip', *Jerusalem Post*, 8 November 2010. Ibrahim Nafe, 'Hamas and Iran after the Invitation to Najad', *al-Ahram*, 10 November 2010.

opposite, to highlight during our visits the importance of national unity. Though we unceasingly explain that the representatives of states are the ones who wish to go to Gaza, and that these visits have mainly humanitarian aims, Ramallah's Authority tries to impede them.'[99] This is a perfect illustration of the diplomatic stakes in the internal Palestinian conflict. By founding the Palestinian Authority, Oslo paradoxically paved the way for the PLO's troubles.

Creating a substitute for the PLO?

'It is great time for the Palestinian people to have a new leadership, the PLO is dead.' These were Khaled Mesh'al's words in February 2009; while in Tehran, he was requesting the foundation of a new structure. One should recall that this disavowal meant more for Fatah than for the PLO, an institution stigmatized above all because it was dominated by the former party. Factional conflict between Fatah and Hamas therefore had repercussions on the conflict between Hamas and the PLO.[100]

Rivalry between Hamas and the PLO goes back to the 1980s and crystallized after Hamas surged on the political stage during the first 1987 Intifada and when the movement asserted itself through various actions: demonstrations, strikes and military operations.[101] The 'peace talks' then played an important part in changes in the relationship between Hamas and the PLO, since it was in the wake of the 1988 Algiers summit, in November 1988, and following its recognition of a Palestinian state within 1967 borders, that the two-state solution met fierce opposition by Hamas.[102] The Islamic Resistance Movement made the PLO responsible for the vanishing of the Palestinian people's gains and the surrender of lands occupied since 1948.[103] The reservations of Hamas deepened with the Madrid and Oslo conferences.[104] Yet, from the start, Hamas' approach towards the PLO was not static, since it was cautious not to discredit it as an organization, but

---

99. Conversation with Ghazi Hamad in Gaza on 17 March 2013.

100. Mahmood Monshipouri, 'The PLO's Rivalry with Hamas: The Challenge of Peace, Democratization and Islamic Radicalism', *Middle East Policy* 4, no. 3 (1996): 84–105.

101. The Charter essentially criticizes the PLOs non-religious nature but does not provide clear new insights on the issue of the organization's legitimacy.

102. The Hamas communiqué, published on 23 October 1991, did not denounce the participation of Arab states, but only that of the PLO. See Hroub, *Hamas, a Beginner's Guide*.

103. According to the memorandum addressed to the PLO on 6 April 1990, Hamas apparently put forward certain conditions to join the organization, notably the adherence of the Palestinian National Council to the principle of 'all of Palestine', the refusal to recognize the 'Zionist Entity', and the obtainment by Hamas of a number of seats proportional to its political weight, which it estimated at 40 or 50 per cent. See Hroub, *Hamas, a Beginner's Guide*, 95.

104. During the Madrid talks, Hamas communiqué number 77 of 3 August 1991 mentioned the PLO's lack of legitimacy; see Hroub, *Hamas, a Beginner's Guide*, 90.

solely in terms of its leadership. Although Hamas had for a long time disputed the PLO its title of 'sole legitimate representative of the Palestinian people', the Second Intifada, which resulted in diminished hopes of establishing a Palestinian state on the lands occupied in 1967,[105] led to the truce of sorts between the two parties.[106] Arafat's death in November 2004 and Mahmoud Abbas's election paradoxically opened a new era in the relations between the two organizations. At the time of the signing of the Cairo Agreements, on 17 March 2005, Hamas accepted to recognize the PLO, while claiming 40 per cent of the seats in the Palestinian National Council.[107]

The issue of proportionality in Hamas' representation at the Palestinian National Council continued to be a pressing one, particularly during the signing of the Prisoners' Document, in June 2006.

Prospects for Hamas' fusion into the PLO, however, diminished with the June 2007 events.[108]

The new souring of relations between the Hamas and the PLO incited the Islamist movement to question once more the PLO's representativeness. Hamas seems then to have chosen to work outside this institution to present itself as an alternative. As of 2007, the option of a parallel institution resurfaced. Though this question was never officially mentioned by its leaders, Khaled Hroub has insisted it was nonetheless present in some speeches. On this matter, he noted, for instance, the statements of Abd al-Azazi al-Rantisi, who, after the Oslo Accords, had said that Palestinians were now facing a void in leadership.[109] The setting up of a body representing the Palestinian people that would substitute for the PLO was mentioned in many communiqués at the time.[110]

105. As early as 2002 Israel had occupied regions ceded to the Palestinian Authority and then besieged Arafat in his general *Muqata'a* headquarters in Ramallah.

106. Khaled Hroub has distinguished three Hamas strategies to face the PLO: to enter the PLO in order to dominate it, form an alternative to the PLO, or choose neither option and abstain from any plan to found a substitute organization.

107. The truce foresaw Hamas' participation in the Palestinian political regime in power at the time, the PLO's reactivation (*taf'il*), and the formation of a Committee that would define its bases and comprise the head of the Palestinian National Council, the members of the PLO's Executive Committees and the general secretaries of all Palestinian factions.

108. Fatah attributed the failure of this fusion to Hamas. According to Ziyad Abou Amr: 'It is amusing to notice that Hamas recognized the PLO as sole legitimate representative of the Palestinians when it was only a simple movement, but that it refused to do when in the government. Generally speaking, a government is more moderate than a party.' Conversation with Ziad Abu Amer in Gaza on 23 March 2013.

109. 'The Palestinian People now have Become Leaderless and therefore it is Necessary to Find Leadership', *al-Destour*, 13 September 1993, cited in Hroub, *Hamas, a Beginner's Guide*, 99.

110. This was notably the case when, in April 1992, following the summit in Madrid, Hamas submitted a proposal to the 'group of ten', calling for the creation of a body (the

An example speaking for itself was Hamas' reaction to the Annapolis summit, in November 2007. The movement reacted to this initiative by organizing a parallel congress in Damascus, reiterating its refusal to abandon the refugees' right of return. It had also planned to send a letter to the PLO leadership stating 'its right of putting into doubt the reality of the PLO's representativeness as regards the Palestinian people'.[111] Another example came after 'Cast Lead', when Khaled Mesh'al declared his wish to reorganize resistance factions upon new foundations. This new stand sparked off much discussion as to the PLO's representativeness and raised doubts about Hamas' will to build a new organization that would be the equivalent of the PLO:

> As for the PLO, which for four years has opposed Hamas' membership and the organization's reconfiguration, it cannot be a reference for Palestinians; it is in a state of powerlessness and exploits, and even weaponizes, the means and tools at its disposal to deepen division among Palestinians; and I must tell you with sincerity today, from Doha, that all Palestinian resistance forces and factions which are around us, particularly since the Gaza victory, will unite to create a new patriotic reference, which will be strong because of a representativeness that will be both an internal and external one, and which will group all the currents of our people and all its patriotic figures.[112]

This approach, which demeaned the PLO, intensified during the visit of the Hamas delegation to Tehran in December 2009.[113]

From the Iranian capital, Mesh'al advised the formation of a new body and command to gather together the Palestinians.

> No legitimacy can be conferred on institutions and formations that are opposed to the deepest choice of our people, which is resistance: this is why we shall try to create a direction of resistance forces inside and outside, until we reach the meeting point between the gun and political organization, as was the case in 1969.

'High Committee of Palestinian Coordination') to streamline the efforts of various factions, and minimized concessions put forward by the PLO; see Khaled Hroub, Arabic version, Appendix 10, Document 7, 328.

111. al-Zubaidi, *Hamas wa-l-hukûm, dukhûl al-nizâm am al-tamarrûd 'alayhi*.

112. *Al-Doha*, 5 February 2009.

113. This official stance was not entirely new, since it was preceded by Osama Hamdan's paper published by the *al-Zaytûna* centre, which stipulated that Hamas was a new political and social force that would eliminate everything obsolete from political structures in place. Hamdan had then added that the PLO was null and void, since it had failed to gather the spectrum of Palestinian political forces.

Hamas had already attacked the PLO from Iran during the First Intifada, a sign that an outside alliance could serve its internal interests:[114] 'What can ensure the Intifada's victory is its organization and control by Islamist groups. No opportunity should be offered to groups favourable to both normalization and opportunism. These groups must follow the general will and adopt Islam. In the reverse case, their leaders must be cast aside for ever.'[115] By uttering threats towards Israel and accusing some Arab countries of complicity, the head of the Political Bureau was, in 2009, once more discrediting the PLO as the Palestinian people's 'sole representative'.

After this episode, several Hamas leaders tried to defuse conflict, explaining that the real goal of Mesh'al's statements was not to create an alternative body to the PLO[116] but only a front for the various factions, forces and figures, which would espouse the political stances of Hamas. These factions, forces and present were those not present inside the PLO. According to them, Khaled Mesh'al simply wished to put pressure on the PLO's direction to achieve the organization's swift reconfiguration and the integration of Hamas within its various bodies. Since 2009 and the crisis caused by the Tehran and Doha speeches, the leaders of Hamas have tried at all costs to avoid appearing as an alternative replacing the PLO and have spoken at large of the necessity of reforming the rival organization.[117]

Statements made by leaders all insist on the urgency of setting up a 'temporary framework of leadership', as stipulated by the Shati reconciliation agreement. Meant to facilitate the holding of discussions and the organization of elections for the Palestinian National Council, this temporary framework was never, however, activated by Mahmoud Abbas.[118] In October 2017, Yahya al-Sinwar reiterated that Hamas had no intention of replacing the PLO while stating that it was the task of the latter to represent all factions.[119] Yet in 2018, following announcements made by the Trump administration regarding the Israeli–Palestinian conflict – recognition of Jerusalem as Israel's capital and suspension of aid for UNRWA – Ismail Haniyeh emphasized from his Gazan residence the need to organize a national conference to reconcile the strategies of the various Palestinian political

---

114. We have already noted the existence of sources indicating that in 1993, an agreement was apparently signed between Hamas and Iran, which stated that Iran recognized Hamas as the only legitimate representative of the Palestinians.

115. *Teheran Press Agency*, 11 January 1988.

116. Although Ismail Haniyeh and Ghazi Hamad had tried to distance themselves from these proposals, other leaders continued to insist openly on the non-representative nature of this institution in the absence of Hamas. Mahmoud al-Zahar denied it any legitimacy, in particular since the end of the mandate of Mahmoud Abbas, who was elected in 2005.

117. See in particular Ismail Haniyeh's tour and his stay in Damascus, where he met various Palestinian factions and mentioned the need to reform the PLO, *Ma'an News*, 28 November 2006.

118. *Al-Monitor*, 17 November 2016.

119. https://www.almanar.com.lb/2806549.

forces, and thus face these challenges effectively.[120] While a few days before, Hamas had refused to participate in the meeting of the Palestinian National Council, held in Ramallah on 14 and 15 January,[121] the announcement of this conference was interpreted by many Fatah officials as an attempt to try to replace the PLO, when all prospects of unification of Palestinian ranks were collapsing.[122]

The role of Qatar in the provision of attributes of sovereignty

The Arab League Summit held in Doha on 16 January 2009 was also called the Gaza Summit (*qimmat al-Ghazza*). It gave Hamas an influential platform to compete against the PLO. Since they were not capable of gathering enough Arab leaders to hold a summit, the Qataris decided to let the meeting go ahead nonetheless and give it the appearance of a consultative assembly.

Khaled Mesh'al, who on this day enjoyed the stature of a chief of state, gave a resounding speech focusing on five claims: a halt to Israeli aggression (concomitantly with the lifting of the blockade and reopening the crossing points), the need to sue Israel at the ICC, the legitimacy of resistance, the appeal to Arab and international efforts for Gaza's reconstruction and finally the opening of a dialogue for national reconciliation with other Palestinian factions.[123]

By showing such goodwill to Khaled Mesh'al, Qatar was making things difficult for the PLO leadership, which had refused to participate in the summit.[124] The absentees were supporting a negotiated solution with Israel and siding with the Palestinian Authority's president, while Qatar, Sudan, Algeria, Iraq, Libya, Lebanon, Turkey, Senegal, Indonesia, Syria and Iran were favourable to Hamas' resistance strategy. The absence of the Saudi and Egyptian delegations was castigated by some, who denounced on this occasion the 'enslavement' of their regimes to the Israelis and Americans.[125]

As demonstrated by French political scientist Bertrand Badie, the 'activation of networks as a means to stigmatise domination allows the most dispossessed to gain a visibility that is not at all proportional to their power'.[126] Dissent is the only way Hamas can survive or even coexist in an order of domination that is impossible

120. https://hamas.ps/ar/post/8494/.
121. Hamas justified its absence by emphasizing that this meeting was held in Ramallah, therefore hampering attendance for many political representatives. He also insisted on the importance of setting up the Temporary Leadership Framework, as stipulated by the Shati Agreement. See Hussam Badran in *Arabi21* on 13 January 2018.
122. *Al-Monitor*, 7 February 2018.
123. *Qatarconferences.org*, 16 January 2009.
124. See Ahmed Azem's interview in *al-Ghad*, 24 April 2013.
125. *Le Quotidien d'Oran*, 17 January 2009.
126. Bertrad Badie, Marie-Claude Smouts, *Le retournement du monde: sociologie de la scène internationale*, Paris, Presses de Sciences-Po, Dalloz, 1999. See also Frédéric Charillon, 'Les politiques étrangères contestataires', *Cahiers de l'Orient* 87 (2007): 25–31.

to question. Action through dissent is a way to position oneself in a game where, without the capacity to exercise power, one must justify one's dissenting posture and even one's permanent deviance.

Qatar's role in the strengthening of Hamas' status could also be felt through its 'diplomatic' presence in Gaza. Both Hamas and Qatar have denied the existence of an embassy in Gaza. The former has mentioned the presence of a simple delegation led by Mohammed al-Imadi, which came to the Strip only to implement an investment project. The opening of this office did not abide by any particular protocol, as opposed to what usual procedure demands. This denial was relayed by the Qataris: in an interview in the *Alresalah* daily, Mohammed al-Imadi emphasized that his action was purely humanitarian and not political and said that what was opened in Gaza was not an embassy. He also argued that the Ramallah *Sulta* (Authority) had favourably greeted Qatar's action in Gaza.[127] Yet one was in fact dealing with a representation office that has never closed its doors since 2007. In the same interview, the journalist himself calls Mohammed Imadi 'ambassador' (*safîr*); this was confirmed by Israeli sources:[128] the Qatari bureau would be under the instructions of an 'ambassador', who would thus politically back Hamas' legitimacy, despite the latter's international non-recognition.

For analysts, the return of a Qatari 'embassy' in Gaza makes Palestinian division durable.[129] Some sources have claimed that this inauguration was done without any coordination with Ramallah, causing a diplomatic rift between the *Sulta* and the Gulf emirate.

Other elements confirm Qatar's attribution of privileged status to the Movement of Islamic Resistance: the visit of Emir al-Thani, for instance, was unprecedented since, until then, no head of state had dared to take the plunge. This visit was apparently food for thought for other chiefs of state, who hurried in sending their ministers to the Strip.[130] The *Jerusalem Post* considered that this visit strengthened Hamas' position on the Palestinian, Arab, Islamic and potentially international stage, while weakening the Palestinian Authority.[131] As for the PLO, reactions were very violent. Although the organization, in spite of everything, saluted the funding of humanitarian projects, Ramallah accused Qatar of ignoring its authority, exacerbating division and strengthening the project for a 'separate entity in the Gaza Strip', coinciding with Israel's agenda. These criticisms were shared by part of the press in the West Bank. In this vein, *Al-Ayyam* newspaper published a caricature with the caption 'The divisor is not welcome'.[132]

---

127. Sources of the Israeli *Yediot Aharonot* daily, republished in *Falastinonline* on 2 October 2012.
128. *Amjad al*-Arab, 3 October 2012.
129. *Zamnpress*, 3 October 2012.
130. Jean-François Legrain, 'Gaza, novembre 2012: une 'victoire' de Hamas pour quoi faire? ', *Carnets de l'Iremam*, 3 February 2013.
131. *al-Jazeera*, 23 October 2012.
132. *al-Jazeera*, 9 May 2012.

In the opinion of Hamas, these reproaches were baseless; it saw Mahmoud Abbas, who continues to blockade Gaza, as the man responsible for division.[133] As for Fatah, it claimed that it had not been associated with preparations during the emir's visit, while its absence was interpreted by its political rival as deliberate withdrawal.[134]

Ismail Haniyeh's grant of a Palestinian passport[135] to Yusuf al-Qaradawi during the latter's visit to Gaza was a new illustration of the 'stately' prerogatives taken over by Hamas.[136] On this issue, Hamas remains largely dependent on Ramallah, since many countries only recognize passports issued by Salam Fayyad's government.[137] Those given by Gaza's Interior Ministry have only limited validity.

Of course, Hamas was not the only side responsible for the deepening of division. Sheikh Hamad and Yusuf al-Qaradawi's visits were authorized by Israel, which was aware that these trips would heighten discord among Palestinians. Providing Hamas with the attributes of sovereignty helps the Jewish State in its efforts to hold in check the prospects of creation of a Palestinian state.

Israel could only rejoice at Qatar's diplomatic recognition of Hamas, which implicitly meant recognition of a Palestinian state in the Gaza Strip only. On 9 January 2017, the Facebook page of Gaza's reconstruction committee (a Qatari body that deals with humanitarian and real estate projects since 2012) announced its intention of building an embassy in Gaza.[138] This information was posted only for a few hours before being replaced by a statement mentioning the fact that Qatar would construct a building meant for its reconstruction committee. This committee's chairman was none other than Mohammed al-Emadi, Qatar's official envoy to Gaza. One should therefore conclude that, beyond Doha's claims that works managed by this committee were being carried out with the government's agreement, this NGO is in fact Doha's official representation in Gaza. Ahmed Yousef sees no real difference between an embassy and the committee's office. As for Fatah, which has emphasized that the official opening of an embassy would be a violation of diplomatic norms, it fears that this move will be followed by similar ones by other countries like Turkey, thus paving the way for Hamas' diplomatic recognition and the establishment of a separate state in Gaza.

In October 2017, when the Cairo Agreement was reached, the rapprochement between Egypt and Hamas had provisionally cooled relations between the movement and Doha.[139] Mohammed al-Emadi's visit to Gaza on 19 December

---

133. Ibid.
134. *Sawt al-Ghad*, 10 May 2013.
135. *Al-Ayyam*, 11 May 2013.
136. Amira Hass, 'Passports are the Latest Weapon in the Struggle between Fatah and Hamas', *Haaretz*, 25 July 2010.
137. Are Hovdenak, 'The Public Services under Hamas in Gaza'.
138. *Al-Monitor*, 18 January 2017.
139. Although Qatar did not recognize the overthrow of Egyptian president Mohammed Morsi, it was above all the rapprochement with Mohammed Dahlan and Hamas that

2017, however, testified to Qatar's wish to reassert its influence in the Palestinian enclave.[140]

Better control of other Islamist factions

Salafis and Islamic Jihad are powerful rivals of Hamas. Each, for its own reasons, is a threat to the Islamist movement. Salafis, whose number is difficult to assess for want of data, originate in part from the organizational base of Hamas, and therefore threaten the Izz al-Din al-Qassam Brigades' cohesion.[141] Islamic Jihad is supported by Iran, and it can be said it sometimes benefits from the Islamic Republic's preference over Hamas. Now, Salafi groups and Islamic Jihad criticized the truce decided since the end of 'Cast Lead'. Although in most cases Hamas was capable of containing these formations and obliging them to respect the lull in the fighting, it did not always have the capacity to repress them and therefore chose to let them take action on their own.

Impossible containment

As of July 2007, a struggle has pitted Hamas against Islamic Jihad, a group always more than willing to rain rockets on Israel.[142] At that time, Ismail Haniyeh tried to force the group's leadership to better monitor its troops.[143] In January 2009, while all of Gaza's armed factions seemed to agree not to fire any more rockets, some Salafi groups, in particular *Jund Ansâr Allah*, refused to abide by the deal. These factions were all the more a menace to Hamas in that some of its members had previously belonged to the movement's armed branch. Khaled al-Banat, *Jund Ansar Allah*'s military chief, had initially been sent to Gaza by the external leadership to train the al-Qassam Brigades.[144] It was the prohibition of firing rockets that had caused the

worried Doha, since Dahlan is one of the advisers of Mohamed Bin Zayed, the UAE Crown Prince, who has decided on an embargo against Qatar.

140. *Al-Monitor*, 29 December 2017.

141. The two main groups which are a menace to Hamas are *Jaysh al-Islâm* and *Jund Ansâr Islam*. The chiefs of these two groups used to belong above all to Hamas. The first group had participated in Gilad Shalit's abduction but been weakened in the wake of the repression against the Dughmush clan. The second confronted Hamas in August 2009. See 'Radical Islam in Gaza'.

142. *Asharq al-Awsat*, 23 October 2007.

143. Sixty per cent of them apparently come from Hamas. According to several sources, in particular Beverly Milton-Edwards and Stephen Farrell, *Hamas: The Islamic Resistance Movement*, Cambridge, UK: Polity Press, 2010.

144. It is rumoured that the defection of Khaled al-Banat (whose *nom-de-guerre* is Abou Abdallah al-Mujahir al-Souri, and who travelled from Damascus to Gaza in 2007 to train the members of the Izz al-Din al-Qassam Brigades) took place following a disagreement

defection of some of them to Salafi movements,[145] who were in particular gathered together under an umbrella group called *jaljalât*.

In early 2010, arrests of Salafis intensified. Though all of the movement's leaders minimized the importance of these groups, considering them numerically weak,[146] it seems that the conflict opposing Hamas to Salafi groups has since 2009 taken precedence over the rivalry between Fatah and Hamas.[147] Some have admitted off the record the tension caused by two contradictory goals: to guarantee security and not hit too hard on those committed to armed operations against Israel. 'In the end Hamas has two choices: fighting the resistance or accepting that the resistance do its job and respond to Israeli attacks. Both choices hurt Hamas. We need military power in Gaza to protect Hamas, and not to fight Israel.'[148] Rafiq al-Masri thus explained: 'Hamas claims to have joined political institutions to protect the resistance. In reality, Hamas uses resistance (*muqâwama*) to protect its political power (*Sulta*).'[149]

Hamas' launching of rockets in March 2011 was part of the increased rivalry with other Islamist groups, who since January had fired tens of rockets on Israel. The head of *Shin Beth* Yuval Diskin announced that these were in large measure actions by radical Islamist groups affiliated not to Hamas but, rather, to al-Qaida.[150] As of this date, however, Hamas could not prevent competing factions from carrying out armed operations against Israel.[151] On 16 March, groups sent a shell on the regional council of Sdot in the Negev; during these attacks, Hamas looked the other way.[152] Israel then accused the movement of being directly responsible

between the Hamas political leadership and himself on the issue of the truce. See *paltoday.com* on 20 August 2009 and *palvoice.com* on 17 August 2009.

145. Abou Hareth, one of the leaders of *Jund Ansâr Allah*, declared that most members of the *jaljalât* group (approximately 70 per cent) are originally from the al-Qassam Brigades. The remainder are originally from Islamic Jihad and the armed branch of the Popular Resistance Committees, that is, the *al-Ansar* Brigades. See *Ma'annews* on 19 April 2010. See also Yezid Sayigh, '*We Serve the People': Hamas Policing in Gaza*, Brandeis University Crown Center for Middle East Studies, Crown Paper 5, April 2011.

146. Most Hamas leaders claim that Salafis are divided into several branches, and that they only represent a handful of people. Conversations with Osama Hamdan, Moussa Abu Marzouk and Yahya Musa. Statistics vary quite markedly, since Hamas minimizes their numbers, while Salafis themselves and even Israel inflate them; see 'Radical Islam in Gaza', *International* Crisis *Group*, Middle East Report No. 104, 29 March 2011.

147. This is Yezid Sayigh's view. He has shown that defections towards Salafi movements have incited Hamas to constantly reformulate its doctrine.

148. Conversation with a Hamas leader who has wished to remain anonymous.

149. Conversation with Rafiq al-Masri, an academic who is not ideologically close to Hamas.

150. *Associated Press*, 19 January 2011.

151. 'Brigade Claims Fire on Israeli Citizens', *Ma'an*, 19 January 2011.

152. 'Radical Islam in Gaza', *International Crisis Group*, Middle East Report n. 104, 29 March 2011.

and eliminated two militants of the al-Qassam Brigades.[153] The latter therefore bore the brunt of Israeli repression for rockets launched by other groups. Hamas police is tired of controlling on a daily basis vehicles driven in the border zone with Israel, while the truce's goals of ending the blockade and diplomatic isolation are not met. This is why it has chosen to in turn send dozens of rockets, the result of armed operations by factions it cannot stop or does not always wish to repress. Following the March escalation, Hamas gathered a large fraction of these groups, as well as Islamic Jihad, to once more negotiate a halt to the shelling of Israel.[154]

Similar events occurred in August 2011, when on the 24th Israel assassinated one of the chiefs of the Islamic Jihad Brigades. While Israel and Hamas had two days before agreed on a provisional cease-fire,[155] this killing reactivated the conflict and incited the al-Qassam Brigades to participate in armed operations side by side with Islamic Jihad, whose militants were bent on revenge. The immense majority of military operations before the elimination of Ahmed al-Jaabari, in December 2012, was also by these uncontrolled groups, even though these are nonetheless tolerated by Hamas despite itself. Hamas' military branch, headed by Ahmed al-Jaabari, therefore had only limited room to manoeuvre. Its inability to control these groups is insufficient, in the minds of some, to whitewash any accusations of collaboration with the occupiers.[156]

In the wake of the November 2012 offensive, while Islamic Jihad had validated the truce between Hamas and Israel,[157] the al-Quds Brigades fired a rocket on 24 June 2013 at the Jewish State. This came after the killing by the Hamas police of one of their militants, Raed Jandiyya. Pointing the finger at the Gaza government's responsibility, Islamic Jihad took advantage of this incident to cut all contact with Hamas. The firing of rockets on the south of Israel the next Sunday and Monday was also a result of the conflict between Hamas and Islamic Jihad. They led to Israeli raids on Gaza and the closure of crossing points with Israel.[158]

Similar mechanisms were operating during 'Protective Edge', during the summer of 2014. On several occasions, the breach of the truce was the result of rockets fired by other factions. On 10 August, while a second truce of seventy-two hours under the aegis of Egypt came into effect and was then prolonged on the 13th for another five days, on 18 August (on the fifth and last day of discussions), three rockets fell on Israel. Benjamin Netanyahu asked his delegation to return to Tel Aviv, declaring that Israel 'does not negotiate under fire'. These rockets were

---

153. 'The Next Israeli-Palestinian War', *International Crisis Group*, Middle East Briefing n. 30, 24 March 2011.

154. 'Gaza Factions Offer Truce if Israel Reciprocates', *Ma'an*, 26 March 2011.

155. *Le Monde*, 22 August 2011.

156. Jean-François Legrain, 'Gaza, novembre 2012: une 'victoire' de Hamas pour quoi faire?', *Carnets de l'Iremam*, 3 February 2013.

157. Israel has weaponized the conflict between both organizations, as shown by the Islamic Jihad's chief Ramadan Shallah's prohibition to enter Gaza, in December 2012.

158. *Al-Quds al-Arabi*, 24 June 2013.

neither from Hamas nor from Islamic Jihad, two movements that were looking forward to negotiate despite the murder of Mohammed al-Deif's wife and son: 'In circumstances where there is no progress, we do not wish to renew the *hudna*, but this does not mean we go back to war.' This statement was proof of the will to cooperate.

On 8 May 2015, the Salafi group 'Followers of the Islamic State in Jerusalem' claimed responsibility for mortar shelling a Hamas military base in Gaza and for firing a rocket towards Ashdod on 26 May. On 7 June, more rocket shelling, this time against Ashkelon, was claimed by another group, the 'Sheikh Omar Hadid Brigade'. Once more, Israel's reaction consisted in squarely blaming Hamas: infrastructure belonging to the al-Qassam Brigades was destroyed, while the crossing points between Israel and Gaza were shut. Salafi groups were seeking to obtain the release of their militants jailed in Gaza's prisons, and targeting Israel was an effective means to force Hamas to negotiate with them.

Hamas can, as well, use groups purportedly affiliated to Islamic State to reinforce its legitimacy by presenting the Jihadi menace as an imminent danger for 'national security'. This manipulation of Jihadism has led, moreover, some to accuse 'the instigator of terrorist attacks, farcically denouncing fake explosions' and condemn the 'premeditated stunts of Hamas', which provide the movement with justifications for the arrest of Salafis.[159]

Islamic Jihad: Rival or partner?

To understand the relationship Hamas maintains with Islamic Jihad, it is necessary to go back in time to the foundation of the latter organization, in the early 1980s. As we have mentioned in the Introduction, the party coalesced around a faction that seceded from the Muslim Brotherhood and put forward its own agenda of armed struggle against Israel.[160] The relationship between the two movements was, from the start, a conflictual one, Hamas describing Islamic Jihad as a dissident group. For all that, there were as from the early 1990s attempts at coordination, Hamas interpreting talks with this aim in mind as the first step towards a complete reabsorption of Islamic Jihad members.

In 2006, the conflict between Islamic Jihad and Hamas continued to fester on the issue of the degree to which one should commit to armed struggle.[161] In some cases, Hamas joined Jihad's operations and described it as a partner in its war against Israel. This was, for instance, the case when Hamas backed an Islamic Jihad operation in 2006. This was also true in August 2011, when several rockets were

---

159. For more details on the relations between Hamas and the Salafis, see Leila Seurat, 'Le Hamas et les djihadistes à Gaza: contôle impossible, trêve improbable', *Politique étrangère* 81, no. 3 (2016): 95–106.

160. Hroub, *Hamas, a Beginner's Guide*.

161. Islamic Jihad also criticized Hamas for its participation in elections and its admission into the institutions of the Palestinian Authority.

fired by both the al-Quds and the Izz al-Din al-Qassam Brigades towards cities in the south of Israel. Both organizations jointly announced in a communiqué responsibility for the attack on the settlement of Ofakim as a response to the assassinations of leaders belonging to the Popular Resistance Committees. Islamic Jihad, through its armed operations, was nevertheless a threat to Hamas' prestige; Islamic Jihad is the recipient of substantial financial and military assistance from Iran and could replace Hamas by appearing as the 'true' resistance movement. In addition, Islamic Jihad has not severed ties with the Syrian regime.

The November 2012 war was the illustration of acute rivalry between both organizations. According to the spokesman of the al-Quds Brigades (Abou Ahmad), Islamic Jihad may have fired some 300 rockets at the time.[162] Israeli military officials had moreover declared that, for the Jewish State, Islamic Jihad was more problematic than Hamas, because the former, not being in power, had greater room to manoeuvre in its commitment to armed struggle.[163] For the first time during this war, on 21 November 2012, a missile with a 70 kilometres range was fired at Tel Aviv. This action was carried out by Islamic Jihad and was immediately followed by rockets launched by the al-Qassam Brigades.[164] Hamas wanted to be the last group to fire at Israel before the conclusion of a truce. During the signing of this *hudna*, Khaled Mesh'al associated Islamic Jihad with it, in his victory speech given while standing next to the group's secretary general Ramadan Abdallah Shallah;[165] nevertheless, this joint parade could not hide the deepening rivalry, especially illustrated at the moment of Israel's assassination of the man responsible for the firing of the missile on Tel Aviv, one year after the events: Mohammed Atzi was killed in Bil'in in the West Bank on 22 October 2013; this deed provoked a conflict between the two Palestinian factions over his identity, each faction considering Atzi as one of its own.[166]

The rapprochement between Hamas and Iran can be explained, moreover, by the desire to avoid the Islamic Republic favouring Islamic Jihad, which had not closed its offices in Damascus or interfered in the Syrian conflict. Witnessing the decline of Iranian backing for Hamas, Islamic Jihad is apparently still the annual recipient of fifty million dollars from Iran.[167] Two months after the assassination by Hamas' police of the militant belonging to *al-Quds*, a new crisis escalated on 25 August 2013 between the two parties in the al-Tawhid mosque of Beit Hanoun, in the northern part of the Strip.[168] The imam's sermon at the mosque was apparently critical of the authoritarian exertion of power by Hamas and its

162. *Asharq al-Awsat*, 13 November 2013.
163. Ibid.
164. Ibid.
165. http://www.facebook.com/video/video.php?v=391669704243359.
166. *Al-Masri al-Youm*, 22 October 2013.
167. *Asharq al-Awsat*, 13 November 2013. Iran apparently also provides assistance to the Ali Abou Mustafa Brigades of the FPLP, *al-Akhbar English*, 21 June 2013.
168. *Firaspress*, 26 August 2013.

responsibility in the continued blockade. This incident also bore the stamp of the Islamic Republic, since this place of worship has benefited from its aid during Ramadan.[169] Hamas then accused Islamic Jihad of disseminating Shia principles in Gaza. A similar incident had also occurred a year earlier when, a few days before Haniyeh's visit to Tehran in February 2012, Hamas forces violently assaulted Shia pilgrims in Gaza.[170] Ismail Haniyeh's visit to Iran may therefore also be explained by Hamas' wish to minimize the impact of its repression of Shia in Gaza.[171]

Similarly, attempts at a rapprochement between Hamas and Islamic Jihad were, apparently, a response to Iranian demands. The Iranians may have wanted to make sure Hamas did not jeopardize Islamic Jihad military forces and wished to secure collaboration with the latter in case of a war between Israel and the Islamic Republic. On 16 September 2013, three years after meetings that had led nowhere,[172] Mahmoud al-Zahar announced in the presence of Islamic Jihad's leader Mohammed al-Hindi that the two organizations would merge.[173] On 17 September, however, this information was denied by Jihad's vice-secretary general Ziad al-Nakhala,[174] who emphasized that the meetings between the two parties to protect the programme of the 'resistance' were actually ancient history.[175] Abou Zouhri, rather than mentioning a 'common direction' (*qiyâda mushtaraka*), used the term 'direction for coordination' (*qiyâda tansîqîya*) to define the horizon for collaboration between these two groups. According to these sources, Hamas tried to convince Islamic Jihad to join it (*indimâj*) by being associated with the running of the Gaza Strip. It was really during 'Protective Edge' that this rapprochement became fact when militants of Jihad's armed branch took part in the al-Qassam Brigades' combat against IDF soldiers in both Gaza and Israeli territory.[176]

The *al-Akhbar* newspaper mentions a distribution of roles between the al-Qassam and al-Qods Brigades during this war, each of the two armed branches favouring a particular type of missile, either short or long range.[177] Joint meetings between both organizations also allowed them to mobilize for the March of Return in March 2018. However, Hamas and Islamic Jihad are still far from being able

---

169. Asma al-Ghoul, *Al-Monitor*, 21 August 2013.

170. *Haaretz*, 17 January 2012.

171. Some of the organization's members apparently converted to Shia Islam following their stay in Tehran. This was the case of Iyad al-Hosni, who was expelled from the movement but then reintegrated. He became one of the most influential members of the *al-Quds* Brigades after the visit of Islamic Jihad members to Tehran two months before his expulsion.

172. *al-Jazeera*, 25 January 2011.

173. *al-Jazeera*, 16 September 2013.

174. *al-Quds*, 17 September 2013.

175. *Asharq al-Awsat*, 18 September 2013.

176. Nicolas Dot-Pouillard, Eugénie Rébillard, Wissam Alhaj, *De la théologie à la libération? Histoire du Jihad Islamique palestinien* (Paris: La Découverte, 2014).

177. Ahmad Hadi, 14 July 2014. https://al-akhbar.com/Arab/34667.

to coordinate their actions. Confrontations between Israel and Hamas, described in Part I, are a reflection of complex and changing relations between Hamas and Islamic Jihad. Some people have witnessed cooperation between the two organizations, as shown by rockets fired jointly by their armed branches on 29 May 2018 – an operation which was followed by the publication of a joint communiqué, which reactivated the idea of forming a common operational cell. Others are the product of shells and rockets launched exclusively by Islamic Jihad, but which Hamas has felt obliged to condone: for instance, on 3 May 2019, when, following exchange of gunfire between Israel and Islamic Jihad, Israel forces pummelled the Gaza Strip and, while publicly admitting that Jihad was the main instigator of 4 and 5 May clashes, it took aim at the commander of Hamas' armed branch Ahmad al-Khodari.

When seeking to preserve the truce, Hamas cannot always approve Islamic Jihad's actions: during clashes opposing the latter and Israel in the wake of the assassination of the Al-Quds Brigades commander Abu al-Ata, Hamas stayed away from the fighting and, for the first time, was spared by Israel. The Israeli Army spokesman Jonathan Conricus stated during the operation that Israel had 'established a distinction between Hamas and Islamic Jihad' with one aim in mind: 'to keep Hamas out of the fighting'.[178] Although rockets fired by al-Ata have enabled Hamas to exert pressure on Israel to accelerate the provision of Qatari aid, without at the same time appearing to be directly responsible for clashes, al-Ata's assassination will not allow the movement to use missile fire by others to push forward its own interests.[179]

---

178. Inès Gil, 'Gaza: un nouveau chapitre s'ouvre entre Israël et le Hamas', *Les clés du Moyen-Orient*, 18 November 2019.

179. *Le Monde*, 12 November 2019.

Part III

PLACE AND FUNCTION OF IDEOLOGY IN THE FOREIGN POLICY OF HAMAS

Hamas most often justifies armed struggle by invoking self-defence against Israeli aggression[1] and as a necessary response to the perpetuation of colonization.[2] This does not exclude the existence of an ideological discourse to describe the conflict with Israel and its relation to the rest of the world.[3] That discourse defines, among other things, Palestine as Arab and Muslim, Gaza as the 'land of ancestors' and Jerusalem as the 'eternal capital' of the Palestinian people.[4]

In this discourse, 'Cast Lead' is described as a 'new Holocaust'[5] and the blockade of Gaza as akin to the Warsaw Ghetto and the deportation of Jews during the Second World War.[6] According to some Hamas leaders, Israeli aggressions are part of a Zionist plan of denial (*al-nahî*) of history, a denial that is openly hostile not only to the Palestinians but also to the entire Arab and Muslim nations, and to all of humanity. Hamas puts forward the Israeli narrative and discourse supposedly revealing the 'true goals' of the Jewish State and its global and total occupation projects:

> Israeli aggression was not just a simple military operation to stop the firing of rockets, win the elections, sort out things with Palestinians and make the

---

1. Mesh'al's speech was given in the presence of Ramadan Abdallah Sallah, the general secretary of Islamic Jihad, during a press conference in Cairo on 21 November 2011. He was describing what had occurred in Gaza as an Israeli adventure (*mughâmara isrâ'îliya*), and the resistance's response as self-defence: http://www.facebook.com/video/video.php?v=3916697043359.

2. See Aude Signoles, *Le Hamas au pouvoir et après?* (Milan actu, 2006), 47.

3. Though the main argument justifying participation in the 2006 elections was that the Oslo peace process was dead, Hamas has also resorted to ideological frames of reference, particularly to *fiqh* (Islamic jurisprudence). See Mohammed Youssef al-Hajj, *Al-hirak 'al-al-fiqhî fî-l-ahdât allatî a'qabat intiqâl Hamâs min mu'âradat ila-l-inhirât fîhi*, No. 20 (March 2008), 9–21.

4. Mesh'al's speech in Gaza on 8 December 2012.

5. Ala Salem, *Filastin al-Muslima*, January 2010.

6. Khaled Mesh'al's interview on the state-owned Syrian TV channel, 12 January 2012.

Hamas government fall. The war's aims were also to freeze Palestinian time, erase Palestinian history, deny the rights of the Palestinian people, and reject Palestinian collective memory. This is the Zionist project from its very origins.[7]

From this reading of the origins of the conflict derives an interpretation of 'resistance', considered by Hamas as a duty (*wâjib*) of all Palestinians, Arabs and Muslims.[8] Only the resistance is capable of getting rid of this project of 'denial'.[9] Thanks to 'resistance', Hamas was able to win the successive wars of 2008–9,[10] 2012 and 2014, military aggression of the Israeli Army against the Gaza Strip. Despite the high number of casualties and the destruction of civilian infrastructure, particularly during 'Protective Edge' in the summer of 2014, truces and cease-fires are always described by Hamas leaders as military victories.[11]

The journal *Filastin al-Muslima* strove to draw up a balance of 'Cast Lead', a year after the end of the offensive. Palestinian defeats were minimized, while, at the military and political levels, the aggression was shown to be a huge Israeli failure: 'This once more placed the Zionist state in front of a situation of moral degradation, which made it from then on the recipient of moral lectures given by the entire set of international players.'[12] Once more, Hamas used Israeli analyses that considered this operation as a setback for the Jewish State,[13] one that allowed Hamas to impose its narrative of 'victory'. Gaza is depicted as the 'knight of the resistance' (*fâris al-muqâwama*) who, on a par with Hezbollah in 2006, won a

---

7. Ala Salem quotes in particular Professor Oren Yiftachel (from Ben Gurion University of the Negev in Beersheba), who accused Israeli elites of participating in a political project of denial (*al-nahî*) of the Palestinian people, see *Filastin al-Muslima*, January 2010.

8. Olivier Carré considers that the ideology of the Palestinian resistance is based on the myth of rebirth through death, see Olivier Carré, *L'idéologie palestinienne de résistance* (Paris: Presses de Sciences Po, 1972).

9. See Khaled Mesh'al's speech in Gaza on 8 December 2012, *al-Zaytûna*, 10 December 2012.

10. According to Osama Hamdan, Olmert's speech was a testimony of Israel's second failure after its setback in Lebanon in 2006: 'The New Reality Shows That Palestinian Resistance Has Beaten Zionist Armed Forces, and That Their Leaders Were Obliged to Put an End to Their Criminal Assault', *markaz al-filastînî lil-i'lâm*, 18 January 2009.

11. The leader of the al-Qassam Brigades Abou, 'Ubayda claimed in *al-Dustur*, on 13 January 2009, that the resistance only had used 30 per cent of its forces, and that it was a regular army of 50,000 soldiers. Ghazi Hamad was the only one among the movement's leaders to argue against these assertions, considering this was mere propaganda: 'It is wrong to say that we won the 2008 war, just as Hezbollah did not win in 2006.' Conversation with Ghazi Hamad in Cyprus on 28 April 2012.

12. Salem, *Filastin al-Muslima*.

13. The report dedicated to the first anniversary of the Gaza War in *Filastin al-Muslima* refers to the Professors of the Hebrew University of Jerusalem Ibrahim Saleg and Aron Barak, who considered that this war was an Israeli setback, January 2010.

'divine victory' against 'the Israeli war machine'. As from the seventeenth day of the war, Haniyeh was mentioning the 'divine manifestation' (*âya muqaddasa*), the 'miracle of God' (*mu'jiza*) and the greatness of the resistance confronting oppression. Triumphalist references to the Qur'an were manifold: 'There are two sides who fight, one fights in the interest of God and one fights against. God sees this with his own eyes and hands victory to the one he will choose.' God is the 'witness of punishments' (*shahîd al-'iqâb*). Haniyeh spoke of the resistance's strength, which apparently was 'solid and impossible to upset like the mountains of Palestine', the collapse of mountains being the sign of Judgement Day in the Qur'an. 'The resistance is silent and filled with pride, while the *Umma* and all free men of the world observe with awe this miracle of God.'

On the day of 21 November 2012, a new speech of 'military victory' was given.[14] 'You will not be able to destroy Gaza because it is impossible to break' were Ismail Haniyeh's words on that occasion.[15] On 22 November, the national day of victory was proclaimed and became an official holiday.[16] Mesh'al's speech in Gaza on 8 December 2010 expressed the idea of a victory granted by God; a verse from the Sura of the Bees was quoted by the head of the Political Bureau: 'Whatever benefit comes to you (O man!), it is from Allah.'[17] As for Usama Hamdan, he said the 'resistance' succeeded in confronting the enemy in large part thanks to Palestinian popular unity around this resistance, but also because of the new regional context and the reconstruction of a solidarity network around the Egyptian, Turkish and Qatari alliance.[18]

During 'Protective Edge', Hamas congratulated itself for its strength, concluding it had built a fortress of resistance capable of making this 'liberated' enclave secure.[19] Hamas' leadership cast the war as one of national liberation, promising residents of the Gaza Strip the loosening of Israel's punishing eight-year siege. One should note, however, that the rendering of this conflict as ideological is far from being specific to Hamas. Israel uses ideology to justify these practices, as attested by the mobilization of messianic references during Operation 'Protective Edge'.[20]

Despite running the risk of being repetitive, the author would like to recall that she takes into account ideology not just in its cognitive dimension (integrating underlying perceptions and beliefs) but in its normative one (as a guide for action). The hypothesis emphasizing that ideas are subordinate to interests should not make one see, without further ado, ideology as a simple trick or as

14. *Asharq al-Awsat*, 23 November 2012.
15. *Asharq*, Doha, 28 December 2008.
16. *Markaz al-filastînî li-l-i'lâm*, 22 November 2012.
17. Mesh'al's speech in Gaza on 8 December 2012.
18. *Markaz al-Zaytûna*, 6 February 2013.
19. Al Qassam Bayan, 13 July 2014 quoted by Tareq Baconi, *Hamas Contained: The Rise and Pacification of Palestinian Resistance* (Stanford: Stanford University Press, 2018).
20. Max Blumenthal, 'Politicide in Gaza: How Israel's Far Right won the War', *Journal of Palestine Studies* 44, no.1 (2014): 14–28.

a justification in retrospect.[21] Its role as justification for action is paramount to convincing, mobilizing and satisfying demands for meaning.[22] While recalling that the setup of coherent and efficient policies necessarily requires the existence of a belief – even if ideological – Max Weber has tried to go beyond the simplistic alternative between non-ideological politics, 'ethics of responsibility' and policies that seek to make the purity of principles triumph ('ethics of belief').[23] Beyond this simple dichotomy, it is possible to identify various types of relationships between ideas and interests.[24] There are indeed four types of relationships between these two variables: coincidence, conflict, adaptation of ideology to interests and finally adaptation of interests to ideology. This last proposal is absent in our study. Analysis of the recourse to ideology in Hamas' foreign policy, however, illustrates the three other types of relationships: affinity, antagonism and redefinition of ideology as function of interests. This last type of purely utilitarian relationship, which consists of a simple adaptation through rational calculations, clearly falls into the category of 'practical rationalization' or 'rationalization by finality',[25] in Max Weber's sense: a player targets his actions as a function of his appreciation of the ends and means, but these actions, to be efficient, must be based on ideological conviction: 'ideology characterizes political parties based on a conception of the world, as opposed to those who are only mere organization of interests, which does not impede that in parties of the former category, ideology is often used to camouflage interests.'[26]

In order to make the author's demonstration coherent, the present chapter is not structured around these various kinds of imbrications but, rather, interwoven with her initial classification of foreign and internal interests.

In this chapter, it is the author's wish to demonstrate that pursuing interests at the external level largely follows the third scenario, the one of 'rationality by finality'. Until 2011, the rhetoric of the 'resistance front' allowed Hamas to reinforce its alliances and produce a discourse permitting it to recognize friends and designate foes. Ideology made Hamas create the impression of a common front, grouping players that share neither the same interests nor the same values.[27]

---

21. Fayez al-Sayegh, 'Islam and Neutralism', in *Islam and International Relations*, ed. Harris Proctor (London, Dunmow: Pall Mall Press, 1965).

22. Bertrand Badie and Marie-Claude Smouts, *Le retournement du monde: sociologie de la scène internationale* (Paris: Presses de Sciences-Po/Dalloz, 1999).

23. Max Weber, *Le savant et le politique* (Paris: La Découverte, 2003).

24. See Stephen Krasner, *Defending the National Interest: Raw Materials Investments and US Foreign Policy* (Princeton, NJ: Princeton University Press, 1978); Peter J. Katzenstein, *The Culture of National Security: Norms and Identity in World Politics* (New York: New York University Press, 1996).

25. Julien Freund, 'L'idéologie chez Max Weber', *Revue Européenne des Sciences Sociales* 11, no. 30 (1973): 5–19.

26. Ibid.

27. Stephen Walt, *The Origins of Alliance* (London: Cornell University Press, 1990).

Ideology constantly adapts to contexts, partners and interlocutors. As of 2011, while Hamas was reassessing its network of alliances to break its isolation, this reformulation of interests led to a redefinition of its ideology: the rhetoric of the 'resistance front' gradually subsided and was replaced by a new narrative structured around the centrality of Hamas in the Arab Spring.

The author shall then show that the pursuit of interests at the internal level illustrates the other cases of rationalization put forward by Max Weber. Beyond the strengthening of regional alliances, the 'resistance front' was also an opportunity to overshadow or weaken nationalist forces by associating Mahmoud Abbas with Egypt and Israel. Regarding the truce, it illustrates the three cases: coincidence, conflict and redefinition of ideology to serve interests.

The *hudna* coincides with the ideology of the movement, which can easily justify this measure as being drawn from Islamic history from the days of the prophet. Yet some elements within the al-Qassam Brigades, who are favourable towards a permanent struggle against the State of Israel, have rejected it outright, considering on the contrary that it goes counter to doctrine.

Although the truce is therefore a reflection of interests conforming to ideology, it also represents a heresy in the eyes of a minority fringe now estranged from Hamas. This once more confirms the relevance of Weber's conceptualization: there is a multiplicity of ideologies, and to each of them corresponds a peculiar rationalization, which is a function of the belief that each places in a specific value. Dominant forces inside the movement and the minority within the armed branch have both adopted antagonistic forms of rationalization. Ideology is both the source of and the antidote to conflictual situations.

Finally, the specific case of the truce illustrates a 'rationality by finality': presented as a form of 'resistance', ideology seeks to minimize criticism originating from Hamas' rivals, namely Salafis and Islamic Jihad. It conceals, as much as it justifies, interests that are hardly acceptable when in the open.[28]

---

28. Jean Baechler, *Qu'est-ce que l'idéologie* (Paris: Gallimard, 1976).

Chapter 6

IDEOLOGY AND DEFENCE OF EXTERNAL INTERESTS

Ideology is a means for Hamas to strengthen its alliances with states and political organizations that do not share identical interests. It also allows justification of a partnership with Iran, which many of its rivals consider unacceptable because it means siding with Shias.

Constrained to readjust its network of alliances to find backers and end its isolation, Hamas adapts its ideology to respond to regional changes beginning in 2011: it emphasizes its central and quasi-exemplary role in the Arab uprisings. Its ideology is also adapted as a function of its interlocutors: a rhetoric of the centrality of Hamas appears during visits to countries which underwent uprisings but disappears in others to those states which have not known dissent or have tried to prevent it.

When ideology goes together with the search
for political and material backers

Allowing an axis to exist

The leaders of Hamas usually dismiss the concept of 'axes', considering it is only American propaganda meant to stigmatize its inclusion in the 'axis of evil' embodied by Iran.[1] In this vein, Khaled Mesh'al declared: 'We did not create a Palestinian, Arab or Muslim axis against another Arab-Palestinian axis. We continue to extend our hand to all, and we wish to communicate and establish relations with all. If there is a break or a chill in relations with somebody, he is the one who has chosen the break or chill, not us.'[2]

Other leaders, nevertheless, state that Hamas and its allies 'congregate to do good, support the Palestinian people, resist the Zionist enemy, counter normalization, resist attempts to infiltrate the nation, fight American hegemony, as well as the occupation of Iraq and Afghanistan.'[3]

---

1. Conversation with Mahmoud al-Zahar in Gaza on 20 March 2013.
2. Interview of Khaled Mesh'al by Silvia Catori, *al-Sabeel*, July 2010.
3. Ibid.

Beyond contradictory discourse, one should note that the blockade and 'Cast Lead' assault have resulted in a polarization of Middle Eastern countries: some states have drawn closer to Hamas while others, described as 'moderate', have joined Egypt and gone with its decision to maintain the blockade. In December 2009, at the time Egypt began the construction of a metal barrier on its border with Gaza,[4] the ideology of 'resistance' was reactivated. Presented as a menace, the building of this wall accelerated the rapprochement of countries and organizations that shared neither the same ideology nor the same interests. Tally Helfont[5] has analysed this trend:

> An entire front has emerged in support of Hamas and its stance on the Egyptian wall. Included in this faction are Iran, Hezbollah, Syria and the Muslim Brotherhood, and more recently, Qatar and Turkey, who have begun to shift their regional alliances in recent years in favor of Hamas and some of the more radical 'resistance' elements in the Middle East. . . . Despite the aggressive criticism of this front, Egypt does not stand alone in its efforts to moderate the more radical elements on its border. Egypt's natural partners in regional anti-radicalization include the Palestinian Authority under Abbas and Salam Fayyad, Jordan, and Saudi Arabia. Its broader coalition includes Israel, the U.S. and the E.U.

This wall is also depicted by Bashar al-Assad as a sign of Egyptian submission to the Americans and Israelis: 'Whoever participates in the siege is responsible for the blood spilt by Palestinians.'[6] According to Hamas spokesman Taher al-Nounou, 'the steel wall is an American racist idea to encircle Gaza':

> It is not surprising that Syria is confronted with challenges and dangers, given that it brandishes the standard of refusal and supports the resistance, to the extent that United States and all those who are in their wake bet that Syria will retract due to the grip of American occupation in Iraq, but Syria has remained committed to its principles, and has been able to go beyond the curve, to take the crisis back to America itself, with its quagmire in Iraq and Afghanistan.[7]

The mobilization of Islamic references helps in consolidating this alliance. Hamas leaders described this wall as a 'sin'[8] and condemned its construction.[9] In a series of

---

4. Egypt apparently built the wall for financial reasons, see House Report 110-497, Section 690, Making Appropriations for the Department of State, Foreign Operations, and related Programs for the Fiscal Year Ending September 30, 2008, 110th Congress, 1st Session, 17 December 2007.
5. Tally Helfont, 'Egypt's Wall with Gaza and the Emergence of a Middle East Alignment', *Orbis* 54, no. 3 (summer 2010): 426–40.
6. L. Barkan, 'Reactions in Arab and Muslim World to Egyptian Steel Barrier along its Border with Gaza', *Memri Inquiry and Analysis Series*, report No. 580, 13 January 2010.
7. *Palestine-info*, 20 December 2009.
8. *Palestinian Information Center*, 4 January 2010.
9. Helfont, 'Egypt's wall with Gaza and the Emergence of a Middle East Alignment'.

articles and statements, they took offence at the Fatwa pronounced by the al-Azhar Islamic institution, which stipulated that this construction was licit (*halal*) from the viewpoint of Muslim jurisprudence.[10] They advised al-Azhar's Ulemas to change their minds and convince Egyptian leaders to open the Rafah crossing.[11] Yusuf al-Qaradawi intervened on Hamas' side, fuelling their condemnation with serious religious credibility:

> The construction of the steel wall is forbidden by Islamic law (*sharia*), because its intention is to seal all entrance and exit gates of Gazans and intensify the siege, humiliate them, starve them, and pressure them to submit to Israel. It is as if Egypt were saying to the Palestinians: 'die and let Israel live'.[12]

Such backing from a renowned religious figure strengthened the 'rejectionist front' and gave it greater credibility. Consistent with religious principles, this anti-Egyptian campaign reinforced criticisms uttered against the Egyptian regime, the latter's supposed abandonment of Palestinians and Muslims, and its submission to American and Zionist 'diktats'. Resorting to Islam and siding with the Egyptian Muslim Brotherhood could also appear as a way to give extra consistency to this 'axis' or to present it as active and operational.

Egypt's construction of the metal barrier appeared as an 'ideological compromise' enabling the various players to position one another. Stephen Walt has demonstrated that only the perception of common danger can allow an axis to exist – the external factor that contributes to create or reinforce an alliance.[13] Perceived by Hamas as a threat, the barrier is a new element on which the region's antagonisms rest, as apparent in statements by one and the other side that reflect the antagonism between unbridgeable and permanent opposing camps.

Providing Islamic justification for an alliance with a Shia state

Hamas has looked around far and wide to find material backers other than Iran. Support from elsewhere could remove all the inconveniencies included in an alliance with the Islamic Republic, an alliance that remains quite unpopular in Palestine. Being friends with Tehran provides an excuse to Israel to tighten the blockade and compromises the eventuality of potential allies, both regional and

---

10. The Egyptian Muslim Brothers have also described this wall in religious terms, considering that it embodies an 'agenda of surrender against resistance and Jihad', statement by Akef, *al-Hayat*, 10 February 2009.

11. 'We disapprove of the al-Azhar Fatwa', Hamas official communiqué published on the website of the *Palestinian Information Center, markaz al-filastinî li-l-i'lâm*, on 2 January 2010.

12. 'Qaradawi: Egypt's Steel Wall Forbidden in Islam', published on the official website of the Muslim Brotherhood on 4 January 2010.

13. Walt, *The Origins of Alliances*.

local: 'Despite the need for military assistance, Hamas wishes to preserve its image of a Palestinian national movement, and in this regard would prefer to remain independent from Iran.'[14]

Since the 2009 episode of the Ibn Taimiyya mosque, many Salafi groups have criticized Hamas for allying with Iran. According to Yezid Sayigh, it is the Wahhabi ideology of these groups that made them excoriate the movement for its 'impious' alliance with the Islamic Republic: *Jaysh al-Umma* has denounced not only Hamas but also Islamic Jihad, for having accepted the backing of 'Shia Persians'.[15]

In the beginning, Hamas and Islamic Jihad did not share the same attitude towards the Islamic Republic. Although the Jihad always attempted to bridge the ideological gap separating it from Iran, Hamas, in contrast, was emphasizing its anti-Shia orientation and its affiliation to the Muslim Brotherhood. The Hamas Charter contains, moreover, no mention whatsoever of the Islamic Revolution. In 1989, Sheikh Ahmed Yasin made it clear that 'Muslims are Sunnis and not Shias'.[16]

The rapprochement between Iran and Hamas became a reality in the early 1990s, when Iran became conscious that the movement, due to its rise to power on the Palestinian stage, was a better candidate than Islamic Jihad for serving Tehran's regional ambitions.[17] Tehran considered this new perspective as a means to reinforce its status and role among the 'Arab masses'.[18] In parallel, Hamas was becoming convinced of the advantage of Iran as an outpost in the struggle against normalization. Two events inaugurated this alliance: the first Gulf War and the opening of a cycle of talks between Palestinians and Israelis under the aegis of the Americans, which ended with the Oslo Accords. Iraq's defeat during the Gulf War meant a defeat for a PLO that had stood with Saddam Hussein. The PLO saw its influence decrease in favour of that of Hamas, as witnessed in the visit of a delegation of the Islamist movement to Tehran in February 1991:[19]

> 'Only one Qur'an and one Islam.' From the start, religion permits justifying the alliance with Iran. According to Hamas leaders, there is moreover no contradiction in the fact of receiving aid from both Iran and Saudi Arabia,

14. Jared Malsin, 'Islamic Jihad Joining Hamas Ceasefire with Israel?', *Ma'anews*, 21 October 2010.
15. *Al-Nahar*, 30 April 1989.
16. The wish to find common ground with Hamas was notably illustrated by Hamas' invitation to two conferences of support to the Intifada in Tehran, in December 1990 and October 1991.
17. Adnan Abu Amer, *Iranian Influence in the Gaza Strip, Evidence and Implications* (Jerusalem: Friedrich Ebert Stiftung, 2011).
18. *Filastin al-Muslima*, March 1991, 19.
19. Martin Kramer, 'Rallying Around Islam', *Middle East Contemporary Survey*, Boulder 17 (1993): 109–53.

since: 'Both believe in Jerusalem and particularly in al-Aqsa, the place Prophet Muhammad rose to Heaven.'[20]

Yet Sheikh Khalil al-Quqa, one of Hamas' early religious authorities, had stated in 1988 that the movement was to have no links with Iran: 'Khomeini's current is superficial, and has seen the end of its transit through Palestine, which was like a small breeze and left no impact whatsoever.'[21] Yet as early as 1991, he changed his stance and spoke in favour of Iran: 'The Islamic Revolution left an impact on the entire region and not only on the Movement of Islamic Resistance. This influence is an answer to those who maintain that the Islamic Revolution is inappropriate.'

Had the Islamic Republic itself not used a similar approach, prescribing the 'export' of the revolution to prevent its lockdown inside Shia doctrine? Khomeini had placed the revolution at the service of Islamic universalism, which played the part of an ideological mantle with a 'utilitarian function'.[22] On the other hand, a rapprochement could also be made with Syria's Alawi community, which had wanted to redefine itself as Shia.[23]

In the early 1990s, when Hamas was expressing its need to redefine its alliance with Iran, it had the advantage of diversified sources of funds. This was no longer the case after its election victory in January 2006, when Hamas was facing an unprecedented cash-flow crisis. With the exception of revenue originating from the Salam Fayyad government, Muslim Brotherhood donations and those of the Gulf Cooperation Council (GCC), Hamas was counting on Iran alone for survival.[24] It therefore gave justifications to its own audience for this alliance, describing it as a religious and moral duty towards the cause and the Holy Places.[25] This is how solidarity towards Iran in case of an Israeli attack, as expressed by Ismail Haniyeh, is to be understood: 'We are one front, united against Islam's enemies.'[26]

Highlighting the Islamic significance of the Palestinian cause

In December 2009, at the time of the construction of the metal barrier, then in 2011, in the wake of Mubarak's fall from power, Hamas drew closer to the Egyptian

---

20. *Al-Anba* (Kuwait), on 8 October 1988, quoted by Meir Hatina, 'Iran and the Palestinian Islamic Movement', *Orient* 38, no. 1 (1997):107–20.

21. Khalil al-Quqa's interview in al-Alam, on 26 January 1991, quoted by Hatina, 'Iran and the Palestinian Islamic movement'.

22. Mohammed Reza Jalili, *Diplomatie islamique, stratégie internationale du khomeynisme* (Paris: Presses Universitaires de France, Paris, 1989).

23. See on this matter Imam Musa Sadr's Fatwa of 1974, identifying the Alawi community as a branch of Shiism.

24. Yezid Sayigh, *We Serve the People: Hamas Policing in Gaza*, Brandeis University Crown Center for Middle East Studies, Crown Paper 5, April 2011.

25. Amer, *Iranian Influence in the Gaza Strip, Evidence and Implications*.

26. Ismail Haniyeh's interview in *markaz al-filastînî li-l-i'lâm*, on 7 September 2010.

Muslim Brotherhood. In a context of rivalry between Sunnis and Shias, however, reasserting an alliance with Iran could be read as an attempt at rebalancing to Tehran's advantage.

When the chronology is looked at more closely, it becomes clear that mobilizing ideological rhetoric in favour of Tehran coincided with these various rapprochements. Mesh'al's meeting with Ahmadinejad in Damascus in February 2010 occurred two months after the Hamas and the Brotherhood's joint mobilization against the building of the metal wall. Sure enough, Iran was an integral part of the 'resistance front', but as has been shown earlier, this particular episode of confrontation against Egyptian authorities (the issue of the barrier) had drawn Hamas closer to the Muslim Brothers.

Ismail Haniyeh's visit to Iran, on 17 February 2012, during which he reiterated the movement's maximalist stance, has to be analysed in the context of Hamas' rapprochement with the Egyptian Brotherhood at the end of 2011. Running the risk of displeasing the Egyptian Brothers, the movement had to keep using the rhetoric of the Islamic resistance bastion to guarantee the continuous backing of its main financial donor. During this visit, Haniyeh recalled the refusal of any sort of agreement with Israel (*taswiya*), as well as the 'great victories' of 2009 and 2011 during the fruitful exchange that led to Gilad Shalit's release. They were possible thanks to Tehran's good offices.

The stances can be explained by Hamas' wish to curry favour with the Iranians, at a time when the movement had refused to support the Syrian regime and had come closer to Egypt by signing the April 2011 Cairo Agreement, while simultaneously declaring its endorsement of 'peaceful resistance'. These statements had been very badly met by the Iranians, who had expressed their anger at Ismail Haniyeh, who, indeed, had gone to Bahrein but had carefully avoided Syria during his diplomatic tour.[27] Conversely, the ideological mantle also served the interests of Iran, which wanted to reassert its loyalty to Palestinian resistance; at a moment its backing of Bashar al-Assad was perceived as sectarian support to an Alawi (and therefore Shia) regime persecuting Syria's Sunni majority.

Perpetual adaptation

It is really from June 2007 onwards, with the tightening of the blockade and the rapprochement with Iran, that Hamas' discourse became loaded with ideological terminology. During the outside leadership's regional tour, between spring 2009 and spring 2010, the movement's chief resorted to the rhetoric of the 'resistance front', a term which was used more than ever in early 2010. The rise of revolutionary movements in January 2011 incited Hamas to redefine its discourse, to structure it around the centrality of Hamas and Palestine in the regional context in formation at the time.

27. Conversations with Mohammed Daraghmeh in Cairo, on 25 February 2012.

Adapting to context

In the wake of its victory in the 2006 regional ballots, Hamas displayed its pragmatic positions,[28] particularly towards Egypt and Jordan. When Amman decided to cancel Mahmoud al-Zahar's visit, pretexting the discovery of an arms cache belonging to Hamas, the movement's spokesman Sami Abou Zouhri merely denied the allegations: 'We regret the use of such methods to cancel al-Zahar's visit at the last minute.'[29] Similar pragmatism was shown when the Egyptian Ministry of Interior denounced the implication of two Hamas members in the 4 April Dahab explosions. Wishing to avoid conflict of any sort, Hamas hurriedly sent to Cairo its Interior Minister Sayyid Siam to speak to Omar Suleiman, then head of Egyptian intelligence.[30] As from 2007, and more precisely following the events of June, Hamas' diplomacy took an ideological turn.

First of all, towards Egypt, when the deterioration of relations between Cairo and Hamas entailed a rapprochement with the Muslim Brothers, whose speeches emphasized the presence of 'plotters' wanting to eradicate Islamism. The Brotherhood's newspapers were publishing articles on Hamas that were very laudatory and which insisted on the importance of 'eradicators' and the reality of their plots against the Palestinian Islamist movement.[31] These 'plotters' were allegedly close to the Americans and Israelis and targeted the Brotherhood rather than al-Qaida. The June 2007 events were presented as the first battle between Islamists and 'eradicators' ready to 'return to the offensive'. Hamas was supposedly not responsible for this division, which was, according to the articles, the result of an American-Zionist conspiracy.[32] The explosion, caused by Hamas, of the wall separating Gaza from Egypt during the night of 23 January 2008, led to an ideological campaign carried out side by side with the Egyptian Muslim Brothers,[33] which focused on the concept of 'resistance'. While mobilizing religious references, the concept was an attempt to involve the 'Arab street' using injunctions of pan-Arab or pan-Islamic solidarity.[34] The need to devise a credible and sellable road map for the 'resistance' option was mentioned by the Muslim Brotherhood Guide Mahdi

---

28. *Al-Joumhouriya al-Masriyya*, 3 January 2006.

29. The spiritual guide of the Jordanian Muslim Brothers, Salem al-Falahhat, was also apparently surprised by the arrest of Hamas officials and the cancellation of the visit, *markaz al-filastînî li-l-i'lâm*, 19 April 2006.

30. Mohammad Jama'a; 'Al-azma al falastînîya wa 'ilâqât- Hamas al-iqlîmîya', *Al-Siyâsat al-Dawlîya*, October 2007, number 42.

31. *Al-Dustur*, 7 July 2007.

32. *Filastin al-Muslima*, January 2010.

33. *Al-Khamis*, 12 July 2007, claims to have obtained sources from the Guidance Bureau of the Brotherhood.

34. It was above all the Egyptian Brothers who led mobilization campaigns in mosques to justify in *shar'i* (legal) fashion the actions of Hamas, and the *fiqh* of the 'resistance', *al-Khamis*, 12 July 2007.

Akef:[35] 'This option must have powerful and multiple international supports. To consolidate it, a universalist humanist narrative is necessary, a discourse that takes this plurality into account, a "theory" that makes it viable, and the means to make it a pressure tool against governments.'[36]

The Brotherhood apparently formulated recommendations, for instance, to announce that Gaza was a liberated region. They may have also advised Hamas to adopt 'adequate "foreign" policies and not be content with shouting simplistic slogans'.[37] After 'Cast Lead', when Egypt accused Hamas of being responsible for the launching of hostilities,[38] the ideological component of statements became more pronounced.

According to Khaled Mesh'al, the 'grouping of which Hamas is part, is a gathering that allows one to avoid submitting to the enemy's diktats, a laudable gathering that cannot be placed at the same level as any other'.[39] The view of reality based on a number of ethical principles provides compensation, at the level of ideas, for values Hamas leaders consider being deprived of and supposes in a utopian manner that they will come true at a future stage, when 'resistance' triumphs at the expense of antagonistic values.

In 2011 the triggering of revolutionary movements in the Arab world incited Hamas to rejuvenate and update its discourse, which now mobilized the concepts of 'freedom' (*hurrîya*) and 'reforms' (*islâh*).

Hamas has often highlighted the failure of Arab policies towards Palestine.[40] It has said it was always expecting regional transformations creating a new balance of power between Israel and Palestine.[41] The Arab Spring appeared as the fulfilment of Hamas' prophecy and helped in depicting the movement as a visionary one.

---

35. According to 'Abd al-Mun'im Mahmud in *al-Dustur* of 28 January 2009, the website of the Muslim Brotherhood announced that a delegation of Brothers, including two members of the Guidance Bureau (al-Katatni and Sa'ad al-Husayni) met, on the direct orders of Mahdi Akef, Khaled Mesh'al and other representatives of the Political Bureau of Hamas.

36. 'Isam al-'Iryan, head of the Political Committee of the Brotherhood', *al-Hayat*, 26 January 2009.

37. The minutes of the 12 October 2009 meeting between the leaders of Hamas and the Egyptian Brotherhood was quoted by *Wafa* on 14 May 2010, and once more by Mohammad Hijazi, 'Hamas Movement between Partnership and Individualism', *Institute for Palestine Studies* 22, no. 87 (2011): 59.

38. Tewfik Aclimandos, 'La onzième plaie d'Egypte', *Outre-terre* 22, no. 2 (2009):159–66.

39. Interview of Khaled Mesh'al by Silvia Catori, *al-Sabeel*, July 2010, English translation by AMEC-*Afro-Middle East* Center.

40. See Charter.

41. In Khaled Mesh'al's opinion, resistance is evolving in an unfavourable atmosphere towards Palestine, due to the regional and international imbalance, and the state of weakness and division of Arab and Muslim countries, see Silvia Catori, 'La nouvelle orientation politique du Hamas', *al-Sabeel*, July 2010.

This rhetoric rested on the retrospective illusion stating that the 'spring' had occurred to save it. The narrative was articulated around a supposed unbreakable link between these uprisings and the Movement of Islamic Resistance, two aspects of an identical phenomenon. According to Hamas, it was the 'heroic resistance' of Gazans which became a model for the Arab peoples, whose oppression was compared to that exerted by Israeli occupiers: 'We are proud to be the spark of this awakening; the Palestinian cause remains the main centre of interests of these peoples, who refused the injustice of regimes in power.'[42]

This link between Gaza and the Arab revolts was emphasized by several leaders who spoke to the author. Mouchir al-Masri, for example, declared:

> The revolutions erupted as a reaction to the tyranny of Arab regimes. Hamas played a part because it was an example to follow, due to its capacity of resistance against the Israelis, as well as being a legend. All this while the regimes ruling these countries were allied to the Israeli enemies besieging Gaza. Hence the desire for revenge of the population against these regimes. Hamas is an integral part of these peoples, it has backed the revolutions in the Arab world. These regimes were against Hamas and the resistance.[43]

In this attempt to link its fate to that of revolutions in progress, Hamas also depicted its 2006 election victory as a precursor to later Islamist victories in the region. By displaying its wish for a long truce with Israel, and its plan to exercise power in the Gaza Strip in 'exemplary' fashion,[44] it reckoned that its example would enable political parties stemming from the Muslim Brotherhood to win elections in Tunisia and Egypt. The Movement of Islamic Resistance was not only a factor of change; it was also its beneficiary:

> We are happy that this spring reinforces the will of popular choices, and we consider it as the prelude to a great rebirth for the Arab nation; which will make it stronger against the Zionist enemy.[45] Arab countries will go through a time of crisis. We think that on this occasion the Muslim Brothers will have a greater part to play. Until now, Arab governments were using Palestine as a propaganda weapon; now, the situation is different and people promote active solidarity. We

---

42. Statement by Salah al-Bardawil, on the occasion of the twenty-fourth anniversary of Hamas, *markaz al-filastînî li-l-i'lâm*, 14 December 2011.

43. Conversation with Mouchir al-Masri in Geneva, on 19 January 2012.

44. Dr Abdou al-Salam, a professor in political science at Al-Najah University in Nablus, also considers that the victory of Islamist parties had a positive effect on Hamas, mentioning 'the giant steps that Hamas will accomplish in various fields, seeing its guideline as victorious in Arab surroundings', *markaz al-filastînî li-l-i'lâm*, April 2012.

45. Khaled Mesh'al, 'The Arab Spring Will Make the Arab Nation Stronger When Confronting the Zionist Enemy', *markaz al-filastînî li-l-i'lâm*, 29 November 2011.

have faith in a positive transformation of the situation in Palestine via these revolutions.[46]

Hamas considers that Islamist parties victorious in the ballot boxes will provide it with inalienable support in the middle and long term.[47] This interpretation of events is expressed by ideological propaganda and a series of political exaggerations.

In December 2011, during his first regional tour, Ismail Haniyeh congratulated the Egyptian and Tunisian peoples for their revolutions and attempted to reinsert the Palestinian cause into the more general quest for dignity and justice attributed to it.[48] When his delegation visited the broadcasting headquarters of the Qatari al-Jazeera TV channel, Haniyeh stated that the victory of Islamists embodied the hopes and ambitions of Arab societies, not only in terms of reforms but also in the struggle against American hegemony in the region. Drawing attention to the generosity of Qatar's emir, who was providing aid and assistance to Gazans faced with the blockade and the practices of 'Zionist terrorism',[49] Ahmad Bahar asserted that the Palestinian–Qatari relationship was founded on religion and history. As for Huda Naim, who was welcomed in Tunisia by the head of the government Hamadi Jebali, she claimed that 'the liberation of Tunisia will lead to the liberation of Jerusalem'.[50]

The exemplariness of Hamas and Palestine was also the focus of Khaled Mesh'al's speeches. On 13 July 2012, from Tunis, he referred to the slogans of the various Arab peoples of the uprisings, saying: 'The people want the liberation of Palestine' (*ash-Sha'ab yourîd tahrîr Filastîn*).[51] Tunisia was supposedly the 'rifle of Palestine' (*Tûnis bunduqîyat al-Filastîn*). He recalled that the 'jewels' (*jawharât*) of these revolutions were Palestine and Jerusalem's liberation. Finally, he reiterated the necessity for Arab states and Hamas to establish relations with the rest of the world but considered that this should not be done at the detriment of interests of these two parties, who need neither the European Union nor the West to reclaim their legitimacy, which can only be conquered by the people. On 20 October 2012, during the AKP's convention in Ankara, he detailed that 'reform and democracy' were at the heart of the movement's internal policy, and 'resistance and confrontation with Israel' were the cornerstone of its foreign policy. In November 2012 in Khartoum, he assured his audience that the enemy was weaker than ever when faced with President Morsi, Rachid Ghannouchi, Libya, North Africa, Yemen, Syria and when confronted with the changes of all these countries, united

---

46. Conversation with Ismail al-Achqar in Ankara, on 20 May 2011.
47. Osama Hamdan claimed that the November 2012 offensive had shown the existence of a strong regional alliance around Hamas, *Markaz al-Zaytûna*, 7 February 2013.
48. *Markaz al-Fiastînî li-l-i'lâm*, 26 November 2011.
49. *Markaz al-Fiastînî li-l-i'lâm*, 3 December 2011.
50. 'Hamas Representative Addresses Tunisia Political Rally', *Asharq al-Awsat*, 15 December 2011.
51. http:///www.youtube.com/watch?v=vTmnSvUU_Bo.

together around the 'rifle of liberation'. According to him, times were changing and Israel was on the verge of collapse.

Adapting to interlocutors

Between the springs of 2009 and 2010, a delegation of the foreign leadership travelled to Sudan, Iran, Libya and Yemen. In Sanaa, Khaled Mesh'al asserted that the only means to fight the occupation was 'the resistance', which was 'the honour of Palestine and the Umma'. In Tehran, he emphasized the notion of 'Islamic community', insisting on religious references, justified as common denominators of identity.[52]

Yet when he spoke to President Ahmadinejad, who had come to meet Bashar al-Assad in Damascus in the summer of 2007, his rhetoric avoided any reference to religion. Likewise, when he met Ali Larijani and Said Jalili in the Syrian capital in January 2009,[53] he thanked Iran for its primaeval role in the 'victory'[54] and once more refrained from alluding to Islam. Regarding Syria, the 'resistance front' did not appear in its Islamic dimension, the onus being placed more on the resistance of a movement whose legitimacy stemmed from it winning the 2006 elections.[55]

Once more in February 2010 in Damascus, religious points were put aside. Khaled Mesh'al announced that any new attack on Gaza would be considered as 'an aggression against the three parties involved in the resistance'.[56] The 'secularist' nature[57] of the Syrian regime, and its antagonism towards the Muslim Brotherhood, explains the absence of any reference to Islam, since Hamas prefers to present the conflict as an anti-imperialist struggle. The 'racist' Zionist project is for Hamas a menace to peoples, both Muslims and others.

While in Turkey, it was this anti-imperialist language that was used during the Israeli assault of the *Viva Palestina* flotilla,[58] an episode that caused the deaths of nine Turkish citizens on 31 May 2010: 'We salute the heroes of the international

---

52. *Filastin al-Muslima*, January 2010.

53. *IRNA*, on 9 January 2009, quoted by Amer, *Iranian Influence in the Gaza Strip, Evidence and Implications*.

54. 'Hamas Leaders Praise Iran for Help in Gaza Fight', *Associated Press*, 2 February 2009.

55. *Filastin al-Muslima*, June 2010.

56. *Filastin al-Muslima*, April 2010.

57. The terms 'secularist' and 'secular' are unsatisfactory when defining the Syrian regime's nature. Al-Assad's Baathist Syria maintains complex relations with local religious authorities and political organizations aligned with religion; for additional details, see Thomas Pierret, *Religion and State in Syria. The Sunni Ulama from Coup to Revolution* (Cambridge: Cambridge University Press, 2013).

58. As early as January 2009, the Egyptian Muslim Brotherhood's Guide Mahdi Akef prescribed the need for Hamas to include Ankara in the 'front'; 'Isam al-'Iryan, *al-Hayat*, 26 January 2009.

'Free Palestine' flotilla. We have much esteem for their courage and their initiative, which reflects the sympathy of all free people towards the besieged Palestinian people.'[59] 'Resistance' was showcased here as a struggle for dignity and against injustice: 'We recall that it is the confrontation with the Zionist entity – thanks to the people and its resistance, as was the case during the Gaza War, in South Lebanon and with the flotilla – that reveals its ghastly face.'[60] The assault was described as an act of piracy: 'We call on the international community and Arab countries to condemn this crime against humanity in a clear-cut way, to work towards legal proceedings against Zionist war criminals who carry out maritime piracy in international waters, and use all kinds of pressure to lift the unjust blockade permanently.'[61]

The onus was placed on the struggle's legalistic aspects. Hamas stated that, in continuity with the Turkish initiative demanding an international enquiry,[62] they wanted to begin juridical and judicial proceedings against Israel: 'Resistance is a legitimate right sanctioned by the United Nations and the international community. We are only doing what France and Great Britain did during the Second World War when they were resisting Hitler.'[63] We note here that, although ideology's versatility has allowed a broadening of the coalition, the nuances of the discourse ran the risk of gradually diluting it.[64]

Hamas' rhetoric of exemplariness gradually changed as a function of interlocutors: it could even disappear when visits were made to countries that had not gone through an uprising; it could also take a more or less religious dimension in accordance with the interlocutor.

Although Ismail Haniyeh, during his December 2011 tour, tried to relate his movement's struggle to the principle of dignity (*karâma*),[65] resorting to this type of normative register was avoided during his second cycle of visits in GCC states. When his trips were to countries that had not been affected by an Arab Spring or to ones that had nipped it in the bud (as in Bahrein), ideology entirely vanished. In

59. Words spoken by Ismail Haniyeh on 31 May 2010, quoted in *Filastin al-Muslima*, July 2010, 35.

60. Press communiqué, *Information Bureau of the Movement of Islamic Resistance*, 31 May 2010.

61. Ibid.

62. The Israeli Army put Reserve General Giora Eiland in charge of the supervision of a 'team of experts', which was responsible for contributing its own conclusions on the sequence of events during the foray into the Gaza Strip, AFP, 14 June 2010.

63. Conversation with Sheikh Bitawi in Nablus on 25 February 2011.

64. Michael N. Barnett, 'Identity and Alliances in the Middle East', in Peter J. Katzenstein, *The Culture of National Security, Norms and Identity in World Politics*.

65. Haniyeh congratulated the Tunisians for their victory in their revolution and mentioned Israeli attempts to make the al-Aqsa mosque Jewish; he also spoke of worries concerning Jerusalem's Morocco Gate and the importance of Maghreb's people in support for the Palestinian cause, *markaz al-filastîni li-l-i'lâm*, 26 November 2011.

Kuwait and the United Arab Emirates, the link between popular uprisings and the Palestinian question was overshadowed by other themes like that of the blockade. This removal of ideological references in favour of pure interests was also obvious when Khaled Mesh'al spoke to Jordan's King Abdullah on 29 January, at a moment when the aim of the Hashemite monarch was to contain popular dissent that might be a prelude to a 'Jordanian Spring'.[66]

One thus witnesses the implementation of an extremely pragmatic policy by the Islamist movement. In contrast with the Tunisian and Egyptian Springs, the Syrian uprising was almost never mentioned until late 2012. Hamas therefore took advantage of the blurred notion of Arab Spring to enter this field, without going into the details of national situations, which would have made things very awkward for the movement.

66. Since the external offices of Hamas were in Amman in the past, normalizing relations with Jordan without sowing distrust and suspicion has always been a priority for the movement, which has often recalled that Jordan will never be a motherland for the Palestinians; interview with Izzat al-Rishq, *al-Hayat*, 22 January 2012.

Chapter 7

INTERNAL INTERESTS AND IDEOLOGY

The 'resistance front' allows Hamas to give credence to the existence of an axis and ensure the loyalty of its foreign backers. We shall see in the present chapter that it is also used to compete against Fatah, assimilated with Egypt to the camp of subjection and surrender to the enemy.

The truce saw the simultaneous occurrence of three types of imbrication between interests and ideology: coincidence, conflict and 'practical rationalization'. This lull in the fighting was all the more sought, since it coincided with a largely shared 'Islamic norm', the concept of *hudna*. Some members of the al-Qassam Brigades, however, rejected the truce and separated from the armed branch following the *hudna*'s approval. Finally, to reduce the risk of seeing the compromise as a dishonourable concession to the enemy, the truce was usually presented as a form of 'resistance'.

Ideology to fight against nationalist forces

The 'resistance front' to fight against Mahmoud Abbas

The 'resistance front' enables Hamas to undermine the credibility of its political rivals in Palestine. The diplomacy of dissent often is vested with internal significance, namely to finalize 'the internal conquest of power',[1] as emphasized by Bertrand Badie.

As of the 2008–9 offensive against Gaza, Mahmoud Abbas's 'complicity' with Egypt was denounced; the 'axis' of occupation was supposedly also the 'axis' of imperialism and Fatah. The Egyptian Muslim Brotherhood's Guide Mahdi Akef criticized Cairo's attitude and considered that it was normal that Hamas call for an 'Arab mediation', and not for an 'Egyptian' one, since 'Cairo prefers Abou Mazen (Mahmoud Abbas) and Mohammed Dahlan'.[2] Akef defended the policies of Damascus, a capital which 'despite occupied Syrian territories, welcomes

---

1. Bertrand Badie, *La diplomatie et l'intrus: l'entrée des sociétés dans l'arène internationale* (Paris: Fayard, 2008).
2. Mahdi Akef's interview in *Al-Hayat*, on 10 February 2009.

and houses the resistance fighters'. He claimed, moreover, that the Brothers had ceased all activities against the Syrian regime: 'When I see the Egyptian regime do something for the resistance, I will cease my activities.'[3]

During a press conference in Gaza, the interior minister warned Palestinians against the 'secret hands' (*al-ayâdi al-khafiya*) and the 'fifth column' (*al-tâbûr al-khâmis*) that were both trying to sabotage the 'resistance front' from the inside. He also blamed the interior enemy in Palestine for what Israel had attempted to paint as a victory in 2009.[4]

Strengthened during the construction of the metal border barrier, the 'resistance front', by stigmatizing Cairo and describing it as Israel's partner, was able to damage the credibility of Abbas, who was Egypt's partner.

The 'axis of imperialism' that included corrupt Arab states and Egypt was also the 'occupation and Fatah's axis'.[5] Accusations thrown at Abbas of complicity with Egypt and Israel were useful in pointing the finger during the nationalist current flowing when the latter was beginning talks with Israel, coined 'Oslo II' by Hamas.[6] This dialectic is sometimes described using a religious expression; 'Haniyeh considers the resumption of negotiations as a sin.'[7] Tareq Baconi has also insisted on the way religious coloration of Hamas' discourse enables it to distinguish itself from the PLO's trajectory, by showing concessions made by the latter since 1988 as blasphemy.[8]

At the end of 2010, Osama Hamdan went even further, considering that the resignation of the 'former President of the Authority' Mahmoud Abbas could pave the way in solving the crisis, since Abbas was the 'man behind the failure of reconciliation and the man guilty of Palestinian division'.[9] He added on the matter:

> Abbas is responsible for the renunciation that took place since the Oslo Accords, and for all that the Palestinians have lost: territories, rights to Jerusalem (occupied al-Quds) as well as in the West Bank, and those relating to the return of refugees, for which he bears direct responsibility. Mahmoud Abbas' absence

---

3. Ibid.

4. *Al-Quds al-Arabi*, 30 December 2008, quoted in 'Abd al-Hamîd al-Kayyâlî, *Dirâsa fî-l-'adwan al-isrâ'ilî 'alâ qitâ' Ghazza*, markaz al-Zaytûna li-l-dirâsât wa-l-istishârât (Beirut, 2009).

5. *Markaz al-filastînî li-l-i'lâm*, 11 September 2010.

6. Khaled Mesh'al's interview on CNN, with questions by Nic Robertson, on 27 September 2010.

7. Markaz al-filastînî li-l-i'lâm, 11 September 2010.

8. Tareq Baconi, *Hamas Contained. The rise and pacification of Palestinian resistance* (Stanford: Stanford University Press, 2018).

9. An attack by Hamas took place on the day of the announcement of the resumption of talks, on 16 October 2010. It caused the deaths of four Israelis in Hebron/Al-Khalil. On 21 October 2010, in *al-Hayat*, Hamas denied any correlation and rejected the idea that it wanted to send a message to negotiators, *markaz al-filastînî li-l-i'lâm*, 31 October 2010.

from the Palestinian political stage would not be bad news for the Palestinians. Quite the opposite, in fact.[10]

On 19 December 2009, in an interview given to the Cairo *Al-Ahram* daily, Mahmoud Abbas expressed his total support for Egypt and stated it had the right to build the border metal barrier in the name of protection of its national sovereignty. He accused certain parties of diverting attention from the causes leading to war and to the blockade's tightening, particularly targeting Iran, which was ordering Hamas. In September 2010, analysts close to Hamas castigated Fatah's anti-Iranian campaign, which was accusing the Islamic Republic of manipulating the Palestinian 'card' to serve its own regional and international interests.[11] According to these sources, this Fatah initiative was an Israeli and American campaign by proxy, with Abbas's goals being identical to those of his allies.

The double ideological justification for conciliation meant to limit Islamist dissent

Since the signing of the truce, Hamas had strictly forbidden other factions to fire rockets at Israel. This decision weakened the movement, whose supposed abandonment of resistance was criticized. Acceptable to Islamic doctrine, the truce appeared as a means to fight Palestinian political forces opposed to it. This was evidently a hugely unpopular measure but was also presented as a form of 'resistance'.

The justification for the truce in Islamic terminology: Coincidence and conflict

The seizure of Gaza heralded the need for the movement to preserve the status quo with Israel. This commitment made some say that Hamas would return after 2007 to its true nature, that of a movement for re-Islamization indifferent to the struggle for national liberation.[12] To impose this unpopular truce on Gaza's population, Hamas took the trouble of describing it from a theological viewpoint; this was all the easier since stopping the fighting was in perfect harmony with 'Islamic doctrine'.

---

10. Osama Hamdan, 'The Zionists are preparing their own team, which will be led by Fayyad', *markaz al-filastînî li-l-i'lâm*, 23 September 2010.

11. *Filastin al-Muslima*, October 2010, 17.

12. Naim al-Achab considers that June 2007 marked a return to the 1967–88 stage, before Hamas took part in national liberation. The 1988–2007 stage that came after the First Intifada and introduced Hamas to armed struggle could be only an interlude, see Naim al-Achab, *Imârat-Hamâs*, (*The Hamas Emirate*) (Ramallah: Dâr al-tanwîr li-l-nashr wa-l-targama wa-l-tawzî', 2007).

For Hamas the term *hudna* is part of the common language of Palestinians, meant to designate the truce. Just as Intifada means the 'uprising', *hudna* would be the literal translation of the word 'truce'. Khaled Hroub also noted that the difference between truce (*hudna*) and peace treaty is largely semantic, both notions implying a limited time span. Hroub nevertheless likewise emphasized the importance of Islamic tradition and the absence of an alternative term to designate a lull in the fighting.[13] This is also what Meir Hatina claimed: Hamas only imagines a 'peace' with the enemy lasting a limited time, just like Prophet Muhammad, who sanctioned the *Hudaybiyya* agreement with his enemies. Hamas has attempted to reinsert the lull with Israel from a historical-religious perspective to give it more legitimacy.

The uses of ideology allow Hamas to limit criticisms and accusations of compromising behaviour in a context where the movement, since the signing of the *hudna*, prevents the various resistance factions from firing rockets towards Israel. To legitimate the truce, the movement's leaders have emphasized the fact that it is sanctioned by Islamic law. Sheikh Yassin had already noted in 1993 that the truce was limited in time (at most ten years); moreover, it did not go counter the prophet's agreement at *Hudaybiyya* and was not in disagreement with 'Islamic doctrine'.[14] Khaled Mesh'al referred directly to the Qur'anic text to explain that Islam did not, from a juridical viewpoint, prohibit the conclusion of truces: 'If the enemy is inclined towards peace, make peace with them. And put your trust in Allah.'[15] According to Khaled Mesh'al, negotiations are the product of jihad, the enemy's only possible path towards peace. This verse (*ayâ*) is the basis for the religious legitimacy of negotiation during conflict:

> [We begin negotiations] when the enemy is obliged to resort to them, when he comes forward to us, ready to negotiate and pay the price, and to respond to our demands. Yet if we are the ones who desperately seek to negotiate and if we consider it our only option, then we are the ones who pay the price. Those who are obliged to negotiate are those who usually pay the price. This why God Almighty says in another verse: 'So do not weaken and call for peace while you are superior.'[16]

Religious justification is also supported by historical precedents, such as the truces granted by the Caliphate throughout its history. Mouchir al-Masri claimed

---

13. Khaled Hroub, *Hamas, Political Thought and Practice* (Washington: Institute for Palestine Studies, 2000), 84.

14. Letter published in *al-Wasat* on 11 November 1993, quoted by Khaled Hroub, *Hamas, Political Thought and Practice*, 82.

15. Qur'an, Sura 8, Verse 61 (*sūrat l-anfāl*). See also Silvia Catori, 'Khaled Mesha'al énonce l'orientation politique du Hamas', *al-Sabeel*, in July 2010.

16. Qur'an, Sura 47, verse 35 (*sūrat muḥammad*). Quoted by Silvia Catori, *al-Sabeel*, July 2010.

that the movement would not recognize the 'structure of oppression' embodied by Israel; he emphasized that though it did occur that the prophet agreed to a truce with the miscreants of the Quraysh tribe, 'this did not mean that he accepted their unbelief'.[17] 'The truce is not direct or indirect recognition of the occupation's legitimacy or the occupier's right of existence on the land of our forefathers or ancestors.'[18]

There is no theological or juridical prescription that forbids a truce with the Israeli enemy since, during their history, Muslim rulers signed some 800 of them. The revitalization of a distant past endowed with mythical status gives these processes credible historical depth:

> In Islamic history, in the time of the Prophet and during the centuries after – the period of Salâh al-Dîn (Saladin), for instance – negotiation with the enemy occurred, but within a clear framework, and it abided by a specific philosophy, took place within a specific context, followed a vision, rules and regulations governing this negotiation. This stands in contrast with the miserable approach adopted by those negotiating professionals, who consider that it is a way of life and the only strategic option whose implementation makes one discard all other options.[19]

This de-historicized reading of Islam gathers and promotes religious values: the aim is to demonstrate that the leaders of Hamas are consistent with other movements in Gaza (mainly Islamic Jihad), which share the same sources of religious inspiration. Hamas' need to justify its decisions in Islamic terms, especially as regards a long-term *hudna*, has been pointed out by Baudouin Long: 'By using this term, Hamas intends to justify its actions religiously while remaining steadfast.'[20]

Although the dominant forces within Hamas expressed their favourable opinion regarding the truce, judging that it was in agreement with ideology, some al-Qassam Brigade members, however, saw it as an ideological drift. The historical justification had trouble convincing those who accuse Hamas of walking in Fatah's footsteps. Since Hamas' seizure of Gaza in June 2007, Salafi thought became increasingly influential, even within the movement. We shall see in the following chapter dedicated to the decision-making process that, though adopted after double consultation, the 2008 truce led to the departure of some members of Hamas' armed branch, who then joined Salafi groups.

17. *Ikhouan online*, 21 October 2006.
18. *Al-Ayyam*, 19 October 2006.
19. Ibid.
20. Baudouin Long, 'The Hamas Agenda: How Has It Changed?' *Middle East Policy* 17, no. 4 (2010): 131–43.

The truce as a form of 'resistance'

The rhetoric of 'resistance' allows repressing internal enemies, be they Salafis or various kinds of 'collaborators'. Yezid Sayigh highlighted that the conflict with Israel could be used by Ismail Haniyeh's government to legitimize its brutal actions, making it part of a global strategy of 'armed struggle'.[21] This was notably the case during the wave of arrests of 'collaborators', carried out with extreme brutality by Hamas security forces between June 2007 and 2011.[22] The Islamist movement controlling Gaza depicted this repressive campaign as part of its policy of 'good governance', itself assimilated to a form of 'resistance'.[23] The Interior Minister Fathi Hamad cleared Hamas of any responsibility by linking the death penalty to the continuation of the conflict with Israel and by considering it a defence mechanism to protect jihad and liberation.[24]

The amalgamation of fighting against Israel with repression of internal enemies also operates in the case of a truce. In order to convince its militant base that this 'abandonment' is only provisional, the truce, supposed to be a stage on the road to armed struggle, is described as a form of 'resistance'.[25] This process appears as a means to justify disengagement from the fighting frontline in a context where many factions contest the truce's legitimacy.

After the Gaza War, Hamas resorted to force against other fighting factions, by putting in place surveillance patrols and observation points to protect borders.[26] The movement apparently demanded from Islamic Jihad and the Popular Resistance Committees that they monitor their own troops themselves, in order to stop anybody engaging in non-authorized attacks.[27] Many statements mentioned

21. Yezid Sayigh, 'Policing the People, Building the State: Authoritarian Transformation in the West Bank and Gaza', *Carnegie Endowment for International Peace*, February 2011.

22. *Palestinian Center for Human Rights*, Press Releases, 15 April and 18 May 2010, and 4 May 2011.

23. See *Filastin al-Muslima*, quoted by Yezid Sayigh, *'We Serve the People': Hamas Policing in Gaza*, Brandeis University Crown Center for Middle East Studies, Crown Paper 5, April 2011.

24. 'Hamas Vows to Keep Executing 'Collaborators' in Gaza', *AFP*, on 19 April 2010.

25. Hamas has mobilized other means to justify the suspension of armed struggle, particularly through a campaign of Islamization of Gazan society and measures of compression of public space (since January 2010). See Wissam Afifeh, 'Le Hamas a réussi à combiner la résistance et le gouvernement', *Filastin al-Muslima* 28, no. 1 (January 2010), or Bilal al-Shobaki, 'Hamas et la dialectique de la résistance et du gouvernement', *Filastin al-Muslima* 27, no. 1 (January 2009).

26. Sayigh, *'We Serve the People': Hamas Policing in Gaza*.

27. Mohammed Hijazi recalled that Hamas had previously accused President Abbas of imposing a truce. On 30 October 2010, Mahmoud al-Zahar declared: 'Those who launch rockets must be considered as rebels to their faction, because no patriotic formation in Gaza endorses this type of action'; see Mohammed Hijazi, 'Hamas Movement between Partnership and Individualism', *Institute for Palestine Studies* 22, no. 87 (2011): 59.

the fact that firing rockets amounted to treason and anti-patriotic behaviour.[28] Hamas thus claimed to have successfully managed to finalize the 'marriage' between good governance and resistance, the '*nuzâwaja*'.[29]

Ideology, however, is not enough to compensate for constraints deriving from the truce's imposition. As we have seen in the pages focusing on the rivalry with Salafi groups and Islamic Jihad, Hamas often sees itself obliged once more to commit to armed struggle in order to avoid losing face with other factions. When the control of borders becomes politically too costly, and the truce's depiction as 'resistance' becomes unconvincing, Hamas can either let other armed groups take action or itself resort to violence. Armed actions thus appear as the symptom of limitations to the principle of ideological reformulation in order to make it correspond to interests.

28. Sayigh, '*We Serve the People*': *Hamas Policing in Gaza*.

29. In January 2009, the *Filastin al-Muslima* newspaper indicated that Hamas was on the road to success, because it had managed to implement 'good governance', which itself was a form of 'resistance'. In November 2010, Fathi Hamed claimed that 'Hamas has managed something unheard of in the world'; quoted by Sayigh, '*We Serve the People*': *Hamas Policing in Gaza*.

Part IV

THE IMPACT OF DECISION MAKING ON HAMAS FOREIGN POLICY

The foreign policy of Hamas illustrates the movement's internal pluralism in an exemplary manner. One should recall that members of the Political Bureau (the central body responsible for foreign relations) are dispersed in various locations, namely the Gaza Strip, the West Bank, Israeli prisons and the 'outside' which until 2012 was located in Damascus. To this geographical spread, moreover, one must add the permanent attempts at interception by host states and Israeli authorities, which render communications between Hamas figures even more difficult. Although the opacity of the movement (which is a characteristic of the Muslim Brotherhood, characterized by concealment and secrecy) does not permit access to the full details of decision-making processes, information is nonetheless available to formulate (partial) elements of analysis regarding the organization's functioning.

The dispersion of Hamas's directive bodies has favoured the adoption of a peculiar decision-making process, consisting of the consultation of Political Bureau members spread in the four above-mentioned locations. Decision, hence, reflects compromise, which is conceived as a form of consensus following negotiations between the various participants, who have chosen to adopt decisions by majority. The choice of this mechanism can be explained by both a wish to display democratic credentials and an acceptance of the Islamic concept of *shura* (consultation).[1] Various sources have confirmed that the signing of the Prisoners' Document in June 2006 and the June 2008 truce was the result of a collective process of consultation.[2]

This mode of governance does not exclude the fact that some decisions reflect the measure of control of certain participants, who have more influence than others. In this process, participants are permanently negotiating, each wanting to

---

1. Jeroen Gunning has noted that Hamas leaders claim that their decision making is 'authentic' and 'democratic', first of all to distinguish it from Fatah's; he has also noted the need for Hamas to appear as a democratic movement after the June 2007 episode. Jeroen Gunning, op. cit.

2. Shaul Mishal and Avraham, Sela, *The Palestinian Hamas: Vision, Violence, and Coexistence*, New York, Columbia University Press, 2000.

reach the decision that best conforms to his interests. Originating from prisons, the Prisoners' Document thus reflected the preferences of the Political Bureau's members then jailed in Israel. In this case, resorting to consultation also served as an excuse for other decision-making centres of Hamas to buy time before expressing an opinion or a stand. This was also the case for the 2008 truce, which was the product of a consultation involving all Political Bureau members, despite the opposition of some of the movement's fringes, as witnessed by the duration of the process and the failure of the initial consultation.

In other circumstances, however, Hamas's foreign policy is the result of unilateral decisions taken by the external leadership. This was the case for the May 2011 Cairo Agreement, the one signed in Doha in February 2012, and the rapprochement with Qatar and concomitant distancing from Iran and Hezbollah. In the cases where only the external leadership decides, the diplomatic orientations of Hamas are then scrutinized and questioned by other bodies. Gaza's leaders are the most critical regarding the confiscation of the decision-making process by the external leadership, because it deprives the former from any effective role but also because of the content of these decisions, which appears contrary to their own interests.

These fracture lines, however, are not exclusively geographical. Thematic coalitions can form independently from the decision-making location, as shown by Moussa Abu Marzouk's alliance with Mahmoud al-Zahar against the Cairo Agreement.

Chapter 8

COLLECTIVE DECISIONS, UNILATERAL DECISIONS

The Political Bureau (*maktab siyâsi*, i.e. the executive organ of Hamas) is the main decision-making body for foreign policy. The Consultative Body (*majlis ash-shûrâ*) nevertheless plays a part in the upstream formulation of general orientations to be followed. Osama Hamdan, in charge of international relations for the external leadership, confirmed this, quoting for instance relations with the United States and the West:

> In the framework of the study of foreign relations, we were placed by the United States on the list of terrorist organizations, and Europe followed suit. The question is still pending: must we battle to take Hamas out of this list? If we are to take a new stand that modifies our strategic orientation, this is not only the matter for officials of the executive, but it must also go through the *majlis ash-shûrâ*. It is only at a later stage that members of the Political Bureau can implement this decision.[1]

Yet, the Political Bureau is the body deciding war and peace, as attested by Imad al-Alami, former official responsible for relations with Egypt: 'The Political Bureau, which is the movement's executive body, conducts foreign policy and deals with issues like the truce.'[2]

Many sources have confirmed that members of this body resort to a consultative process (*mushâwara*).[3] According to Osama Hamdan, this method of decision making prevents a single leader from monopolizing power over the whole movement and allows him to remain in agreement with the Qur'anic principle of consensus (*ijmâ'*), which rules that legitimacy is ensured by the

---

1. Conversation with Osama Hamdan, Damascus, 29 January 2011.
2. Conversation with Imad al-Alami in Gaza on 18 March 2013.
3. Concerning the debate on the possible participation of Hamas in the election and the PA'institutions, see the secret document which circulated in July 1992 among Hamas' senior member (a reflection on the movement's procedure of decision making) furnished by Shaul Mishal and Sela Avraham, 'Participation without Presence, Hamas, The Palestinian Authority and the Politics of Negotiated Coexistence', *Middle Eastern Studies* 38, no. 3 (2002): 1–26.

entire community's agreement. Hamdan emphasized, moreover, that the more numerous the disagreements, the more it is legitimate to resort to extensive consultation.[4] The extent of consultation would therefore be proportional to the potential level of disagreements it causes. This therefore opens a first breach in a decision-making method described as deliberative. One should also mention the existence of a second breach, relating to logistics of consultation, equally guaranteed by the external leadership, who are in charge of this matter by organizing the vote among the three other bodies: Gaza, Israeli prisons and the West Bank.[5] These two biases mean that specific prerogatives are attributed to members of the outside leadership, as confirmed by a number of sources (including Hamas members themselves). Osama Hamdan put it in this way: 'Although foreign policy is managed by the Political Bureau, the management of day-to-day decisions (*qarârât yawmîya*) is the prerogative of the Damascus decision-making leadership: the *hudna* (truce) is obviously not part of these day-to-day decisions.'[6]

This tendency was also confirmed by Egyptian diplomats, as well as by Palestinian analysts,[7] for example, by Mohammed Daraghmeh, a specialist of the movement based in Ramallah: 'Bureau members debate and then take decisions. It is the Damascus group, however, who takes charge of daily management of diplomacy and sensitive issues of foreign policy.'[8]

Additional attributions left to the outside leadership have made the author question the degree of recurrence in consultation. It appears that, in addition to managing consultation proceedings and communicating their outcome, the external leadership sometimes takes decisions on its own. First of all, in 2009, when Khaled Mesh'al refused to validate the signing of the reconciliation agreement concluded by Mahmoud al-Zahar; then in 2011 and 2012, when the president of the Political Bureau signed the Cairo and Doha Agreements without consulting members of the Gaza leadership. These reconciliation agreements thus appeared in the eyes of some leaders as a decision taken by Khaled Mesh'al alone. Finally, the rapprochement with Qatar, as well as the communiqué calling for Hezbollah's withdrawal from Syria, was also met with intense criticism by the various players: by part of the Gaza leadership, Mahmoud al-Zahar, but also some leaders and officials abroad.

---

4. Ibid.

5. 'Many are those who think that decisions are taken abroad, because it is Khaled Mesha'al or Moussa Abu Marzouk who announce decisions, while in reality these are decisions taken by the entire group of Bureau members. It is not because they announce a decision that they have taken it alone.' Conversation with Imad al-Alami in Gaza, on 18 March 2013.

6. Conversation with Osama Hamdan, Damascus, 29 January 2011.

7. *Asharq al-Awsat*, 26 June 2010.

8. Conversation with Mohammed Daraghmeh in Ramallah on 25 February 2011.

Collective decisions

The Prisoners' Document

Signed in June 2006 by Hamas and other Palestinian factions, the Prisoners' Document implicitly recognized the June 1967 borders, agreed on the construction of a Palestinian state with Jerusalem as a capital and accepted limitations to the resistance in the territories occupied in 1967. It was approved on 28 June 2006, following consultations with the entire Political Bureau, whose extensive participation was confirmed by Khaled Hroub,[9] Alvaro de Soto and Paola Caridi.[10]

A part of the external and internal leadership was against this document. This refusal was first expressed by the opposition of some to the referendum proposed by Mahmoud Abbas. These opponents asserted that pending issues like prisoners could not be discussed via a referendum, a process considered 'inadequate' and 'forbidden', because it de facto excluded Palestinians of the Diaspora. For all that, these same leaders could not, however, ignore this document, because it originated from the leadership held in Israeli jails. According to Alvaro de Soto, 'The document pushed Hamas into a corner, since it could neither reject it, nor accept it entirely without first consulting all its constituencies.'[11] As for Paola Caridi, she thought 'The problem for the leaderships in Ramallah and in Gaza City was rather how not to take into account – even diminish its importance, if possible – that document written by the prisoners who in the eyes of Palestinian society were the living definition of suffering and of heroism.'[12]

Conversations with the author reminded her that prisoners have a similar right to participate in decision making, and their opinions should be taken into account with all the more attention because of the penitentiary environment they live in, which allows them to dialogue more easily with other Palestinian factions. Normal delays resulting from consultations with all parties can be exploited, however, as in the case of the Prisoners' Document: it does seem that Hamas used time for consultation to change paragraphs of the text's initial version, which it deemed inconvenient. Paola Caridi explained the details of the matter to us:

> The Prisoners' Document, once modified, was approved on 28 June 2006: it makes any compromise on the borders impossible, just like on the issue of refugees,

---

9. Khaled Hroub, Khaled Hroub, *Hamas, Political Thought and Practice* (Washington: Institute for Palestine Studies, 2000).

10. Paola Caridi, *Hamas, From Resistance to Government* (New York: Seven Stories Press, 2012).

11. Alvaro de Soto, 'End of Mission Report-Confidential', May 2007, https://image.guardian.co.uk/sys-files/Guardian/documents/2007/06/12/DeSotoReport.pdf, 21–2.

12. According to Paola Caridi, the fact that the Prisoners' Document was from prisons was an important element, which clarified how consultations were organized. Paola Caridi, *Hamas, From Resistance to Government* (New York, Seven Stories Press, 2012), 233.

adding conditions that render any negotiation very difficult. According to the modified version, refugees would have 'the right to return home, to the land from which they were expelled', and receive compensation. This shows to what extent the Gaza and Damascus leaderships wanted to leave their mark on the document.[13]

The time Hamas took to make its decision public[14] was criticized by Fatah, which considered that consultation was only an excuse to refrain from answering immediately. For Fatah, this was an unbearable postponement, reflecting the impasse and contradictions of Hamas alone, since the consultation was a logical response to the communication difficulties caused by occupation and dispersion of its members. Again according to Osama Hamdan:

> We can neither discuss a decision by telephone nor by mail, because these are confidential matters. It is true, therefore, that Hamas needed additional time to make its decisions. We are faced with this dilemma: either Hamas preserves its unity by taking into account decentralization, extra-territoriality, or we become a dictatorial movement. We should accept neither becoming a dictatorship nor be made up of clans and factions. We therefore take the necessary time, and at least we can say this decision is right.[15]

Be it either to buy time or to transform or amend the document before its approval, what is important here is that the consultation process was truly implemented.

Consultation to reach a truce

Nor were Hamas members unanimous about the truce. Although most leading bodies considered it as a provisional decision on the path to liberation, there was within the movement a broad range of viewpoints between the followers of armed struggle at all costs, and those favouring the search for a compromise with Israel, even if a temporary one.[16] Some rejected the truce outright;[17] others,

---

13. The external leadership apparently tried to minimize this document's importance, and then forced modifications on its content before approving it.

14. In Janis and Mann's model, the most decisive resource affecting a decision-making process is the time available. Irving L. Janis and Leon Mann, *Decision Making: A Psychological Analysis of Conflict, Choice and Commitment* (London: Collier Macmillan, 1977).

15. Conversation with Osama Hamdan, 29 January 2011.

16. Moussa Abu Marzouk went as far as mentioning the possibility that Hamas accept Israel's legitimacy in the case a Palestinian state was established in the West Bank and the Gaza strip with Jerusalem as its capital.

17. According to Basim al-Zubaidi, from early 2005 to late 2007, 24 per cent of the leadership of Hamas rejected the truce. See *Hamâs wa-l-hukûm, dukhûl al-nizâm am al-tamarrûd 'alayhi*, Palestinian Center for Policy and Survey Research, March 2010.

although a minute minority, accepted direct negotiations;[18] others again thought it was necessary to accept Israeli–Palestinian accords to become part of Palestine's internal institutional balance. This latter stance was illustrated by elements of Ismail Haniyeh's speech:

> We propose this message: were Israel ready to negotiate in a serious and honourable way, were Israel to find a solution at the heart of the matter of 1948, instead of being satisfied with that of 1967 (which for us is of secondary importance), we could agree on a just and permanent peace. This could give the Holy Territories an opportunity to be a genuine land of peace and fertility, also from the economic viewpoint. It would be a stable land for all of the region's Semitic peoples. If only Americans knew the truth, this possibility would become reality.[19]

As for the Prisoners' Document, a consultation of the whole set of Political Bureau members is what really took place to ratify the decision in favour of the June 2008 truce. The same decision-making procedures had been set in motion for the previous truces.[20]

Discussions for the June 2008 truce apparently began as early as March. The question asked to the various parties and currents by members of the external leadership was: Should one implement the truce only in the Gaza Strip (a territory the movement considered 'liberated' since 2005), or should it be broadened to include the West Bank? After a second examination, the truce was finally accepted and signed in June. The first consultation seems not to have led to the expected results. The French diplomat (and former ambassador to Tunisia and Iraq) Yves Aubin de la Messuzière, who stayed twice in Gaza in 2008,[21] has left his testimony on the matter: 'To avoid splitting the movement, they resorted to a process of consultation. This was implemented in particular for the 2008 truce: the first consultation was negative, and this is why they proceeded to another consultation.' This was also what Mohammed Daraghmeh explained: 'For the 2008 truce, consultation was carried out twice, which proves that disagreements were many. It is in part for this reason, moreover, that the decision process extended over two months to validate this *hudna*.'[22]

These observations support the model put forward by Graham Allison, who highlights the importance of a movement's organizational structure to understand its decisions in matters of foreign policy: each person's place in the process explains the preferences of players, according to the formula 'where you stand depends

---

18. Basim al-Zubaidi mentioned only one statement, which was that of Ghazi Hamad.
19. Ismail Haniyeh's interview in the *Washington Post*, on 11 July 2006.
20. Jeroen Gunning, *Hamas in Politics* (New York: Columbia University Press, 2009).
21. La Messuzière's visit to Gaza, in March 2008, was reported by French journalist Georges Malbrunot on 19 May 2008, in the French *Le Figaro* daily.
22. Conversation with Yves Aubin de La Messuzière in Paris, on 15 January 2010.

on where you sit'.[23] They also confirm Margaret Hermann's conclusions,[24] which emphasize that the processes can vary within a given movement as a function of context and the nature of the decision. In addition, this author mentions the existence of various options to solve conflicts that go from granting concessions to saving face for the other parties, to compromises from both sides so as not to completely lose the thread of the decision-making process. Both options were chosen in turn for the Prisoners' Document and the 2008 truce, with the majority of leading bodies finally approving them.

Divergences of interest rather than ideological differences

There were many disagreements regarding the truce, these essentially concerning its duration: though the common viewpoint was that the *hudna* could last more than ten years, some thought it could be prolonged for approximately fifty years.[25] Other divergences related to the commitment to abide by the truce: most leaders like Ghazi Hamad, Yahya Musa and Faraj Roumana considered it must be implemented with meticulousness so long as Israel respected it, but others like Mahmoud al-Zahar, Abou Ubaida, Mouchir al-Masri and Mohammad Nazzal saw it as useful only as preparation for the next coming stage, namely Israel's destruction. These differences in approach were not frozen but changed as function of the context.

As shown by Basim al-Zubaidi, between 2005 and 2006 there was within Hamas a tendency to oppose the truce, which could be explained by the resurgence of Israeli attacks against Gaza and West Bank villages and by the numerous assassinations of Hamas officials and civilians in Jenin, Nablus and Gaza.[26] After June 2007, declarations against the truce became much rarer. In the author's view, this evolution can be explained by a contingent change creating a redefinition of interests: in 2006, the al-Qassam Brigades would have spoken against the truce, because they feared being marginalized by the formation of a Hamas government that prescribed a fusion of resistance and conciliation (*taswîya*). They would have liked to preserve their identity as resistance fighters. Harsh statements against the truce by Abu Obeida, the spokesman of the al-Qassam Brigades, therefore

---

23. Graham Allison, *Essence of Decision: Explaining the Cuban Missile Crisis* (New York: Harper Collins, 1972).

24. Margaret G. Hermann, "'How Decision Units Shape Foreign Policy, A Theoretical Framework", in Leaders, Groups and Coalitions: Understanding the People and Processes in Foreign Policymaking', *International Studies Review* 3, no. 2 (2001): 47–81.

25. Sayyid Abou Musameh, from Gaza, in May 2008. See Basim al-Zubaidi, *Hamas wa-l-hukûm, dukhûl al-nizâm am al-tamarrûd 'alayhi* (Palestinian Center for Policy and Survey, 2010).

26. Eleven per cent of statements made by Hamas leaders were made up of this type of declaration. Basim al-Zubaidi, *Hamas wa-l-hukûm, dukhûl al-nizâm am al-tamarrûd 'alayhi*.

mostly appeared after Hamas' participation in elections. In contrast, following Gaza's seizure in June 2007, these declarations disappeared from the *Alresalah* newspaper, and Abu Obeida (but also Said Siam, Oussam al-Mazini, Mouchir al-Masri, Mahmoud al-Zahar and Mohammad Nazzal, who had expressed their opposition to truce) adopted stances favourable to such a policy.[27]

These dissensions could also reflect ideological conflicts within the movement. It was on the issue of the truce in particular that the opposition of part of the al-Qassam Brigades crystallized: despite Abu Obeida's rallying to the *hudna* after June 2007, other members of the armed branch still did not accept the lull in the fighting.[28] They therefore joined the Salafi *Jund Ansâr Allah* movement led by Sheikh Abd al-Latif Moussa. Khaled Banat, who became responsible for this group's armed operations, had in the past been in charge of military training of al-Qassam Brigade members. He was thus able to mobilize his contacts with Hamas' armed wing to recruit new personnel willing to join him. Fahd Moussa, Abd al-Latif Moussa's son-in-law, is an example of a fighter who, in the wake of the June 2008 truce, split from Hamas to become a *Jund Ansâr Allah* activist.[29]

Unilateral decisions

Although the Political Bureau is the institution in charge of foreign policy decisions, in practice, this model is usually adaptable, depending on the nature of the decision. In the Shalit affair, for instance, the intervention of the leadership held in prisons was apparently of crucial importance.[30] As for the question of the temporary lull in the fighting (*tahdîya*), decisions were most often taken very quickly by the Gaza leadership only.[31] Osama Hamdan justified this adaptability by the hazards of occupation and the need to preserve the confidentiality of decision-making models:

---

27. According to Basim al-Zubaidi who has analysed articles published in *Alresalah* between 2005 and 2007, there was an increase in the number of Hamas leaders favourable to appeasement, even after 2006, at the time Israeli leaders were increasing pressure on Hamas. The results of the analysis show a weekly rise in their number, particularly after June 2007. Basim al-Zubaidi, *Hamas wa-l-hukûm, dukhûl al-nizâm am al-tamarrûd 'alayhi*.

28. Basim al-Zubaidi, *Hamas wa-l-hukûm, dukhûl al-nizâm am al-tamarrûd 'alayhi*.

29. 'Radical Islam in Gaza', *International Crisis Group*, Middle East Report n. 104, 20 March 2011.

30. 'Although theoretically one must have the approval of the entire group of the Bureau's members, for some decisions it is not always necessary to consult everybody, like for instance going through the prisons'; conversations with Imad al-Alami and Ayman al-Taha in Gaza on 18 and 19 March 2013.

31. Prisoners apparently delegated their votes via a mandate process (*tawqîl*).

We have a problem of geography: we are dispersed throughout the world. [. . .] Overcoming this situation of dispersion supposes flexibility in the implementation of decisions. Central decisions taken by the leadership in light of the results of consultation must remain pliable and adaptable, because the very nature of the struggle against Israel implies a certain flexibility in the implementation of a decision.[32]

Contested unilateral foreign policy

Some Gaza leadership members apparently introduced as of 2008 a project of reconciliation with Fatah, which included both the signing of a new truce with Israel and Gilad Shalit's release.[33] These leaders had attempted to convince the outside leadership of more flexibility towards Fatah.[34] A month after 'Cast Lead', a delegation from Gaza headed by Mahmoud al-Zahar went to Damascus, and then to Cairo, to respond to truce proposals formulated by Israel.[35] At the end of 2009, al-Zahar once more travelled to Damascus, Sudan and Cairo to negotiate with Egyptian and German mediators. The success of these talks made him sign an Egyptian Document planning new inter-Palestinian reconciliation and the freeing of the abducted IDF private. Khaled Mesh'al, then residing outside the territories, nevertheless prevented implementation of the already signed deal. According to him, no compromise could be approved in a context where Mahmoud Abbas had conformed to American wishes to postpone examination of the Goldstone report at the United Nations Human Rights Council, in October 2009.[36]

In March 2010, Mahmoud al-Zahar was forced to permanently suspend negotiations for eventual reconciliation,[37] because his 'advances' were described as

32. Conversations with Osama Hamdan in Damascus on 29 January 2011.
33. *Asharq al-Awsat*, 29 August 2007.
34. According to *asharq al-Awsat* published on 24 August 2007, Ghazi Hamad criticized the external leadership for not having taken any measure likely to favour entente with Fatah. He claimed to have requested that Hamas 'make the first step towards' reconciliation.
35. *al-Jazeera.net*, 11 February 2009.
36. On 15 September, a UN report under the direction of judge Richard Goldstone, focusing on the 2008–9 Gaza War, accused Israel and Hamas of 'war crimes' and possible 'crimes against humanity'. The report recommended that the Security Council refer to the International Criminal Court's attorney general. On 6 October, faced with the defensive reactions provoked by the 2 October decision, Mahmoud Abbas announced his intention to refer the file to the UN. On 16 October, the Human Rights Council adopted a resolution referring the file to the Security Council.
37. Mahmoud al-Zahar apparently accepted Israel's conditions, notably that of changing the names of some prisoners on the list proposed by Ahmed al-Jaabari. In addition, al-Zahar would have agreed with Israel to prevent the return of the freed prisoners to the West Bank, approving their deportation to Gaza; *Palvoice.com*, 2 March 2010.

'concessions' that were too substantial. Many Fatah officials have mentioned these internal conflicts inside Hamas to explain the failure of reconciliation (*musâlâha*) in 2009:[38] 'It is indeed Khaled Mesh'al who sabotaged the agreement, despite Mahmoud al-Zahar's support for the signing of the document. Unfortunately, Mesh'al wants to reach an agreement that would seem ideal, but this is simply impossible.'[39]

Nabil Shaath, a former member of Fatah's Central Committee, considered that the decision in favour of reconciliation was beyond the Gaza leadership's grasp: 'Hamas, inside (Palestine), wishes to attain reconciliation, but the position of Hamas in Damascus is different. I am not saying there is a battle between the inside and outside leadership, but there are two different perspectives.'[40] The Fatah Central Committee member Mohammed Shtaya added: 'Some are interested in reconciliation, but at the same time the Damascus leadership keeps the agreement dangling and refuses to sign the Egyptian Document.'[41]

The outside leadership's unilateralism resurfaced as of 2011, but this time Mesh'al was in favour of reconciliation. The Cairo and Doha Agreements, which foresaw a transfer of the negotiations file to the PLO,[42] were signed without consulting the members in Gaza. During the signing ceremony of the Cairo Agreement, Khaled Mesh'al announced he was ready to grant Mahmoud Abbas an additional year to carry out negotiations with Israel:[43] this initiative was unacceptable to many leaders in Gaza.[44] Different sources confirmed that the signatories of the Cairo Agreement were not political figures from the Gaza Strip.[45]

Some Gazan leaders, moreover, expressed their displeasure concerning Khaled Mesh'al's new place of residence, namely Doha. The presence of Mesh'al next to Yusuf al-Qaradawi during his sermon on 3 May 2013 was also problematic:[46] insults hurled at Iran and Hezbollah by the Egyptian sheikh led Mahmoud al-Zahar to send a letter to Mesh'al, urgently requesting him to clarify his position and express

---

38. The September 2009 Egyptian Document was apparently modified by Egypt on 10 October, prior to acceptance by Fatah on 15 October. The document had to be approved by Hamas before validation on 25 October; *al-Ayyam*, 12 September 2009.

39. *Palvoice*, 3 April 2010.

40. *Al-Ayyam*, 25 March 2010.

41. Statement by Mohammed Shtaya, a member of the Fatah's Central Committee, *al-Hayat al-Jadida* on 23 February 2010.

42. 'Light at the End of their Tunnels? Hamas and the Arab Uprisings', Middle East Report, *International Crisis Group*, n. 129, 14 August 2012.

43. *al-Jazeera*, 4 May 2011.

44. 'Hamas in Gaza, Damascus Spare over Unity Deal', *Ma'an News Agency*, 2 June 2011.

45. *Al-shorouk online*, 'Details on the conflict between Mahmoud al-Zahhar and Khaled Mesha'al', 6 April 2011; see also sources close to Fatah, for example, Jamal Muhaysen, a member of Fatah's Central Committee.

46. *Al-Quds al-Arabi*, 3 June 2013.

disapproval at al-Qaradawi's words.[47] Other Gazan leaders had additionally stated their opposition to the visit to Gaza of the president of the World Union of Ulemas: Imad al-Alami, returning to the Strip after his departure from Damascus, had tried to convince Haniyeh to cancel this visit, as an emergency measure against declarations made a few days prior in Doha.[48] These attempts were fruitless: a little after his virulent speech against Hezbollah, the Egyptian sheikh went to Gaza anyway, provoking the displeasure of the Strip's leadership.

The latter dismissed the communiqué broadcast by Mesh'al on 17 June 2013, which called for Hezbollah's retreat from Syria. The Gaza leaders asked the Political Bureau's chairman to make amends for this mistake.[49] Responding to claims that the Hezbollah had neglected resistance to Israeli occupation in favour of fighting Sunni 'brothers' in Syria, a large fraction of the al-Qassam Brigades once more insisted on its loyalty to the Lebanese Shia Party, saying that the latter was an Islamic faction and not an apostate movement.[50]

The divisions relating to the durability of the Iranian alliance and its Lebanese Shia surrogate were now such that Mahmoud al-Zahar and his delegation, consisting of twenty-two people who wished to go to Iran, were forbidden from leaving Gaza. Fathi Hamad, who was then interior minister, prevented them from going through the Rafah crossing when they were at the beginning of their journey to Tehran.[51] The movement's spokesman then denied this prohibition, saying it was just propaganda orchestrated by Fatah, which was trying to spread the image of a divided Hamas.[52]

While in the early 1990s a few internal leaders had expressed doubts on the need to pursue an alliance with Iran, fearing that it would be at the expense of relations with Arab states,[53] it was now the outside leadership who did not want to prolong the strategic alliance with a country backing the regime in Damascus. In a context where civil war in Syria was polarizing regional conflicts around a sectarian Sunni/Shia split, Hamas' leaders outside Palestine chose to operate a rapprochement with Egypt and Qatar,[54] two Sunni regional players.

Decisions contested by various players

From 2009 onwards, several Hamas officials began to complain publicly about the Damascus leadership's autocratic management and more specifically about

---

47. *Al-Quds al-Arabi*, 3 June 2013.
48. *Al-Badil*, 4 November 2013.
49. *Palpress*, 21 June 2013.
50. 'Hamas-Hezbollah Split over the Syrian War', *Alakhbar English*, on 21 June 2013.
51. *Fatehmedia*, 24 June 2013.
52. *Palpress*, 24 June 2013.
53. Meir Hatina in 'Hamas and the Oslo Accord: Religious Dogma in a Changing Political Reality', *Mediterranean Politics* 4, no. 3 (1999):37–55.
54. 'Hamas-Hezbollah Split over the Syrian War', *Alakhbar English*, on 21 June 2013.

Khaled Mesh'al's. In February, a Gaza leader protested against his statements on an alternative PLO, describing it as 'a grave mistake, both illogical and unacceptable'.[55]

The reconciliation deal signed in Cairo in 2011 was criticized by part of the Gaza leadership, a criticism echoed in the media. During a robust tirade, Mahmoud al-Zahar asserted that Hamas had not changed its stance and was opposed to talks with Israel:

> The position of Hamas regarding negotiations and the resistance has not changed. Negotiations go counter to the aspirations of the Palestinian people, who voted in favour of Hamas in 2006. Nowadays some are claiming we have given Abou Mazen (Mahmoud Abbas) the option to open a new round of negotiations. We have not agreed on that, and have never encouraged him to negotiate. Quite the opposite, we annoy him night and day on the issue of negotiations. Accordingly, what happened on the day the agreement was signed was not approved by Hamas. We do not recognize this deal and I think it does not reflect the position of the movement, whose platform is based on resistance and not negotiation. We were surprised by these words. The world must know there is no change in our position. We want to negotiate within the framework of resistance only. Any person who claims that we authorize the Authority to hold negotiations does not represent Hamas.[56]

In November 2011, when Khaled Mesh'al met Mahmoud Abbas in Cairo and adopted the notion of 'peaceful resistance', Mahmoud al-Zahar's criticisms resumed. In al-Zahar's mind, this expression was only a slogan: 'We have mentioned this concept only as a slogan that cannot be applied to Gaza.'[57]

On 1 June 2011, two months after the signature of the Cairo Agreement, the Damascus leadership invited some of Gaza's Hamas' chiefs to the Syrian capital to discuss once more its contents and resorb the tensions it had sparked. The presence at the meeting of both Khalil al-Hayya and Nizar Awadallah (despite Mahmoud al-Zahar's exclusion)[58] showed that, well as being a conflict between the two decision-making headquarters, this was a dispute pitting two leaders.[59] Political Bureau members residing in Damascus sought to categorize Mahmoud al-Zahar's position as marginal.[60] They published the following communiqué:

---

55. *Asharq al-Awsat*, 13 February 2009.
56. *Al-Quds*, 17 May 2011.
57. *Ma'an News Agency*, 3 January 2012.
58. *al-Jazeera.net*, 2 June 2011.
59. Even though al-Zahar tried to minimize the importance of these disagreements and claimed he was on a trip to Algeria during the Damascus meeting, 'The Difference with Mesha'al has Passed', *al-Riyadh*, 8 June 2011.
60. According to Hamas leaders interviewed by the daily *al-Hayat* on 3 June 2011, the presence of two figures from Gaza countered the idea of a rift within the movement; while

The Political Bureau met in Damascus on Wednesday June 1st to discuss several important points, in particular those of Palestinian reconciliation and its implementation, in coordination with the brothers from Fatah and those from other Palestinian organizations. The Bureau's members have in addition discussed the question that has most interested the media on the occasion of the speech given by Political Bureau's chairman Khaled Mesha'al during the ceremony in Cairo. In this respect, the Bureau wishes to emphasize various points: first of all, the declarations made by Khaled Mesha'al reflect and represent the movement's positions and principles, and any other statement originating from another source that contradicts the Bureau's statements does not represent the movement's positions. The Bureau is the only body authorized to amend the chairman's declarations, if need be.[61]

Yet the February 2012 Doha Agreement that foresaw, in addition to the transfer of the file on negotiations to Mahmoud Abbas, the formation of a provisional government inside which the Palestinian Authority's president would also acquire the status of prime minister was again the target of harsh criticism from the Gaza leadership. Although Mahmoud al-Zahar was the first to express his rejection, adding that his opposition was not because of Mahmoud Abbas's personality but due to the agreement's contents,[62] many thought that it went against Palestinian Fundamental Law, which stipulates that the same person cannot be both president and prime minister.[63] These fractures also led to a rift inside the al-Qassam Brigades, part of the latter pledging allegiance to Khaled Mesh'al, with another sympathetic to Mahmoud al-Zahar's stand.[64]

In the wake of the Damascus meeting (whose aim was to smooth out divergences caused by the Cairo accord) and after the Doha Agreement, another discussion between the two decision-making centres was organized in the Egyptian capital. The goal was the same: to renegotiate the relevance or validity of this Palestinian reconciliation. This encounter in Cairo took place on 23 February 2012, and, in contrast with that in Damascus, Mahmoud al-Zahar was one of the Gaza leaders invited. This is what one of the external leadership's members communicated to the author when they met in the *City Star* Hotel in Cairo's Nasr City neighbourhood: 'The Political Bureau met for around thirteen hours, which reflects the importance and depth of internal differences. There were four Gaza representatives present: Mahmoud al-Zahar, Ismail Haniyeh, Nizar Awadallah and Khalil al-Hayya.'[65]

Mahmoud al-Zahar's position was marginal, he stood for no one else and therefore did not constitute an opposition.

61. *Al-Riyadh*, 3 June 2011.
62. *Maannews*, 12 February 2012.
63. 'Doha Agreement Divides Political Opinion', *Ma'an News Agency*, 7 February 2012.
64. *Al-Quds al-Arabi*, 21 February 2012.
65. Conversation with a Hamas official who has preferred to remain anonymous, Cairo, 23 February 2012.

Many were those who denounced the appropriation (*tafarrud*) of decision making by Khaled Mesh'al. This is how Mahmoud al-Zahar expressed the matter via the press:

> We were not aware of Khaled Mesha'al's position. He never consulted anybody on the matter. This position is bad. We never gave Fatah the opportunity of negotiating in the name of the Palestinian people. We had no prior knowledge of Mesha'al's position, no one consulted us on the issue.[66]

While minimizing the importance of this internal opposition and criticisms which were personally addressed to it, Khaled Mesh'al mentioned a confusion (*iltibass*) around the choice of Mahmoud Abbas as prime minister. Mesh'al emphasized on internal discussions held in Cairo to overcome controversy (*jidal*):

> There perhaps has been a confusion (*iltibass*) on the choice of Mahmoud Abbas as Prime Minister of a national unity government, in addition to his responsibilities as President of the Palestinian Authority. Some inside Hamas considered that this choice was not desirable. We then gathered the entire group of Political Bureau members of both inside and outside Gaza to discuss and overcome this contention (*jidal*). We finally agreed on implementing what I had signed with Abou Mazen and the Emir of Qatar.[67]

In May 2012, a compromise was finally reached, which ensured that Mahmoud Abbas would not stay as prime minister in case an agreement to form a national unity government was not found. Finally, although some decisions seem to have been taken unilaterally, their efficient implementation was hampered by the opposition of one or the other side, which most of the time led to attempts to recalibrate these same decisions to make them more agreeable to the group of leading bodies. These unilateral decisions, therefore, could not be adopted without additional discussion and renegotiation between the leaders inside and outside Palestine. This happened on two occasions, nonetheless: in Damascus, following the signing of the Cairo Agreement, and in Cairo regarding the Doha one. The movement thus ultimately went back to a consultation process, an 'ex-post' concertation of sorts.

Differing from a typical political party, Hamas is a movement in which resources are spread out not only in quantitative terms but also in qualitative ones. Though one of the decision-making centres controls important material resources, it will lack some symbolic resources held by the other centre: the dispersion of resources is such that it is very difficult for one of the leaderships (including the one outside Palestine) to impose its will on the others.

---

66. *Al-Akhbar*, 24 May 2011.
67. Conversations with Khaled Mesh'al in Doha on 17 April 2017.

The stances of various members often went beyond a simplistic internal/external fracture. The alignments of other leaders were partly organized around the al-Zahar/Mesh'al antagonism. On the issue of the Doha Agreement, it was noticed that Moussa Abu Marzouk (the Political Bureau's vice-president and a member of the external leadership) joined Mahmoud al-Zahar in his refusal to back this agreement. Another example of overcoming of the internal/external fracture was Ismail Haniyeh's rally in favour of the regional realignment prescribed by Khaled Mesh'al. Haniyeh was initially one of the most outspoken apologists of the alliance with Iran and went to Tehran when Mesh'al was signing the Doha Agreement (the visit to Iran was made without the Political Bureau chairman's permission).[68] He finally aligned himself with the Political Bureau's stance when the latter visited Gaza on 7 December 2012, and from then on supported disengagement from the Iranian alliance and rapprochement with Qatar.

---

68. According to a talk with Mouchir al-Masri in Geneva on 19 January 2012, Khaled Mesh'al had not been informed of Haniyeh's visit to Iran. On the same topic, see *al-Arabiyya*, on 11 February 2012.

Chapter 9

CAUSES OF DISSENT

Despite the geographical separation of its decision-making centres, the political apparatus of Hamas has succeeded, by consultation, to preserve certain cohesion. However, the internal/external fracture, which is regularly expressed by Gaza's opposition to initiatives from the outside, as well as the antagonism between Mahmoud al-Zahar and Khaled Mesh'al, has often sparked interrogations on many of Hamas' decisions. Dissent can be explained by the existence of diverging interests inside the organization.

Since the 2006 election victory and the formation of a government, Gaza leaders have expressed their wish for a better distribution of powers between the various decision-making centres. The seizure of Gaza in June 2007, and the accumulation of duties and revenue through taxation of trade via tunnels, has in addition decreased the economic dependence of the internal leadership on external Hamas decision-making centres. This competition was finally exacerbated by changes in 2011 in the regional context, which affected the ratio of forces between the two centres of power.

Beyond issues of procedure, the problem for part of the Gaza leaders also derived from the very content of these decisions, since they were perceived as hindrances to the preservation of their interests. The Gaza leadership sought to stay in power at all costs in the Strip and strengthen its position by allying with Iran. In addition, they criticized Khaled Mesh'al for yielding to pressure from foreign powers. Although these pressures did exist prior to 2011, they had not led to any dissent because the context was not favourable.

Finally, this dissent was sparked by some important figures, independently from their belonging to such-and-such a leadership. It illustrated processes of alignment or realignment of positions in the context of conflict between Mahmoud al-Zahar and Khaled Mesh'al. This conflict reflected individual stakes in the struggle for power, and its geographical aspects were of rather secondary importance.

Defending and reinforcing the Gaza leadership

Gaza's search for greater participation in the decision-making process

Opposition from the Gaza leadership first of all focused on issues of procedure. Dominating governmental institutions since 2006, it considered that a new balance in its favour was all the more justified.¹ Despite these demands, however, the external leadership continued to think that the centre of power had to stay outside Palestine.² On 25 May 2011, Al-Zahar told the Lebanese *al-Akhbar* daily: 'the real center of Hamas is located in the occupied land and its real weight is there. Blood was spilled there, the leadership is there, and the complementary part is outside.'³

The question of the centre of gravity (*markaz al-quwâ*), which has opposed the Gaza and outside leaderships, has existed since the latter's creation, the result of numerous waves of the arrest of the movement's officials between the late 1980s and the early 1990s. This repression had led the Diaspora to restructure the organization outside Palestine, first under the supervision of Moussa Abu Marzouk, then under Khaled Mesh'al. Moving to Amman until 2000 and then to Damascus until 2012 had made the outside leadership enjoy a certain freedom of action but also earn material and political support, thus creating the conditions for rivalry between the two decision-making centres.⁴ Even when the internal leadership regained part of its influence at the moment of Sheikh Yasin's release in 1997, the outside leaders remained predominant because of their capacity to send resources to the territories, a capacity itself allowing internal figures to reinforce their prestige and compete against nationalist leaders in the West Bank and Gaza.⁵ The importance of these material resource capabilities in explaining the external leadership's hegemony was clarified by Qaddura Fares, a former minister affiliated to Fatah and a member of the Palestinian Legislative Council until 2006: 'Though the members of the external leadership are a minority, they are the ones who decide because they provide the money.'⁶

It was therefore after Gaza's seizure in June 2007, when the economic dependency of the Gaza leadership on the external one diminished because of the expansion of the tunnel economy, that this rivalry was exacerbated. This is how Adnan Abu Amer, a professor at Gaza's al-Umma University, expressed the matter: 'The coup (*inqilâb*) helped the Gaza leadership, since from now on the government and the members of the internal Political Bureau were benefitting from their own sources of funding, thanks to smuggling networks via the tunnels. Controlling an entire

---

1. *Dar al-Hayat*, Ramallah, 1 January 2012.

2. Jonathan D. Halevi, 'Power Dynamics inside Gaza: The Increasing Weight of the Gaza Leadership', *Jerusalem Center for Public Affairs* 11, no. 4 (16 June 2011). See also Mohamed Gomaa, *Al Ahram Center for Political and Strategic Studies*, 3 June 2013.

3. https://www.al-akhbar.com/Arab/88920.

4. Shaul Mishal and Avraham Sela, *The Palestinian Hamas: Vision, Violence and Coexistence* (New York: Columbia University Press, 2000).

5. Ibid.

6. Conversation with Fatah member Qaddura Fares in Ramallah on 7 February 2011.

territory from Beit Hanoun to Rafah, internal leaders considered that they were the only ones legitimate in taking decisions.'[7]

Offensive 'Cast Lead' in the winter of 2008–9 also increased competition between the two leaderships, Gaza now claiming, as well as the government, the means of military action against the Israeli enemy. Journalist Mohammed Daraghmeh put forward the importance of armed struggle as a symbolic resource:

> In theory, Gaza is one of the four centres of authority, but technically, it has an influence and weight that are more important, simply because it controls the government, the parliamentary majority and also the fighters. Khaled Mesha'al knows he must listen attentively, and give Gaza more latitude in the decision-making process to avoid conflict.[8]

This evolution in the ratio of force, however, did not lead to an undisputed supremacy of the internal leadership, since the Gaza Strip was cut off by the Israeli blockade.

By offering Gaza members the opportunity to travel and be welcomed abroad, the advent of the Arab Spring provided them with a new chance to change the balance in the ratio of force.[9] The relative opening of the Rafah border crossing in the wake of Hosni Mubarak's fall allowed them to go abroad and raise funds, decreasing the over-representation of diplomats from the external leadership. At the same time, one saw a loss of influence of leaders from the outside who, after their departure from Damascus, found themselves geographically separated: Khaled Mesh'al had gone to Qatar, while Moussa Abu Marzouk had moved to Cairo. Imad al-Alami, a Political Bureau member residing in Damascus until February 2012, who then returned to Gaza where he came from in the first place,[10] admitted that although the departure from Syria had not weakened the outside leadership, dispersion had made the situation more complex by further multiplying decision-making centres. This conclusion was also shared by Ghazi Hamad, deputy minister of Foreign Affairs of the Gaza government.[11] The external leadership could no longer (as had previously been the case) control most of the decision-making process or marginalize its Gaza counterpart.[12] The conclusion of the 'Loyalty of the Free' Agreement, immediately preceding Gilad Shalit's release in October 2011, had also permitted the return to Gaza of charismatic figures of

---

7. Conversation with Adnan Abu Amer in Gaza on 24 March 2013.
8. Conversation with Mohammed Daraghmeh in Ramallah on 28 February 2011.
9. Larbi Sadiki, 'Test and Contest: Hamas without Syria', *al-Jazeera*, 12 March 2012. See also Mohamed Gomaa, *Al Ahram Center for Political and Strategic Studies*, 3 June 2013.
10. In 2018, he was shot in the head during what Hamas described as an accident, as he was inspecting his personal weapon at home.
11. Conversations with Imad al-Alami and Ghazi Hamad in Gaza, on 17 and 18 March 2013.
12. Halevi, 'Power Dynamics inside Gaza'.

the armed branch who possessed huge symbolic capital, such as Yahya al-Sinwar and Rawhi Mushtaha; these returns were factors that decreased the external leadership's influence over the al-Qassam Brigades.[13] The fallouts on Hamas due to the Arab Spring, varied as they were, were instrumental in accelerating the change in balance that had begun before 2011. The Political Bureau and Palestinian Legislative Council member Mouchir al-Masri described this rebirth of the Gaza leadership: 'Yes, it is true that since the Arab uprisings, there was a form of novelty in Gaza's importance. Nowadays, after the Arab revolutions, the Gaza direction can exit the Strip, and this increases joint work.'[14]

Although Adnan Abu Amer admitted that leaving Syria has helped Gaza figures to a great extent, he explained that the centre of power still was in the outside leadership's hands, as demonstrated by decisions relating to reconciliation agreements in 2011–12 and regional alliances.

One could compare these rifts to those that had affected the PLO, whose direction after 1967 had moved in succession to Amman, Beirut and Tunis. Establishment outside the borders of Palestine allowed draining financial resources towards the West Bank and Gaza, and giving Palestine a voice on the international stage; it simultaneously sparked a feeling of superiority of the external leadership over that of the interior.[15] Arafat was not ready to accept players from the territories in the decisional mechanisms, even after the triggering of the First Intifada, which had nevertheless rectified the balance between the two centres of power, giving more influence to leaders from the inside.[16] Marginalized in relation to public figures in Palestine who, after the first Gulf War, were participants in the Madrid Conference, Tunis PLO headquarters were still exerting their control over decisions taken.[17] In March 1991, PLO heads of staff outside the territories had forbidden Palestine's public figures from joining the talks (with American State secretary James Baker) without their authorization. The following year, the interior delegation around Abd al-Shafi had violently criticized the Tunis offices, lashing out at the non-democratic character of the Fatah-dominated organization.

---

13. 'Light at the End of Their Tunnels? Hamas and the Arab Uprisings', *International Crisis Group* 129, 14 August 2012.

14. Conversation with Mouchir al-Masri, Gaza, 16 March 2013.

15. Nadine Picaudou and Isabelle Rivoal (ed.), *Retours en Palestine: Trajectoires, rôles et expériences des returnees dans la société palestinienne après Oslo* (Paris: Karthala, 2006).

16. A first change in the balance had occurred after the departure of PLO heads of staff from Beirut in 1982, when Arafat focused more on activities in the territories. This induced a political shift, since in 1984 as a result Arafat made a rapprochement with Jordan and became more open to a negotiated solution.

17. The external PLO headquarters were not able to impede this participation, despite the fact that they were fearful of excessive independence of the delegation from the territories and were entirely mistrustful of its loyalty.

These observations support the theoretical reasoning of Brecher,[18] who distinguishes leaders with ultimate prerogatives in decision making (the ruling elite) from other segments of the decision-making unit, who often promote an alternative foreign policy (the competing elite). Inside Hamas, the former are the members of the external leadership, while the latter are the Political Bureau members belonging to the three other decision-making bodies: Gaza, Israeli prisons and the West Bank. The only peculiar aspect of Hamas is that all of its leaders agreed for reasons of convenience to grant specific prerogatives to a few of them, namely the members of the outside leadership; this did not mean, however, that Hamas leaders approved the permanent nature of these prerogatives.

The will to remain in power in Gaza

Together with issues of procedure, the refusal to submit to the external leadership's unilateral decisions shows multiple interests specific to Gaza leaders, who have feared that the Cairo and Doha Agreements could erode their gains in the coastal strip.

Gaza has its own interpretation of costs and benefits, considering that power (*hukûm*) is more important than reconciliation (*musâlaha*). An International Crisis Group report correctly noted that the two decision-making centres had diverging judgements on the profound regional changes affecting the movement.[19] Although all members considered that these revolutions would lead to the victory of Islamists supporting Hamas, the Cairo and Doha Agreements were rejected by some leaders, who thought reconciliation implying the return of Abbas's security services to Gaza had to entail compensation for Hamas in the West Bank. According to Adnan Abu Amer, this reconciliation was perceived as submission. This view was confirmed by Azzam Tamimi, a British scholar of Palestinian origin, member of Hamas and the director of the Institute for Islamic Political Thought: 'Some think that the only horizon is reconciliation, while others view reconciliation as capitulation to Fatah, which wants to obtain what it could not by other means.'[20]

This analysis was shared by Hamas leaders who expressed themselves anonymously: 'Mesha'al has trusted too much to Abbas and made superfluous concessions. We in Gaza are afraid that reconciliation could be a manoeuvre by Abbas to retake Gaza. Hamas can make concessions on Gaza only if its role in the West Bank is guaranteed.'[21]

Others acknowledged this difference in judgement, while assessing it had no influence on the movement's political line. For example, Mouchir al-Masri

18. Michael Brecher, *The Foreign Policy System of Israel: Setting, Image, Process* (London: Oxford University Press, 1972).
19. 'Light at the End of Their Tunnels? Hamas and the Arab Uprisings'.
20. Azzam Tamimi's interview in *Palestine-info*, 23 March 2010.
21. Conversation with a Hamas leader who wanted to remain anonymous, Cairo, 23 February 2012.

mentioned the discrepancies of 'vision' between the two Hamas decision-making centres:

> Fatah imprisons our militants, summons our wives and closes our associations. Hamas outside is not going through this and cannot follow these details of daily life. Hence a kind of differential approach in discourse.[22] Huda Naim, who is a member of Gaza's Palestinian Legislative Council, emphasizes the differences in environment: a political direction is often influenced by the geographical and regional context and environment in which it develops. We in Gaza often have a way of thinking different from that of our brothers in Syria.[23]

The report of the International Crisis Group concluded that despite viewing reconciliation as a scam, part of the members in Gaza wanted to wait for the results of elections in Egypt before reaching a decision. This is how the report quoted the words of some Gazan leaders:

> Hamas does not need to make any concession whatsoever to Abbas, and certainly not before the Egyptian presidential elections in May. The Brothers are the main political force in Egypt and, after the elections, this force will become a real power structure. Egypt will provide great support to Hamas and its regime in Gaza, though it is difficult to say how much time the military junta ruling Egypt will remain in power. In Gaza, people think that all these movements will come to support and help Hamas.[24]

The same leaders were also making an analogy with the precedent of June 2007, when Palestinian Authority security forces had tried to expel Hamas from the Gaza Strip. Memories of this episode, which had caused Hamas to take complete control of the territory by force, explained the leaders' reluctance.[25]

These observations are a confirmation of the relevance of works by Morton H. Halperin: to understand decision-making processes in foreign policy, one needs to identify how differences in environment influence 'decision making'. According to the location he finds himself in, a leader will interpret the problem differently:

> Each one of the participants, according to the location he finds himself in, will see a different side of the problem, because his perception will be influenced by his own preoccupations. What is an economic issue for a player will represent a problem of foreign relations for another. Each, therefore, focuses on one of the

---

22. Conversation with Mouchir al-Masri in Geneva, on 19 January 2012.
23. Talk with Huda Naim in Ankara, on 19 May 2011.
24. 'Light at the End of Their Tunnels? Hamas and the Arab Uprisings'.
25. Ibid.

aspects of a problem, and sees differently dangers and opportunities. The place where he is will largely determine the manner he perceives the problem.[26]

Yet whatever the importance of the issue of perceptions (also largely supporting conclusions by Robert Jervis),[27] it is difficult to explain the Gaza leadership's opposition to reconciliation simply by the historical precedent of 2007. What was expressed by its refusal to approve the Cairo and Doha Agreements was above all a will to remain in power in this part of Palestine.

The strengthening of the Gaza leadership through alliance with Iran

Gaza wishes to preserve its relations with Iran and Hezbollah, since it considers Iran as the only power willing to back Hamas both financially and militarily. Ruling over more than 1,800,000 Palestinians, the Gaza Strip must ensure the support of Tehran to be able to continue paying for its common expenses, especially since the Egyptian military has begun sealing a series of tunnels between its border and the Gaza Strip in September 2011.[28] As Nathan Brown put it,

> The Gaza government now views itself as bearing responsibility (quite happily, it should be added) for the administration of over one million Palestinians and may fear that the weight of its concerns are given insufficient attention.[29]

The existence of a strong popular base was a factor whose importance Jean-François Legrain emphasized to clarify the opposition between Hamas inside and outside of Gaza, on the issue of cooperation with the Palestinian Authority in the mid-1990s: he explained the hostility of Hamas leaders in Amman towards any rapprochement with the Palestinian Authority by the environment in which its members residing abroad were living, stressing that they were far from their base.[30]

---

26. Halperin concentrated on explaining the various viewpoints inside the American administration during the Cold War on the acquisition of an anti-ballistic missile. See Morton H. Halperin and Priscilla A. Clapp, *Bureaucratic Politics and Foreign Policy* (Washington DC: Brookings Institution Press, 2006).

27. Robert Jervis, *Perception and Misperception in International Politics* (Princeton: Princeton University Press, 1976).

28. The decision was made after a violent cross-border incident with Israel. On 18 August, militants, who Israel said had criss-crossed from Gaza into Egypt and back again, attacked an Israeli resort town, killing 8. *The Washington Post*, 4 September 2011.

29. Nathan Brown, 'Is Hamas mellowing?', *Carnegie Endowment for International Peace*, 17 January 2012.

30. Jean-François Legrain, 'Hamas: Legitimate Heir of Palestinian Nationalism?', in *Political Islam: Revolution, Radicalism or Reform?* Ed. John J. Esposito (Boulder, CO: Rienner, 1997).

One can thus see that the search for foreign backers can reflect the interests of a single faction and not of the whole set of Hamas' various components.[31]

Ismail Haniyeh's visit to Tehran on 10 February 2012 was, for example, the result of a disagreement between Hamas executives inside and outside of Palestine. The outside leadership had not planned this visit, which was decided in impromptu fashion during a tour of the Gulf states by the Gaza government's prime minister. According to Mkhaimer Abusada, a professor of political science at al-Azhar University in Gaza, this visit exacerbated internal tensions within the organization.[32] It was carried out by Haniyeh without prior concertation with Khaled Mesh'al, a testimony of the Gaza leadership's discontent regarding the Doha Agreement signed two days before in Qatar by the Political Bureau's chairman. Mesh'al apparently tried fruitlessly to convince Ismail Haniyeh to cancel his visit at the last minute. This example shows that the defence of interests by one of the leaderships (in this case Gaza's) can also imply the mobilization of outside support (in this case Iran's).

Part of the Gaza leadership (the al-Qassam Brigades in particular) asserts, moreover, that it was Iran that helped them to resist Israel during the November 2012 aggression. A camp was formed in Gaza around Ahmed al-Jaabari: it considered that the path to free Palestine went through Iran and not Qatar. *Al-Quds al-Arabi* reported that the chiefs of Hamas' armed branch had written to Mesh'al to warn him against an alignment with Qatar at Iran's expense, stating that it was Tehran's military support (and not the Gulf states' subsidies) that had permitted resisting Israeli military occupation.[33] As for Mahmoud al-Zahar, he declared that relations with Iran were always the same, despite what the media were claiming. He added that there had been no change even after Rohani's election to the presidency of the Islamic Republic.[34]

Reasserting the Iranian alliance also implied guaranties to Lebanon's Hezbollah. Confronted with Sheikh al-Qaradawi's heated statements in Khaled Mesh'al's presence, Gaza leadership members took several measures to appease the crisis with Hezbollah: two days before the Egyptian sheikh's visit, a delegation of the al-Qassam Brigades led by Marwan Issa went to Tehran. Mahmoud al-Zahar sent a letter to Hezbollah's secretary general with the following words: 'You are a Sheikh of Islam and Qaradawi does not represent Islam.'[35] These divergences over the alliance with Hezbollah would later be confirmed by Hassan Nasrallah himself: during his 15 January 2015 speech preceding the re-establishment of relations with Hamas, he mentioned previous disagreements not only within Hamas' political leadership but also inside the al-Qassam Brigades. For Hezbollah's secretary

31. *BBC Arabic*, 12 February 2012.
32. *Al-Arabiya*, 11 February 2012.
33. *Al-Quds al-Arabi*, 19 June 2013.
34. *Palpress*, 21 June 2013.
35. *Alarab.co*, 4 June 2013.

general, the internal and external leaderships of Hamas were not agreeing on the need to mend bridges and improve relations with his movement.³⁶

Finally, the evolution of the situation in Egypt at the end of 2012 also supported the idea that alliance with Iran's Islamic Republic was unavoidable. Part of the Gaza leadership feared that the Brotherhood's discredit on the Egyptian national stage would hinder the Palestinian movement's ambitions, all the more so since Hamas was perceived by many Egyptians as an integral part of the internal strife affecting their country. Now, this discredit occurred at a moment when the external leadership was implementing an increasingly clear strategy of rapprochement with Mohammed Morsi, oblivious of the popular discontent this would entail in Egypt and elsewhere. This analysis is shared by Mohammed Daraghmeh: 'Mesha'al has tried to pull Hamas away from Iran and Syria and to bring it closer to its ideological family, the Muslim Brothers, who are on the rise in the region since 2006.'³⁷

Morsi's fall on 3 July 2013 confirmed to the Gaza leadership the absolute necessity of maintaining resuming relations with Iran, in a context where Egyptian armed forces were once more destroying border tunnels.³⁸ Rumours of Moussa Abu Marzouk's expulsion from Egypt had even circulated before being dismissed.

The author has attempted here to describe the interests specific to the Gaza leadership that are likely to cast light on dissent relating to certain unilateral decisions taken outside of Palestine. Reciprocally, the external leadership also has specific interests; these can be summarized in a single sentence: weakened by its dispersion after leaving Damascus, it wants to find new outside backers. Several analysts insist on Hamas' will to enter the PLO: 'The main interest of Mesh'al and his colleagues is to promote reconciliation with Fatah to enable Hamas to join the PLO, and take control of this organization known on the international stage as the only legitimate representative of the Palestinian people.'³⁹ According to Nathan Brown, the members of the external leadership have been pushing Hamas towards reconciliation and adherence to the concept of 'peaceful resistance', with the aim of favouring 'international diplomacy'. They have run the risk, however, of undermining the Gaza leadership's position without offering any benefits whatsoever in return.⁴⁰

Retrospectively, one notices that the outside leadership was acted on the basis of 'misperceptions', in the sense developed by Jervis.⁴¹ According to him, in many cases, decisions are the result of mistaken interpretations that bias the deciding

36. *Al-mayadeen*, 15 January 2015.
37. *Associated Press*, 18 March 2012.
38. 'Light at the End of their Tunnels? Hamas and the Arab Uprisings'. See also Leila Seurat, 'L'Égypte étend la 'guerre contre le terrorisme' à Gaza', *Orient Xxi*, January 2014.
39. Halevi, 'Power Dynamics inside Hamas'.
40. Nathan Brown, 'Gaza Five Years on: Hamas Settles in', *Carnegie Endowment for International Peace*, 11 June 2012.
41. Robert Jervis, *Perception and misperception in International Politics* (Princeton, NJ: Princeton University Press, 1976).

person or body's rationality. By favouring rapprochement with Egypt and Qatar at Iran's expense, the external leadership yielded to 'wishful thinking', by dismissing alternative information and scenarios that contradicted its expectations, representations and beliefs. It was thus satisfied with interpreting reality through a single interpretative prism: the supposed inevitability of the victory of Islamist movements after the start of the Arab Spring, which would rehabilitate Hamas on the international stage.

Outside pressure

Hamas leaders unceasingly repeat that decision making inside the movement is completely impervious to external pressure. They often cite as example relations with Egypt, which still continue, the state of Egyptian–Israeli relations notwithstanding. Another example often put forward is that of alliance with Syria: the latter had accepted the peace plan presented in 2002 by Saudi Arabia, while Khaled Mesh'al had rejected it. This is how Osama Hamdan spoke on the matter:

> Some of the countries that point the finger of blame at our relationship with Damascus and Iran do so because they have tried to influence us, and they could not. Some wanted Hamas to be their puppet. That is not the way we operate. They are puppets for others, so they can't accept that a movement such as ours make its own decisions. Before being in Syria, we were in Jordan and the decisions were taken in the same way. Does that mean we were the Jordanians' puppets at that time?[42]

Mahmoud al-Zahar has also taken great care to emphasize the independence of decision making, despite settlement in a host country.

> There is a Hamas leadership in Syria, but we remain independent (of Damascus) and we simply have common interests with Syria. Claiming the Syrian regime exerts pressure over Hamas so that the latter becomes opposed to Fatah is illogical. Why would Syria be against Fatah, and why would it pressure us?[43]

The very existence, however, of a Hamas decision-making body abroad, and more specifically its dispersion to several countries as of 2012, exposed it to more outside pressure than a typical political organization. Settled in Damascus until February 2012, external leadership members were for a long time permeable to the preferences of the Syrian and Iranian regimes. The influence of these two

---

42. Osama Hamdan's interview by Manuela Paraipan, *Open-Democracy*, 24 May 2010.
43. Mahmoud al-Zahar's interview in *al-Masri al-Youm*, 3 May 2011.

states could partly explain the reason why Hamas was opposed to reconciliation in October 2009.[44]

At the time, this pressure was nevertheless not a matter of dissent. It was after 2011 that the receptiveness of the Damascus leadership to outside influences began to be really criticized by a fraction of Hamas Gaza officials. In particular, they questioned Egyptian and Qatari entreaties inciting Mesh'al and his colleagues to sign the Cairo and Doha Agreements.

Outside pressure before 2011

Many authors have already noted the need to take into account the priorities of other state players close to Hamas in order to better understand its foreign policy. They have interpreted, for instance, the 2003 and 2005 truces as the signs of a strategic U-turn of Hamas' traditional regional backers, which after 9/11 were displaying a political line in tune with the expectations of the United States. Syria and Iran, for different reasons, had become more cautious.[45] Subjected to robust international pressure in the wake of Lebanese prime minister Rafiq Hariri's assassination, the Syrian regime was not in a position to support the absolutist and maximalist camp inside Hamas.

Many sources have confirmed the existence of Syrian pressure to stop the June 2008 truce.[46] Although its acceptance took time, this was not only because there were disagreements inside Hamas but also because external leadership members were attempting to convince Syria and Iran to approve it. On 18 April, Khaled Mesh'al and Moussa Abu Marzouk met former American president Jimmy Carter and expressed their commitment in favour of conciliatory measures towards Israel. Carter then tried to influence Syrian decision-makers who, in June, announced through their Foreign Affairs minister Walid Mu'allem that Damascus backed the *hudna* between Hamas and Israel.[47] Displaying support for a truce initiative shows that Syria's part was not irrelevant in the decision-making process.

Other sources spoke of external pressure to explain the failure of the reconciliation process launched in 2008 by Mahmoud al-Zahar. Egyptian officials[48] mentioned the presence of a branch led by Khaled Mesh'al opposed to any deal with Fatah and that relied very much on the Damascus–Tehran axis. A broad sector of the Egyptian administration at the time was even considering that Hamas' agenda was not national, but could be better explained by the strategies of external actors located outside Palestine.[49] This conclusion was shared by Palestinian analyst Mohammed Hijazi:

---

44. According to Fatah, *BBC Arabic*, 12 October 2009.
45. 'Hamas: Diplomatic Pressure vs. Popularity', *Stratfor*, 19 June 2003.
46. Jeroen Gunning, *Hamas in Politics* (New York: Columbia University Press, 2009).
47. *BBC Arabic*, 18 June 2008.
48. According to Egyptian officials quoted by Johad al-Khazin, *al-Hayat*, 30 May 2008.
49. *Al-Arab*, 27 June 2010.

There were structural changes within Hamas after the coup (*inqilâb*), notably the creation of political and military forces with weapons and money. These forces were largely from the Iranian political axis, but were asserting their demands regarding the necessary independence of Hamas's political decision-making. All this certainly explains the absence of reconciliation.[50]

Fatah spokesman Ahmad Assaf also noted the dependency of Hamas in terms of decision, which he opposed to the 'autonomy' of Fatah and Abou Mazen:

> It is under the pressure of Iran and Qatar that Hamas decided not to sign the document. They told the movement that Barack Obama was against the agreement, and Hamas therefore refused to sign the document. On the contrary, Abou Mazen has always rejected pressure regarding the question of reconciliation, and in 2009, refused to yield to foreign entreaties on this file, preferring the withdrawal of Congressional aid. The direction (*qiyâda*) in Damascus has other interests in mind, linked to regional powers. Why does Iran give more than a hundred million dollars each year to Hamas? This is political geography: the external leadership lives in Damascus in a magnificent region called '*mitaqa khadrâ*'. Now, according to the Syrian constitution, any person belonging to the Muslim Brotherhood can be sentenced to death. There are therefore political, geographical and financial divides.[51]

Uttered by the Fatah's spokesman, these words must necessarily be put into the right perspective, since the context is one of harsh political rivalry. It should be noted, however, that the hypothesis of Syrian interference in the choices of decision-makers residing in Damascus was also shared by Azzam al-Ahmad, responsible within Fatah for the file of Palestinian reconciliation. Less categorical than Assaf, he did admit that when political backing and military and economic support enter the equation, any player (Hamas included) is subjected to the pressure from other parties.[52]

To Khaled Mesh'al's question asking 'Do you think that Hamas in Gaza wants reconciliation, and we in Damascus are against it because of Syria and Iran?', Azzam apparently answered: 'This does not interest me, I want the official position.'

During his visit to Tunisia on 13 March 2010, the president of the Palestinian Authority Mahmoud Abbas had declared that Iran was responsible for the failure

---

50. Mohammad Hijazi, 'Hamas Movement between Partnership and Individualism', *Institute for Palestine Studies* 22, no. 87 (2011): 59.

51. Conversation with Ahmad Assaf in Ramallah, on 20 February 2011.

52. Azzam al-Ahmad, a PLO member in charge of Palestinian reconciliation inside Fatah, highlighted that other political players are also dependent on foreign powers. He said no one wished reconciliation, not even the European Union, which threatened Mahmoud Abbas with an immediate end to financial aid if there was an agreement with Hamas; conversation with the author in Ramallah in January 2011.

of reconciliation. Agreement on the latter essentially implied the organization of presidential and parliamentary elections in June of the same year.[53]

Inversely, Hamas leaders have emphasized Western interference and that of some Arab players, who have refused to back the efforts of the two main Palestinian factions to form a national unity government.

According to Khaled Mesh'al, it was the American veto and Western pressure that were above all responsible for the failure of reconciliation. He insisted on the nefarious role of Egypt, which he said was adjusting its position as a function of Abou Mazen's. Mahmoud al-Zahar also has criticized the actions of Egyptian Foreign Affairs minister Abou al-Gheit, while Fawzi Barhoum has pointed the finger at Egypt's inefficiency on the matter.[54] This was also Osama Hamdan's opinion:

> We thought we were going to implement the agreement, but not only did the United States act against this, as unfortunately we had expected, but a regional power, Egypt, also acted against it, just because the agreement was not coordinated by themselves. Both Syria and Iran, by contrast, consider what will benefit our cause. Till now, they have accepted that what we call for is in the interests of the Palestinians. Sometimes we discuss matters with them: on other occasions, we don't. We don't really consult them much. There are limits for everything and everyone involved.[55]

During a personal conversation, Hamdan reiterated the fact that contrary to the West and Egypt, Iran and Syria have always proven to be supportive of reconciliation:

> As allies, one could think that they will always support Hamas against Fatah. In fact, they have always only backed national unity plans. The Syrians welcomed the Fatah-Hamas summit in February 2007. But we signed the Mecca Agreement, because had we signed a deal in Damascus, we would not have received the support we needed. Knowing the regional leverage of the Saudi kingdom, we went there and secured some gains.[56]

Hamas is not the only movement to be subjected to pressure from Syria. This phenomenon recalls the interferences of Hafez al-Assad's regime in the mid-1980s. The Syrian president was then constantly meddling in Palestinian decision making via his 'client factions' (the PFLP-General Command and Fatah Intifada).[57]

---

53. *Al-Riyadh*, 13 March 2010.
54. *Al-Arab*, 27 June 2010.
55. Osama Hamdan's interview by Manuela Paraipan, *Open-Democracy*, 24 May 2010.
56. Conversation with Osama Hamdan in Damascus on 29 January 2011.
57. Foreign Affairs minister Farouq al-Qaddoumi had in addition refused the Fahd plan (a stance prescribed by Damascus) without Arafat's approval. It was only after 1982 and

Pressure from new backers after 2011

After 2011, outside pressure did not vanish, but its reconfiguration sparked increasing dissent among the Gaza leadership. The fact that Hamas leaders were spread out in several countries gave them more visibility, if only because this allowed a greater number of foreign players to become involved in its decisions. The February 2012 Doha Agreement was the result of winning over new backers of the dispersed leadership abroad: Egypt and Qatar.

Members of the outside leadership now largely depended on Qatar, which became a 'substitute ally' to compensate for the end of the alliance with the Syrian regime. Qatar, in the first place, apparently put pressure on Khaled Mesh'al to accept the Doha Agreement. A fraction of Hamas leaders in Gaza was opposed to the deal precisely because they perceived it was the product of a Qatari decision. Prime Minister Ismail Haniyeh's refusal was just as adamant as that of Mahmoud al-Zahar and part of the al-Qassam Brigades, the armed branch that since June 2007 had acquired crucial power in the Gaza Strip.[58] According to Mohammed Daraghmeh, 'Mesha'al's detractors within Hamas believe that he signed the Doha Agreement under the pressure of Qatar, which was Mesha'al's new asylum country since leaving his base in Syria.'[59]

On the other hand, one can explain these criticisms targeting the rapprochement with Qatar by the fear of it entailing Hamas military interference in the Syrian conflict. Part of the media, moreover, revealed the presence of the armed branch of Hamas fighting on the insurgents' side, in particular during the Battle of al-Qusayr in the spring of 2013.[60] Although on 15 June 2013, Ismail Haniyeh asserted that there were no Hamas fighters in Syria,[61] many sources persistently mentioned the participation of elements from the movement in the conflict.[62] Sheikh al-Qaradawi's position towards Syria was one of the reasons for these militants joining the Syrian uprising. Indeed, he was echoing other ulemas who had called from Cairo for jihad in Syria and spoken in favour of Western intervention to overthrow Assad's regime.[63] Mahmoud al-Zahar responded harshly to these statements, considering that these ulemas had 'to bear responsibility for their call'.

when the PLO left Beirut that this rejectionist front sponsored by Syria lost its importance. See Rashid Khalidi, *Under Siege: PLO Decision Making during the 1982 War* (New York: Columbia University Press, 1985).

58. In early March Ahmed al-Jaabari may have sent a letter to Khaled Mesh'al, complaining about the part Brigade members were now obliged to play. He emphasized that the Brigades were not prepared to become border guards. See Yezid Sayigh, *'We Serve the People': Hamas Policing in Gaza*, Brandeis University Crown Center for Middle East Studies, Crown Paper 5, April 2011.

59. *Associated Press*, on 18 March 2012.
60. *Al-Arab*, 4 June 2013.
61. *Markaz al-Zaytûna*, 15 June 2013.
62. *Al-Quds al-Arabi*, 11 June 2013.
63. http://www.youtube.com/watch?v=-RLvEzF4gSU.

He recalled the imperative of non-intervention by referring to the PLO's meddling in the affairs of Arab states, which had been greatly detrimental to the Palestinian cause.[64] Mahmoud al-Zahar was apparently even assaulted by unidentified people because of his opposition to Yusuf al-Qaradawi's visit to Gaza.[65]

This pressure on the external leadership was all the more criticized because it had repercussions on the one in Gaza. In order to come to Mesh'al's rescue when faced with robust dissent from Gaza leaders, Qatar applied strong influence to convince them to approve the agreement. As for Egypt, it also attempted to push for acceptance of the Doha Agreement by Hamas leaders in Gaza by cutting off electricity in the Strip: an energy crisis began with a suspension of petrol deliveries from Egypt via the smuggling tunnels, which resulted in the closure of Gaza's electricity plant and power cuts of up to eighteen hours a day.[66] The Gaza leadership then accused Egypt of inflicting this punishment on the coastal strip because they opposed the deal in Doha. Many were those in Gaza who considered that Egypt was implementing the same policies as under Hosni Mubarak's rule, and that the decision to block oil deliveries was a way of pressuring Hamas leaders: this was notably the case of Mouchir al-Masri, who said:

> Some players continue to pressure Gaza, Hamas and its government, believing that this can bring about concessions. Neither electricity nor anything else will lead the Gazan people to make concessions. Egypt keeps petrol, partly to push Gaza towards reconciliation. Hamas began to buy petrol from Egypt via the tunnels fourteen months after a crisis with Israel on oil deliveries. Today, the Supreme Council of Armed Forces tries to use oil, as well as other goods, as leverage to accept reconciliation. They insist we buy petrol from the Kerem Shalom crossing, but Hamas does not want to continue obtaining supplies through a road controlled by Israel.[67]

According to some sources, the Guidance Bureau of the Muslim Brothers intervened to put pressure on the Gaza leadership. The Brotherhood's former Supreme Guide Mahdi Akef, and the current one Mohammed Badie, apparently sent Hamas figures in Gaza a letter demanding support for the Doha Agreement and a stop to the campaign against Mesh'al. The Muslim Brothers reproached Hamas for acting as a 'free-rider' while remaining outside the moderate line they themselves stood for, which was enjoying substantial successes in the region in the wake of the Arab revolutions.[68] This process translated into interference of the Brotherhood in internal electoral consultations of Hamas, when Mahdi Akef and Mohammed Badie demanded that Mesh'al's re-election be favoured. Mohammed

---

64. *Palpress*, 21 June 2013. See also *al-akhbar*, 24 May 2011.
65. *Syrianow*, 11 May 2013.
66. This crisis was solved in June after the delivery of fuel from Qatar via Israel.
67. Conversation with Mouchir al-Masri in Gaza, on 16 March 2013.
68. Mohamed Gomaa, *Al Ahram Center for Political and Strategic Studies*, 3 June 2013.

Badie apparently wished Khaled Mesh'al's victory, because he considered Mesh'al to be the representative of the 'pragmatic current' within Hamas; he wanted to marginalize Mahmud al-Zahar, whom he assimilated to the movement's 'radical wing' in Gaza.[69]

Finally, while affecting the Gaza leadership, these pressures from outside would conflict with one another. Gaza's opposition to the Doha Agreement could thus be explained by pressure from Iran, which was against its implementation. Already in 2007, when Hamas had just received important financial backing from Qatar, Tehran had accused Hamas of refusing to mention publicly the delivery of Iranian aid.[70] According to Palestinian sources, obstacles hampering the Doha Agreement's implementation were due to interference by the Islamic Republic, which had communicated to the Gaza leadership its complete hostility on the matter.[71]

Although international politics have an important place in the decision-making process of all of Hamas members, there are also internal factors capable of unsettling cohesion in concertation proceedings.

Power games independent of the internal/external rift

The antagonism between Mesh'al and al-Zahar

Several factors have led the author to look differently at the apparent central rift affecting the internal and external leaderships. First of all, there are multiple underground and secret currents (*khafi*), notably inside the al-Qassam Brigades, which cannot be attributed to the inside/outside divide.[72]

Another fault line that cannot be conflated with this divide: the socio-economic factor. The social origins and levels of income of Hamas leaders differ not only as a function of their belonging (or not) to the Diaspora; within the Gaza leadership itself, various groups have coalesced more or less according to socio-economic criteria. These criteria played a part in defining the various viewpoints on issues like Palestinian reconciliation or the truce. A figure who owned one or several tunnels did not consider the truce in necessarily the same way as another who did not: a softening of the blockade (i.e. a partial opening of crossing points) would mean for the former a loss in profits earned by his participation in informal trade.

On this matter, Nicolas Pelham has noted that the levying of taxes from the tunnels is a bone of contention between the people in the Gaza government and some members of the movement.[73] According to him, only the latter (based in Rafah) have largely benefited from taxes. These conflictual interests inside the

---

69. *Al-Masri al-Youm*, 5 April 2013.
70. *Al-Hayat*, 28 July 2007.
71. *Al-Mustaqbal*, 21 February 2012.
72. *Asharq al-Awsat*, 12 July 2006.
73. 'Diary, how to Get by in Gaza', *London Review of Books* 31, no. 20 (22 October 2009).

Gaza authority could partly explain why the latter were in favour of a continuation of smuggling, while the former were more inclined towards the lifting of the blockade.[74]

The various points of view inside the movement can also be explained by the existence of personal antagonisms between leaders. The conflict between Mahmoud al-Azhar and Khaled Mesh'al goes back to at least 2006, when the latter nominated Ismail Haniyeh as prime minister, at a time when the former thought of himself as the principal figure in Gaza. In the end, Zahar inherited only the position of head of diplomacy. A year later, when the national unity government was formed, he still had no ministerial portfolio.[75] In October 2009, Khaled Mesh'al also curtailed the ambitions of the former Foreign Affairs minister when he signed the Egyptian Document. Khaled Mesh'al sent him a letter to warn him against signing the deal.[76] As of 2009, Mahmoud al-Zahar openly challenged the authority of the chairman of the Political Bureau.[77] During the signature of the Cairo Agreement, the Gazan leader put brakes on the hopes of Mesh'al, just as the latter had done a year before by refusing the ratification of the Egyptian Document that he had himself signed. During an interview for al-*Masri al-Youm*, Mahmoud al-Zahar declared that what had been agreed in Cairo in 2011 was equivalent to what he had argued in favour of two years before.[78]

These hypotheses confirm the conclusions of Halperin,[79] which state that a foreign policy decision is often the result of a confrontation between leaders, some favourable and others hostile to change, and is also related to their personal ambitions. This scholar has emphasized that, in order effectively to oppose a decision and protect his interests, a leader must choose the appropriate moment. This is what happened in 2009, when Khaled Mesh'al rejected Mamoud al-Zahar's signature of the Egyptian Document: the chairman of the Political Bureau could thus personally benefit from the outcry provoked by the withdrawal of the Goldstone report, using this argument to justify his hostility to any reconciliation deal. This is how he was able to exclude Mahmoud al-Zahar from the decision-making process. The sidelining of the latter was a recurrent phenomenon: he was again pushed aside when the Cairo and Doha reconciliation agreements were

---

74. The identity of groups locally collecting taxes is unclear. It seems there are local and federal taxes. What is known, however, is that the 2009 figure of all of the taxes collected was between $4 and $6 million per month, that is, 17 per cent of the monthly budget of thirty million. Liam Stack, 'For Hamas, an end to Gaza's tunnel trade may be only the beginning', *The Christian Science Monitor*, August 2010. See also Nicolas Pelham, 'Diary, how to Get by in Gaza', *London Review of Books* 31, no. 20 (22 October 2009).

75. *Al-Hayat*, 6 February 2008.

76. 'You have Nothing to do with the Prisoners' Portfolio', *Palvoice*, 2 March 2010.

77. Halevi, 'Power Dynamics inside Hamas'.

78. Mahmoud al-Zahar's interview *in al-Masri al-Youm*, 3 May 2011.

79. Morton Halperin and Priscilla Clapp, *Bureaucratic Politics and Foreign Policy* (Washington DC: Brookings Institution Press, 2006).

reached. Once more, Mesh'al had chosen the right time to impose a reconciliation he had himself rejected in 2009: the Arab Spring and increasingly louder claims from Palestinian public opinion demanding an 'end to division' (*inhâ' al-inqisâm*) allowed him to finalize what al-Zahar had wanted to set about doing more than two years beforehand. Halperin has enumerated various strategies designed to exclude certain participants from a decision: invoking security, raising questions about the level of responsibility of each official, or simply not disseminating the information that a decision is being examined. He has also referred to the necessity of widening the circle of participants to avoid criticisms.[80] It was precisely with this goal in mind that a meeting was organized in Damascus on 1 June 2011, to which two members of the Gaza leadership (but not Mahmoud al-Zahar) were invited.

Another illustration of the conflict between the two personalities was the diplomatic mission to Switzerland on which Mahmoud al-Zahar had to be sent a few days after the Damascus meeting on 1 June 2011. Mahmoud al-Zahar's acceptance of the invitation of Daniel Roch (the Swiss special delegate for the Middle East), without prior consultation with Khaled Mesh'al, was interpreted as an inadmissible mark of autonomy. Hamas' sources quoted in the *al-Hayat* daily have confirmed this. The refusal to grant a visa to al-Zahar and the Swiss decision to cancel the visit could be related to Mesh'al's intervention.[81] When he was Foreign Affairs minister, Mahmoud al-Zahar could not, moreover, travel to a country without the prior go-ahead of the Political Bureau's chief.[82] This also occurred in the summer of 2013, when Interior Minister Fathi Hamad, acting on Mesh'al's orders, prevented al-Zahar from using the Rafah crossing to go to Iran. Even the members of the government intervened to stop al-Zahar from doing as he pleased. Some Hamas officials apparently broke with him after the May 2011 Cairo Agreement, reproaching him for having thought that as former Foreign Affairs minister of the Gaza government, he was also foreign minister of Hamas.[83] The antagonism pitting Khaled Mesh'al against Mahmoud al-Zahar was particularly noticeable during the former's visit to Gaza since, during the speeches commemorating Hamas' twenty-fifth anniversary, al-Zahar was not present next to the Political Bureau's chairman.

Alignments and realignments

The divide between the inside and outside should not make one analyse these decision-making centres as two distinct categories. The internal/external rift is also relative because of the existence of alignments and realignments that make it partly irrelevant. Part of the Gaza leadership was also favourable to Mesh'al, while outside some were opposed and refused the Doha Agreement.

80. Ibid.
81. Quoted by Halevi, 'Power Dynamics inside Hamas'.
82. Conversation with Adnan Abu Amer in Gaza on 24 March 2013.
83. *Al-Akhbar*, 25 May 2011.

It was this rivalry and these power games that explained contention over the Doha Agreement, as formulated by the Political Bureau's vice-president and external leadership member Moussa Abu Marzouk. His increased vying for the chairmanship of the Political Bureau could explain his choice regarding the Doha deal. The latter was indeed negotiated at a moment when internal elections were in process to renew Hamas' Political Bureau. As a candidate for the position of Political Bureau chairman, Moussa Abu Marzouk, whose opinions were generally close to those of Khaled Mesh'al, wanted to compete against him by backing Mahmoud al-Zahar's opposition to the Doha Agreement. Some leaders from outside in fact suspected Khaled Mesh'al of signing this deal not only to compensate for his departure from Syria but also to ensure his re-election at the head of the Political Bureau. Mohammed Daraghmeh expressed the issue in this way:

> One notices that Moussa Abu Marzouk, the Bureau's number two, became aligned with the Gazans. He was against the Doha Agreement. The reason for this refusal is to be found in his rivalry with Mesha'al. He wanted to receive the backing of Gaza for the coming April 2012 internal elections. He therefore clearly expressed his disapproval of Mahmoud Abbas becoming Prime Minister. He considered that Mesha'al had made a mistake by giving the enemy a chance to put a knife under our throats.[84]

Moreover, Mahmoud al-Zahar's re-election as member of the consultative assembly (*majlis al-shûrâ*) may have gone ahead because of Moussa Abu Marzouk's support. Without this backing, the Gaza leader might have lost his seat.[85] Mustafa Liddawi, a former Hamas representative in Lebanon, Iran and Syria (and now a dissident opposing Hamas), gave details of the stakes of these April 2012 internal elections in an interview published in *al-Hayat al-Jadida*:

> Al-Zahar went through difficult moments, which threatened his presence in the *majlis al-shûrâ*. He apparently called on Abu Marzouk to continue being a player on Gaza's political stage and, without the latter's intercession, would have probably not been re-elected. The arrival of Abou Khaled (al-Zahar) was

---

84. Conversation with Mohammed Daraghmeh in Cairo on 25 February 2012.

85. The election of the seventy-seven *majlis al-shûrâ* members took place in Gaza on 12 April 2012. The *majlis al-shûrâ* was supposed to choose fifteen of its elected members to fill vacancies in the Political Bureau. According to forecasts, these included Ismail Haniyeh, Imad al-Alami, Khalil al-Hayyat, Nizar Awadallah, Ahmed al-Jaabari, Marwan Issa, Ismail al-Achqar, Abdel Fattah Dukhan, Yahya al-Sinwar, Touhi Mouchtaha and Osama al-Mazzini. Once formed, the Political Bureau was then meant to choose for Gaza six members to form the Executive Bureau (*maktab tanfidhîya*). According to forecasts, these six were: Haniyeh, al-Alami, al-Hayya, Nizar Awadallah, Yahya al-Sinwar and Rouhi Mouchataha. Some figures were elected to the Political Bureau, for instance, Mahmoud al-Zahar, Fathi Hamad, Ghazi Hamad and Ahmed Yousef; *al-Hayat al-Jadida*, 20 April 2012.

arduous and troublesome. People consider him as the 'rag' meant to pick up the garbage and wipe the furniture after welcoming outside visitors. Elections were held in an atmosphere of tension between Ismail Haniyeh's current and Imad al-Alami's. Al-Zahar had no influence in this choice and was at the margins of this struggle. [. . .] Despite all, he continued to consider himself the movement's most legitimate representative, after Abu Marzouk and before Mesha'al.[86]

To make sure he gained more influence in the decision-making process, Mahmoud al-Zahar sought the backing of other Hamas leaders, including members of the movement's armed branch. This demand for al-Qassam Brigades' support was particularly clear following the November 2012 war, when al-Zahar paraded on the streets of Gaza in military costume, side by side with Hamas fighters, during the victory celebration.[87]

Apart from Moussa Abu Marzouk rallying to the camp (led by Mahmoud al-Zahar) rejecting the Doha Agreement, one could also notice Ismail Haniyeh's realignment in favour of stances on regional policy prescribed by Khaled Mesh'al. Ismail Haniyeh had indeed reiterated his backing of the Iranian alliance during his February 2012 visit to Tehran; yet his later gradual progression in favour of a rapprochement with Qatar could be partly explained by his new status inside the movement, which was granted to him on the occasion of Mesh'al's visit to Gaza in December 2012: Haniyeh became vice-president of Gaza's Political Bureau.[88] Khaled Mesh'al actually mentioned this in his 8 December 2012 speech, when he introduced Ismail Haniyeh (*Abou al-Abd*) as prime minister and Hamas president in Gaza.[89] Haniyeh was, at the beginning, one of the most adamant defenders of the alliance with Iran. He had gone to Tehran without Khaled Mesh'al's approval, not even informing him, at the time when the Political Bureau chairman was signing the Doha Agreement.[90] It was only from spring 2012 that Haniyeh sided with Mesh'al's programme and supported a position of relative disengagement from Iran and Hezbollah. According to Azzam al-Ahmad, Prime Minister Haniyeh needed regional backing to fulfil his political ambitions in Gaza.[91]

In June 2013, Ismail Haniyeh gathered in Khan Yunis's Saqa mosque several of the movement's political officials to let them know that Iran and Hezbollah did not share the same interests as Hamas. Many leaders, however, reacted to these watchwords (Younes al-Astal, for instance) and made it clear they would not permit severing links with Iran and Hezbollah, pillars of the 'resistance'. Many

86. *Al-Hayat al-Jadida*, 20 April 2012.
87. *Al-Taqwa*, 24 November 2012.
88. Although this status was not new, it now became official. According to interviews carried out by the author, Haniyeh was already vice-president of the Bureau, but this information is now known by all.
89. *Markaz al-Zaytûna*, 10 December 2012.
90. Conversation with Mouchir al-Masri in Gaza on 16 March 2013.
91. Azzam al-Ahmad's interview in *al-Ghad*, on 24 April 2013.

Hamas leaders in Gaza shared this stance against the line defended by Mesh'al and Haniyeh, who in this framework were supported by Gulf states. As for Salah al-Bardawil, it seems he rallied the pro-Iranian group.[92]

This reconfiguration had a very negative impact on Ismail Haniyeh's relations with Mahmoud al-Zahar. One should note on this issue the latter's absence during Haniyeh's 19 October 2013 speech in Gaza, on the day of the *'îd al-adhâ* festival.[93] Al-Zahar may have declined Haniyeh's invitation for personal reasons. It seems one could link his absence to his opposition on Syrian and Iranian matters. One should recall that a few months before, Mahmoud al-Zahar had not been authorized to leave Gaza to travel to Tehran. This diversity of stances is therefore partly related to the support of some for dissent and of others in favour of Khaled Mesh'al's agenda.

The geographical divide is therefore secondary when looking at the different individual strategies of Hamas officials, strategies that are at times unrelated to the states that these officials reside in. These elements confirm Putman's 'two-level game' theory,[94] which exposes how a leader must be aware of both the external and organizational environments to make sure his preferences in matters of foreign policy are taken into account. Concerning the Doha Agreement, Khaled Mesh'al had to consider the interests of the other decision-making centres of Hamas: particularly Gaza's, which was largely against the deal, but also those of his own leadership, who were not unanimously in favour of it.

92. *Fatehwatan*, 26 June 2013.
93. *Firas Press*, 20 October 2013.
94. R. Putman, P. Evans, and H. Jacobson, *Double-Edged Diplomacy, International Bargaining and Domestic Politics* (Berkeley, CA: University of California Press, 1993).

CONCLUSION

Fifteen years after the victory of Hamas in the 2006 parliamentary elections and the imposition of a new blockade on Gaza, the total failure of boycott strategies has become obvious. Of course, most Western states consider the Islamist movement as a pariah, with which it is unthinkable to establish standard diplomatic relations.[1] Yet at the international and regional level, the movement has managed to gain a form of implicit recognition, even from the Egyptian regime whose reputation nevertheless is that of the fiercest opponent to the Muslim Brotherhood, from where Hamas emerged. The tightening of the blockade was not unrelated to this quasi-normalization, which paradoxically was beneficial for Hamas: the worsening of the humanitarian situation in the Gaza Strip, and the threat to the territory's stability in terms of security, forced Egypt to take Hamas into account as both a partner in the struggle against Takfiris in the Sinai Peninsula and a political player ready to negotiate with Israel in indirect talks under Cairo's aegis. While displaying the scarecrow of Islamist agitation at its borders, Israel has also sought to keep Hamas in power in Gaza, not only to make Palestinian political division long-lasting but also to guarantee its security: Hamas does indeed often carry out police operations on the borders to keep the peace and stop the launching of rockets and incendiary balloons. Israel, moreover, considers Hamas as a lesser evil, in comparison with other Palestinian factions with a more 'radical' reputation (Islamic Jihad, for instance). The neologism 'frenemy', used by former Mossad director Efraim Halevy, neatly encapsulates this Israeli ambivalence towards Hamas, both a friend and a foe.

This dynamics of separate deals has resulted in accusations of secessionism (and even anti-patriotic behaviour) being levelled at Hamas. Moreover, Hamas has been blamed for finalizing the fragmentation of Palestine by building a separate state in Gaza. Without denying that Hamas has duplicated Palestinian institutions by organizing, with Israel's tacit approval, the management of administration and security in this territory, this accusation nonetheless neglects a double dynamics of refusal: Israel's rejection of the formation of a national unity government and Mahmoud Abbas's refusal to regain control of the Gaza Strip. Ultimately, these are

---

1. Even though as early as 2008 many experts have recommended the US administration to abandon its policy of non-negotiation with Hamas. ZUHUR, Sherifa Zuhur, 'Hamas and Israel: Conflicting Strategies of Group-Based Politics', Army War College (US), Strategic Studies Institute, 2008.

nothing more than accusations based on the supposed original schemes of Hamas, which are indifferent to the political aims of other players.

Countering these interpretations tinged with political and ideological bias, this book was an attempt to analyse the diplomacy of Hamas from 2006 by looking at aspects that do not turn a blind eye to its ambiguities. The choice of this year should not make one consider that, after its victory in parliamentary elections, the movement suddenly shifted from intransigence to conciliation, abandoning wholesale its past ideological stances. As early as the 1990s, Hamas was able to conciliate armed struggle with non-violent forms of resistance (*Sumud*),[2] which were peaceful tools that did not suddenly spring out in Khaled Mesh'al's statements in the wake of the 2011 Arab Spring, or even in the publication of the 2017 Document of General Principles. The display of discourse on the struggle against occupation, based on international law, goes back at least to the expulsion of Islamist militants to South Lebanon in 1992, an event seen by movement's leaders as marking the birth of its foreign policy, when Hamas had called for the respect of UN Security Council Resolution 799 requesting the immediate return of deportees.

Hamas' admission to the institutional game marked a shift nonetheless in both the formulation and the implementation of its foreign policy. It was as from this date that Hamas regularly recognized – in the framework of inter-Palestinian reconciliation agreements – the validity of 1967 borders and deals signed between Israel and the PLO. This book is based on three main factors providing explanations for changes in this foreign policy since 2006: interests, ideology and decision-making processes.

The political orientations of Hamas – towards both Israel and other countries – essentially respond to interests that are both external and internal: to obtain international recognition, find material resources and funds to ensure the functioning of its government, reform its security apparatuses and get ahead of political rivals. This book is thus largely based on the concept of linkage formulated by James Rosenau, meant to emphasize imbrications between foreign and internal policy. Bringing with it the administrative and security reorganization of the Gaza Strip, the unilateral seizure of this territory in June 2007 required, as much as was then possible, the preservation of a truce with Israel. The need to carry out internal reform thus restricted any possibilities of implementing a proactive military policy at the external level. The triggering of the March of Return in 2018 inaugurated a period of major strategic change: the dynamics of war and peace became the favoured tool to try to obtain a lifting of the blockade, gaining (even symbolic) recognition and obtaining material resources.

It would be wrong to separate these aims entirely from the ideology that Hamas has always tried to associate them with. The quest for outside backers always

---

2. Aude Signoles, 'Le Hamas, organisation de résistance ou organisation terroriste?', in *Résistances, insurrections, guérillas*, dir. Corentin Selin, 55–76 (Presses Universitaire de Rennes (PUR), 2010).

went in tandem with a 'resistance' discourse, which enabled the strengthening of regional alliances by creating the impression of an axis or common front between players: yet these shared neither the same interests nor the same ideology. Ideology has also provided a justification for the alliance with Iran by emphasizing the common Islamic denominator between Sunnis and Shias and by camouflaging the existence of conflictual doctrine between both major branches of Islam. An in-depth analysis of speeches given by leaders allowed the author to emphasize the idea of predominance of interests over ideology, ideological proposals being always articulated, reformulated, strengthened or understated as a function of context and interlocutors. At the internal level, ideology has also provided justification for unpopular measures like the truce, which, though abiding with Islamic norm (*hudna*), go counter to the ideological bedrock that resistance embodies. In order to minimize the sidelining of armed struggle, the truce was thus introduced as a form of 'resistance'. Finally, ideology has also and above all been a means to stand out from the PLO's diplomatic trajectory, considered as a dismal failure.

The predominance of interests in relation to ideology cannot hide the importance of decision-making processes within the movement, which filter interests and ideological stances of the various Hamas members participating in the elaboration and implementation of foreign policy. Far from being a homogeneous political organization, Hamas is in fact made up of leaders who each have their own experience and background, their own supporters and their own perceptions of what the movement's priorities should be. One of the newest aspects of the book is to have sought to expose the various currents coexisting within Hamas, which partly reflect the geographical and political contexts in which each of the leaderships has developed. Attention focusing on the decision-making processes allowed the author to grasp these discrepancies: though certain decisions provide a glimpse of the consultation process involving the entire group of Political Bureau members – like the truce or the Prisoners' Document – others reflect the predominance of the outside leadership. Ratified by the external leadership only, without consulting other Political Bureau members, the 2012 Doha Agreement was contested by part of the Gazan leaders, who were worried that too many concessions to Fatah would jeopardize Hamas' long-lasting hold on power. Gaza's disapproval was also the product of another preoccupation, that of a gradual loss of autonomy of the outside leadership, which was weakened by its departure from Damascus, a factor that rendered more apparent its susceptibility to pressure from regional players like Egypt and Qatar. Although, from a historical viewpoint, the set of Hamas leaders was committed to grant more prerogatives to the outside leadership, recognition of these prerogatives was not conceived as acceptance of its domination. The dissent that the Doha Agreement triggered can be thus understood, more generally, as an attempt on behalf of the Gazan leadership to re-establish a redistribution of authority more in its favour within the organization.

While highlighting the structural aspects of the internal/external divide inside Hamas, this book is careful to avoid falling into the trap of over-assessing its importance, or of exaggerating its supposed ideological colours. As part of the context of the 2013 Hamas internal elections, the acceptance or refusal of the Doha

Agreement exposed coalitions of players whose cooperation went well beyond this geographical rift: as a member of the outside leadership, Moussa Abu Marzouk, had opposed the Doha Agreement, siding with the rejectionist stand of the Gaza leaders; in contrast, Ismail Haniyeh, who was nonetheless a Gazan member and at the beginning one of the fiercest opponents to the deal, finally rallied to it, gaining new status inside the movement, namely that of the vice-president of the Political Bureau in Gaza. The way the Gaza leadership in the mid-1990s was favourable to a rapprochement with the Palestinian Authority (rejected by the outside leadership) has already been emphasized in the Introduction. This example is sufficient to undermine any attempt at ordering these various leaderships into two frozen and ineffective categories: a 'radical' Gaza versus a 'moderate' exterior.

These preliminary observations deserve deeper scholarly exploration. In this respect, the movement's internal elections are a favoured analytical tool to decipher the ratio of forces and the tensions and rifts inside Hamas. In any event, the 2013 and 2017 elections emphasized the increasing power of the Gaza leadership, in relation to that of the outside.

As of 2013, in his race to the Hamas presidency, Moussa Abu Marzouk (who hails from Rafah in the Gaza Strip) had mobilized his Gazan ascendancy to gain backers and compete against Khaled Mesh'al. The latter, during his campaign, had used his December 2012 visit to Gaza to garner support, highlighting the centrality of Gaza as a symbolic territory and a place of sacrifice. These elements thus confirmed the importance, to a political player in the search for political backers, of benefiting from loyalties based on common geographical connections, as well as from the social uses of geographical spaces. Although Khaled Mesh'al won these elections, the admission to the Political Bureau of members of Hamas' armed branch was significant in that it reflected an internal transformation in Gaza's favour, which would be further confirmed by the 2017 elections.

Having declared his intention to not run during the 2017 elections for the Hamas presidency,[3] Khaled Mesh'al left two candidates originating from Gaza to compete against each other: Ismail Haniyeh and Moussa Abu Marzouk. The former resides in the territory, and the latter was born there; although he belongs to the external leadership, he has regularly stayed in the coastal strip since he was put in charge of relations with Egypt. Though the geographical origin of the candidates is, in itself, a sign of inflection in favour of Gaza, Ismail Haniyeh became a major player in this transformation. For the first time in the history's movement, Hamas was led by a representative from inside Palestine, who would nevertheless be forced to operate largely from the outside. This can be explained by the need to be able to both circulate freely and ensure diplomatic representation, without depending on the Egyptians' goodwill. Another explanation for the ascent to power of Gaza's

---

3. According to Osama Hamdan, whom the author met in Beirut in 2017, the period between 1996 and 2009, during which he was already the movement's president, did not count, because it was before the official promulgation of the new Hamas internal election law.

leadership lies in the concentration of power in the hands of Yahya al-Sinwar, who became Gaza's strongman in the wake of the 2017 elections.

Yahya al-Sinwar's rise to the summit Gaza's leadership no doubt heralded a break, both in the way of governing and policies implemented: leaving little space for dissent, he was able, thanks to his close links with the al-Qassam Brigades, to carry out at his discretion policies of war and peace. After succeeding in imposing a reconciliation agreement with Fatah among Hamas' ranks – an accord which like the previous ones has never been implemented – he engaged in a cunning policy of talks and negotiations with Israel: by alternating the firing of rockets and the launching of incendiary balloons with moments of calm, Sinwar's method consisted in forcing Israel to return to the negotiation table and concede a number of guarantees to Hamas. This policy approach has also given the internal leadership a central role regarding the purchase of material resources: indeed, the granting of the Qatari funds to the Islamist movement depended more on a strategy put in place in Gaza than on good relations established by the external leadership operating from Doha.

In any case, these elements confirm that Hamas must be seen as a political player like any other. This is what this book has attempted to demonstrate, going against many written works produced by experts and their academic institutions, describing Hamas as a terrorist organization. By no means has the author's goal been to rehabilitate Hamas; she has rather wished to expose the movement's political practices for what they are, with neither prior judgements nor preconceived ideas. From a scientific viewpoint, there is moreover no consensual definition of 'terrorism'. Though some consider it a violence emanating exclusively from non-state players, others have noted the impossibility to relate one specific type of violence to a particular type of player.[4] Charles Tilly, who was warned against the reification of terrorism in political discourse, has even asked scholars to question the existence of a specific and consistent category of players (the terrorists), who are specialized in a predetermined form of political action (terror).[5] As a form of political violence like any other,[6] 'terrorism' would deserve to be grasped not as a function of political and media demands but as a social and discursive construction circulating beyond national borders. In a framework where, since

---

4. Richard Jackson, 'Knowledge, Power and Politics of Political Terrorism', in *Critical Terrorism Studies – A New Research Agenda*, dir. R. Jackson, M. Breen-Smyth and J. Gunning (Londres: Routledge, 2009).

5. Charles Tilly, 'Terror, Terrorism, Terrorists', *Sociological Theory* 22, no. 1 (2004): 5–13 quoted par Ami-Jacques Rapin, 'L'objet évanescent d'une théorie improbable: le terrorisme et les sciences sociales', *Cahiers du réseau multidisciplinaire d'études stratégiques* 5, no. 1 (2008): 165–223.

6. Pierre-Alain Clément, 'Le terrorisme est une violence politique comme les autres: vers une normalisation typologique du terrorisme', *Etudes internationales* 45, no. 3 (2014): 355–78.

9/11, the struggle against 'Islamist' terrorism has taken a global dimension,[7] labelling Hamas as such reflects the wish to blur and conflate national liberation with terrorism. Now, a simple effort of historical contextualization enables one to grasp how, well before the foundation of Hamas, Israel had seen the Gaza Strip as an 'enemy entity', a policy leading to the imposition, as from the days of Egyptian occupation in 1948, of blockades, bombings and (re)occupations meant to contain Palestinian nationalism as expressed via the operations of Fedayin fighters.

7. Andrew Silke, 'The Impact of 9/11 on Research on Terrorism', in *Mapping Terrorism Research – State of the Art, Gaps and Future Directions*, dir. M. Ranstorp (Londres: Routledge, 2007).

POSTSCRIPT

On 10 May 2021, a new Israeli assault began against the Gaza Strip. As in 2009, 2012 and 2014, this military attack is to be understood in the context of both Palestinian reconciliation and elections in Israel. While Mahmoud Abbas had just announced, on 29 April, the cancellation of parliamentary elections planned for 22 May, the prospects of Palestinian unity were a matter that did not worry Benjamin Netanyahu any more.

What seemed to count more in the Israeli prime minister's mind was his incapacity to form a government after four parliamentary elections in less than two years. In East Jerusalem, Netanyahu was also confronted with demonstrations of militants of all kinds, mobilized against the eviction of Palestinian families from the neighbourhood of Sheikh Jarrah. Criticized internationally and overtaken on the right by violent religious nationalists favourable to the expulsion of Palestinians, he then tried to depoliticize the issue by transforming it into a matter of religion and security: in front of the Damascus Gate, Israeli security forces installed metal barriers preventing the daily gatherings of Palestinians during the month of Ramadan. As in 2017, these barriers led to protests by Palestinians, who were brutally repressed by police and extremist Jewish civilians.

The police's entry inside the walls of the al-Aqsa mosque itself, during prayers on 7 May, was seen by Hamas as a violation of a red line. On 10 May, the spokesman of the al-Qassam Brigades, Abu Obeida, published a communiqué stipulating that abuses against Jerusalem's Arab inhabitants were equivalent to aggression against all Palestinians. By resuming repression in Jerusalem, Netanyahu had thus invited Hamas to armed confrontation, displacing the conflict from al-Aqsa to Gaza. Once more, brandishing the Islamist terrorist menace on the borders of the State of Israel allowed the prime minister to try to foment national unity around his persona.

Weakened on the internal political stage, Netanyahu once more played the card of diversion, but this time the situation was notably different. In several respects, the May 2021 offensive was a fifth U-turn in the foreign policy of Hamas. It marked a number of breaks, both at the strategic and ideological levels.

- In contrast to what had occurred during previous Israeli military attacks, Hamas fired the first shots, while emphasizing that its decision to do so was to be seen in the frame of legitimate defence. On 11 May, the al-Qassam Brigades, as well as other armed factions in Gaza, launched more than a thousand rockets with a range of up to 250 kilometres: these were fired towards the very heart of Israel, which had never yet been confronted to such a military response.

- This response was part of a major strategic reset by Hamas. Since its seizure of the Gaza Strip in 2007, Hamas had essentially mobilized military means to respond to the imperatives of its management of the coastal strip and to attempt to soften the blockade. It often saw itself being accused of serving only its partisan aims at the expense of the general interest. Repression in Jerusalem by Israeli forces thus became an opportunity in the eyes of the Islamist movement, a chance to use rockets as tools to protect all Palestinians, wherever they live. By establishing an intimate link between Gaza, al-Aqsa and Sheikh Jarrah, Ismail Haniyeh, in his 12 May speech, went beyond a local rationale to introduce himself as the guarantor of the unity of Palestinians.[1]
- This strategic shift is to be understood in the context of the unprecedented uprising of all Palestinians, who massively mobilized to support their fellow-citizens in Jerusalem. Without any direct link with the actions of Hamas, these protests occurred both in Jerusalem and in many cities of the West Bank, making demonstrators march towards al-Aqsa; above all – and this is the first occurrence of its kind – protests were by Palestinian citizens of Israel. On the night of 11 May, Palestinians from Lydda, Akka and Wadi Ara entered into confrontations with police, making Israeli authorities declare a state of emergency. The intensity of the rocket barrage between 12 and 16 May was thus an answer to this unheard-of situation whereby Hamas was attempting to accompany a spontaneous uprising taking place well beyond the limits of the 'autonomous' Territories imposed by the Oslo process. Mohammed Deif and Yahya al-Sinwar were thus portrayed as genuine nationalist leaders, and support for the resistance was quasi-unanimous, although this did not mean a partisan adherence to Hamas.

These trends went hand in hand with an ideological renaissance. Although Jerusalem has always had a central importance in Palestinian speeches, narratives and iconography – including those of the PLO[2] – Hamas was now insisting on its predominant place by giving its offensive against Israel the name of 'Sword of Jerusalem'. Yet this identification with Jerusalem did not derive merely from religious attachment; the city is described as the heart of the Palestinian nation. The conditions for a cease-fire stated on 15 May by Khaled Mesh'al were not, moreover, limited to the retreat of Israeli soldiers from the esplanade of the Mosques; they also mentioned the halt of attempts to evict families from Sheikh Jarrah.[3] During a press conference on 26 May, Yahya al-Sinwar paid tribute to Sheikh Yassin, but also to Yasser Arafat (Abu Ammar), and congratulated all

1. https://www.youtube.com/watch?v=IgTfcmwVaKQ.
2. In 2000 Yasser Arafat issued in statement declaring that 'Jerusalem is the essence of the Palestinian issue. It is the right and responsibility of all Muslims.' See Beverley Milton-Edwards, 'Political Islam and the Palestinian-Israeli Conflict', *Israel Affairs* 12, no. 1 (2006): 65–85.
3. https://www.youtube.com/watch?v=5g5Ti4KQJec.

Palestinians, those of Jerusalem and the West Bank, but also those of 1948 and the Diaspora, who gathered on the borders to highlight their attachment to the homeland (*watan*). He assured that he would not abandon Palestinians subjected to colonization in the West Bank, congratulated the brave (*qabadayat*) fighting for dignity (*karama*) and for the restoration of their rights (*huquq*).[4] Responding to accusations of extremism, al-Sinwar also pointed a finger towards provocations by Jewish radicals during parades organized during 'Jerusalem Day', warning against risks of a possible religious war whose responsibility would fall entirely on Israel.

As during previous offensives, Hamas hurriedly proclaimed 'victory'. Although Israel claimed to have reached its limited goals, the 'victory' of Hamas was undoubtedly more tangible than in 2009, 2012 or 2014: despite the blockade, Hamas had managed to impose a new ratio of force by pushing Israelis into shelters and bringing civilian air traffic and airports to a grinding halt. Osama Hamdan also declared that the cease-fire had been obtained under specific conditions (the cessation of incursions into al-Aqsa and the abrogation of the decision to dispossess the families from Sheikh Jarrah), although the wave of arrests in the wake of the cease-fire would tend to counterbalance the impact of these concessions.[5]

This newly regained legitimacy on the Palestinian stage enabled Hamas to display its stance in favour of national unity, while sidelining Mahmoud Abbas.

Many analyses have interpreted the armed action of Hamas as a response to Mahmoud Abbas's cancellation of Palestinian parliamentary elections, meant for 22 May.[6] More importantly than its participation in the elections, Hamas was counting on its integration into the PLO's bodies to gain recognition as one of the Palestinian people's legitimate representatives. The agreement signed in Beirut in September 2020 between Salah al-Arouri (the vice-president of Hamas' Political Bureau) and Jibril Rajoub (the general secretary of Fatah's Central Committee) had led to a compromise between both political organizations, stating that Hamas would not present a candidate during presidential elections but would nevertheless participate in the renewal of the PLO's Palestinian National Council. The cancellation of elections was thus a significant setback for the movement, which described this measure as a Coup (*inqilab*).[7] Prevented from gaining increased legitimacy through the ballot box, Hamas chose to do so by military means.

Far from introducing itself as the only player confronting occupation, Hamas made this military action part of an agenda shared by all armed factions present in the Gaza Strip. The al-Qassam Brigades are indeed an integral part of a common operation 'chamber' (*ghurfat al-mushtaraka*), which since its creation in

---

4. https://www.youtube.com/watch?v=GccfGKsSZjs.

5. Osama Hamdan declared, in an interview with *Al-Monitor*, that the cease-fire was not unilateral, contrary to Israeli allegations. *Al-Monitor* on 21 May 2021.

6. Khaled Hroub, *Le Monde*, on 15 May 2021.

7. Official communiqué of Hamas, published on 30 April 2021: https://hamas.ps/ar/post/13186.

2018 groups together Islamist factions, the Left, but also Fatah.[8] It is in the name of this chamber that Abu Obeida published his communiqué. Ismail Haniyeh also insisted on the strategic dimension of this battle as a point of entry towards the creation of a Palestinian 'home' and the re-foundation of the PLO under a common programme.

Through this regained internal legitimacy, Hamas has tried to obtain recognition outside Palestine.

Hamas saw itself propelled to the centre of negotiations meant to reach a truce, as shown by the meeting in Doha between Tor Wennesland, the UN Special Coordinator for the Peace Process in Israel, and Ismail Haniyeh. Several Western political figures expressed their doubts on the relevance of resuming negotiations with Abbas, while ignoring Hamas altogether.[9] Some have also emphasized the shift in Egypt's stance, which, in the wake of an improvement of its relations with Qatar, appears to have shown more leniency towards Hamas, setting up a more impartial mediation and opening its border with Gaza to bring medical assistance to the wounded. Egypt's change in tone was also perceptible in state media, which described Hamas as a legitimate resistance movement; during previous Israeli military offensives, these media had accused the movement of damaging the country's national security.[10]

These changes, which follow the taking into account of Hamas by Egyptian authorities since 2017, should not be overrated, however. Cairo continues to consider Ramallah's Palestinian Authority as the legitimate representative of the Palestinian people, as testified by the visit to Ramallah of Egyptian Intelligence chief Abbas Kamel. Egyptian authorities also went to great lengths to dissociate Hamas from Cairo's material backing of $500 million, meant to reach Gaza, further mentioning that their own firms and organizations would take charge of reconstruction.[11] Once more, the issue of international aid crystallizes the division between Ramallah and Gaza, each entity having set up its own committee to assess in economic terms the extent of destructions. Supported by the United States, the European Union and the United Nations, Ramallah insists on its legitimacy as a state to take charge of reconstruction; as for Hamas, it has accused Abbas of confiscating funds allocated to Gaza in the wake of the 2014 Israeli offensive and claims a place in mechanisms of reconstruction, to make the latter effective, as opposed to what occurred in the past.[12]

---

8. Nicolas Dot-Pouillard, 'Tremblement de terre pour le mouvement national palestinien', *Orient Xxi*, 15 May 2021.

9. On 20 May, Angela Merkel declared she was favourable to the opening of direct talks with Hamas.

10. https://www.lorientlejour.com/article/1264067/pourquoi-le-caire-a-change-de-regard-sur-le-hamas.html.

11. *Ahramonline*, 10 June 2021.

12. Rasha Abou Jalal, 'Hamas, PA compete for Gaza reconstruction', *Al-Monitor*, on 6 June 2021.

The last military offensive on Gaza also once more brought to the fore attempts by Hamas to maintain a delicate balance between conflicting regional powers. The consolidation of its strategic alliance with Iran must indeed not compromise the backing of other countries such as Egypt, Qatar and Turkey. While in his 21 May speech Ismail Haniyeh thanked Iran for its 'financial and military' support, the issue of a total re-establishment of the 'resistance front' also became relevant with Bashar al-Assad expressing that the gates of Syria were open to all factions, without exceptions.[13] At present, the re-establishment of relations with Damascus is a matter of disagreement within Hamas:[14] in favour of normalization, Osama Hamdan was contradicted by Khaled Mesh'al, who dismissed the existence of talks with Iran and Hezbollah on the eventual return of Hamas to Damascus.[15]

Hamas has also measured the 'costs' implied by the return of part of its leadership to Damascus, in particular in terms of image. All the more so since Ismail Haniyeh's visit to Morocco, on 16 June, at the invitation of the Justice and Development Party, had already been a matter of substantial criticism against the movement. While Hamas had loudly criticized the normalization accord between Israel and Morocco, the movement was once more accused of favouring its partisan interests at the expense of the national cause.[16]

In his 21 May speech, Ismail Haniyeh also called to 'strengthen relations with the international community' and take into account the 'great changes in European and Western societies'.[17] The last military offensive against Gaza had indeed aroused unprecedented support in favour of the Palestinians. Thousands of demonstrators met in Madrid, London, Los Angeles, Washington and Paris, mobilized around slogans like 'We can't breathe since 1948' or 'Palestinian lives matter', to condemn Israeli colonial occupation, assimilated to a form of Apartheid. South African president Cyril Ramaphosa having compared the situation in Gaza to that of his country during Apartheid, the French minister of Foreign Affairs, Jean-Yves le Drian, also made the analogy with the South African regime by mentioning the 'risk of Apartheid' in Israel. In the United States, many voices were raised to denounce the delivery of American weaponry to Israel, pointing the finger at the United States' eventual complicity in war crimes committed against Gaza's civilian population. Hamas, which accused President Biden of deliberately postponing a UN Security Council meeting to enable Israel to continue its assault on Gaza, is betting on these changes, hoping that they will favour the movement in the long run.

---

13. Welcoming to Damascus on 20 May a delegation of Palestinian factions, Bashar al-Assad paid homage to not only Islamic Jihad fighters but also those of Hamas, *Al-Akhbar*, 21 May 2021.

14. Adnan Abu Amer, 'Syria'Assad, Hamas weigh rapprochement', *Al-Monitor*, 29 May 2021.

15. Conversation between Khaled Mesh'al and *Russia Today*, 13 May 2021.

16. See Khaled Hroub, 'Hamas Won and the Homeland Lost', *Palestine Forum*, 19 June 2021.

17. https://www.youtube.com/watch?v=R-J9XYym4xs.

It is far from certain, however, that these current changes in Western societies will benefit Hamas. Inspired by the anti-colonial and Afro-American movements in favour of civil rights, this new support for Palestine is part and parcel of a narrative centred on the struggle against any form of discrimination (of class, race and gender). Opposed to the recognition of sexual minorities – anathema to any Islamic society – Hamas is at best ignored, at worst accused of its 'oppression' against its own population.

In the framework of this liberal 'conception' centred around the imperative protection of human rights, Hamas is also accused of indiscriminate shooting against civilians and war crimes. During her conversation with the head of American diplomacy, Ilhan Omar, a representative of the Democrats in the US Congress thus lamented the inaction of the International Criminal Court regarding crimes perpetrated by the United States, Israel, Hamas and the Taliban.[18] Now, some criticized her for creating a moral equivalence between Israeli crimes and those of Hamas, and thus indirectly recreating the classic mechanisms of de-legitimation of the fight of Palestinians by denying the legal character of armed struggle against colonial occupation.[19]

The 'for or against' Hamas debate became a substitute for one on the legality of armed struggle;[20] as had been the case for the PLO, the criminalization of Hamas is part of a recurrent pattern that aims to discredit Palestinian players in order to sabotage and undermine the contents of their rights to self-determination. Praised by Ismail Haniyeh, these great changes in Western societies nevertheless contribute to the selective treatment of players and strategies that the national Palestinian struggle should take, de facto excluding Hamas. It could try to adapt to this renewal of paradigms, although one can hardly see how an Islamist movement could become an advocate for the rights of sexual minorities.

Hamas may rather become a beneficiary of the radicalization of Israeli society, which has just elected Naphtali Bennett as prime minister, a man who had declared a few years before: 'I have killed many Arabs in my life, and this has not posed any problem whatsoever.' The ascent to power of a far-right coalition in Israel weakens the narrative based on an 'extremist' Hamas and could thus allow the movement to reclaim control over its image.

18. https://twitter.com/ilhan/status/1401985884191404041.

19. See Ali Abunimah, 'It's Time to Change Liberal Discourse about Hamas', *Electronic Intifada*, 10 June 2021.

20. Haim Malka advocates that Hamas 'must halt the smuggling, production and development of rockets' and that 'these activities should be criminalized by all Palestinians', Haim Malka, 'Forcing Choices: Testing the Transformation of Hamas', *The Washington Quarterly* 28, no. 4 (2005): 37–53.

BIOGRAPHIES

Military branch

Ahmed al-Jaabari

Born in 1960, Ahmed al-Jaabari was one of the executive leaders of the Izz al-Din al-Qassam Brigades. In a context where Hamas was attempting to prevent other movements, as well as Salafis, from launching military operations against Israel, he was in charge of keeping the borders calm. Involved in Shalit's abduction, he returned the Israeli private to the Israelis on 18 October 2011. He was assassinated on 14 November 2012 during a targeted air strike at the start of 'Pillar of Defence'.

Mohammed Deif (Mohammed Diab al-Masri)

Born in Khan Yunis in 1965, Mohammed Diab al-Masri, better known under his nom de guerre as Mohammed Deif, was a member of the Muslim Brotherhood before he joined Hamas in 1987. He was arrested the first time during the 1989 wave of detentions. After his release, he took part in the formation of the Izz al-Din al-Qassam Brigades, together with Yahya Ayyash. He was arrested again in 2000 by the Preventive Security Force. Freed by the Palestinian Authority's president when the Second Intifada began, he became the brains behind the wave of suicide attacks in the mid-2000s. His name appears on the Israeli list of members of the movement to be eliminated and was several times a target. After the death of Salah Shehadeh in 2002, Mohammed Deif was apparently one of the main commanders of the al-Qassam Brigades, with Ahmed al-Jaabari. In 2014, during 'Protective Edge', an umpteenth attempt to murder him was ordered by the Shin Bet. Mohammed Deif's home was hit, but it was one of his two wives and his seven-month-old son who were killed in the attack. His family name Deif ('guest' in Arabic) derives from his habit of always changing his place of residence. Attempts to assassinate Mohammed Deif continued, in particular during the military offensive against Gaza in May 2021, when according to Israeli sources the occupation army tried to liquidate him twice (unsuccessfully). On 4 May, Deif spoke in an allocution, warning that if Palestinian families from Sheikh Jarrah were expelled, Israel would pay a heavy price.

Marwan Issa

Born in Gaza in 1965, he is one of the founders of the Izz al-Din al-Qassam Brigades. Jailed in succession by Israel and the Palestinian Authority, he directed special operations (*al-'amaliyyât al-khâssa*) carried out by Hamas' special branch. In 2006, Marwan Issa (Abou Bara by *his* nom de guerre) participated in Shalit's kidnapping. He played a part in negotiations, and then in attempts to have Palestinian prisoners released, in return for the freeing of the young abducted Israeli private. Marwan Issa is one of those who, together with Mahmoud al-Zahar, attempted to re-establish relations between Hamas and Iran. He replaced Ahmed al-Jaabari as executive head of the Izz al-Din al-Qassam Brigades after the assassination of the latter in November 2012. In early June 2021, Marwan Issa appeared for the first time in the al-Jazeera TV programme *What Is Hidden Is Greater*. A little after the last Israeli assault on Gaza and the 21 May cease-fire, he highlighted the necessity of unity for all Palestinians during the 'Sword of Jerusalem' battle. He also elaborated on details of the conditions in which, in 2006, Israeli Army Private Gilad Shalit was captured and mentioned the conditions for a new exchange of prisoners against four Israelis (among them two dead bodies).

Abu Obeida

Abu Obeida is the spokesperson of the al-Qassam Brigades who, despite his regular appearances, has never shown his face. His first appearance dated from 2006 when he claimed Shalit's abduction, together with the Popular Resistance Committees and the Army of Islam. He was also active during military assaults against Gaza in 2008, 2012 and 2014. His popularity became stellar during confrontation in May 2021, particularly when he sent Israel an ultimatum on 10 May. Thanks to social networks, he became a national hero for many Palestinians, seen as a man of his word capable of subverting the ratio of force against Israel. Inspired by Israeli methods of speaking and giving interviews when curfews are lifted, he thus announced on 15 May a halt of rockets for a duration of two hours.

Hamas leadership in prisons

Abd al-Khalek al-Natsheh

AL-Natsheh was born in Hebron (Al-Khalil) in 1954. After his studies in Saudi Arabia, he returned to the West Bank, where he was considered as a religious authority and the central figure of the Hebron notability. He was arrested several times by Israeli authorities for his membership in Hamas. He was one of the 415 deportees to Marj al-Zouhour. In 1996, he attempted to establish a dialogue between Hamas and the Palestinian Authority. In 2000, he became the movement's spokesman in the district of Hebron. He is one of the Hamas representatives in Israeli jails and one of the first, together with Marwan al-Barghouti, to sign the June 2006 Prisoners' Document.

Yahya al-Sinwar

Born in the camp of Khan Yunis in 1962, he studied there and then went to the Islamic University of Gaza, where he became secretary of the Department of Sports, and then of the Union of Students. Imprisoned the first time in 1982, he was put in solitary confinement. After his release in 1985, he formed *al-Majd*, a cell of the Association of Palestinian Brothers in charge of hunting down collaborators with the occupation forces. He was arrested a second time in 1989 and sentenced to 426 years in jail. In October 2011, Yahya al-Sinwar was part of the batch of detainees freed in the wake of the signing of a prisoner exchange agreement with Israel.

Between 1989 and 2011, he was the head of Hamas in Israeli prisons. When he was freed in 2011, he had served twenty-two years of his sentence. He was then elected member of the Political Bureau and became the coordinator between the political and military wings of the movement.

In February 2017, he was elected as the head of the Political Bureau of Hamas in the Gaza Strip. He considers the union with Fatah as a strategic option and has therefore pushed towards an agreement with reaching a deal in Cairo in October 2017. Although Hamas leaders have unanimously stressed his respect for principles of consultation, some nevertheless have stated that Sinwar was always able to impose his choices on the rest of the movement by means that sometimes include threats. He maintains good relations with Egypt, which sees him as a real Palestinian national leader prioritizing national considerations over partisan and ideological affiliations. In 2021, al-Sinwar was re-elected as head of the Gaza leadership. His popularity grew during the 2021 attack on Gaza, and he now has a true nationalist stature among all Palestinians.

Gaza leadership

Sheikh Ahmed Yasin

Born in 1938 in al-Joura near Ashkelon, Ahmed Yasin and his family emigrated to the Gaza Strip after the 1948 war. Growing up in Egypt, he was wounded in a sports accident that left him paralysed. Despite his disability, he read religious studies at Al-Azhar University in Cairo and joined the Muslim Brotherhood. Returning to Gaza under Israeli occupation in the wake of the Six-Day War, he founded the *Mujama' al-Islâmî* (Islamic Society) in 1973 and was in charge of an entire network of dispensaries, schools, clinics and sports clubs. As from the early 1980s, Yasin sought to create a political branch in the institution, an attempt that resulted in his first arrest in 1984 by the Israelis. Despite the prison term to which he was sentenced, for possession of weapons, he was released the following year in the framework of an agreement on the exchange of prisoners. It was at the moment of the First Intifada's eruption, in December 1987, that the *Mujama' al-Islâmî* changed its name to become Hamas. Detained once more in 1989, he was sentenced to eight years. The failed assassination attempt against Khaled Mesh'al in Amman caused the Israelis to free him in compensation. On 2 March 2004, as he was exiting the mosque adjacent to his home, he was killed by missiles fired from Israeli military helicopters. The initiative of this targeted assassination was attributed to Prime Minister Ariel Sharon.

Said Seyam

Born in 1959 in the Shati camp, Seyam graduated with a doctorate in Islamic studies. From the moment of Hamas' foundation, he was an active member of the movement and participated in the First Intifada. He was arrested on four occasions, then exiled in 1992 to Marj al-Zouhour in South Lebanon. Upon his return, he was taken in for questioning by the Palestinian Authority's security services. In March 2006, appointed Interior Minister of the Tenth Government, he set up the Executive Force and closely collaborated with Khaled Mesh'al, whom he accompanied during his first visit to Moscow in March 2006. Accused of being one of the instigators of the June 2007 coup in Gaza, Said Seyam was assassinated by the Israelis on 15 January 2009, during 'Cast Lead'.

Ahmed Yousef

Born in 1960 in Rafah, Ahmad Yousef left Gaza for Cairo in 1973 and graduated in engineering at al-Azhar University. He left to work in the Gulf states and then to the United States, where he wrote a doctorate in political sciences. He replaced Moussa Abu Marzouk as director of the UASR think tank (*United Association for Studies and Research*), which he managed for fifteen years. He holds American citizenship and speaks English fluently. Once again in Gaza, he became one of Ismail Haniyeh's closest advisers. Ahmad Yousef has directed the 'House of Wisdom' (*dâr al-hikma*) in Gaza, a think tank which many Europeans seeking to establish a dialogue with Hamas have visited. He is a respected journalist and the author of more than ten works on political Islam.

Ahmad Bahar

Born in Khan Younis in 1950, Bahar joined the Muslim Brotherhood in the 1970s. He was active at the time in the *Mujama' al-islâmî*. A member of the *al-Khalâs* Party in the 1990s, he was elected in January 2006 on the 'Change and Reform' list and became vice-president of the parliament. Following Aziz Dweik's 2006 arrest by the Israelis, Ahmad Bahar ascended to the position of interim president of the Palestinian Legislative Council. An influential preacher, he is also imam in Gaza's *Palestine* Mosque.

Sayed Abu Musameh

Born in 1948 and a member of the Palestinian Muslim Brothers since the early 1970s, Abu Musameh studied at the University of Damascus. In 1989, he was appointed chief of the Political Bureau for a year, following the arrest of Sheikh Ahmad Yassin and Ismail Abou Shanab. Arrested in 1992 by the Israelis, sentenced to twelve years in prison, he was released three-and-a-half years later in the framework of a prisoner exchange, only to be arrested again, this time by Palestinian Authority security forces. Director of the a*l-Watan* newspaper, he is one of Hamas' oldest recruits.

Ayman Mohammed Salah al-Taha

Born in 1970, Ayman al-Taha studied religious jurisprudence (*fiqh*) at Gaza's Islamic University. He then went on to read political sciences and public affairs. He was seventeen at the eruption of the First Intifada, in which he participated. In 1988, he was elected president of the Committee of Students of Gaza's Islamic University. In 1989, he was arrested by the Israelis and subsequently deported in 1992 to Marj al-Zouhour in South Lebanon. After the establishment of the Palestinian Authority, he was detained by its security forces and incarcerated for some four years. Once more arrested in 2003 by Israel, he was freed in 2007. If one adds all the sentences together, Ayman Taha has spent, in total, eleven years in jail. In 2007, he was in charge of negotiations with Fatah. In February 2009, in Cairo, he began discussions on the possibility of a truce between Israel and Hamas. He was detained at the border with approximately one million dollars; the Egyptians then prevented him from returning to Gaza. Since Hosni Mubarak's fall in 2011, al-Taha has been in charge of relations between Egypt and Hamas. He was the owner of several tunnels and was very involved and experienced in smuggling; he was therefore held in February 2014 for illegal profits and espionage on behalf of Egypt. During Operation 'Protective Edge', he was apparently executed by members of the al-Qassam Brigades, who are thought to have taken advantage of the context of war to make Israel responsible for his killing.

Basem Naim

Born in Beit Hanun, Basem Naim finished his secondary schooling in Gaza and then travelled to Germany to study medicine. Graduating in 1963, he went to Jordan for a short while and then returned to Gaza, where he was in charge of public hospitals. He was appointed health minister during the formation of the 'Tenth Government' and then became the national unity government's sports minister. After the June 2007 events, he was once more the Gaza government's health minister. In tandem with his political activities, he had been practising at al-Shifa hospital. His son Naim, who was a member of the Izz al-Din al-Qassam Brigades, was killed at the age of seventeen during an Israeli foray. From 2012 Basem Naim has been in charge of the movement's Foreign Relations Department. He stepped down in 2012 and became the head of the Council on International Relations in Gaza.

Huda Naim

Born in Gaza in 1969, she is the mother of five children and lives in the al-Burj camp. Graduating with a BA in sociology, she directed the Islamist movement's 'kindergarten' sections in the camp. Nominated on the 'Change and Reform' list in 2006, she became a member of the Palestinian Legislative Council. From 2002 to 2005, she was responsible of the orientation unit at the rectorate of the University of Gaza. She was also a member of the committee in charge of education and social affairs and responsible for the commission of supervision and of human rights. A member of several social organizations, she is also president of several boards of directors, notably one of the *al-Thurayya* foundations for communication and the media.

Mahmoud al-Zahar

Born in Gaza in 1945 of a Palestinian father and an Egyptian mother, he spent the greater part of his childhood in Ismailia (on the Suez Canal). In 1965 he returned to Gaza and then went back to Egypt to study medicine. From Cairo, he witnessed the mobilization of the country to confront Sinai's invasion by Israel during the Six-Day War. In 1972, back in Gaza, he worked at the al-Shifa hospital and in the Khan Younis refugee camp. He is one of the founders of Gaza's Islamic University and one of the oldest members of Hamas. He was arrested for the first time by Israeli authorities during the 1989 wave of incarcerations. In 1992, he was deported to Marj al-Zouhour in Lebanon, where he became a spokesman for the camp. In 1995, he was jailed in the Palestinian Authority's detention centres. His two sons Khaled and Hussam would later be casualties of the Israelis. The first died of his wounds during an attack aimed against his home, and the second disappeared during Operation 'Cast Lead'. He was appointed minister of Foreign Affairs in March 2006 and was the only holder of this portfolio from Hamas to benefit from full recognition and to have been officially welcomed in many countries. In the national unity government formed in the wake of the Mecca Agreement in February 2007, he lost his position of minister and was replaced by Ziad Abu Amer. In 2011 and 2012, he violently opposed the Cairo and Doha Agreements and adamantly expressed his disapproval of the rapprochement with Qatar prescribed by Khaled Mesh'al. As he was leaving for Iran, Interior Minister Fathi Hamad forbade his delegation from exiting the Gaza Strip. In tandem with his political activities, al-Zahar has written film scenarios and books. He was not re-elected as Political Bureau member in the movement's April 2013 internal elections.

Ghazi Hamad

Born in Rafah in 1964, Ghazi Hamad joined the Muslim Brothers in 1982. He spent five years in Sudan to study veterinarian sciences. Upon his return to Gaza, he participated in the First Intifada and, in 1989, was jailed for five years by the Israelis. This period in detention enabled him to establish relations with other

Palestinian factions and learn Hebrew. After being released, he was appointed spokesman for Hamas. Chief editor of the *al-Watan* weekly, he was also a columnist for *Alresalah*, the main showcase of the movement. Between 1996 and 2000, he was a member of the *al-khalâs* Party which grouped several members of Hamas who wished to participate in elections. After becoming Ismail Haniyeh's adviser, he resigned after the June 2007 seizure of Gaza orchestrated by Hamas. He then was in charge of crossings between Gaza and the outside (Egypt and Israel). After that he was deputy Foreign Affairs minister of Hamas, having nevertheless stated that he did not want to be minister of a government that was the outcome of the 2007 division.

Fathi Hamad

Born in 1961, Fathi Hamad hails from Beit Lahia. He joined the Muslim Brotherhood in 1983 and was in charge of several charities. He joined Hamas' security force *al-Majed* in 1984 and formed the group's first military presence in the Jabaliyya refugee camp in 1988. He spent six years in Israeli prisons from 1988 to 1994 in addition to being arrested three times by the PA. Elected in 2006 on the 'Change and Reform' list, he was one of the members of the Palestinian Legislative Council and the manager of the *al-Aqsa* TV channel. He helped to establish several Islamic media institutions and charities focusing on prisoners and people with injuries and special needs. From April 2009 to 2014, he replaced Interior Minister Said Seyam, who had been murdered by the Israelis during 'Cast Lead'. Since the formation of a unity government in 2014, he has had no institutional position. Since 2017 he is a member of Hamas' politburo.

Ismail Haniyeh

Born in 1962 in the camp of Shati, Haniyeh studied Arabic literature at the Islamic University of Gaza. In the early 1980s, he joined the Muslim Brotherhood and directed the Islamic Block, later participating in the First Intifada. He was arrested first in 1988 and then once more in 1989, both times by Israeli authorities. In 1992, he was part of the group of 415 Palestinian deported by the Israelis to Marj al-Zouhour in South Lebanon. After his return to Gaza in 1993, he became a close friend of Sheikh Ahmed Yassin and took part as an independent candidate in the 1996 parliamentary elections. In February 2006, he was appointed prime minister of the 'Tenth government'; in this capacity, he made several visits abroad. He was also prime minister of the national unity government, formed in March 2007. He was sacked on 14 June 2007 by Mahmoud Abbas and replaced by Salam Fayyad. In December 2011, he went on a diplomatic tour (his first one since the seizure of Gaza in June 2007). He travelled in particular to Tunisia, Egypt and then to the Gulf states. On 11 February 2012, he went to Tehran, where he reasserted the maximalist stance of Hamas. After the internal elections of 2017, he became the head of Hamas' Political Bureau, replacing Khaled Mesh'al. In December 2019, he left Gaza for a diplomatic tour taking him to Turkey, Qatar, Oman, Lebanon, Koweit, Indonesia, Malaysia, and Iran (to attend General Soleimani's funeral in Tehran on 6 January). One year after his departure from Gaza, he has still not returned home. On the occasion of the 21 May 2021 cease-fire, Haniyeh made a speech in which he saluted the 'victory' and thanked Iran for its financial and military support, while calling to reinforce links with the 'international community'. He recalled that 'resistance' was the best way of ending the occupation and promoting the Return of Palestinians, insisting on the fact that this last Israeli attack made any attempt to normalize Israel illusory.

Khalil al-Hayya

Born in Gaza in 1960, he undertook religious studies in Sudan and graduated with a doctorate. He became professor at Gaza's Islamic University and then member of the Union of Palestinian Ulemas; he was elected in 2006 on the 'Change and Reform' list. He negotiated many agreements between Hamas and Fatah between 2006 and 2007. In May 2007, an Israeli raid targeting his home killed seven members of his family. He played a key role in negotiating a cease-fire with Israel during the 2014 Gaza offensive. He is a member of Hamas' politburo and deputy head of Hamas' leadership in Gaza since 2017.

West Bank leadership

Samir Abou Eisheh

Born in 1960 in Nablus, Samir Abou Eisheh graduated with a PhD in engineering from the University of Pennsylvania. He has directed the Department of Engineering at al-Najah University in Nablus. In 2006, he was appointed minister of Planning and Cooperation during the formation of the 'Tenth Government'. Arrested in June 2006 together with other members of the Palestinian Legislative Council, he was released two weeks later. He was then appointed interim finance minister and then again minister of Planning and Cooperation in the national unity government.

Sheikh Hamid al-Bitawi

Born in 1944 in Bita, Hamid al-Bitawi studied Islamic Jurisprudence at Amman University. He was also part of the group of deportees at Marj al-Zouhour in South Lebanon. For forty years, he was a judge in a sharia court and *khatib* at the al-Aqsa Mosque in Jerusalem. As president of the Union of Palestinian Ulemas, he was in charge of the organization of the collection of *zakat* in Nablus. Elected on the 'Change and Reform' list, he was a member of the Muslim Brotherhood before he joined Hamas. He died in 2013.

Nasser al-Din al-Shaer

Born in 1961 in Nablus, specialized in Islamic studies, Nasser al-Din al-Shaer is one of the most appreciated intellectuals in the West Bank. After graduating from Manchester University, he returned to Nablus, where he presided over the council of students of al-Najah University in 1980 and 1981 and then directed the sharia department for five years. He was arrested several times by Israeli authorities. Deputy prime minister of the 'Tenth Government', al-Shaer saw himself as a moderate and refused any association with Hamas. He was detained in August 2006, together with other ministers, and released two months later. He became Minister of Education in the national unity government and was then once more under arrest in 2009 before being freed.

Aziz Dweik

Aziz Dweik comes from Hebron (al-Khalil) but was born in 1948 in Nablus. Graduating with a PhD in Urban Planning from the University of Pennsylvania, he was professor of geography at the al-Najah University in Nablus. A member of Hamas since it was founded, he was expelled to Marj al-Zouhour in South Lebanon in 1992. Elected on the 'Change and Reform' platform in 2006, he became president of the Palestinian Legislative Council, succeeding Ahmad Qorei. In June 2006, during the Israeli 'Summer Rain' military operation, he was arrested by the IDF at his Ramallah home. On 12 September, the Ofer Military Tribunal ordered his provisional release, but on 15 September, an Israeli military court of appeal of the West Bank overturned the decision. This arrest was condemned by the European parliament. He was freed in June 2009.

Sheikh Hassan Yousef

Born in Janiya near Ramallah in 1955, he is the most important religious figure in the West Bank. He was one of the 415 Islamists deported in 1992 to Marj al-Zouhour in South Lebanon. A member of the Political Bureau, he was arrested by Israeli authorities in 2002 and then in 2005. In 2006, he was elected on the 'Change and Reform' list.

Salah al-Arouri

Born on 19 August 1966 in Aroura in the West Bank, Salah al-Arouri was one of the founders of Hamas' armed branch. Elected in 1985 at the head of the Islamic faction of the University of Hebron, he became very much involved in the formation of the al-Qassam Brigades during the first years after the foundation of Hamas. Arrested the first time in November 1990, he spent some fifteen years in jail in Israel. In 2007, he was once more imprisoned, then released in March 2010 to facilitate the conclusion of a deal on the exchange of prisoners, even though Israel considered him as one of the main threats to its security.

At the time of IDF soldier Gilad Shalit's liberation in 2011 – which enabled the freeing of 1,027 Palestinians, among whom Yahya al-Sinwar – al-Araouri had already left Palestine to join Khaled Mesh'al in Syria. As from 2012, following the closure of Hamas offices in Damascus, al-Arouri moved to Turkey and established his own bureau in Istanbul, which at certain times operated independently of the movement's leadership. For instance, during the summer of 2014, al-Arouri encouraged a faction of the Qawashmeh clan in Hebron to kidnap three Israeli teenagers without coordinating with the leading bodies of Hamas. During a conference in Turkey on 20 August 2014, he claimed in the name of Hamas the abduction and murder of the three teenagers. The movement would later, via its president, deny any involvement in this crime without actually condemning it.

In 2016 a rapprochement between Israel and Turkey brought the latter to close al-Arouri's office in Istanbul. Moving between Lebanon and Qatar, al-Arouri is now itinerant, which allows him to take part in many official meetings, regularly leading Hamas delegations during their diplomatic tours.

Considered one of the representatives of the al-Qassam Brigades in the West Bank, Salah al-Arouri is, since 2010, a member of the Hamas Political Bureau and, since 2017, the vice-president of Hamas. He is also in charge of the reconciliation file in negotiations with Fatah. Thanks to his good relations with Jibril Rajoub (the secretary of Fatah's Central Committee), Arouri was successful in fomenting an agreement on a fragile reconciliation between PLO member and non-member factions. This agreement was concluded in Beirut in September 2020. The vice-president of Hamas was also re-elected as head of Hamas in the West Bank during internal elections held in 2021.

Outside leadership

Moussa Abu Marzouk

After the 1948 war, the Abu Marzouk family, which hails from Yibna (nowadays Yavne in Israel), was forced to join the refugee camp of Rafah, where Moussa was born on 9 January 1951. The young Abu Marzouk studied engineering in Cairo, travelled to the Gulf states and then to the United States, where he obtained a master's and a PhD in industrial engineering at the University of Colorado. As of 1968, Moussa Abu Marzouk was involved in the charity activities of the *Mujama' al-islâmî*. Following the massive waves of the arrest of Hamas officials in 1989, the part he played in the movement's reorganization was crucial. Thanks to wealthy donors in the United States and Europe, he managed to reconstruct the movement's infrastructure in Gaza. His brother Mahmoud was then, under Yasser Arafat's presidency, the first head of civilian defence of the Palestinian Authority. Between 1991 and 1995, he was chairman of the Political Bureau and resided in Amman. In 1995, he was arrested at JFK airport in New York, but no charges were laid against him. It was only two years later, in 1997, that the Israelis dropped their demands for extradition and he was released by the United States. He then went looking for a residence in Arab states, but none of them agreed to welcome him. Accused in 2002 of illegal transfer of funds from a business in Texas, his name is on the US government's list of specially wanted terrorists. Abu Marzouk is one of the main decision-makers of Hamas. He was, in particular, one of the artisans of the June 2008 truce signed with Israel for a duration of six months. In February 2012, the departure of the outside leadership from Syria brought him to Cairo. In April of the same year, from his Egyptian home, he accepted to give an interview to the *Forward* daily, which was conducted by several specialists of the Palestinian–Israeli conflict, including Yossi Alpher and Nathan Brown. In April 2014, Moussa Abu Marzouk travelled to the Gaza Strip to negotiate a reconciliation agreement with Fatah. At the end of 'Protective Edge', he announced that direct negotiations with Israel were possible, a statement that was nevertheless contested by Mesh'al from Doha. In both the 2013 and 2017 internal elections of Hamas, he declared himself a candidate but failed once more to become the leader of the Political Bureau. In 2021, Abu Marzouq became Mesh'al deputy for the external leadership.

Imad al-Alami

Born in Gaza, Imad al-Alami studied there in primary and secondary school. From 1988 to 1990, he was jailed in Israeli prisons. In January 1991, he was expelled from Gaza and deported to Marj al-Zouhour in South Lebanon. In 1992, Imad al-Alami became Hamas' representative in Tehran, the location of the first representation office of the movement outside Palestine. In 1993, he travelled to Amman, from where he was expelled three years later. In 1998, he became the representative of Hamas in Damascus. In February 2012, with his wife and six children, he left the Syrian capital for the Gaza Strip. During the 2014 war, following an incident whose circumstances remain unclear, Imad al-Alami was seriously injured. According to the official version, the elevator of a smuggling tunnel fell on him while he was hiding with Ismail Haniyeh to protect himself from the bombing. Others have asserted that it was an assault by one of the members of the al-Qassam Brigades. Al-Alami then went to Turkey for healthcare before returning to Gaza. In 2018, he was shot in the head during what the militant Palestinian group described as an accident, as he was inspecting his personal weapon at home.

Ibrahim Ghosheh

Born in Jerusalem in 1936, Ibrahim Ghosheh did his secondary studies at the *al-Râshidîya* school. He then went to Egypt for university tuition. He became a member of the League of Palestinian Students in Cairo and joined the Muslim Brotherhood when he returned to Palestine in 1950. He graduated with an engineering diploma from Cairo University and then participated in the construction works on the *Jûr al-Sharqîya* canal in Jordan. After four years of residence in Kuwait, he returned once more to Jordan where, until 1971, he was part of the team involved in the construction of the *Sadd Khâlid* dam. Then once again in Kuwait, he worked for a business specializing in public works. Between

1972 and 1978, he was appointed director of the *Sadd al-Malik Talâl* dam project and then founded his own consultancy in civil engineering. In 1989, he decided to dedicate himself exclusively to Hamas and became, in 1992, its official spokesman. In 1999, he was expelled to Qatar by the Jordanian government. Only in the early 2000s did he go back to Amman, having resigned from Hamas, an essential prerequisite for his readmission into the Hashemite Kingdom.

Mohammad Nazzal

Born in Amman in 1963 and originally from Qalqilya, Mohammad Nazzal went to secondary school in Kuwait and was a contributor for the Kuwaiti *al-Mujtama'* magazine, ideologically close to the Muslim Brotherhood. He was then accepted into Karachi University, where he graduated with a master's in chemistry; he was also in charge of welcoming foreign Islamist students. During his return to Kuwait, he was placed in charge of the Palestinian Charity Committee. In 1989 he joined Hamas, opposed Iraq's invasion of Kuwait, which he described as 'occupation', the neutrality displayed by Hamas notwithstanding. When the movement's outside leadership settled in Amman, Mohammad Nazzal was appointed as head of the representation bureau opened in 1992. Following his multiple appearances on al-Jazeera in defence of suicide operations, Nazzal became one of the movement's main figures. He played an essential part in divulging the news of the assault on Khaled Mesh'al to AFP offices in Amman. In 1999 he was put on trial by Jordanian authorities, which had decided to expel all Hamas representatives residing in Amman. In 2001, he left Jordan's capital for Syria, where he was in charge of communication for the movement. This was a period that coincided with the creation of the two TV channels: al-Quds and al-Aqsa. During 'Cast Lead', Nazzal appeared approximately 100 times on television in less than a month. Since the closure of the offices of Hamas in Damascus, he has left Syria and now follows an itinerant life between various Arab capitals.

Osama Hamdan

Born in the al-Burj camp in the Gaza Strip in 1964, Osama Hamdan studied in Kuwait and then in Jordan. In the early 1980s, he joined the Islamic Bloc at Yarmouk University in Irbid, where he studied chemistry. He returned to Kuwait to work in the petrochemical sector. In 1990, at the beginning of the Gulf War, he joined the representation office of Hamas in Tehran as the assistant of Imad al-Alami, whom he replaced in 1993 when the latter went back to Jordan. He was then appointed representative of the movement in Lebanon. In 2010, he returned to Damascus, where he directed the newly created Department of International Relations. He notably met Western diplomats, whom he regularly invited to Hamas premises in Mashru' Dummar (in the western suburbs of Damascus). Since Hamas' departure from Damascus in 2012, he has resettled in Beirut's southern suburbs. As opposed to Mesh'al, Hamdan announced on several occasions that the return of Hamas to Damascus was on the agenda and was a matter of discussions within the movement. Following the Israeli 21 May assault on Gaza, Hamdan declared that the 21 May cease-fire had been reached under certain conditions (a stop to incursions in the al-Aqsa mosque and the abrogation of the decision to expropriate families from Sheikh Jarrah).

Khaled Mesh'al

Born in Silwad in 1956, Khaled Mesh'al did his school studies in Kuwait, where he read physics at university. He participated in the creation of the Palestinian League of Islamic Students. In 1990, after the Gulf War, he travelled to Jordan and was deputy chairman of the Political Bureau until 1995, the year of Moussa Abu Marzouk's arrest. He then became the latter's successor. On 25 September 1997, he was the victim of a murder attempt by the Mossad. Two Israeli agents with Canadian passports were successful in injecting a poisonous substance into his ear. They were neutralized and handed over to the Jordanian intelligence services. Under King Hussein's pressure, who threatened to rescind the 1994 Wadi Araba peace treaty, Israeli authorities not only provided Mesh'al with an antidote but also released Sheikh Ahmed Yasin. In 1999, Khaled Mesh'al was expelled to Qatar. At that time, Syria was welcoming the members of the external leadership and their families, so he went to live in Damascus. Between 2005 and 2008, he took part in successive negotiations with Fatah. He was, in particular, a main player in the Mecca Agreement of 2007. After attempting to mediate between the Arab League and the Syrian regime, he left Damascus for Doha in February 2012. Although he had announced that we would not be a candidate to his own success as chairman of the outside leadership, he was nevertheless reappointed on 1 April 2013, during the internal elections for the Political Bureau, which took place in Cairo. While emphasizing that he would still play a role in politics, he decided not to run in the 2017 internal elections, allowing Ismail Haniyeh to replace him as the head of Hamas' Political Bureau. After hesitations as to a possible candidacy to retake the leadership of Hamas during the 2021 elections, Mesh'al finally decided to abstain from standing for the presidency of the Political Bureau. In April 2021, he became the head of the outside leadership. On 15 May, during the Israeli offensive against Gaza, Mesh'al announced a set of conditions for a cease-fire, among others the withdrawal of Israeli soldiers from the Esplanade of Mosques and the halting of evictions of families from Sheikh Jarrah.

Izzat al-Rishq

Izzat al-Rishq was born in Hebron (Al-Khalil) in 1960. His family emigrated to Kuwait in the wake of the Six-Day War. Graduating with a BA in political science, he participated in the creation of the Islamic Bloc and the Islamic League of Palestinian Students at the University of Kuwait. During his entire stay in this Gulf state, Izzat al-Rishq worked in the field of communications, for both private and governmental foundations. Arrested a first time in Jordan in 1996 because of his active role inside Hamas, he was expelled to Doha at the end of 1999 with other representatives of the movement. When Syria chose to welcome Hamas allowing all the members of its external leadership to settle in Damascus, he moved to the Syrian capital. He is a member of the General Secretariat of the Congress of Arab Parties, a member of the council of the *al-Quds al-Dawliyya* foundation and of the Council of the Islamic National Congress. Since the departure of Hamas' external leadership from Syria, he resides in Doha (Qatar). He is a member of Hamas' politburo.

Hussam Badran

Born in Nablus in 1966, he was in the mid-1980s a member of the Islamic Block of al-Najah University. Considered one of the main figures of the al-Qassam Brigades in the West Bank during the Second Intifada, he was in 2002 the target of a failed assassination attempt. He spent some fourteen years in Israeli jails, during which he was member of the Prisons' Leadership Bureau. After a brief stay with Khaled Mesh'al in Damascus, he settled in Qatar, where he now lives. He is a member of Hamas' Political Bureau.

Translator

Martin Makinson is an Australian and French translator specializing in political science, archeology and history.He has lived in Syria, Lebanon, Yemen, Jordan and Iraq, and has worked and excavated in the above-mentioned countries as well as in Saudi Arabia, Sudan and Turkey. His interests, focus and research are on the Middle East in antiquity and modern times. Often joining expeditions east or south of the Mediterranean, his main base, however is Paris. The foreign policy of Hamas is the fifth book he has translated.

CHRONOLOGY

2006

26 January: Hamas victory in parliamentary elections.

28 January: Khaled Mesh'al's press conference in Damascus.

31 January: Ismail Haniyeh sends a letter to the Quartet members asking them to accept collaborating with Hamas.

19 February: Ismail Haniyeh is appointed prime minister.

28 February: A delegation of British MPs travels to the Gaza Strip.

March: The Quartet decides a blockade on the Gaza government unless the latter submits to three conditions.

March: Sayed Abu Musameh and Ahmad Yousef's visit to London.

2 March: A delegation of European parliamentarians visits Gaza.

3–5 March: Hamas leaders visit Moscow.

April: Israeli bombings on the Gaza Strip, killing more than twenty people.

4 April: Dahab attack; Egypt accuses two Hamas members of being involved.

7 April: Suspension of direct aid from the European Union to the Palestinian government.

April: Operation carried out by Islamic Jihad. Hamas backs the operation.

14 April: First regional tour by Foreign Affairs minister Mahmoud al-Zahar, who travels to Saudi Arabia, Syria, Kuwait, Bahrein, Qatar, the United Arab Emirates, Yemen, Libya, Algeria, Sudan and Egypt.

20 April: Cancellation of Minister al-Zahar's visit to Amman by Jordanian authorities.

May: New letter sent by Ismail Haniyeh to Quartet members.

10 May: Palestinian figures jailed in Israel – including Marwan al-Barghouti and Sheikh Abd al-Khalek al-Natsheh – make proposals to end the crisis opposing Hamas and Fatah.

19 May: A Hamas spokesman is detained at the Rafah crossing in Gaza, in possession of a million dollars.

May: Creation of the Executive Force by Interior Minister Said Seyam.

27 May: Second tour of the Foreign Affairs minister Mahmoud al-Zahar. He travels to Indonesia, Malaysia, Brunei, Pakistan, China, Sri Lanka and Iran.

May–June: Palestinian Authority president Mahmoud Abbas refuses to transfer to the Hamas-led government the control of security services. Confrontation and fighting between the two factions cause the death of more than twenty people.

22 May–12 June: Israeli prime minister Ehud Olmert's tour to Washington and Europe, where he presents his plan to definitively establish Israel's borders before 2010.

5 June: Mahmoud Abbas announces a referendum on an initiative to solve the crisis.

9 June: Ten Palestinians are killed in an Israeli bombing on a beach in Gaza.

12 June: Palestinian government offices are set on fire in the centre of Gaza and Beit Lahia, causing the deaths of eleven Palestinians.

14 June: Parliament is taken by force by public servants deprived of their wages for four months. Mahmoud Abbas and Prime Minister Ismail Haniyeh reach an agreement on the inclusion of a Hamas paramilitary force into Palestinian police.

16 June: The European Union approves a special fund for Palestinians that bypasses their government.

25 June: Abduction of Gilad Shalit at the Kerem Shalom border post.

27 June: Signing of the Prisoners' Document.

28 June: Israel launches the 'Summer Rains' offensive in retaliation for Gilad Shalit's kidnapping: sixty-four Hamas officials, including eight ministers and twenty-six MPs (notably including Aziz Dweik), are arrested in the West Bank.

6 July: The land and air offensive carried out by Israel causes the destruction of a large amount of infrastructure, including the only electricity plant of the Gaza Strip, and kills several tens of Palestinian civilians.

1 September: Faced with the strikes of Palestinian public servants demanding their salaries, the international community promises to send $500 million in aid to the Palestinians during a meeting of donors in Stockholm.

30 October: In Israel the prime minister broadens his coalition, admitting the Far Right Russian-speaking Israel Beitenou Party, led by Avigdor Lieberman.

1–8 September: Israeli ground and air offensive, nicknamed 'Autumn Clouds' and taking place in the north of the Gaza Strip: during the bombing of Beit Hanun, twenty-four Palestinians are killed, including nineteen civilians.

26 November: A cease-fire is reached after five months of military offensive in the Gaza Strip. By then, Operations 'Summer Rain' and 'Autumn Clouds' will have claimed the lives of 400 Gazans.

28 November: Ismail Haniyeh leaves on a regional tour.

14 December: While Prime Minister Ismail Haniyeh returns from his regional tour, his convoy is targeted on the border between Egypt and Gaza. Hamas accuses Fatah of being responsible. Armed clashes erupt between militants of both movements. In nine months, inter-Palestinian violence has caused 320 deaths.

16 December: Mahmoud Abbas announces anticipated general elections following the failure of dialogue with Hamas to solve the political and financial crisis paralysing the Palestinian Authority. This decision is rejected by Ismail Haniyeh and sparks a wave of violence in Gaza between Hamas and Fatah militiamen. Mortar shells are fired against the seat of the presidency in Gaza; a convoy of the Palestinian Foreign Affairs minister is fired on. A colonel of Fatah's National Security Service is abducted and executed.

30 December: Ahmad Bahar travels with Ismail Haniyeh to Saudi Arabia to meet King Abdullah and do the Haj pilgrimage.

2007

21 January: Mahmoud Abbas meets Khaled Mesh'al in Damascus.

28 January: Saudi king Abdullah invites rival Palestinian leaders to come and start talks in Mecca.

29 January: A suicide operation in Eilat kills four people. This is the first attack of this kind since April 2006.

8 February: Hamas and Fatah sign the Mecca Agreement.

17 March: Reappointed as prime minister, Ismail Haniyeh forms a national unity government with Fatah.

March: Kidnapping of British journalist Alan Johnston in Gaza (freed in June of the same year).

May–June: New clashes between Hamas and Fatah in the Gaza Strip.

8–14 June: Hamas seizes the Gaza Strip by force.

15 June: Mahmoud Abbas declares a state of emergency, sacks the national unity government and asks Salam Fayyad (former finance minister) to form a new emergency cabinet.

18 June: The European Union and the United States decide to resume their financial aid to the Palestinian Authority and normalize its relations with it. These had been suspended since the formation by Hamas of the 'Tenth Government', in March 2006.

21 July: Heads of the external leadership meet Mahmoud Ahmadinejad in Damascus.

28 October: Israel imposes economic sanctions on Gaza, which is decreed 'enemy entity'.

26–28 November: International Conference of Annapolis (United States); Olmert and Abbas commit to the signing of a peace treaty before the end of 2008.

December: Ismail Haniyeh sends a letter to the White House, emphasizing that Hamas is ready for dialogue with the United States.

2008

11 January: Ismail Haniyeh sends a letter to French president Nicolas Sarkozy.

January: Visit to Tehran of members of the external leadership.

23 January: Hamas opens a breach in the border separating Egypt from the Gaza Strip.

February–March: Israeli Army offensive against the Gaza Strip.

21 February: The European parliament calls for the end of the siege of the Gaza Strip.

18 April: Meeting between the former US president Jimmy Carter, Moussa Abu Marzouk and Khaled Mesh'al in Damascus.

May 2008: A Hamas representative reveals that Norwegian, French and Italian officials have requested meeting the Hamas government.

16 June: Jimmy Carter's visit to the Gaza Strip.

19 June: After months of Egyptian mediation, a six-month truce between Hamas and Israel is concluded; Israel commits to gradually lifting the blockade.

July–August: Following a deadly attack in Gaza blamed on Fatah, Hamas begins implementing repressive measures and attacks the bastion of the Helles clan.

25 August: Israel releases 198 Palestinian prisoners.

September–December: Release of Aziz Dweik and other members of the Palestinian Legislative Council, who had all been captured during Operation 'Summer Rain', in June 2006.

September: After the death of a policeman shot in Gaza by members of the Dughmush clan, Hamas security forces attack the clan's bastion.

November: A letter by Khaled Mesh'al, addressed to US president Barack Obama, is handed to the emir of Qatar, via Mohammad Nazzal, during the latter's trip to Doha.

4 November: The Israeli Army makes a foray into Gaza, causing the death of six Palestinian activists. Hamas retaliates by firing some fifty rockets in the direction of Israeli territory.

14 December: Khaled Mesh'al announces that the truce with Israel will not be renewed.

19 December: The armed branch of Hamas claims the mortar shells over Israel fired since the end of the truce.

27 December: Israel announces the launching of Operation 'Cast Lead'.

2009

3 January: Beginning of the Israeli ground offensive on the Gaza Strip.

6 January: Forty people sheltering in a school run by the UN in the Jabaliyya refugee camp are killed by Israeli fire.

16 January: Khaled Mesh'al is invited to the 'Gaza Summit' held in Doha.

17 January: Unilateral Israeli cease-fire. The Israeli operation has killed 1,330 Palestinians.

January: End of the official mandate of President Mahmoud Abbas.

January: Meeting of the outside leadership with Iranian authorities in Damascus.

February: Visit to Tehran by representatives of the outside leadership.

February: Regional tour of Gaza's parliamentarians.

4-5 March: Fourth Jerusalem Summit in Tehran, named 'Victory of Gaza'.

15 September: The UN report on the Gaza War headed by Richard Goldstone accuses Israel and Hamas of war crimes.

2 October: Mahmoud Abbas accepts the postponement of the examination of the Goldstone report's contents by the UN Human Rights Council.

6 October: Mahmoud Abbas announces his intention to refer the report to the UN.

October: Dismissal of the Egyptian Document's ratification, which was signed by Mahmoud al-Zahar.

16 October: The UN Human Rights Council adopts a resolution approving the Goldstone report and refers the file to the UN Security Council in New York.

23 October: Mahmoud Abbas calls for parliamentary and presidential elections in January 2010. Hamas refuses the holding of elections in Gaza.

5 November: The UN General Assembly adopts a resolution giving three months to Israel and the Palestinians to open independent enquiries on allegations of war crimes committed during Operation 'Cast Lead'.

12 November: The Palestinian Authority decides to postpone the elections planned in January 2010.

16 December: The PLO's Central Council decides to prolong the mandates of Mahmoud Abbas and the Palestinian parliament to avoid a political and institutional crisis.

December: Egypt begins the construction of an underground steel wall separating Sinai from the Gaza Strip.

2010

6 January: Clashes erupt on the border between Egypt and the Gaza Strip during a demonstration of Palestinians against the construction of the underground wall.

19 January: Assassination in Dubai of Mahmoud al-Mabbouh, a member of the armed branch of Hamas.

February: The external leadership meets with President Mahmoud Ahmadinejad in Damascus.

February: The external leadership's visit to Moscow.

April: Meeting in Damascus between Khaled Mesh'al and Amr Moussa.

May: Israeli attack on the *Viva Palestina* flotilla.

May: Meeting in Damascus between Dimitri Medvedev and the members of the external leadership.

June: Amr Moussa's visit to Gaza.

2011

January: al-Jazeera's revelations on the negotiations.

March: Mohammed Awad is appointed Foreign Affairs minister of the Gaza government, following a cabinet reshuffle carried out by Ismail Haniyeh.

14 March: Demonstrations in Gaza's central square of Palestinians demanding the 'end of division'; Hamas reacts violently and assaults the demonstrators.

15 March: Demonstrations in downtown Gaza.

16 March: Two militants of the armed branch of Hamas are killed by Israeli air strikes.

16 March: Abbas favourably answers Haniyeh's invitation to travel to Gaza.

16 March: Members of Hamas security forces beat up several students of al-Azhar University in Gaza, who were about to exit the building's premises to demonstrate.

19 March: The armed branch of Hamas fires a series of rockets at Israel.

21 March: Members of the al-Qassam Brigades declare they are ready to sign a truce.

22 March: The Israeli Air Force bombs the Gaza Strip. Ismail Haniyeh calls on the UN Security Council to take action regarding the crimes committed by occupying forces and adopt a resolution similar to that taken for Libya.

26 March: Several Hamas officials let it be known they will not be able to guarantee Mahmoud Abbas's security were he to travel to Gaza.

29 March: A Hamas delegation meets the new Egyptian Foreign Affairs minister Nabil al-Arabi.

29 March: Ammunition is fired from the Gaza Strip after two days of calm. Israel retaliates by killing two militants of Islamic Jihad's armed branch, the *al-Quds* Brigades.

April: Israel demands the withdrawal of the Goldstone report after the expressions of regret made by the South African judge. The UN refuses.

2 April: A Hamas communiqué lauds the Syrian regime, stating that the latter has backed the resistance of the Palestinian people and welcomed resistance forces.

3 April: Meeting in the Gaza Strip of two Hamas delegations (led by Khalil al-Hayya) with Fatah (led by Ismail Redwan) to discuss the issue of reconciliation.

7 April: An anti-tank shell is fired at an Israeli school bus. Violent Israeli retaliation causing nineteen deaths in Gaza.

10 April: Israel and Hamas declare they are ready to sign a truce.

14 April: Assassination of an Italian pro-Palestinian militant by the *Tawhid wa-l-Jihâd* group.

4 May: Signing of the Cairo Agreement between Fatah and Hamas.

May: Ismail Haniyeh regrets Ben Laden's death. The Saudi Jihadi is described as a 'fighter of Islam'.

14 May: US president Barack Obama's speech on the Middle East.

15 May: Day of commemoration of the Nakba.

5 June: Day of commemoration of the Naksa (defeat in the 1967 war); twenty-three people are killed in the Golan Heights as they get close to the Israeli–Syrian border.

17 June: The spokesman of the organizers of an international humanitarian flotilla to Gaza announce that the Turkish *Mavi Marmara* ship will not be part of it. Warming up of Turkish–Israeli relations, which had been strained since the flotilla incident.

21 June: Announcement of the postponement of the Cairo meeting for the formation of a Palestinian government, following disapproval of Salam Fayyad's nomination.

August: Armed confrontation between Hamas and Israel.

1 October: International summit of support for the Intifada organized in Tehran. Ahmad Bahar, Mahmoud al-Zahar, Khaled Mesh'al, Osama Hamdan and Izaat al-Rishq are present.

18 October: Release of Gilad Shalit.

29 October: A delegation of the Egyptian Muslim Brotherhood travels to the Gaza Strip.

November: Cairo meeting between Mahmoud Abbas and Khaled Mesh'al, during which the latter declares himself favourable to peaceful resistance.

December: Ismail Haniyeh's regional tour.

2012

January: Ismail Haniyeh's second diplomatic tour.

January: Visit to Geneva of a delegation of Gazan parliamentarians.

January: Khaled Mesh'al's visit to Jordan.

February: Closure of Hamas's offices in Damascus.

6 February: The Doha Agreement between Hamas and Fatah is signed.

11 February: Ismail Haniyeh's visit to Tehran. The same week, Moussa Abu Marzouk travels to Beirut.

24 February: Ismail Haniyeh's speech at al-Azhar University in support of Syrian insurgents.

4 March: Ahmad Bahar, leading a parliamentary delegation notably including Sayed Aby Musameh and Khamis al-Najjar, travels to Tunisia, Morocco and Qatar. He addresses a letter to the president of the Arab Parliamentary Union, requesting the inclusion on the following day's agenda of the file on the imprisonment of MPs and Aziz Dweik (the president of the Legislative Council).

Summer 2012: First wave of destruction of the tunnels between Gaza and Sinai, carried out by the Egyptian Army.

Summer 2012: First decrease in Iranian economic support.

July: Khaled Mesh'al's visit to Tunisia.

5 August: Attack of the Kerem Shalom border outpost.

September: Khaled Mesh'al's visit to Turkey.

14 November: Ahmed al-Jaabari is assassinated by Israel. Beginning of Israeli Operation 'Pillar of Defence' in the Gaza Strip.

16 November: Khaled Mesh'al's visit to Khartoum.

16 November: The Egyptian prime minister Ahmad Qandil visits Gaza.

17 November: The Tunisian Foreign Affairs minister visits Gaza.

20 November: The Turkish Foreign Affairs minister visits Gaza.

21 November: Truce.

7 December: Khaled Mesh'al's visit to the Gaza Strip to celebrate the twenty-fifth anniversary of the foundation of Hamas, as well as the November 'victory'.

2013

January: Second wave of flooding of the smugglers' tunnels by the Egyptian Army.

22 January: Malaysia's prime minister visits the Gaza Strip.

28 January: Khaled Mesh'al asks the king of Jordan to transmit a message to US president Barack Obama, reasserting his attachment to the recognition of 1967 borders.

16 March: Khaled Mesh'al visits the premises of the Egyptian Muslim Brotherhood in Mokattam near Cairo and meets Supreme Guide Mohammed Badie.

31 March: Internal elections of the Political Bureau of Hamas in Cairo.

3 May: Presence of Mesh'al next to Sheikh Yusuf al-Qaradawi during the sermon given at the al-Doha Mosque, violently criticizing Iran and Hezbollah.

8 May: Al-Qaradawi's visit to Gaza.

18 May: Congress on the right of return organized in Brussels, in the presence of Palestinian MP Khoudari and Tunisia Ennahda leader Rached Ghannouchi.

May: Battle of al-Qusayr in Syria; probable participation of members of the al-Qassam Brigades.

17 June: Communiqué of the Political Bureau of Hamas calling for Hezbollah's retreat from Syria.

June: Hezbollah requests the closure of Hamas representation offices in Beirut's southern suburbs.

30 June: Mohammed Morsi's speech, interpreted by Hamas as unflagging support for the movement.

June: Two Hamas delegations travel to Tehran and Beirut.

3 July: Overthrow of Egyptian president Mohammed Morsi.

Summer 2013: New decrease in Iranian economic support.

3 October: Mesh'al's speech in Beirut; inflection of his stance regarding the conflict in Syria.

15 October: Cancellation of Mesh'al's visit to Tehran by Iranian authorities. The visit takes place but Mesh'al is not part of the delegation.

27 October: The Gaza government's finance minister Ala al-Rafati declares that the closure of the tunnels between Egypt and the Strip since July has made Gaza lose $230 million per month.

11 November: The mobilization of a 'Palestinian *tamarrod*' (rebellion), planned for this day (the anniversary of Yasser Arafat's death), does not take place.

16 November: Khaled Mesh'al's visit to Khartoum.

9 December: Mahmoud al-Zahar declares that relations between Hamas and Egypt are severed.

25 December: The Muslim Brotherhood is labelled as a 'terrorist organization' by the new Egyptian power structure.

2014

23 April: Signing of the Shati Agreement, which stipulates the formation of a unity government, the holding of elections within six months, the control of the Rafah crossing by Mahmoud Abbas's Presidential Guard, and finally the payment of Hamas public servants by the Palestinian Authority.

2 June: Formation of a 'consensus' government led by Rami al-Hamdallah, comprising independent figures and technocrats (seventeen ministers, including five from Gaza, but none affiliated to Hamas). This ministerial cabinet is recognized for the first time by the United States and the European Union.

2 June: Israel prevents Gaza ministers from going to Ramallah to pledge allegiance and pressures President Abbas to stop paying salaries, following Qatar's proposal of providing funds.

12 June: Kidnapping of three Israeli students in the West Bank near Kfar Etzion. The bodies of Eyal Yifrach, Gilad Shaer and Naftali Frenkel are later found on 30 June.

14 June: Israel carries out several operations in the West Bank's cities as reprisals for the kidnapping of the three young Israeli men. More than 100 Islamist militants are detained by the Israelis, in particular those who had been freed in the wake of the prisoner exchange leading to Gilad Shalit's release (including several of the Palestinian Legislative Council MPs and Aziz Dweik). An Israeli air strike is also carried out in the Gaza Strip.

2 July: Abduction of the young Palestinian Mohammed Abou Khdeir in East Jerusalem. His body is discovered a few hours later near a forest in the Western sector of Jerusalem.

8 July: Beginning of Operation 'Protective Edge'.

15 July: Hamas refuses the Egyptian cease-fire proposal. It accuses Egyptian authorities of not having bothered to inform the Palestinian movement beforehand and states that Hamas leaders learnt about the cease-fire proposal through the media.

16 July: Ten-point Egyptian cease-fire proposal presented by Hamas and Islamic Jihad. Demands relate to the lifting of the blockade, the release of prisoners and the provision of a more extensive fishing zone; several points of this proposal mention a control, shared between Qatar and Turkey, of the crossing points into Gaza.

31 July: A first 72-hour cease-fire is to take effect on Friday, 1 August. The hope of a lull in the fighting ends when Israel uses as a pretext the capture of one of its soldiers to extend its military operations to Rafah.

1 and 18 August: A round of negotiations begins in Cairo.

5 August: Palestinian factions agree on a 72-hour truce under Egyptian aegis. On the morning of Friday, 8 August, new firing of rockets from the Gaza Strip.

10 August: A second 72-hour truce under Egyptian aegis comes into effect. It is extended for another five days on Wednesday, 13 August.

18 August: Three rockets fall on Israel. Israel leaves Cairo, saying it will not negotiate under fire.

19 August: The home of Mohammed Deif is targeted by an Israeli missile. His wife and his four-year-old son die in the attack.

21 August: Israel carries out a military operation during which three members of the al-Qassam Brigades are killed: Mohammed Abou Chamala, Raed al-Attar and Mohammed Barhoum.

22 August: Salah al-Arouri, a Hamas official who was exiled to Turkey, claims the kidnapping of the three Israeli students.

22 August: Hamas executes eighteen Palestinians accused of collaboration with Israel.

26 August: Signing of a cease-fire agreement and end of Operation 'Protective Edge'.

25 September: Hamas says it is ready to leave aside some aspects of its control (of all ministries and security) of the Gaza Strip if in return Mahmoud Abbas commits to paying public servants.

9 October: In the framework of the conference for Gaza's reconstruction, which is being held in Cairo, the government meets in the Gaza Strip for the first time since its formation. Hamas and Fatah still do not agree on the return of the Presidential Guard to the crossing points.

8 December: A Hamas delegation comprising Mohammed Nasr, Osama Hamdan and Khaled al-Qaddoumi travels to Tehran.

12 December: Attack against the French Institute in Gaza, closed since the criminal arson on 7 October. Although claimed by a Salafi group, many observers suggest the hypothesis of a responsibility of Hamas or some of its leaders.

17 December: Because of a procedural error, the European Court of Justice cancels the European Council's decision to keep Hamas on the list of terrorist organizations. The Court of Justice highlights that this erasure from the list 'does not imply any in-depth estimation on the question of the classification of Hamas as a terrorist group'.

28 December: Khaled Mesh'al's visit to Turkey. In July, Hamas had denied Mesh'al's unofficial visit to Istanbul. In September, Turkey had stated it was ready to welcome on its territory representatives of the Egyptian Muslim Brotherhood who had been expelled from Qatar in September because of pressure exerted on this emirate by other Gulf states.

30 December: Rejection of Mahmoud Abbas's proposal to adopt a resolution of the UN Security Council, which would have given three years to the Israelis to evacuate the territories occupied since 1967. The text was approved by only eight of the fifteen members of the Council.

31 December: Mahmoud Abbas signs the Rome Status to become a member of the International Criminal Court (ICC). In retaliation, Israel stops paying the money from taxes collected by the Palestinian Authority, which is estimated at $120 million per month. One hundred and fifty thousand Palestinian public servants are not paid their wages as a result.

2015

19 January: Some 200 Salafi militants demonstrate in front of the French Institute in Gaza in support of the terrorist attack against the *Charlie Hebdo* magazine in Paris, brandishing portraits of the Kouachi Brothers and Amedy Coulibaly, who committed the crimes.

28 February: An Egyptian law court places Hamas on the list of terrorist organizations.

11 March: The president of the Iranian parliament, Ali Larijani, meets Khaled Mesh'al. This is the first time that the head of the Political Bureau of Hamas meets an official representative of the Islamic Republic since the cooling of their relations, a consequence of Hamas's relations with Bashar al-Assad since March 2011.

30 March Publication of a communiqué of Hamas on the war in Yemen.

April: Seizure of Yarmouk Camp in Damascus by Islamic State fighters.

May: Khaled Mesh'al speaks to former British prime minister Tony Blair in Doha.

2 May: Mobilization of young Gazans gathered in the Shujariyya neighbourhood to demand 'the end of division', and the reconstruction of the Gaza Strip. Harsh repression by Hamas.

May: Attack on the headquarters of Hamas National Security, claimed by the 'Followers of the Islamic State in Jerusalem'.

June: Egypt overrules its decision to place Hamas on the list of terrorist organizations.

6 June: Rockets fired towards Ashkelon by the 'Sheikh Omar al-Hadid' Brigade.

17 July: Visit to Saudi Arabia of a delegation led by Khaled Mesh'al.

19 July: Explosion of cars in Gaza, belonging to members of the armed branches of Hamas and Islamic Jihad.

August: Abduction of four Palestinians by Egyptian security services.

1 August: Russian foreign minister Serguei Lavrov meets Khaled Mesh'al in Qatar.

2016

January: A telephone conversation between Moussa Abu Marzouk is leaked. Abu Marzouk speaks of Iranian lies on the issue of the funding of Islamist Palestinian resistance.

February and March: Osama Hamdan and Ismail Haniyeh's visit to Iran.

12 March: During the visit of a Hamas delegation to Cairo, the movement reiterates its commitment to guarantee the stability of Egypt and protecting the latter's borders.

14 December: Official communiqué of Hamas condemning the genocide in Aleppo.

2017

January: Moussa Abu Marzouk speaks with Hassan Nasrallah, conversations he will have repeatedly with the Hezbollah leader between the months of January and June.

February: Yahya al-Sinwar is elected as head of the Political Bureau in Gaza.

April: Mahmoud Abbas imposes sanctions on the Gaza Strip.

1 May: A Document on Principles and General Policy is announced in Doha.

May: Ismail Haniyeh is elected as head of the Political Bureau of Hamas.

June: Qatar expels Hamas members.

June: Five-week visit of Yahya al-Sinwar to Cairo. Opening of the Rafah border crossing and supplying of cement and fuel to Gaza.

July: Decision of the European Union's Court of Justice of keeping Hamas on the list of terrorist organizations.

July: Osama Hamdan and Sami Abou Zouhri's visit to Algeria.

17 September: Hamas announces the dissolution of its administrative committee.

18 September: A delegation of the external leadership travels to Russia to talk to Mikhail Bogdanov.

September: Ismail Haniyeh's visit to Cairo, the first since his victory in the May elections.

12 October: Reconciliation agreement signed in Cairo.

15 November: The Rafah crossing is handed over to the Ramallah Authority.

20 November: Hamas supports Hezbollah, labelled as 'terrorist' by the Arab League.

December: Khaled Mesh'al's tour to North Africa.

2018

February: The al-Qassam Brigades officially display their support for the Damascus regime, when the latter orders the shooting down of an Israeli warplane flying over Syrian territory.

30 March: The March of Return begins.

30 March: Meeting between Moussa Abu Marzouk and Mikhail Bogdanov in Moscow.

14 May: The US Embassy is transferred from Tel Aviv to Jerusalem on the day of the commemoration of the seventy years of the foundation of the State of Israel and on the anniversary of the Nakba. Sixty Palestinians are killed in Gaza along the border fence.

25 June: Moussa Abu Marzouk meets Mikhail Bogdanov in Moscow.

13–15 July: Attacks from the Gaza Strip with kites set alight, provoking fires on the Israeli side. Israel responds by launching air raids.

20 July: An Israeli soldier is killed during demonstrations near the border fence separating Israel from the Gaza Strip. This death is the first of an Israeli soldier since the 2014 war. As a response, Israel intensely bombs the military command of Hamas in Khan Younis, in the southern part of the enclave. Four Palestinians are killed, including three members of the al-Qassam Brigades.

7 August: Two other militants of the Brigades are killed during an Israeli air strike, this time in the north of the Gaza Strip, a strike that, according to Israeli military command, is the result of a mistake. In response, more than 180 rockets are fired at Israel, resulting in reprisals by the Israeli Air Force, which bombs more than 150 sites in the Gaza Strip. A young pregnant woman is killed, as well as her eighteen-month-old girl. This escalation is the most grievous since the 2014 war.

15 August: Cease-fire following the UN and Egypt's mediation. It reiterates the principles of the August 2014 cease-fire: cessation of hostilities, enlargement of the fishing zone, reopening of the Kerem Shalom crossing closed since July.

November: Egyptian mediation, backed by the United Nations and Qatar, which permits the reaching of a first appeasement agreement between Israel and Hamas.

11 November: An Israeli commando is spotted near Khan Younis, when a local officer of the al-Qassam Brigades is killed during exchange of fire.

2019

January: The employees of the Palestinian Authority in Ramallah leave the Rafah crossing.

January: Hamas rejects the third payment by Qatar, pretexting non-abidance of the truce by Israel. This payment had strongly angered Egypt. Hamas is also accused of having 'sold' the March of Return.

February: Mesh'al welcomes a Russian delegation in Doha.

3-27 February: Ismail Haniyeh visits Cairo.

8-9 March: The IDF responds to incendiary balloons launched from the Gaza Strip.

14 March: Two rockets are fired towards Tel Aviv, an attack unheard of since 2014. Hamas attempts to appease the situation indicating via the Egyptians that this was a mistake related to a maintenance operation.

14 March: Hamas violently represses peaceful demonstrations against the high cost of living in Gaza.

25 March: A rocket lands in Mishmeret, north of Tel Aviv. The firing is not claimed by any Palestinian faction. Israel responds by a huge bombing campaign on the Gaza Strip, hitting both military and civilian sites.

30 March: During the commemorations of the anniversary of the March of Return, Hamas deploys its men in orange suits to prevent demonstrators from getting involved in confrontations with Israeli armed forces.

1 April: New appeasement deal reached between Israel and Hamas, under the aegis of Egypt.

3 May: Exchanges of fire between Israel and Islamic Jihad. Tsahal pummels the Gaza Strip, causing the deaths of twenty-five Palestinians, including two pregnant women. Seven hundred rockets are fired from the Gaza Strip towards Israeli urban centres, such as Ashkelon, Ashdod and Beersheba, resulting in four Israeli deaths. Israel resumes its practice of targeted assassinations, killing Hamad al-Khodori.

6 May: New cease-fire implemented, reiterating the main clauses of previous deals.

July: Diplomatic tour headed by Salah al-Arouri, who travels to Moscow and then to Iran.

22 July: The Hamas delegation has talks with Khamenei, who had not welcomed the movement's representatives since 2012.

12–14 November: Confrontation between Islamic Jihad and Israel. Hamas stays out of this exchange of fire.

16 November: Israel authorizes the passage of fuel trucks to Gaza, extends the fishing zone and reopens the Kerem Shalom crossing.

December: Haniyeh's diplomatic tour to Turkey, Qatar, Oman, Kuwait, Lebanon, Mauritania, Indonesia and Malaysia.

18 December: Khaled Mesh'al travels to Kuala Lumpur.

2020

6 January: Ismail Haniyeh is present at Qassem Soleymani's funeral in Tehran.

15 January: Khaled Mesh'al meets Robert Malley in Doha.

18 February: Khaled Mesh'al holds talks with Serguei Lavrov and Mikhail Bogdanov in Doha.

1 March: Ismail Haniyeh and Moussa Abu Marzouk's visit to Moscow.

June: Israel agrees on the transfer of $50 million given by Qatar to Hamas, in exchange for calm at the border.

3 July: Conversations via videoconference between Jibril Rajoub, Fatah's general secretary, and Salah al-Arouri, on countering the Israeli annexation project.

6 August: Beginning of the confrontation between Israel and Hamas.

13 August: Normalization agreement between Israel and the United Arab Emirates.

22 August: Ismail Haniyeh and Salah al-Arouri meet Recep Tayyip Erdogan in Istanbul.

31 August: Cease-fire agreement between Israel and Hamas, under the aegis of Qatar.

2 September: While visiting Lebanon, Ismail Haniyeh participates via videoconference in an anti-normalization meeting held at the Palestinian Embassy in Beirut. He then speaks to Nabih Berry, Abbas Ibrahim, Walid Jumblatt and Hassan Nasrallah.

20 September: Meeting between Fatah and Hamas in Istanbul.

18 October: Israel normalizes relations with Bahrein.

22 December: Normalization agreement between Israel and Morocco.

2021

January: Israel normalizes relations with Sudan.

10 March: Yahya al-Sinwar is re-elected as Gaza's leader.

12 April: Khaled Mesh'al elected at the head of Hamas's outside leadership.

29 April: President Mahmoud Abbas cancels parliamentary elections.

10 May: Abou Obeida, the spokesman of the al-Qassam, sends Israel an ultimatum.

11 May: Hamas fires the first rockets towards Tel Aviv and Jerusalem.

15 May: Khaled Mesh'al elaborates on the conditions for a cease-fire: the withdrawal of Israeli troops from the Esplanade of Mosques and the withdrawal of the settlers from Sheikh Jarrah.

21 May: Cease-fire concluded between Israel and armed Palestinian factions.

16 June: Ismail Haniyeh's visit to Morocco.

21 June: Ismail Haniyeh's visit to Nouakchott (Mauritania).

27 June: Ismail Haniyeh's visit to Lebanon.

BIBLIOGRAPHY

General Bibliography

Allison, Graham T. (1972), *Essence of Decision: Explaining the Cuban Missile Crisis*, New York, Harper Collins, 352p.
Al-Sayegh, Fayez (1965), 'Islam and Neutralism', in J. Harris Proctor (dir.), *Islam and International Relations*, London, Dunmow, Pall Mall Press. 221p.
Anderson, Paul A. (1987), 'What do Decision-Makers Do When They Make a Foreign Policy Decision? The Implications for the Comparative Study of Foreign Policy', in Charles F. Herrman, Charles W. Kegley and James N. Rosenau, *New Directions in the Study of Foreign Policy*, Boston, Allen and Unwin, 450p.
Aspaturian, Vernor (1966), 'International Politics and Foreign Policy in the Soviet System', in R. Barry Farrell, *Approaches to Comparative and International Politics*, Evanston, Northwestern University Press, 368p.
Badie, Bertrand (2008), *Le diplomate et l'intrus: l'entrée des sociétés dans l'arène internationale*, Paris, Fayard, 283p.
Badie, Bertrand and Smouts, Marie-Claude (1999), *Le retournement du monde: sociologie de la scène internationale*, Paris, Presses de Sciences-Po, Dalloz, 238p.
Baechler, Jean (1976), *Qu'est-ce que l'idéologie*, Paris, Gallimard, 416p.
Bar-Siman-Tov, Yaacov (1983), *Linkage Politics in the Middle East: Syria between Domestic and External Conflict, 1961–1970*, Boulder, Westview, 186p.
Barnett, Michael N. (1996), 'Identity and Alliances in the Middle East', in Peter J. Katzenstein, *The Culture of National Security: Norms and Identity in World Politics*, New York, Columbia University Press, 580p.
Braillard, Philippe and Senarclens, Pierre de (1981), 'Idéologie et relations internationales, le cas des relations soviéto-américianes', *Relations Internationales*, vol. 25 (2), pp.113–33.
Bloom, Mia (2005), *Dying to Kill: The Allure of Suicide Terror*, New York, Columbia University Press, 251p.
Brecher, Michael (1973), 'Images, Processes and Feedback in Foreign Policy: Israel's Decisions on German Reparations', *The American Political Science Review*, vol. 67 (1), pp.73–102.
Brecher, Michael (1972), *The Foreign Policy System of Israel: Setting, Images, Process*, London, Oxford University Press, 693p.
Brecher, M., Steinberg, B. and Stein, J. (1969), 'A Framework for Research on Foreign Policy Behaviour', *The Journal of Conflict Resolution*, vol. 13 (1), pp.75–101.
Carlsnaes, Walter (1986), *Ideology and Foreign Policy: Problems of Comparative Conceptualization*, Oxford, Basil Blackwell, 234p.
Charrett, Catherine (2019), *Hamas, the EU and the Palestinian Elections: A Performance in Politics*, Abingdon/New York, Routledge, 249p.
Charillon, Frédéric (2002), *Politique étrangère: nouveaux regards*, Paris, Presses de Sciences-Po, 437p.

Charillon, Frédéric (2007), 'Les politiques étrangères contestataires', *Cahiers de l'Orient*, vol. 87, pp.25–31.

Christler, Jonsson (2002), 'Essence of Diplomacy', in Walter Carslnaes, Thomas Risse-Kappen and Beth Simmons, *Handbook of International Relations*, London, Sage, 688p.

Clement, Pierre-Alain (2014), 'Le terrorisme est une violence politique comme les autres: vers une normalisation typologique du terrorisme', *Etudes internationales*, vol. 45 (3), pp.355–78.

Dawisha, Adeed I. (1983), *Islam in Foreign Policy*, Cambridge, Cambridge University Press, 191p.

Dehousse, Renaud (1989), 'Fédéralisme, asymmétrie et interpdépendance: Aux origines de l'action internationale des composantes de l'Etat federal', *Etudes Internationales*, vol. 20 (2), pp.283–309.

Der Derian, James (1987), *On Diplomacy: A Genealogy of Western Estrangement*, Oxford, Basil Blackwell, 288p.

Dimaggio, Paul J. and Powell, Walter W. (1991), *The New Institutionalism in Organizational Analysis*, Chicago, University of Chicago Press, 486p.

Djalili, Mohammed-Reza (1989), *Diplomatie islamique, stratégie internationale du khomeynisme*, Paris, Presses Universitaires de France, 241p.

Donner, Fred M. (1991), 'The Sources of Islamic Conceptions of War', in John Kelsay and James Turner Johnson, *Just War and Jihad: Historical and Theoretical Perspectives on War and Peace in Western and Islamic Traditions*, Westport, Greenwood Press, 271p.

Dupret, Baudouin (ed.) (2012), *La charia aujourd'hui: Usages de la référence au droit islamique*, Paris, La Découverte, 240p.

Duroselle, Jean-Baptiste (1992), *Tout empire périra: Théorie des relations internationales*, Paris, Armand Colin, 346p.

Eickelman, Dale F. and Piscatori, James (2004), *Muslim Politics*, Princeton, Princeton University Press, 235p.

Esposito, John L. (1992), *The Islamic Threat: Myth or Reality?* Oxford, Oxford University Press, 243p.

Freund, Julien (1973), 'L'idéologie chez Max Weber', *Revue Européenne des Sciences Sociales*, vol. 11 (30), pp.5–19.

Gabel, Joseph (1984), 'Idéologie', *Encyclopædia Universalis* [en ligne], consulté le 11 septembre 2021. URL: https://www.universalis.fr/encyclopedie/ideologie/

Groth, Allon (1995), *The PLO's Road to Peace: Processes of decision Making*, London, Royal United Service Institute for Defence Studies, 96p.

Halperin, Morton H. and Clapp, Priscilla A. (2006), *Bureaucratic Politics and Foreign Policy*, Washington, Brookings Institution Press, 400p.

Hamilton, Keith and Langhorne, Richard (2010), *The Practice of Diplomacy*, London, Routledge, 328p. .

Hermann, Margaret G. (2001), 'How Decision units Shape Foreign Policy: A Theoretical Framework', in Margaret G. Hermann, 'Leaders, Groups and Coalitions: Understanding the People and Processes in Foreign Policymaking', *International Studies Review*, vol. 3 (2), pp.47–81.

Hill, Christopher (2003), *The Changing Politics of Foreign Policy*, New York, Palgrave Macmillan, 376p.

Hinnebusch, Raymond and Ehteshami, Anourshiravan (2002), *The Foreign Policy of Middle East States*, Boulder/London, Lynee Rienner, 400p.

Hocking, Brian (1993), *Localizing Foreign Policy: Non-Central Governments and Multilayered Diplomacy*, New York, Saint Martin's Press, 249p.

Hocking, Brian, (2001), 'Non-State Actors and Transformation of Diplomacy', in Bas Arts, Math Noortmann and Bob Reinalda (dir.), *Non-State Actors in International Relations*, Burlington, Ashgate, 334 p.

Hoffman, Stanley (1968), *Gullivers' Troubles, or The Setting of American Foreign Policy*, New York, McGraw-Hill, 556p.

Hollis, Martin and Smith, Steve (1991), *Explaining and Understanding International Relations*, Oxford: Clarendon Press, 226p.

Holsti, Ole R. (1976), 'Foreign Policy Decision-Makers Viewed Psychologically', in James Rosenau, *In Search of Global Patterns*, New York, The Free Press, 389p.

Honneth, Axel (2012), 'La reconnaissance entre Etats, l'arrière-plan moral des relations interétatiques', *Cultures et Conflits*, vol. 87, pp.27–36.

Jackson, Richard (2009), 'Knowledge, Power and Politics of Political Terrorism', in R. Jackson, M. Breen-Smyth and J. Gunning (dir.), *Critical Terrorism Studies – A New Research Agenda*, London, Routledge, 292p.

Jackson, Robert H. (1993), *Quasi-States, Sovereignty, International Relations and the Third World*, Cambridge, Cambridge University Press, 238p.

Janis, Irving L. and Mann, Leon (1977), *Decision Making: A Psychological Analysis of Conflict, Choice and Commitment*, London, Collier Macmillan, 488p.

Jervis, Robert (1976), *Perception and Misperception in International Politics*, Princeton, Princeton University Press, 464p.

Kalberg, Stephen (2010), *Les valeurs, les idées et les intérêts. Introduction à la sociologie de Max Weber*, Paris, La Découverte, 276p.

Karabell, Zachary (1996), 'Fundamental Misconceptions: Islamic Foreign Policy', *Washington DC: Carnegie Endowment for International Peace*, vol. 105 (105), pp.77–90.

Keating, Michael and Aldecoa, Fransisco (1999), *Paradiplomacy in Action: The Foreign Relations of Subnational Governments*, Portland, Frank Cass Publishers, 232p.

Keohane, Robert O. and Goldstein, Judith (1993), *Ideas and Foreign Policy: Beliefs, Institutions and Political Change*, Ithaca, Cornell University Press, 304p.

Khadduri, Majid (1965), 'The Islamic Theory of International Relations', in J. Harris Proctor, *Islam and International Relations*, London, Dunmow, Pall Mall Press, 221p.

Kienle, Eberhard (1990), *Ba'th vs. Ba'th: The Conflict between Syria and Iraq, 1968–1989*, London, I.B. Tauris, 176p.

Kirby, Stephen (1973), 'National Interest versus Ideology in American Diplomacy', in Robert Benewick, R.N. Berki and Bhikhu C. Parekh, *Knowledge and Belief in Politics: The Problem of Ideology*, London, Allen and Unwin, 327p.

Kissinger, Henry (1957), *Nuclear Weapons and Foreign Policy (abridged)*, New York, Harper and Brothers, 276p.

Korany, Bahgat (ed.) (1986), *How Foreign Policy Decisions are made in the Third World: A Comparative Analysis*, Boulder, Westview, 332p.

Kramer, Martin (1993), 'Rallying Around Islam', *Middle East Contemporary Survey*, Boulder, vol. 17, pp.109–53.

Krasner, Stephen D. (1978), *Defending the National Interest: Raw Materials Investments and US Foreign Policy*, Princeton, Princeton University Press, 424p.

Kratochwill, Friedrich and Lapid, Yosef (1996), *The Return of Culture and Identity in IR Theory*, Boulder, CO, Lynne Rienner, 255p.

Labedz, Leopold (1982), 'Idéologie et politique étrangère sovéitique', in Christoph Bertram (ed.), *La menace soviétique*, Paris, Berger-Levrault, 208p.

Lavau, Georges (1982), 'Le rapport entre l'idéologie et la politique extérieure', *Pouvoirs*, vol. 21, pp.125–38.

Laroui, Abdallah (1982), *L'idéologie arabe contemporaine*, Paris, la Découverte, 225p.
Levi, Werner (1970), 'Ideology, Interests, and Foreign Policy', *International Studies Quarterly*, vol. 14 (1), pp.1–31.
Lindemann, Thomas (2010), *Causes of War: The Struggle for Recognition*, Colchester, ECPR Press, 176p.
Lindemann, Thomas (2012), 'Théories de la reconnaissance dans les relations internationales: enjeux symboliques et limites du paradigme de l'intérêt', *Cultures et Conflits*, vol. 87, pp.7–25.
Mannheim, Karl (1957), *Idéologie et utopie*, Paris, Rivière, 272p.
Morgenthau, Hans J. (1954), *Politics Among Nations: The Struggle for Power and Peace*, New York, Alfred A. Knopf.
Norton, Augustus R. and Greenberg, Martin H. (1989), *The International Relations of the Palestine Liberation Organization*, Carbondale, Southern Illinois University Press, 233p.
Pape, Robert A. (2005), *Dying to Win: The Strategic Logic of Suicide Terrorism*, New York, Random House, 368p.
Paquin, Stéphane (2004), *Paradiplomatie et relations internationales: Théorie des strategies internationales des regions face à la mondialisation*, Brussels, PIE-Peter Lang.
Putman Robert, D., Evans Peter, B. and Jacobson Harold, K. (1993), *Double-edged Diplomacy, International Bargaining and Domestic Politics*, Berkeley, University of California Press, 508p.
Ramazani, Rohallah K. (1983), 'Khumayni's Islam in Iran's Foreign Policy', in Adeed I. Dawisha, *Islam in Foreign Policy*, Cambridge, Cambridge University Press, 204p.
Rapin, Ami-Jacques (2008), 'L'objet évanescent d'une théorie improbable: le terrorisme et les sciences sociales', *Cahier du réseau multidisciplinaire d'études stratégiques*, vol. 5 (1), pp.165–223.
Rodinson, Maxime (1966), *Islam et capitalisme*, Paris, Le Seuil, 302p.
Rosenau, James N., Kegley, Charles W. and Hermann, Charles F. (1987), *New Directions in the Study of Foreign Policy*, Boston, Allen and Unwin, 450p.
Rosenau, James N. (1969), *Linkage Politics: Essays on the Convergence of National and International Systems*, New York, The Free Press, 352p.
Roy, Olivier (1993), 'Sous le turban, la couronne. La politique étrangère', in Olivier Roy, Fariba Adelkhah and Jean-François Bayart, *Thermidor en Iran*, Bruxelles, Éd. Complexe, 139p.
Safieh, Afif (2004), *On Palestinian Diplomacy*, London, Palestinian General Delegation to the UK and the Office of Representation of the PLO to the Holy See, 36p.
Schemeil, Yves (2010), *Introduction à la science politique: objets, methods, résultats*, Paris, Presses de Sciences-Po/Dalloz, 531p.
Schurmann, Franz (1974), *The Logic of World Power: An Inquiry into the Origins, Currents, and Contradictions of World Politics*, New York, Pantheon Books, Random House, 593p.
Seliger, Martin (1976), *Ideology and Politics*, New York: Free Press, 352p.
Snyder, Richard C., Bruck, Henry W. and Burton, Sapin (1962), *Foreign Policy Decision Making: An Approach to the Study of International Politics*, New York, Free Press of Glencoe, 286p.
Soldatos, Panayotis (1990), 'An Explanatory Framework for the Study of Federated States as Foreign-Policy Actors', in Hans J. Michelmann and Panayotis Soldatos, *Federalism and International Relations: The Role of Subnational Units*, Oxford, Clarendon Press., 334p.

Starkey, Brigid A. (1992), 'Foreign Policy in the Muslim World: A Dialogue between State and Society', *Political Communication*, vol. 9 (1), pp.31–45.
Taylor, Philip. (1984), *Non-State Actors in International Politics. From Transregional to Substate Organizatios*, New York, Routledge, 247p.
Tilly, Charles (2004), 'Terror, Terrorism, Terrorists', *Sociological Theory*, vol. 22 (1), pp.5–13.
Vatikiotis, Philip J. (1965), 'Islam and Foreign Policy in Egypt', in J. Harris, *Islam and International Relations*, London, Pall Mall Press.
Walt, Stephen M. (1990), *The Origins of Alliances*, London, Cornell University Press, 336p.
Walter, Barbara F. and Kydd, Andrew (2002), 'Sabotaging the Peace: The Politics of Extremist Violence', *International Organization*, vol. 56 (2), pp.263–93.
Weber, Max (2003), *Le savant et le politique*, Paris, La Découverte, 210p.
Weber, Max (1971), *Economie et société*, Paris, Plon.

Works and Articles Focusing on Palestine and Hamas

Abu Amer, Adnan (2011), *Iranian Influence in the Gaza Strip, Evidence and Implications*, Jerusalem, Friedrich Ebert Stiftung, 40p.
Abu Amr, Ziad (1994), *Islamic Fundamentalism in the West Bank and Gaza: Muslim Brotherhood and Islamic Jihad*, Bloomington and Indianapolis, Indiana University Press, 192p.
Abu Amr, Ziad (1993), 'Hamas: A Historical and Political Background', *Journal of Palestine Studies*, vol. 22 (4), pp.5–19.
Aclimandos, Tewfik (2009), 'La onzième plaie d'Egypte', *Outre-Terre*, vol. 22 (2), pp.159–66.
Ahmad, Hisham H. (1994), *From Religious Salvation to Political Transformation: The Rise of Hamas in Palestinian Society*, Jerusalem, PASSIA (Palestinian Academic Society for the Study of International Affairs).
Al-Awaisi, Abd al-Fattah Muhammad (1998), *The Muslim Brothers and the Palestine Question, 1928–1947*, London/New York, I.B. Tauris, 256p.
Alhaj, Wissam, Rebillard, Eugénie and Dot-Pouillard, Nicolas (2014), *De la théologie à la liberation? Histoire du Jihad Islamique Palestinien*, Paris, La Découverte.
Alhaj, Wissam and Dot-Pouillard, Nicolas (2015), 'Pourquoi le Hamas et le Hezbollah restent quand même alliés?', *Orient Xxi*. online: https://orientxxi.info/magazine/pourquoi-le-hamas-et-le-hezbollah-restent-quand-meme-allies,0831
Baconi, Tareq (2018), *Hamas Contained. The Rise and Pacification of Palestinian Resistance*, Stanford, Stanford University Press, 368p.
Balawi, Hassan (2008), *Dans les coulisses du movement national palestinien*, Paris, Denoël, 208p.
Barghouti, Iyad (1996), 'Islamist Movements in Historical Palestine', in Abdel Salam Sidahmed and Anoushiravan Ehteshami, *Islamic Fundamentalism*, Boulder/Oxford, Westview Press, 304.
Blumenthal, Max (2014), 'Politicide in Gaza: How Israel's Far Right won the War', *Journal of Palestine Studies*, vol. 44 (1), pp.14–28.
Brenner, Björn (2017), *Gaza Under Hamas. From Islamic Democracy to Islamist Governance*, London, I.B.Tauris, 251p.

Brown, Nathan J. (2010), 'Principled or Stubborn? Western Policy towards Hamas', *The International Spectator*, vol. 43 (4), pp.73–87.
Brown, Nathan J. (2011), *Palestine: The Fire Next Time?*, Washington, Carnegie Endowment for International Peace, 6 July.
Brown, Nathan J. (2012), *Gaza Five Years On: Hamas Settles In*, Washington, Carnegie Endowment for International Peace, 11 June.
Bucaille, Laetitia (2003), 'L'impossible stratégie palestinienne du martyre: Victimisation et attentat suicide', *Critique Internationale*, vol. 20 (3), pp.117–34.
Carré, Olivier (1972), *L'idéologie palestinienne de résistance*, Paris, Presses de Sciences Po, 276p.
Caridi, PAOLA (2010), *Hamas, from Resistance to Government?*, Jerusalem, PASSIA (Palestinian Academic Society for the Study of International Affairs), 416p.
Chehab, Zaki (2007), *Inside Hamas, The Untold Story of Militants, Martyrs and Spies*, London, I.B. Tauris, 240p.
Cohen, Ammon (1982), *Political Parties in the West Bank Under the Jordanian Regime, 1949–1967*. London, Cornell University Press, 344p.
Danino, Olivier (2009), *Le Hamas et l'édification de l'Etat palestinien*, Paris, Karthala, 300p.
Dot-Pouillard, Nicolas (2013), 'Les Palestiniens déchirés par la crise syrienne', *Orient Xxi*. https://orientxxi.info/magazine/les-palestiniens-dechires-par-la-crise-syrienne,0389
Dot-Pouillard, Nicolas (2015), 'Yarmouk, divisions palestiniennes face à l'organisation de l'Etat islamique', *Orient Xxi*. https://orientxxi.info/magazine/yarmouk-divisions-palestiniennes-face-a-l-organisation-de-l-etat-islamique,0870
Dot-Pouillard, Nicolas (2021), 'Tremblement de terre pour le mouvement national palestinien', *Orient Xxi*. https://orientxxi.info/magazine/tremblement-de-terre-pour-le-mouvement-national-palestinien,4787
Dunning, Tristan (2015), 'Islam and Resistance: Hamas Ideology and Islamic Values in Palestine', *Critical Studies on Terrorism*, vol. 8 (2), pp.284–305.
Egre, Anne Laure (2008–2009), *Le recours à la violence par le Hamas à l'aune de l'offensive israélienne sur Gaza pendant l'hiver 2008–2009*, Masters in International Relations, University of Paris I Panthéon-Sorbonne.
Enderlin, Charles (2009), *Le grand aveuglement: Israel et l'irrésistible ascension de l'Islam radical*, Paris, Albin Michel, 384p.
Feldman, Ilana (2015), *Police encounters: Security and Surveillance in Gaza Under Egyptian Rule*, Stanford: Stanford University Press, 224p.
Filiu, Jean-Pierre (2014a), *Gaza: A History*, London, Oxford University Press, 424p.
Filiu, Jean-Pierre (2014b), 'The Twelve Wars on Gaza', *Journal of Palestine Studies*, vol. 44 (1), pp.52–60.
Goerzig, Carolin (2010), 'Transforming the Quartet Principles: Hamas and the Peace Process', Occasional Paper, Vol. 85, Published by the European Union Institute for Security Studies, Paris, 32p., Western European Union (Print) available online: https://op.europa.eu/en/publication-detail/-/publication/b86a44a9-6cfb-47fe-a4ee-e3ce62ab5441/language-en
Gunning, Jeroen (2007), *Hamas in Politics: Democracy, Religion Violence*, London, Hurst and Company, 320p.
Halevi, Jonathan D. (2011), 'Power Dynamics inside Hamas: The Increasing weight of the Gaza Leadership', *Jerusalem Center for Public Affairs*, vol. II (4), 16 June.
Hamed, Qossay (2021), 'The Constant and Variable in the Ideology of Hamas (2006–2018)', Thèse de science politique, Université de Bordeaux, sous la direction de Laetitia Bucaille.

Hatina, Meir (1997), 'Iran and the Palestinian Islamic Movement', *Orient*, vol. 38 (1), pp.107–20.
Hatina, Meir (1999), 'Hamas and the Oslo Accords: religious Dogma in a Changing Political Reality', *Mediterranean Politics*, vol. 4 (3), pp.37–55.
Helfont, Tally (2010), 'Egypt's Wall with Gaza and the Emergence of a New Middle East Alignment', *Orbis*, vol. 54 (3), pp.426–40.
Herzog, Michael (2006), 'Can Hamas be Tamed?', *Foreign Affairs*, vol. 85 (2), p.83.
Hijazi, Mohammad (2011), 'Hamas Movement between Partnership and Individualism', *Institute for Palestine Studies*, vol. 22 (87), p.59.
Hovdenak, Are, (2009), 'Hamas in Transition: The Failure of Sanctions', *Democratization*, vol. 16 (1), pp.59–80.
Hovdenak, Are (2010), 'The Public Services under Hamas in Gaza: Islamic Revolution or Crisis Management? ', Prio Report, 3. Oslo: PRIO.
Hroub, Khaled (2000), *Hamas: Political Thought and Practice*, Washington: Institute for Palestine Studies, 329p.
Hroub, Khaled (2004), 'Hamas after Shaykh Yasin and Rantisi', *Journal of Palestinian Studies*, vol. 33 (4), pp.21–38.
Hroub, Khaled (2006a), *Hamas, a Beginner's Guide*, London, Pluto Press, 224p.
Hroub, Khaled (2006b), 'A "new" Hamas through its New Documents', *Journal of Palestine Studies*, vol. 35 (4), pp.6–27.
Hroub, Khaled (2008), 'Conflating National Liberation and Socio-Political Change', *The International Spectator*, vol. 43 (4), pp.59–72.
Hroub, Khaled (2017), 'A Newer Hamas? The Revised Charter', *Journal of Palestine Studies*, 46, pp.100–11.
Jaradat, Muhammad (1992), 'Islamic Resistance Movement (Hamas) in the Territories Occupied in 1967', *News From Within*, vol. 8 (8), August issue.
Jarbawi, Ali (2005), 'Le Hamas, un parti politique pragmatique', *Confluences Méditerranée*, vol. 4 (55), pp.105–12.
Jensen, Michael I. (2009), *The Political ideology of Hamas: A Grassroots Perspective*, London/New York, I.B. Tauris, 240p.
Karmon, Ely (2009), 'Gaza/Hamastan, plateforme de déstabilisation du monde arabe par l'Iran', *Outre-Terre: revue française de géopolitique*, vol. 22 (2), pp.41–53.
Khalidi, Rashid (1985), *Under Siege: PLO Decision Making during the 1982 War*, New York, Columbia University Press, 241p.
Klein, Menachem (2007), 'Hamas in Power', *Middle-East Journal*, vol. 61 (3), pp.442–59.
Kristianasen, Wendy (1999), 'Challenge and Counterchallenge: Hamas' Response to Oslo', *Journal of Palestine Studies*, vol. 28 (3), pp.19–36.
Legrain, Jean-François (1991a), 'A Defining Moment: Palestinian Islamic Fundamentalism', in James Piscatori, *Islamic fundamentalisms and the Gulf crisis*, Chicago, American Academy of Arts and Sciences.
Legrain, Jean-François (1991b), *Les voix du soulèvement palestinien, 1987–1988*, Cairo, Dossier du CEDEJ, Centre d'Études et de Documentation Economique, Juridique et Sociale.
Legrain, Jean-François (1997), 'Hamas: Legitimate Heir of Palestinian Nationalism?', in John Esposito, *Political Islam: Revolution, Radicalism, or Reform?*, Boulder/Colorado, Lynne Rienner, 310p.
Legrain, Jean-François (2007a), 'L'impasse politique et institutionnelle palestinienne', *Critique Internationale*, vol. 36 (July–September), additional documents available online.

Legrain, Jean-François (2007b), 'La dynamique de la "guerre civile" en Palestine', *Critique Internationale*, vol. 36, pp.147–65.

Legrain, Jean-François (2009), 'Pour une autre lecture de la guerre de Gaza', EchoGéo, Sur le Vif, available online: https://journals.openedition.org/echogeo/10901.

Legrain, Jean-François (2010), *Palestine: un État? Quel État?*, Paris, Notes de l'IFRI, Janvier issue.

Legrain, Jean-François (2013), 'Gaza, novembre 2012: une 'victoire' de Hamas pour quoi faire?', *Carnets de l'IREMAM*, 3 February, [En ligne] http://iremam.hypotheses.org/1835

Legrain, Jean-François (2017), 'Le 'Document' de Hamas (2017) ou l'ouverture comme garante des invariants', *Carnets de l'IREMAM*, Open Edition, 2020. ⟨hal-02941056⟩

Levitt, Matthew (2006), *Hamas, Politics, Charity and Terrorism in the Service of Jihad*, New Haven/London: Yale University Press, 336 p.

Litvak, Meir (1998), 'The Islamization of the Palestinian-Israeli Conflict', *Middle Eastern Studies*, vol. 34 (1), pp.148–63.

Long, Baudouin (2010). 'The Hamas Agenda: How Has It Changed?', *Middle East policy*, vol. 17 (4), pp.131–43.

Mcgeough, Paul (2009), *Kill Khalid: The Failed Mossad Assassination of Khalid Mishal and the Rise of Hamas*, New York, New Press, 464p.

Malka, Haim (2005), 'Forcing Choices: testing the Transformation of Hamas', *The Washington quarterly*, vol. 28 (4), pp.37–53.

Mayer, Thomas (1990), 'Pro-Iranian Fundamentalism in Gaza', in Emmanuel Sivan and Menachem Friedman, *Religious Radicalism and Politics in the Middle East*, Albany, State University of New York Press, 254p.

Milton-Edwards, Beverley (1992), 'The Concept of Jihad and the Palestinian Islamic Movement: A Comparison of Ideas and Techniques', *British Journal of Middle Eastern Studies*, vol. 19 (1), pp.48–53.

Milton-Edwards, Beverley (1996a), 'Political Islam in Palestine in an Environment of Peace?', *Third World Quarterly*, vol. 17 (2), pp.199–226.

Milton-Edwards, Beverley (1996b), *Islamic Politics in Palestine*, London, I.B. Tauris, 272p.

Milton-Edwards, Beverley (2006), 'Political Islam and the Palestinian-Israeli Conflict', *Israel Affairs*, vol. 12 (1), pp.65–85.

Milton-Edwards, Beverley (2008a), 'The Ascendance of Political Islam: Hamas and its Consolidation in the Gaza Strip', *Third World Quarterly*, vol. 29 (8), pp.1585–99.

Milton-Edwards, Beverley (2008b), 'Order without Law? An Anatomy of Hamas Security: The Executive Force (*Tanfithya*)', *International Peacekeeping*, vo. 15 (5), pp.663–76.

Milton-Edwards, Beverley and Crooke, Alastaire (2004), 'Elusive Ingredient: Hamas and the Peace Process', *Journal of Palestinian Studies*, vol. 33 (4), pp.39–52.

Milton-Edwards, Beverley and Farrell, Stephen, (2010), *Hamas: The Islamic Resistance Movement*, Cambridge: Polity Press, 340p.

Mishal, Shaul (2003), 'The Pragmatic Dimension of the Palestinian Hamas: A Network Perspective', *Armed Forces and Society*, vol. 29 (4), pp.569–89.

Mishal, Shaul and Sela, Avraham (2000 and update 2006), *The Palestinian Hamas: Vision, Violence, and Coexistence*, New York, Columbia University Press.

Mishal, Shaul and Sela, Avraham (2002), 'Participation without Presence, Hamas, The Palestinian Authority and the Politics of Negotiated Coexistence', *Middle Eastern Studies*, vol. 38 (3), pp.1–26.

Monshipouri, Mahmood (1996), 'The PLO Rivalry with Hamas: The Challenge of Peace, Democratization and Islamic Radicalism', *Middle East Policy*, vol. 4 (3), pp.84–105.

Mukhimer, Tariq (2012), *Hamas Rule in Gaza: Human Rights under Constraint*, Basingstoke, Palgrave Macmillan.
Muslih, Muhammad (1999), *The Foreign Policy of Hamas*, New York, Council on Foreign Relations.
Nofal, Mamdouh (1995), 'La crise entre l'Autorité nationale et l'OLP', *Revue d'études palestiniennes*, vol. 56 (4), p.3.
Nüsse, Andrea (1998), *Muslim Palestine: The Ideology of Hamas*, Amsterdam, Harwood Academic Publishers, 204p.
Picaudou, Nadine and Rivoal, Isabelle (ed.) (2006), *Retours en Palestine. Trajectoires, rôles et expériences des returnees dans la société palestinienne après Oslo*, Paris, Karthala, 289p.
Rabbani, Mouin (2008), 'Interview Part I – and Part II, Khalid Mishal: The Making of a Palestinian Islamic Leader', *Journal of Palestine Studies*, vol. 37 (3) and (4), pp.59–81.
Rashad, Ahmad (1993), *Hamas: Palestinian Politics with an Islamic Hue*, Occasional Paper serie n°2, Springfield, VA: United Association for Studies and Research.
Roy, Sara (2007), *Failing Peace: Gaza and the Palestinian-Israeli Conflict*, London, Pluto Press.
Roy, Sara (2009), 'If Gaza Falls…', *London Review of Books*, vol. 31 (1), 1447 words.
Roy, Sara (2011), *Hamas and Civil Society in Gaza*, Princeton: Princeton University Press.
Sayigh, Yezid (2010), '"Hamas Rule in Gaza: Three Years On", Brandeis University, Crown Center for Middle East Studies', *Middle East Brief*, vol. 41, March issue, 8 p.
Sayigh, Yezid (2011a), *Policing the People, Building the State: Authoritarian Transformation in the West Bank and Gaza*, Washington: Carnegie Endowment for International Peace, February issue.
Sayigh, Yezid (2011b), '"We Serve the People": Hamas Policing in Gaza', *Brandeis University, Crown Center for Middle East Studies*, vol. 5, pp.177.
Seurat, Leila (2014), 'L'Égypte étend la "guerre contre le terrorisme" à Gaza', *Orient Xxi*.
Seurat, Leila (2017), 'Révolution dans la révolution au Hamas', *Orient Xxi*.
Seurat, Leila and Bonnefoy, Laurent (2018), 'Les islamistes dans les relations internationales. Des acteurs transnationaux comme les autres?" in D. Allès, R. Malejacq and S. Paquin, *Un monde fragmenté. Autour de la sociologie des Relations internationales de Bertrand Badie*, Paris, CNRS Éditions, 282p.
Seurat, Leila and Younes, Mohamed (2017), 'Un accord entre le Fatah et le Hamas à l'ombre du parrain égyptien', *Orient Xxi*. https://orientxxi.info/magazine/un-accord-entre-le-fatah-et-le-hamas-a-l-ombre-du-parrain-egyptien,2043
Shakkura, Majdy, 'Le Hamas, de la résistance armée à l'exercice du pouvoir', Thèse de doctorat en science politique, sous la direction de Jean-Paul Chagnollaud, Université de Cergy soutenue le 9 décembre 2012.
Signoles, Aude (2006), *Le Hamas au pouvoir: et après?*, Milan actu, 2006, 112p.
Signoles, Aude (2010), 'Le Hamas, organisation de résistance ou organisation terroriste?', in Corentin Selin (dir), *Résistances, insurrections, guérillas*, Presses Universitaires de Rennes (PUR), pp.55–76.
Silke, Andrew (2007), 'The Impact of 9/11 on Research on Terrorism', in M. Ranstorp (dir.), *Mapping Terrorism Research - State of the Art, Gaps and Future Directions*, Londres, Routledge, 352p.
Singh, Rashmi (2013), *Hamas and Suicide terrorism, Multi-Causal and Multi-Level Approaches*, London, Taylor and Francis, Routledge, 224p.
Susser, Asher (2010), *The Rise of Hamas in Palestine and the Crisis of Secularism in the Arab World*, Brandeis University, Crown Center for Middle East Studies, vol. 1, p.78.

Tamimi, Azzam (2007), *Hamas: A History from Within*, Northampton, Olive Branch Press.
Zuhur, Sherifa (2008), *Hamas and Israel: Conflicting Strategies of Group-Based Politics*, Army War College (US), Strategic Studies Institute, US Army War College, Carlisle.

Works and Articles in Arabic focusing on Hamas

Arbaʿ sanawât min al-ʿita raghm a-hiṣâr (2006–2010), 'Four Years of Sacrifice despite the Blockade', *Majlis al-tashrîʿi al-falasṭînî*, 2010, p.367.
Abû Al-Umrayn, Khâlid (2001), *'Ḥamâs: Ḥarakat al-Muqâwama al-Islâmîya. Juḏuruhâ, Nashʾatuhâ, Fikruhâ al-Siyâsî', ["Hamas: The Movement of Islamic Resistance. Its Roots, Activities and Political Thought"]*, Markaz al-Ḥaḏâra al-ʿArabîya.
Abû ʿAmr, Ziyâd (1992), 'Al-Islaâmiyyûn al-falasṭîniyyūn: taʾadûdîya wal-dîmûqrâṭîya', ['Palestinian Islamists: Pluralism and Democracy'], *Majallat al-dirâsât al-falasṭînîya*, Ramallah, vol. 12, autumn 1992, pp.88–101.
Abû ʿAzza (1992), *Maʿa al-ḥaraka al-islâmiyya fî-l-aqṭâr al-ʿarabîya, ["The Islamist Movement in its Regional Environment"]*, Kuwait, Al Qalam.
Abû Ghanîma, Ziyâd (1985), *Al-ḥaraka al-islâmîya wa qaḏîyat Filasṭîn, ['The Islamist Movement and the Palestinian Cause']*, Amman, Furqan House.
Abû ʿissâ, Wisam (2011), 'Ḥamâs wa Rûsiyâ', ['Hamas and Russia'], *Markaz al-Zayt11 na li-l-dirâsât wa-l-istishârât*, Beirut, p.60.
ʿAbd Al-Raḥman, Aḥmad (2008), 'Ḥamâs khârij al-sirb...wuṣûlan ilâ-l-hudna l-majjânîya', ['Hamas astray from the Right Path...towards Truce without Compensation'], Seyasat, Ramallah, summer, pp.65–70.
Ashniyûr, Râʿid Kamâl Aḥmad (2010), 'Al-taqqarub bayn Îrân wa Ḥamâs: Bayn al-ḍarûra wa-l-khiyâr', ['The Rapprochement between Hamas and Iran: Between Choice and Necessity'], Kânûn al-awwall, Birzeit University.
Ashtiyye, Muḥammad (2000), 'Al-fikr al-siyâsî li-l-ḥarakât al-islâmiyya, tajribat-Miṣr wa-l-Urdun wa Falasṭîn', ['Political thought of Islamist movements: the Egyptian, Jordanian and Palestinian experiments'], *Al-Markaz al-falasṭînî li-l-dirâsât al-iqlîmîya*, pp.140–51.
ʿAduwân, Bîsâm (2007), 'Ḥarakat-Ḥamâs bayn al-huwiyya al-waṭanîya, wa-l-ḥiṭâb al-"aqîdî', ['The Hamas Movement between National Identity and Ideological Discourse'], Seyasat, Ramallah, winter issue, pp.27–41.
Al-Ashhab, Naʿîm (2007), *Imârat-Ḥamâs, ['The Emirate of Hamas']*, Dâr al-tanwîr li-l-nashr wa-l-tarjama wa-l-tawzîʿ, Ramallah, p.91.
Al-Barghûṭî, Iyâd (1992), 'Al-Ḥaraka al-islâmiyya al-filasṭînîya wa-l-niẓâm al-ʿâlamî al-jadîd', ['The Palestinian Islamist Movement and the New World Order'], *Al-Jamʿiya al-Falasṭînîya al-Akâdîmîya li-l-Shuʾûn al-Dawlîya*, Jerusalem.
Al-Barghûṭî, Iyâd (1997), *Jawâd al-Ḥamad, Ḥamâs 1987–1996, ['The Political Thought of Hamas']*, Markaz dirâsât al-sharq al-awsaṭ, Nablus.
Al-Fallûjî, ʿImâd (2002), *Darb al-achouak, Ḥamâs, al-Intifâḍa, al-Sulṭa, ['The Thorny Path, Hamas, Intifada and the Authority']*, Dâr al-Shurûq li-l-nashr wa-l-tawzîʿ, Ramallah.
Al-Ḥâjj, Muḥammad Yûsuf (2008), 'Al-ḥirak al-fouqhi fî-l-aḥdâṯ allatî aʿqabat intiqâl Ḥamâs min muʿâraḍat-al-sulṭa ila-l-inḥirâṭ fîhi', ['Religious Polemics following Hamas' Transition from Opposition to Power'], *Tasâmuḥ*, vol. 20, March issue, pp.9–21.
Al-Jarbâwî, ʿAlî (1989), 'Al-Intifâḍa wa-l-qiyâda al-siyâsiyya fî-l-ḍiffa al-gharbîya wa qiṭâʿ Ghazza', ['The Intifada and the Political Leadership in the West Bank and the Gaza Strip'], *Dâr al-ṭalîʿa*, Beirut, p.175.

Al-Kayyâlî, ʿAbd al-Ḥamîd (2009), *Dirâsa fî-l-ʿaduwan al-isrâʾilî ʿalâ qiṭâʿ Ghazza*, [*'On the Israeli Aggression in the Gaza Strip'*] Markaz al-Zaytûna li-l-dirâsât wa-l-istishârât, Beyrouth.

Al-Kîlînî (1995), *Al-ḥaraka al-islâmîya fî-l-Urdun wa-Falasṭîn*, [*'The Islamist Movement in Jordan and Palestine'*], Amman, Al-Risala Institute.

Al-Madhûn, Rabʿî (1988), 'Al-ḥaraka al-islâmîya fî Falasṭîn 1928–1987', ['The Islamist Movement in Palestine 1928-1987'], *Shuʾûn Falasṭînîya*, vol. 187, October issue, pp.21–37.

Al-Nawâtî, Aḥmad (2002), *Hamâs min al-dâkhil*, [*'Hamas from Inside'*], Dâr al-Shurûq li-l-nashr wa-l-tawzîʿ, Gaza, p.247.

Al-Shîkâkî, Fatḥî (1979), *Al-Khumaynî: al-ḥâl al-islâmî wa-l-badîl*, [*'Khomeini, the Islamic Solution and its Alternative'*], Dâr al-mukhtâr al-islâmî.

Al-Zubaidî, Bâsim (2010), 'Hamâs wa-l-hukûm, dukhûl al-niẓâm am al-tamarrûd ʿalayhi?', [*'Hamas and Participation or Boycott?'*], Palestinian Center for Policy and Survey, p.184.

Bakr Abû Bakr (2008), *Ḥamâs, suyûf wa manâbir*, [*'Hamas, Pulpits and Swords'*], Dâr al-Shurûq li-l-nashr wa-l-tawzîʿ, Ramallah, p.180.

Bilqzîz, ʿABD Allâh (2006), 'Azmat-al-mashrûʿ al-waṭanî al-falasṭînî, min Fataḥ ila Ḥamas', ['The Crisis of the Palestinian National Project, from Fatah to Hamas'], *Markaz dirâsât al-waḥda al ʿarabîya*, pp.93–123.

Ghûshê, Ibrâhîm (2008), *Al-Miʾdina al-ḥamrâʾ*, [*'The Red City'*], autobiography, Markaz al-Zaytûna li-l-dirâsât wa-l-istishârât, Beirut, p.343.

Ḥijâzî, Muḥammad (2008), 'Madkhal li-qirâʾa tajribat-Ḥamâs fî-l-ḥukm', ['On the Experience of Hamas in Power'], *Awrâq falasṭînîya*, vol. 2, summer issue, pp.99–115.

Jamʿa, Muḥammad (2007), 'Al-Azma al-falasṭînîya wa ʿilâqât-Ḥamâs al-iqlîmîya', ["The Palestinian Crisis and Hamas' Regional Relations], *Al-Siyâsat al-dawlîya*, vol. 42, October issue, pp.138–41.

Majdî Najm, Muḥammad ʿÎsâ (2007), *Al-Mushâraka al-siyâsîya li-ḥarakat-Ḥamâs fî-l-niẓâm al-siyâsî al-falasṭînî, mâ bayn al-tamassuk al-îdiyûlûjî wa al-bragmâtîya al-siyâsîya*, [*The Participation of Hamas in the Palestinian Political Regime: Between Ideological Adherence and Political Pragmatism*], Birzeit University.

Mashâqî, Munḏir (2010), 'Al-Ṯâbit wa al-mutaghayyir fî khiṭâb Ḥamâs, mâ qabl al-intikhâbât 2006 wa mâ baʿd', ['Continuities and Changes in the Discourse of Hamas, before and after the 2006 Elections'], *Tasâmuḥ*, vol. 28, pp.57–75.

Maṣlaḥ, Aḥmad (2007), 'Al-sayṭara al-ʿaskarîya li-Ḥamâs ʿala qiṭâʿ Ghazza', [*'The Military Domination of Hamas in the Gaza Strip'*], Seyasat, Ramallah, pp.65–70.

Ṣâfî, Khâlid (2007), 'Ittifâq Makka: wâqiʿ wa tahdîya', [*'The Mecca Agreement: Realities and Challenges'*], Seyasat, Ramallah, pp.43–51.

INDEX

9/11 attacks 141, 237
1979 revolution 24
1988 Charter 13, 14, 16–18, 17 n.80, 39, 62

Abbas, Mahmoud 2, 13, 32, 34, 35, 48, 48 n.12, 50, 56–63, 71, 85, 107, 109, 110, 117, 118, 123, 124, 133–8, 134 n.84, 144, 146–54, 156, 158, 161, 173, 176, 188–90, 199, 204, 204 n.36, 205, 207–9, 215, 222, 229, 232, 239, 241, 242
Abdullah (king) 71, 81, 132, 187
Abdullah II (king) 77
Abou al-Gheit, Ahmad 70, 102, 116, 223
Abou Aysh, Ammar 60 n.54
Abou Eisheh, Samir 36, 252
Abou Mazen. *See* Abbas, Mahmoud
Abou Musameh, Sayyid 37, 48 n.11, 67, 79, 103
Abou Shamala, Mohammed Ibrahim 61, 105
Abou Zouhri, Sami 102, 167, 181
Abu Ammar. *See* Arafat, Yasser
Abu Marzouk, Moussa 9, 16, 28, 29, 31, 36, 47, 49, 54, 67, 68, 75 n.49, 77, 83, 85, 99, 100, 104, 126, 131, 132, 196, 210, 212, 213, 219, 221, 229, 230, 235, 254–5
Abu Musameh, Sayed 248–9
Abusada, Mkhaimer 218
al-Achqar, Ismail 121
al-Adli, Habib 70
Agency for National Security 140
agreement (*taswîya*) 77, 180, 202
al-Ahmad, Azzam 58, 71, 222, 222 n.53, 230
Ahmadinejad, Mahmoud 74, 75, 95, 96, 180, 185
Akef, Mahdi 11, 102, 127, 181–2, 188, 225

Aknaf Beit al-Maqdis Brigades 94 n.39
al-Ahram 41, 93, 105, 190
al-Akhbar 167, 212
al-Alami, Imad 9, 197, 206, 213, 255
al-Aqsa Mosque 239, 252, 257
al-Aqsa TV 41, 56, 251
Alaraby TV 85
Alawi community 179, 180
Al-Ayyam 160
al-Azhar Islamic institution 177
al-Azhar mosque 93
al-Azhar University 77, 126
Aleppo bombings (2016) 99
Algiers summit (1988) 155
al-Hayat al-Jadida 41, 228, 229
Ali Mustafa Brigades 61
al-Jazeera TV 46, 54, 73, 184
Allison, Graham 27, 201
al-Masri al-Youm 41, 227
al-Mayadeen 94, 98
al-Nosra 95
al-Qaeda 95, 106, 107, 138, 163, 181
al-Qassam mortar shells 54
al-Qods Brigades 167
al-Quds al-Arabi 41, 218
al-Quds Brigades 164, 166, 168
al-Ramel camp 92
Alresalah 41, 81, 159, 203, 203 n.27
Al-Sharq al-Awsat 41, 54 n.39
al-Shourouk 105
al-Watan 55
al-Zaytouna 40
Amer, Adnan Abu 212, 214, 215
Amer, Ziad Abu 117, 153 n.90
American State Department 85
American-Zionist conspiracy 181
Annapolis summit (2007) 148, 157
Annex II, of Declaration of Principles 150 n.75
Ansar al-Jihad Egyptian armed group 106

anti-Brotherhood media campaign   105
anti-Egyptian campaign   177
anti-imperialist struggle   185
anti-Iranian campaign   190
anti-normalization symposium   85
anti-Shia orientation   178
Apartheid   243
appeasement (*tahdîya*)   54, 87, 140
appropriation (*tafarrud*)   209
Aqel, Ashraf   72
Arab countries   31, 66, 78, 115–17, 121, 122, 129, 158, 183, 186
al-Arabi, Nabil   90
Arab League   90, 116, 125, 128
Arab League Summit (2009)   75, 159
Arab Parliamentary Federation   71
Arab Parliamentary Union   78
Arab revolutions   103, 214, 225
Arab Spring   34, 55–61, 66, 76–81, 115, 125, 173, 182, 186, 187, 213, 214, 220, 228, 233
  2011   31, 32
  2012   120
Arab States   16, 21, 22, 39, 40, 70, 184, 189, 206, 225
Arab support and Hamas   128–9
Arab uprisings   66, 121, 175
Arafat, Moussa   137 n.2
Arafat, Yasser   8, 17, 30, 32, 107, 144 n.44, 145, 156, 214, 240
armed struggle   3, 6–8, 17, 20, 32, 39, 46, 51, 52, 57, 123, 124, 136, 149, 150, 164–6, 169, 193, 193 n.25, 194, 200, 233, 244
Arouri, Salah   2
al-Arouri, Salah   60, 60 n.54, 67, 82–5, 100, 241, 253–4
al-Ashkar, Ismail   103
al-Ashqar, Omar   78
al-Assad, Bashar   36, 69, 88–100, 125, 126, 131, 176, 180, 185, 224, 243
al-Assad, Hafez   10, 87, 88, 223
Assaf, Ahmad   222
Assembly for Strategic Affairs   83
al-Ata, Abu   168
al-Attar, Raed   61, 105
Atzi, Mohammed   166
authority (*Ṣulṭa*)   15

Awad, Mohammed   76, 120, 121, 146, 153
Awadallah, Nizar   207, 208
Ayyash, Yahya   8
al-Azhar, Mahmoud   227

Baathism   24
Baathists   6
Baconi, Tareq   189
Badie, Bertrand   12, 159, 188
Badie, Mohammed   78, 104, 109 n.123, 127, 225–6
Badran, Hussam   39, 83, 258
Bahar, Ahmad   71, 71 n.29, 73, 74, 78–80, 128, 184, 248
Baker, James   214
Bakr, Ahmad   72
Balawi, Hassan   147
al-Banat, Khaled   162, 162 n.144, 203
Ban Ki-Moon   82
al-Banna, Hassan   5
Barak, Ehud   58
Baraka, Rajah   73 n.36
Barakat, Ali   97
Barakat, Hisham   109, 109 n.123
al-Bardawil, Salah   73 n.36, 90, 93, 231
al-Barghouti, Marwan   56, 147
Barhoum, Fawzi   54, 102, 148, 223
al-Bashir, Omar   73
Basic Law (2003)   46
Baskin, Gershon   55, 58
Battalions of Justice   6
Battle of al-Qusayr (2013)   93, 96, 132, 224
Battle of the Camel (2011)   105
al-Bayanouni, Ali Sadr al-Din   88, 90
Beirut   77, 85, 94, 97, 132, 214, 241, 254, 256
Benkirane, Abd al-Ilah   78
Benn, Aluf   58
Bennett, Naphtali   244
Berry, Nabih   86
Biden, Joe   243
bilateral meetings   59, 66, 74, 75, 110
Bin Mohammed, Mahathir   84
al-Bitawi, Hamid   36, 252
Blair, Tony   82
Bogdanov, Mikhail   83
Brecher, Michael   215
Brown, Nathan   124, 217, 219

Cairo 2, 33, 40, 83, 84, 87, 100, 102–4, 107–9, 111, 123, 127, 133, 134, 188, 189, 242
  and Hamas 181
  reconciliation agreements of Doha and 56–7
Cairo Agreement 161, 205, 209, 215, 216, 221, 227
  2005 17, 32, 47, 47 n.8, 61, 133–5, 156
  2011 17, 124, 133, 180, 196, 198, 207, 228
Camp David Agreement (1978) 58
Camp David negotiation (2000) 9
Caridi, Paola 199
Carter, Jimmy 74, 221
'Cast lead' 53–4, 60, 73, 75, 76, 95, 102, 123, 148, 157, 162, 169, 170, 176, 182, 204, 213
cease-fire (*waqf itlâq an-nâr*) 54, 61, 74, 108, 170
Center for Mediterranean Integration (CMI) 37
'Change and Reform' group 71
China 70
Civilian Defence (*al-difâ' al-madanî*) 140
civilian police (*shurta*) 140
civil rights 244
civil society 128
civil war 85, 93, 206
Clinton, Bill 53
Cold War 24
collective decisions 199–203
  consultation to reach truce 200–2
  divergences of interest 202–3
  Prisoners' Document 199–200
colonization 8, 169
Communist militants 6
complementarity (*takammul*) 119
Congress for the Right of Return 153
Conrad, Gerhard 55
Conricus, Jonathan 168
consensus (*ijmâ'*) 197
consultative assembly (*majlis al-shûrâ*) 229, 229 n.86
Consultative Body (*majlis ash-shûrâ*) 197
consultative process (*mushâwara*) 197
controversy (*jidal*) 209

Corriere della sera 68
Council on International Relations 40
coup (*inqilâb*) 34, 50, 117, 222, 241
Covid-19 pandemic 1, 39, 65, 85, 111

Dahab attack (2006) 70
Dahlan, Mohammed 109, 110, 137 n.2, 188
Damascus 27, 36, 54, 66, 69, 80, 87–92, 96, 100, 116, 119, 125, 126, 136, 140, 157, 166, 180, 195, 206, 220, 221, 234, 243
Daraghmeh, Ayman 35, 229
Daraghmeh, Mohammed 198, 201, 213, 219, 224
Daroubi, Melhem 94
Davutoglu, Ahmet 80, 81
day of commemoration of the Naksa 92
'Deal of the Century' American project 85
decision-making 226
  centres 196, 208, 209, 211, 216
  process 26–8, 31, 33, 35, 149, 192, 195–6, 198, 202, 209, 211–15, 234
Declaration of Independence of the Palestinian National Council (1988) 12, 12 n.51, 50
de facto recognition 50
al-Deif, Mohammed 61, 98, 165, 240, 245
de la Messuzière, Yves Aubin 53
democratization 69
Dera'a uprising (2011) 36, 90
Desagneaux, Frédéric 37
de Soto, Alvaro 199
DFLP 126
Diaspora Palestinians 28, 29, 39, 153, 199, 241
dignity (*karâma*) 186
diktats 177, 182
Dimertis, Idir 74 n.41
diplomacy of demarcation 143–6
diplomatic recognition 115–22
diplomatic visits 70, 71, 115, 128
Diskin, Yuval 163
dissent causes
  alignments and realignments 228–31
  Gaza and decision-making process 211–15

Gaza leadership strengthening 217–20
  Mesh'al and al-Zahar 226–8
  outside pressure before 2011 220–3
  power in Gaza 215–17
  pressure after 2011 224–6
dissociation, principle of 146
division (*inqisâm*) 34, 50, 117, 154
Djalili, Mohammed-Reza 24
Document of General Principles and
  Policies (2017) 11, 14, 17, 38, 39,
  61–3, 233
Document of National Entente 49
Doha 29, 31, 34, 57, 79, 82, 83, 98, 115,
  161, 209, 236
Doha Agreement (2012) 17, 31, 37, 125,
  126, 131, 133, 198, 205, 208, 210,
  215, 216, 218, 221, 224–6, 228–31,
  234–5
Dughmush family 137, 138
Dukhan, Abd al-Fattah 7
Dunning, Tristan 26
duty (*wâjib*) 170
Dweik, Aziz 36, 49, 59, 71 n.29, 72, 74,
  78, 253

East Jerusalem 5, 239
Egypt 2, 35, 45, 50 n.21, 51, 53–5, 58,
  61, 64, 81, 83, 84, 91, 94, 104, 115,
  122, 124, 125, 127–9, 133–5, 145,
  147 n.57, 173, 176, 180, 181, 183,
  188–90, 206, 216, 220, 224, 225,
  234, 235, 242
Egypt and Hamas 87, 100–11, 161, 182
  anti-Morsi campaign 105–6
  conflictual relationship under
    Mubarak's rule 100–3
  fight against Takfiris 108–9
  involved in Palestinian
    reconciliation 109–11
  limited coordination during Morsi's
    presidency 103–6
  war against terrorism to Gaza 106–8
Egypt(ian)
  administration 87, 107, 116
  security forces 108, 109, 122–3
Egyptian Army 104, 105, 107
Egyptian Association 10, 107
Egyptian Document (2009) 204, 205,
  205 n.38, 227

Egyptian Muslim Brotherhood 10, 11,
  34, 101–4, 107, 108, 123, 124, 127,
  177, 179–81, 188, 232
Egyptian Spring 187
Egyptian Workers' Party 74
al-Emadi, Mohammed 1, 161
Erdogan, Recep Tayyip 78, 84, 85
Europe 68, 120, 131, 197
European Court of Justice 82
European Union (EU) 33, 34, 59, 68, 69,
  72, 82, 125, 129, 133, 242
Executive Force (*al-qiwa
  al-tanfîdîyâ*) 139 n.17, 140

fait accompli (*amr wâqi'*) 50, 122
falatan 137 n.2
Fares, Qaddura 212
Fatah 2, 3, 5–7, 13, 17–19, 21, 30–35,
  45, 47, 48, 50, 50 n.21, 56, 57, 62,
  63, 102, 107, 108, 110, 115, 116,
  126, 130, 133, 134, 136, 137, 143,
  144, 147, 148, 150, 153, 155, 161,
  188–90, 200, 204, 208, 215, 219–22,
  234, 236, 242
  agreements with (2007–2012) 123–5
  Central Committee 205
  and Hamas 2, 17, 35, 48, 62, 102, 150,
    155, 163
  mistakes 144, 145
Fatah-Hamas summit (2007) 223
fawda 137 n.2
Fawzi, Khaled 109
Al Faysal, Saud 69, 132
Fayyad, Salam 51, 139, 148, 161, 176,
  179
Fedayin fighters 237
Filastin al-Muslima 40, 41, 170
al-Filastini, Abou Qatada 137–8
financial management and
  rearmament 140–3
First Intifada (1987) 7, 20, 155, 158, 214
Five Years On 39
Followers of the Islamic State in
  Jerusalem 165
Foreign Affairs of Arab States 70
Foreign Affairs of Gaza 55
Forum for Cooperation 70
Fourth Jerusalem Summit. *See* 'Victory of
  Gaza' (2009)

Fraenkel, Naphtali 59 n.54
France 24, 37
freedom (*hurrîya*) 182
'Free Palestine' flotilla 186
Free Syrian Army 93
fruitless negotiations ('abathîya) 15
Fundamental Law 39, 46, 208
funds/funding 33, 128–31, 140, 242

Galloway, George 74 n.41
Garnier, Paul 82
Gaza government 35, 40, 72, 77, 116–19, 129, 130, 138, 164, 217, 218, 226, 228
Gaza leadership 28–9, 31, 33, 198, 203–5, 208, 211, 224, 226, 228, 234–6
 participation in decision-making process 211–15
 power (*hukûm*) 215–17
 strengthening through Iran alliance 217–20
Gaza Strip 2, 5, 27, 38, 39, 45, 47, 50–4, 59, 63–5, 71, 74, 79–82, 87, 91, 100–3, 105, 106, 110, 113, 115, 116, 118, 126–9, 132, 135, 137, 159, 161, 168, 170, 171, 195, 198, 201, 205, 232
 2012 assault on 149
 2012 'Pillar of Defence' offensive on 57–8
 2014 military assault against 59–61
 and Abbas 133–5
 administrative and financial management 136
 and Arab revolts 183
 Israeli attacks against 202, 239
 Israeli offensive on 16, 34, 73, 150, 188
 Israel's occupation (1956 and 1957) 6
 Israel's withdrawal from 33, 34
 and outside leadership 76–8
 Qatari 'embassy' in 160
 seizure and change in relations 3, 13, 32, 34, 50–4, 66, 122, 190, 192, 203, 211, 212, 240
 siege of 148
 success of Hamas over 146
 war against terrorism to 106–8

Gaza Summit (*qimmat al-Ghazza*). See Arab League Summit (2009)
Gaza War (2008–9) 186, 193, 204 n.36
Geneva Inter-Parliamentary Federation 37
genocide 99
German Federal Intelligence 65
Germany 143
al-Ghannouchi, Rashid 79, 184
al-Gharbi, Anwar 74 n.41
Ghosheh, Ibrahim 9, 22, 255–6
Golan Heights 92, 98
Goldin, Hadar 61, 65
Goldstein, Baruch 8
Goldstone, Richard 204 n.36
Goldstone report 204, 227
good governance and foreign policy 136–43, 193, 194
 planning financial management and rearmament 140–3
 re-establishing order and reforming security system 136–40
Grad missiles 54
Grand Mufti of Jerusalem 5
'Guardians of our Brothers' 59
Guidance Bureau of the Muslim Brothers 225
Gulf Cooperation Council (GCC) 100, 179, 186
Gulf states 2, 99, 129, 132
Gulf War (1991) 8, 28, 144, 178, 214

Haaretz 58
Habib, Mohammed 102
Hadi, Mansour 98
Halevy, Efraim 232
Halperin, Morton H. 216, 227, 228
Hamad, Fathi 41, 132, 193, 206, 228, 251
Hamad, Ghazi 36–7, 41, 55, 58, 70, 97, 118, 120, 132, 133, 154, 158 n.116, 161, 202, 213, 250–1
Hama massacre (1982) 88
Hamas Charter 178
Hamas genesis 5–7
Hamas government 41, 116–17, 124, 137, 153, 154, 170, 202
Hamas MPs 36, 37, 39, 71–2, 120, 121, 145
al-Hamdallah, Rami 58

Hamdan, Osama   36, 38, 81, 83, 88, 89,
    97, 144, 149, 157 n.113, 171, 189,
    197, 198, 200, 203, 220, 223, 241,
    243, 256-7
Haniyeh, Ismail   1, 29, 38, 39, 46, 49, 50,
    58, 65-72, 74, 76, 77, 83-6, 93, 96,
    98, 100, 100 n.75, 111, 117, 118,
    121, 126, 128, 129, 143, 146, 149,
    153, 154, 158, 158 n.116, 161, 162,
    167, 171, 179, 180, 184, 186, 193,
    201, 206, 208, 210, 218, 224, 227,
    230, 231, 235, 240, 242-4, 251-2
Hashemite Kingdom   9, 77, 187
Hatina, Meir   191
al-Hayya, Khalil   61, 83, 84, 99, 207, 208,
    252
Helfont, Tally   176
Hermann, Margaret G.   27, 202
Hezbollah   86, 92-9, 99 n.67, 100, 130,
    132, 133, 136, 196, 198, 205, 206,
    217, 218, 230, 243
al-Hibash, Mahmoud   154
Hijazi, Mohammed   193 n.27, 221
Hill, Christopher   12
al-Hilwa, Ain   86
al-Hindi, Mohammed   167
Hiroshima   144
'historical' Palestine   30
homeland (*watan*)   241
House of Commons   71-2
Hroub, Khaled   4, 14, 20, 22 n.104, 156,
    156 n.106, 191, 199
Hudaybiyya agreement   191
hudna (truce)   15, 16, 30, 32, 45, 46, 58,
    64, 82, 102, 110-11, 136, 142, 143,
    162, 164-6, 168, 170, 173, 183, 188,
    195, 198, 203, 234
    consultation to reach   200-2
    as form of 'resistance'   193-4
    with Israel   204
    June 2008   51-3, 58, 138, 140, 142,
        196, 201-3, 221
    justification in Islamic
        terminology   190-2
humanitarian aid   54, 61, 85
humanitarian disaster   82
human rights   244
Human Rights Watch   74
al-Husseini, Amin   5

'id al-adhâ festival   231
ideology
    concept of   19-23
    in Hamas' foreign policy   169-73
ideology and defence of external
        interests   175-87
    adapting to context   181-5
    adapting to interlocutors   185-7
    concept of 'axes'   175-7
    Islamic significance of Palestinian
        cause   179-80
    providing Islamic justification   177-9
ideology and defence of internal
        interests   188-94
    justification for truce in Islamic
        terminology   190-2
    'resistance front' against
        Abbas   188-90
IDF forces   53, 60 n.54, 61, 64, 65
ikhtisâsât (specialties)   119
al-Imadi, Mohammed   159, 160
imperialism   188, 189
incarceration   27, 28, 78
Independence Declaration   8
informal economy   141 n.27
Institute for Islamic Political
        Thought   215
'The Interim Policy of Hamas and its
        Political Relations'   13-14
Interior Ministry   161, 181
internal elections   11, 29, 31, 38, 66, 83,
    104, 127, 229, 234-6
internal pluralism   195
International Asian Summit for Peace
    (2006)   71
International Congress (2011)   131
International Criminal Court (ICC)   60,
    244
International Crisis Group   215, 216
International Federation of Muslim
        Ulemas   80
international law   17, 233
International Parliamentary
        Federation   120
International Parliamentary Union   79
international relations   2-4, 11, 12, 14,
    24, 40, 88
Intifada   47, 131, 191
Introductory Memorandum   13, 16, 39

Iran   34, 35, 81, 88, 89, 95–100, 115, 126, 129–32, 136, 140, 150, 158, 162, 166, 167, 175, 190, 196, 205, 206, 210, 221–3, 230, 243
  Gaza leadership strengthening through   217–20
  and Hamas   177–80
Iranian Fars Press Agency   98
Iranian Shoura Council   98–9
Iraq   21, 178
Islam   158, 177, 185, 234
Islamic community   185
Islamic Conference Organization   147
Islamic doctrine   13–19, 190, 191
Islamic foreign policy   24
Islamic Forum in Saudi Arabia   70–1
Islamic Jihad   7, 57, 61, 63, 65, 94, 98, 99 n.67, 108, 135, 136, 147, 162, 163 n.145, 164–8, 173, 178, 193, 194
Islamic Jihad and Hamas   22, 57, 61, 63, 164, 165, 167–8, 178
Islamic Republic   22, 29, 30, 34, 74, 81, 95–7, 115, 129, 132, 133, 162, 166, 167, 177–9, 190, 218, 219, 226
Islamic Republic of Iran   87
Islamic Resistance   100
Islamic Revolution   7, 24, 99, 178, 179
Islamic State   94–5, 165
Islamic Summit (2006)   71
Islamic tradition   191
Islamism   181
Islamist factions, control of   162–8
  impossible containment   162–5
  Islamic Jihad   165–8
Islamist movement   19, 21, 33, 45, 51, 59, 60, 63, 81, 105, 117, 122, 143, 156, 162, 178, 187, 193, 232, 236, 240, 244
Islamist parties   124, 125, 184
Islamization   7, 193 n.25
Israel   1, 3, 8, 9, 35, 39, 95, 116, 123, 124, 134, 135, 153, 158, 159, 163–4, 167, 171, 182, 189, 232, 237
  aggression   169, 170
  American weaponry to   243
  conflict with Palestine   110, 158
  deals with PLO   233
  and Islamic Jihad   168
  negotiations with America   60
  relations with Egypt   220

Israel and Hamas   2, 19, 30, 45–65, 82–4, 87, 102, 108, 136, 140, 147–9, 161, 164, 165, 168, 169, 193, 221
  Document of General Principles and Policies and new reconciliation agreement   61–3
  Gaza seizure and change in relations   50–4
  liberation of Shalit   55–6
  March of Return and negotiation and confrontation   63–5
  Mecca Agreement (2007)   48–50, 48 n.13
  military assault against Gaza Strip (2014)   59–61
  National Conciliation Document (Wathîqat al-Wifâq al-watani)   47–8
  'Pillar of Defence' offensive on Gaza (2012)   57–8
  power exercising and imperative of resistance   45–7
  reconciliation agreements of Cairo and Doha   56–7
  resumption of talks on prisoner exchange   65
  Shati reconciliation agreement (2014)   58–9
  tensions between   109–11
Israeli Air Force   57, 64
Israeli Army   8, 170
Israeli F-16 warplane   100
Israeli prisons   27, 36, 130, 195, 198, 199, 215
Israel-Jordan peace treaty (1994)   21
Issa, Marwan   46, 132, 245–6
Izz al-Din al-Qassam Brigades   8, 28–30, 41, 45, 46, 57, 58, 60, 64, 93, 94, 96, 98, 100, 139, 141, 148, 162, 164–7, 173, 188, 192, 202, 203, 206, 208, 214, 218, 224, 226, 230, 236, 239, 241
al-Jaabari, Ahmed   55, 57, 58, 143, 164, 218, 245

Jabr, Tawfiq   139
Jackson, Robert   13
Jalili, Said   75, 185
jaljalât   163
al-Jamil, Abdel Rahman   73 n.36
Jandiyya, Raed   164

Japan 143
al-Jarr, Abou Ubayda 139
Javad, Mohammad 100 n.75
Jaysh al-Islâm group 46, 137, 138, 162 n.141
Jaysh al-Umma 178
Jebali, Hamadi 184
Jerusalem 63, 78, 158, 199, 240, 241
Jerusalem Day 241
Jerusalem Post 159
Jews 17, 169
Jibril, Ahmed 89, 94
Jihadism 165
Johnston, Alan 137, 138
Jordan 6–9, 70, 71, 77, 127
Jordanian Muslim Brothers 9, 10
Jordanian Spring 187
Judaization 78
Judgement Day 171
Jumblatt, Walid 86
Jund Ansâr Allah movement 162, 162 n.141, 163 n.145, 203
Justice and Development Party (AKP) 74, 78, 81, 184, 243

Kamel, Abbas 242
Katiba Square 149
Kaufman, Gerald 74
Kawasme, Marwan 60 n.54
Kerem Shalom attack (2012) 104 n.105, 105, 105 n.107
Kerem Shalom border crossing 1, 110, 135
Kerry, John 59
Khamenei, Ali 22, 75, 83, 95, 131
Khan Younis refugee camp 93
Kharazi, Kamal 22, 83
Khartoum Summit (2006) 128
Khatami, Mohammed 22
Khater, Sami 28, 81
Khawasneh, Awn 77
al-Khodari, Ahmad 65, 168
al-Khoudari, Jamal 79
Khroub, Khaled 51 n.23, 53, 191
Kuala Lumpur 71, 81, 84, 144, 152
Kuala Lumpur Islamic Summit (2019) 84
Kuwait 21, 144, 145, 187

la Messuzière, Yves Aubin de 201
Larijani, Ali 75, 81, 97, 100 n.75, 185

Lavrov, Sergei 83, 85
Lebanese Security Services (*Sûreté Générale*) 86
Lebanese Shia Party 100, 206
Lebanon war (2006) 53
le Drian, Jean-Yves 243
Legrain, Jean-François 217
licit (*halal*) 177
Liddawi, Mustafa 229
Lindemann, Thomas 113, 123
linkage 2, 113, 122, 233
Livni, Tzipi 102
Long, Baudouin 192
'Loyalty of the Free' Agreement 213

Madrid Conference 214
Malley, Robert 53
March of Return (2018) 1, 45, 63–5, 116, 134, 135, 167, 233
marginalization 20, 30, 110
marja'îya (reference) 119
marriage (*nuzâwaja*) 194
martyrdom operations (*istishhâd*) 47
Marzouqi, Moncef 78
Masar Palestinian centre 39
al-Mashal, Tamer 46
Mashru' Dummar 88
al-Masri, Mohammed Diab. *See* Deif, Mohammed
al-Masri, Mouchir 37, 79, 128, 146, 148, 183, 191, 202, 203, 214, 215, 225
al-Masri, Rafiq 163
al-Mazini, Oussam 203
Mecca 102
Mecca Agreement (2006 and 2007) 17, 48–50, 48 n.13, 56, 115, 124, 125, 133, 223
Mechal, Khaled 76
Medvedev, Dimitri 76
Mengistu, Avera Avraham 65
al-Mesh'al, Khaled 9, 10, 17, 18, 28–31, 38, 40, 49, 52, 54, 56, 57, 60 n.55, 61, 62, 66–9, 74–8, 75 n.49, 80–4, 88, 90–102, 104, 109, 119, 124–7, 129, 131, 133, 143, 148, 149, 154, 155, 157–9, 166, 171, 175, 180, 182, 184, 185, 187, 191, 198, 204–13, 215, 218–31, 233, 235, 240, 243, 257
Mesh'al-Larijani meeting (2015) 98
metal border barrier 189, 190, 239

Middle Eastern Greek Orthodoxy   24
'Miles of Smiles 2'   74
military escalation   148–50
Military Intelligence Services   137 n.2
military operations   5, 34, 39, 40, 51, 135, 155, 164, 169
military support   129–31
Mille, Gieri   72
Milton-Edwards, Beverly   142
Minbar al-Islâh   46
Ministry of Foreign Affairs   12, 33, 39, 40, 72, 118, 150–3
Ministry of Planning and International Cooperation   12, 150 n.75
'*mitaqa khadrâ*'   222
Montevideo Convention (1933)   3 n.4, 150 n.75
moral principles and values   20
Morgenthau, Hans J.   113
Morsi, Mohammed   11, 34, 58, 59, 80, 87, 103–9, 126, 127, 133, 184, 219
Moscow   76, 85
Motlanthe, Kgalema   75
Mouslih, Mahmoud   35
Moussa, Abd al-Latif   203
Moussa, Amr   74, 75
Moussa, Fahd   203
Movement of Islamic Resistance   8–12, 36, 60, 62, 89, 99, 103, 106, 108, 155, 159, 179, 180, 183
Mu'allem, Walid   221
Mubarak, Hosni   55, 87, 90, 100–3, 108, 122, 179, 213, 225
Mughniyeh, Imad   98
Mughniyeh, Jihad   98
Mujam'a al-islâmi (Islamic Society)   6
Mukhimer, Tareq   137
municipal elections (2005)   69
Musa, Yahya   47, 48 n.12, 135, 202
Mushtaha, Rawhi   214
Muslih, Mahmoud   25
Muslim Brothers/Brotherhood   5–7, 9–11, 17, 58, 78, 87, 104, 108, 109 n.123, 122, 124, 125, 127, 140, 165, 178–80, 182, 183, 185, 219, 222, 225. *See also* Egyptian Muslim Brotherhood; Jordanian Muslim Brothers; Syrian Muslim Brotherhood
Muslim states (*Dâr al-Salâm*)   14

Nagasaki   144
Naim, Basem   40, 145, 146, 249
Naim, Huda   122, 184, 216, 250
Naim al-Achab   50 n.21
Naji, Talal   89
al-Najjar, Khamis   79
Nakba   3, 63, 79
al-Nakhala, Ziad   167
al-Nashar, Issa   7
Nasr, Mohammed   81, 97
Nasrallah, Hassan   77, 86, 98, 100, 126, 132, 218
Nasser, Gamal Abdel   5, 6
National Assembly   49
National Conciliation Document (*Wathîqat al-Wifâq al-watani*)   17, 39, 47–8, 61–2, 115, 123–5, 156, 195, 196, 199–202, 234
nationalism   23, 237
national liberation   52, 171, 190, 237
national reconciliation   148, 159
National Security Force (*quwat al-amn al-watanî*)   140
National Unified Council   20
national unity government   45, 48, 50, 56, 62, 117, 125, 133, 146, 149, 223, 227, 232
al-Natsheh, Abd al-Khalek   246
al-Nayrab, Kamal   57
Nazzal, Mohammad   9, 77, 102, 119, 202, 203, 256
Netanyahu, Benjamin   2, 55, 61, 135, 150, 164, 239
neutrality   19, 92, 98
Nofal, Ayman   105
Nofal, Mamdouh   151 n.77
non-interference (*tadakhkhul*)   19, 92, 104, 106, 126, 144, 145
non-Muslim states (*Dâr al-Ḥarb*)   14
non-state players   4, 12, 236
al-Nounou, Taher   125, 176
nuclear programme   81, 97
nuzâwaja   194

Obama, Barack   75, 78, 222
Obeida, Abu   202, 203, 239, 242, 246
Occupied Palestinian Territories   3, 8, 20, 22, 23, 28, 32, 85
Olmert, Ehud   50 n.21, 53, 148

Omar, Ilhan 244
Oriental Christians 24
Orient-News 94
Oslo Accords 8–9, 12, 13, 21, 33, 39, 46, 48–50, 150, 151 n.76, 155, 156, 178, 189
'Oslo II' 189

Palestine 5, 61, 180, 182, 188, 189, 201
   factions 3, 32, 47, 56, 57, 59, 63, 64, 94, 102
   foreign policy and political Islam 11–26
   government 45, 73, 83
   and Hamas 184
   and Qatari relationship 79, 184
Palestine Preventive Security (PPS) 137 n.2
Palestinian Authority 2, 3, 12, 13, 30–5, 32 n.154, 45, 47, 57–60, 63, 82, 84, 107, 113, 116, 123, 133–6, 139, 142, 143, 148–55, 159, 176, 208, 209, 216, 217, 235, 242
Palestinian centre for Information communiqués, of Izz al-Din al-Qassam Brigades 55, 57
Palestinian Civilian Police 139
Palestinian Constitution 49
Palestinian Declaration of Independence in Algiers 151
Palestinian Embassy 85
Palestinian Information centre (*Markaz al-filastînî li-l-i'lâm*) 40
Palestinian Islamist movement 4, 127, 181
Palestinian Islamist organization 88
Palestinian Left 3
Palestinian Legislative Council (PLC) 36, 37, 39, 48, 56, 59, 71–4, 73 n.36, 78, 120, 212, 216
Palestinian movement 9, 95, 109, 178
Palestinian MPs arrest 74
Palestinian National Council 49, 155 n.103, 156, 158, 159, 241
Palestinian people 16, 36, 52, 71, 79, 144, 145, 155–7, 169, 186, 209, 241
   resistance 68
   rights 40, 46, 147, 170
Palestinian Presidency 108

Palestinian reconciliation 2, 18, 34, 60, 83, 85, 102, 109–11, 127, 133, 149, 204, 208, 222, 226, 233, 239
   National Conciliation Document (*Wathîqat al-Wifâq al-watani*) and agreements with Fatah (2007–2012) 123–5
   regional realignment 125–7
parliamentary elections 2, 49, 57, 103, 239, 241
   1989 9
   1996 21, 32
   2006 2, 3, 10, 12, 13, 28, 32, 33, 45, 46, 129, 130, 151, 152, 179, 181, 183, 185, 211, 232, 233
   2009 53
peaceful/popular resistance 17, 56, 57, 62, 124, 180, 207, 219
peace talks 39, 46, 155
peace treaty 9, 15, 21, 191
Pelham, Nicolas 226
Peres, Shimon 15
'Pillar of Defence' (2012) 45, 57–8, 60, 96
PLO 3, 6, 8, 9, 12, 13, 17, 22, 30, 32, 40, 46–50, 56–8, 61, 67, 71, 89, 118, 124, 136, 143, 146, 159, 178, 214, 219, 225, 240–2, 244
   delegitimize 150–5
   substitute for 155–9
Political Bureau (*maktab al-siyâsî*) 1, 2, 18, 27, 27 n.134, 28, 30, 35, 36, 38, 56, 60, 60 n.54, 67, 76, 78, 81, 83, 84, 90, 97, 98, 104, 144, 158, 171, 195–9, 203, 206, 208, 212, 214, 227–30, 234, 235
Political Department 151
political identity 26
political Islam 124
political parties 3, 35
Popular Front for the Liberation of Palestine (PFLP) 56, 57, 98, 99 n.67, 126
Popular Front for the Liberation of Palestine-General Command (PFLP-GC) 94
Popular Resistance Committee 46, 57, 163 n.145, 166, 193
power, externalization of 27–8
Prakash, Ohm 72

presidential elections 2, 84, 103
Prisoners' Document. *See* National
    Conciliation Document (*Wathîqat
    al-Wifâq al-watani*)
Prodi, Romano 68
'Protective Edge' (2014) 32, 35, 45,
    59–62, 66, 82, 87, 107, 108, 111,
    133, 164, 167, 170, 171
Public Salvation government 51
public sector employees 130

al-Qaddoumi, Farouq 71, 151, 152
al-Qaddoumi, Khaled 81, 83, 89, 100
Qandil, Hisham 80
al-Qaradawi, Youssef 66, 80, 92, 96, 126,
    133, 154, 161, 177, 205, 206, 218,
    224, 225
Qatar 1, 2, 27, 29, 73, 75, 77, 82–3,
    91, 94, 97, 99, 110, 115, 125, 126,
    132, 134, 135, 150, 184, 196, 198,
    206, 210, 218, 222, 224, 226, 230,
    234, 242
    aid 116, 133–5
    role and sovereignty 159–62
al-Qidwa, Nasser 151
al-Qneita, Mohammed 93
Quai d'Orsay (French Ministry of Foreign
    Affairs) 72
Quartet 33, 34, 67–9, 67 n.1, 82, 120,
    124
al-Quqa, Khalil 179
Qur'an 21, 171
Quraysh tribe 192

Rabbo, Yasser Abed 107
radical but inevitable decision
    (*hâsim*) 34, 50, 117
radical Islamist groups 163
Rafah border crossing 58, 63, 66, 71, 76,
    77, 80, 87, 101, 102, 109, 116, 123,
    125, 133, 177, 206, 213, 228
al-Rafati, Ala 133 n.83
al-Rahim, al-Tayeb Abd 148
Rajoub, Jibril 2, 38, 241
Ramallah 2, 13, 34, 36, 38, 51, 59, 62,
    72, 110, 115, 117, 118, 130, 136,
    143–50, 154, 159–61, 242
Ramallah Authority (*Khamsa-
    Khamsa*) 38, 58, 140, 148, 155

Ramaphosa, Cyril 243
al-Rantisi, Abd al-Azazi 7, 156
al-Razzak, Mohammed Najil Abd 80,
    154
rebellion (*tamarrud*) movement 107
recognition (*i'tirâf*) 50
reconciliation (*musâlâha*) 205, 215
Redwan, Ismail 83, 154
reforms (*islâh*) 182
re-Islamization 190
rejectionist front and Syrian
    crisis 95–100
    Islamic Republic 95–6
    relations with Shia partners 97–100
    time of dissent 96–7
religious justification 191
resistance
    concept 181, 186
    discourse 234
    ideology 176
    programme 39, 143
    truce as form of 193–4
resistance front 6, 36, 99, 172, 173, 180,
    185, 188–90, 243
respect (*ihtirâm*) 50
Revue d'études palestiniennes 36
al-Rishq, Izzat 28, 74, 83, 257–8
Riyadh 85
Roch, Daniel 228
Rohani, Hassan 84
Rosenau, James 2, 113, 122, 233
Roumana, Faraj 202
Roy, Olivier 24
Roy, Sara 53
Roz 127
Russia 24, 83, 85, 88, 118

Saadat, Ahmed 56
al-Sa'ati, Abd al-Rahman 5
sabr (patience) 21
Saddam Hussein 22 n.103, 178
Safa, Wafiq 97
Saher, Gilad 59 n.54
Said, Mohammed Qadri 106 n.112
Salafi movements 163
Salafis 136, 147, 162, 163, 163 n.146,
    165, 173, 178, 192–4
al-Salam, Rafiq Abd 80
Saleh, Maher 83

Salman (king)   98
Saraya al-Quds   57
Sarkozy, Nicolas   72
Saudi Arabia   6–7, 73, 81, 82, 84, 98, 99, 108, 127, 220
al-Sawwaf, Mustafa   41
al-Sayed, Hisham   65
Sayigh, Yezid   138, 139, 178, 193
Second Intifada   9, 137, 137 n.2, 156
Second World War   5, 143, 144, 169, 186
security system   136–40
Seta, Suleyman Abou   153
sexual minorities   244
Seyam, Said   248
Shaath, Nabil   102, 150 n.75, 151, 205
al-Shaer, Nasser al-Din   253
al-Shafi, Abd   214
Shalit, Gilad   45–7, 55–6, 59, 61, 76, 113, 127, 136, 146–7, 180, 204, 213
Shallah, Ramadan Abdallah   166
Sham'a, Mohammed   7
Shanab, Ismail Abou   30
al-Shaqfa, Mohammed Riyad   90
sharia (Islamic law)   21, 177, 191
Shati reconciliation agreement (2014)   2, 58–9, 62, 133–5, 158
Shaul, Oron   61, 65
Shehadeh, Salah   7, 10
Sheikh Omar Hadid Brigade   165
Shia Lebanese Party   96
Shia Persians   178
Shia principles   167, 179
Shia republic   125
Shias   175, 180, 234
Shin Beth   163
al-Shiqaqi, Fathi   7
Short, Clare   79
Shoukry, Sameh   109
Shtaya, Mohammed   205
shura (consultation)   195, 196, 198–202, 204
Siam, Sayyid   70, 71, 138, 139, 181, 203
al-Sinwar, Yahya   18, 38, 65, 100, 110, 134, 158, 214, 236, 240, 241, 247
al-Sissi, Abd al-Fattah   11, 34, 66, 87, 107–9, 133

Snyder, R.   26 n.131
Soleimani, Qassem   84, 100 n.75, 111
sovereignty (*tawrît*)   12, 13, 15, 25, 38, 106, 159–62, 190
Special Security (*al-amn al-khass*)   140
Square of the Unknown Soldier   149
Stack, Liam   141 n.27
Starkey, Brigid   25 n.119
Steinmeier. Frank-Walter   82
suicide attacks   8, 47
Suleiman, Omar   54, 70, 181
Sulmiyya, Abou   47
'Summer Rains' operation (2006)   72
Summit for Democracy (2009)   71
Summit of Non-Aligned States   71, 152
Summit of 'Victory of Jerusalem and of the Palestinian people' (2006)   71
Sunnis   180, 234
Sunni/Shia split   206
Supreme Council of Armed Forces   225
Switzerland   120
symbolic recognition   122–3
Syria   9, 35, 36, 38, 81, 85, 125, 126, 131, 176, 185, 198, 206, 220, 223, 229
    foreign policy of (1960 and 1970)   122
    regime   87, 96, 99, 131, 180, 185, 185 n.57, 189, 221, 224
Syria and Hamas   87. *See also* rejectionist front and Syrian crisis
    Damascus, capital of Hamas diplomacy   87–9
    Syrian uprising   92–5
    tawâjud ('presence in absence')   89–91
Syrian Army   92, 100
Syrian Muslim Brotherhood   88, 90, 94
Syrian revolution   78, 93, 99, 126
Syrian uprising   34, 36, 126, 187, 224

al-Taha, Ayman Mohammed Salah   54, 117, 129, 145, 154, 249
Takfiris   87, 108–9, 232
Taliban   244
Tamimi, Azzam   215
tawâjud ('presence in absence')   89–91
al-Tawil, Hissam   73 n.36
taxes   141–2

Tehran 74, 84, 95, 96, 98–100, 130–3, 178, 180, 185, 210, 217, 218, 226
Tenth Government 13, 29, 68, 71, 116, 117, 128, 129
territory (*buqʻa*) 15
terrorism 82, 85, 106–9, 236
    Islamist 237
    Zionist 79, 184
al-Thani, Sheikh Hamad ben Khalifa 79
al-Thani, Tamim Bin Ahmad 84
Tilly, Charles 236
Times 93
al-Tohamy, Muhammad Farid 108
Toledano, Nassim 8
transnational ideology 4, 23–4
Trump, Donald 83
Trump administration 158
Tunisia 40, 124, 125, 183, 184
Tunisian Spring 187
tunnels and commerce 141, 142, 212
Turkey 40, 60, 66, 74, 76–8, 81, 82, 85, 91, 93, 94, 99

Ubaida, Abou 202
ulemas 126, 177, 224
UN Council for Human Rights 121, 204, 204 n.36
underground economy 141
UN General Assembly 17, 147
    Resolution 799 23, 233
    Resolution 2621 (XXV) 14
unilateral decisions 196, 203–10, 215, 219
    contested by players 206–10
    foreign policy 204–6
unilateralism 147, 205
United Arab Emirates 1, 82, 108, 127, 154, 187
United Nations (UN) 17, 60, 64, 101, 110, 134, 135, 147–50, 186, 242
United States 22–3, 59, 68, 85, 107, 120, 125, 127, 131, 133, 143, 145, 197, 221, 242–4
    hegemony 79, 175, 184
    NGOs 140
UNRWA 140, 158
UN Security Council 23, 63, 146, 233, 243

UN Special Coordinator for the Peace Process 242
US Embassy 1, 63
Usher, Graham 103 n.95
US State Department 75

'Victory of Gaza' (2009) 73
Viva Palestina flotilla 73, 74, 185

Wadi al-Natrun 105
Wahhabi ideology 178
Walt, Stephen 177
waqf 15, 20
Waqf and Religious Affairs 154
war crimes 243, 244
Warsaw Ghetto 169
Warsaw summit 85
Weber, Max 26, 172, 173
Wennesland, Tor 242
West Bank 2, 5, 6, 8, 27, 35, 36, 38, 39, 51, 59, 62, 105, 118, 148, 160, 195, 198, 201, 202, 212, 214, 215, 240, 241
Western Foreign Affairs Ministries 68
'What Is Hidden Is Greater' (documentary) 46
world and Hamas 19, 66–86, 169
    active diplomacy 72–4
    al-Arouri's diplomatic tour 83–4
    centrality of Hamas Damascus head office 74–6
    consolidating Doha leadership 82–3
    diplomacy 80–1
    Gaza and outside leadership 76–8
    Hamas MPs 71–2
    Haniyeh's departure from Gaza 84–6
    limited interactions with West 67–9
    recognition 79–80
    visits by MPs 78–9
    al-Zahar and Haniyeh tours 69–71
World Federation of Ulemas 154, 206
Wright, Iain 72

Yang Wei 72
Yarmouk camp 92, 94, 119
Yassin, Ahmad 6, 7, 9, 10 n.42, 15, 22, 28, 30, 32, 51, 51 n.23, 80, 93, 132, 178, 191, 212, 240, 247–8
al-Yazouri, Ibrahim 7

Yemen 99
Yemen war 98
Yifrach, Eyal 59 n.54
Yousef, Ahmed 37, 67, 68, 72, 74, 82, 96, 97, 106, 118, 119, 124, 130, 131, 142, 147, 161, 248
Yousef, Hassan 253
YouTube 58

al-Zahar, Mahmoud 14, 29, 31, 66, 68–71, 76, 77, 97, 99, 102, 116, 117, 119–22, 128, 129, 132, 143–6, 152, 158 n.116, 167, 181, 193 n.27, 196, 198, 202–12, 218, 220, 221, 223–31, 250
zakat committees 141
Zionism 6, 14, 17
Zionist entity 19, 52, 55, 153, 155 n.103, 186
Zionist project 170, 185
Zionist war criminals 186
al-Zouhour, Marj 16, 23
al-Zubaidi, Basim 140, 140 n.21, 202, 203 n.27

www.ingramcontent.com/pod-product-compliance
Ingram Content Group UK Ltd.
Pitfield, Milton Keynes, MK11 3LW, UK
UKHW022325011025
463500UK00009B/268